QUEEN ELIZABETH 2

Bernard M. Patten, MD

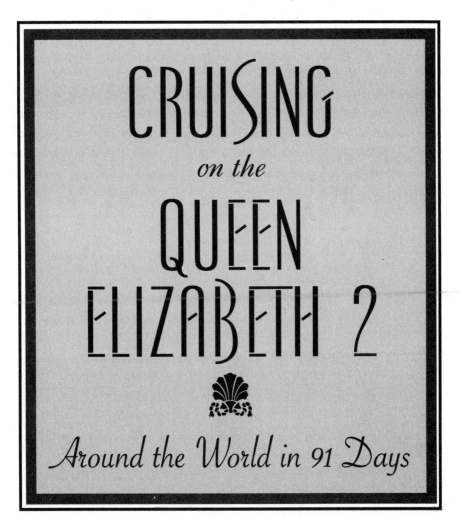

CRUISING
on the
QUEEN
ELIZABETH 2

Around the World in 91 Days

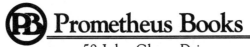

Prometheus Books

59 John Glenn Drive
Amherst, New York 14228-2197

Published 2006 by Prometheus Books

Inquiries should be addressed to
Prometheus Books
59 John Glenn Drive
Amherst, New York 14228–2197
VOICE: 716–691–0133, ext. 207
FAX: 716–564–2711
WWW.PROMETHEUSBOOKS.COM

10 09 08 07 06   5 4 3 2 1

Library of Congress Cataloging-in-Publication Data

Patten, Bernard M.
    Cruising on the Queen Elizabeth 2 : around the world in 91 days / by Bernard M. Patten.
        p. cm.
    ISBN-13: 978–1–59102–432–3 (pbk. : alk. paper)
    ISBN-10: 1–59102–432–3 (pbk. : alk. paper)
    1. Queen Elizabeth 2 (Ship). 2. Ocean travel. I. Title. II. Cruising on the Queen Elizabeth two.

G550.P29 2006
910.4'1—dc22

2006012122

Printed in the United States of America on acid-free paper

To Mark Twain, whose book Life on the Mississippi *(1883) introduced me to the beauty and mystery of ships and the magic of the sea and whose much-praised—but little read—classic cruise chronicle* The Innocents Abroad *(1869) provided much amusement and some inspiration.*

CONTENTS

8   CONTENTS

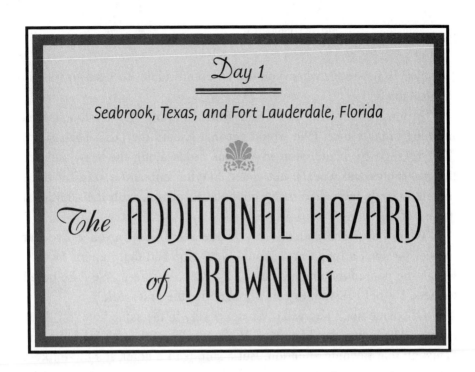

Day 1

Seabrook, Texas, and Fort Lauderdale, Florida

The ADDITIONAL HAZARD *of* DROWNING

"OK. Let's go." That's what Ethel, my wife of thirty-one years, finally said.

Her reluctance based itself on good reasons. We would miss our favorite calico cat, P.J.

Not having P.J. around to pet for ninety-one days would devastate not only P.J.'s psychology but also, and more importantly, could devastate our own mentality, cat-dependent people that we are.

And what about the house plants? We wish they could travel, too. We love the herb bed, the basil, the Mexican marigold mint. And we love our fresh garden vegetables—carrots, tomatoes, five types of lettuce (romaine, black-seeded Simpson, ruby, oak leaf, and buttercrunch), and the beautiful cabbages, cauliflowers, scallions, and so forth. Ethel and I inspect the plants every day—pet them, too, the way we pet P.J. Aboard ship, could we do that?

Is it wrong to love material things so much? Is it wrong to be so comfortable? Is it wrong, when you are so comfortable, to want to remain comfortable?

"Around the world, yes," said Ethel, sipping her fresh-squeezed morning orange juice. (We would get that aboard the *QE2*, I felt sure.) "But let's go by plane, stop in various cities along the way, and see things—wings and wheels, not water. Staying onboard a ship for three months sounds more like being confined to prison, with the additional hazard of drowning."

"Would we," she added, "stay in the same hotel, even a five-star palace, for such a long time? Would we?" She had that inquiry face on her as she poured me another cup of Kenya AA coffee. "We'll be bored to tears. I'll bet I'll want to come home after the first week."

"Of course not," I agreed. "We never stay in the same hotel for three months. The luxury would cloy us. We'd get sick of the rich food, the servants, all that fawning attention. But a ship isn't a hotel. It's more like a city, I would say, a traveling city, with lots of things to do and see. And a chance to experience all sorts of levels of happiness. It would be an adventure, a once-in-a-lifetime adventure."

I was speaking, as I often do, from the vantage point of sheer ignorance. I had no idea what awaited us aboard the world cruise. I had no idea what would happen, what adventures or misadventures would befall us, and whether or not we would like it.

Then I thought of something. "Hey, why not start in the worst cabin and work our way up? Every two weeks or so, we could recapitulate our marriage from rags to riches. That would keep us on the move and give us the illusion of travel, even though we would still be on the same ship. By starting in the lowest class and lowest deck, we could have something to look forward to as we advanced, a kind of linear development. It would be romantic."

I was getting carried away by my own rhetoric, as usual. But Ethel fell for it. She goes for anything with a little romance attached.

Around the world on the *Queen Elizabeth 2,* the most sophisticated ship afloat. Where did I get the notion?

Perhaps it was in first grade when Mrs. Voight mentioned that the world was round. More likely the idea occurred in 1978, after our crew—

Ethel and our two kids, Allegra and Craig—settled in the Queen Anne suite as we crossed the North Atlantic on *Queen Elizabeth 2*. That five-day crossing cost a pile. Never mind how much. But we had a ball. What good is money if you don't spend it?

The last evening, at dinner in the Queens Grill in the sunken center of the restaurant, the section known to the cognoscenti as the fish bowl, Allegra, age ten, started to cry. When asked why, Allegra said, "I don't want to leave the ship. I want to cruise forever."

Ethel, with an unusually nasty tone in her voice, reproved our child. "Don't be a baby. All good things must come to an end."

But when Ethel got back to the Penthouse suite, she cried, too. She didn't want to leave the ship. She wanted to cruise forever.

And so one dark, dank, dreary day in January, when the weatherman predicted the temperature in Texas would fall into the twenties, when there was a damp drizzle in our souls, a sadness about leaving P.J., the calico cat, and our too comfortable lives, we left Seabrook, Texas, our home, and set out on our journey to circumnavigate the globe like Ferdinand Magellan.

Well, I hoped not *exactly* like Magellan. In 1521, he got into a rather negative situation at Mactan, the Philippines, when the local inhabitants ate him for supper.

At 9 AM, Trent, my chauffeur, met us at the door and carried our stuff, eight bags full, out to our black stretch limo.

Surprise!

Our neighbors, Lennie and Vince, Martha and Frank, had turned out en masse to toast our departure with Moët and Chandon. I like the smell of champagne in the morning. I like its taste, its fizz and tickle, particularly good champagne like Moët. Earl Long, when he was governor of Louisiana, used to drink Champagne with breakfast. His wife disapproved. But Long was, I now realize, on to something.

Riding to the airport felt like the old days, with one significant difference—no work. Now instead of working in the limo, talking on the portable phone, typing on the computer, or dictating letters, I enjoyed myself much as P.J. would have, looking dumbly out the window at the scenery. Relaxed meditation, that's one of the great lessons, perhaps the only lesson, cats teach us.

"Champagne for breakfast," I told Ethel. "Remind me to order it on *QE2*."

Ethel was, as usual, worried. This time the worry concerned Continental Airlines. She feared the airline wouldn't accept our overweight and over-limit baggage, which probably came in close to a ton, carry-ons excluded. But I told Ethel that I would take care of any problems with a special note from the United States Government, a note that I hoped would work miracles.

At curbside, the check-in man eyed our bags dubiously. His concern showed more clearly when he tried to lift my suitcase. It pulled him back hard. "Books," I explained apologetically and handed him my special note, a green and black piece of linen from the United States Federal Reserve Bank of Dallas, Texas. The man stared at the twenty-dollar bill as if he were reading what it said: "This note is legal tender for all debts, public and private." He smiled, pocketed the twenty, and, without ado, tagged our bags.

On the plane, we met fellow travelers, all gray heads over sixty and none going around the world. These people had signed up just for the eleven-day Florida-to-California segment through the Panama Canal.

Patti Silva, the friendly hostess from Cunard, the famous ocean liner company, met us at Fort Lauderdale airport and piled us in a bus, while Cunard people assembled the baggage.

Nope! We weren't on Patti's list for free transportation to the ship, so Patti just wrote in our names. Patti said, "I've got lists coming out my eyeballs today, but they're not always right."

Ethel poked her elbow into my ribs. Oh, yes, now I remembered. I was supposed to sign us up for (and presumably pay for) transport from airport to the ship, but I had forgotten.

As the bags rolled by, I spied our lavender tags labeled M5, the worst class. M stands for Mauretania, and the 5 is the lowliest and the lowest of the Mauretania divisions.

I looked away. I tried to appear nonchalant, pretending our bags don't belong to us. But you know what? Nobody cared. All the bags, the ones I saw anyway, they were all 5s and 4s, the lower decks, the Mauretania group.

Ethel and I are among our friends the plebs, I thought. We relaxed.

But what is this? All our stuff has priority tags on it from Continental Airlines. Ethel said, "Only first class gets that. Must be a mistake."

"No way, José. It's not a mistake. It's the effect of the twenty. See?" I pointed my right index finger at her and smiled. "The little people in this world have the power. They make things happen."

It was only two miles from the Fort Lauderdale airport to Port Everglades's docks, so the *QE2* springs into view rather quickly. At dockside, *QE2*'s massive shape loomed over us. I admired her single red funnel, white top glistening in the Florida noontime sun, and the dark blue hull. On the front in big, red capital letters the word *CUNARD* appeared, followed by the famous red racing stripe from front to rear. Front to rear? I meant forward to aft.

QE2—her shape is the shape of a classic ship—not the upside-down layer-cake design, the new-fangled innovations of marine architecture that would have floating hotels indistinguishable from apartment houses. *QE2* represented the eternal ship of the imagination, the ship of dreams, the ship I repeatedly drew as a child. I knew she was to be our primal mother whose warmth protects us against the roughness of wind and storm, a ship, a very capable ship, by which to sail the ocean seas. And to us, she was also to be a pleasure dome, a traveling machine dedicated to making us happy.

Check-in occurred at the speed of light. Well, maybe not that fast, but faster than at the airport. Times have changed. It used to take hours to get onboard a superliner, and there was always all that hustle-bustle and confusion (I have seen that remark somewhere) and fuss, getting the porters and the embarkation cards. And I remember my father running around, getting table and deck-chair reservations, and frantically tipping stewards and the dockside hands to get our bags into the rooms.

Not now. All that's over, a thing of the past.

I showed our tickets, listened to the four-piece string quartet play

Haydn, smelled the gorgeous arrangements of hundreds—no, thousands —of flowers assembled in the reception hall, and opened our passports for customs review. Two minutes later, away we went, aided by a small army of crew finely dressed in white and gold naval uniforms.

Oh, yes, forget New York. Forget the messy commotion of those West Side piers, the longshoremen hauling (and hurling) bags, the beeping taxis, the multiple ramps, and passengers bewildered and visitors bewildered tottering under "Bon Voyage" canvas-sided gangplanks. Forget all that hubbub. Embark in Florida.

From the gangway, we spotted the men loading supplies dockside. I counted eighty-nine cases of Idaho potatoes, forty-six cases of carrots, and seventeen crates of Rice Krispies. Who eats all those Krispies? And what in the world was this? We spied innumerable gigantic tins of sauerkraut. What's that for?

For just five days at sea, the *QE2* took on, among other things: 625 pounds of strawberries, 600 pounds of tomatoes, 855 pounds of duck, 1,150 pounds of bananas, 33 pounds of caviar, 60 pounds of foie gras, 2,000 pounds of sausages, 329 pounds of rack of lamb, 2,000 pounds of pork, and 2,395 pounds of beef. We had seventy-nine chefs aboard to prepare the food, twenty-two wine stewards, ten dancers, and eight gentlemen hosts.

Gentlemen hosts?

If you don't know what a gentlemen host is, don't feel bad. They are gentlemen who balance out the numbers for dancing, since there are more single and unaccompanied women aboard than men. Gentlemen hosts pay 10 percent of the usual fare and in return must hang around at night and amuse the ladies. They passed a test in dancing and conversation, but the regulations prohibit romancing the customers. We entered on Two deck. Hands clasped behind my back (like Prince Charles reviewing a parade), I walked past the immaculately uniformed crew members lined up to greet us. They pointed the way to Five deck and our M5 cabin.

"Did you detect any disdain when we asked the way to M5?" I asked Ethel.

"None."

Nichola, a twenty-five-year-old, pixie-faced room stewardess met us in our room but refused to share the strawberries and Perrier-Jouet champagne left there by who knows who. Champagne for lunch—that's the ticket. We toasted again. "To all our dreams doubled!"

The room was functional, light, and happy. It smelled fresh and clean but had no view. It was our love nest. Although it measured 145 square feet, smaller than part of our bathroom at home, we liked it.

At first glance, it seemed impossibly cramped, but after things were unpacked, suitcases stowed beneath beds, belongings hung in closets, the cabin became an ideal seagoing home away from home. And without a porthole, this cabin has a great advantage: it's impossible to tell whether it's too dark, too cold, too rainy, too foggy, or too anything outside.

We expected the worst, but this was much better than we expected.

Nichola spoke with a British accent, but we forgave her; she can't help it. She hails from Liverpool. In that accent she explains that she left the ship a while back to return home. A few months of reality back there on land in squalid, industrial Liverpool made her appreciate her job at sea onboard *QE2*. So she's back and happy. Nichola explained everything about the room, including where to find the lead-bottom tissue box (Holy cow! Do the seas get that rough?) and where the life preservers were hidden in the closet under the baseboard.

Nichola left, while Ethel and I continued toasting with the champagne: "To joy and fresh new days of love," I said, misquoting the Bard. We emptied the glasses in one draught. I replenished us. We clinked again. "To big ships and big dreams," I said, correctly quoting myself. That toast has a kind of 1920s ring to it. I like it.

We killed the bottle before Nichola returned with an arrangement of flowers, pink carnations, white orchids, Scottish heather, and birds of paradise, a gift from Lennie and Vince, our travel agents.

By the way, around-the-world cruise passengers, whether in M5 (the worse class) or the Q1 Penthouse (the best class), get a $2,000 onboard credit. That means, in the unlikely event Ethel and I could control our drinking to $2,000 worth of booze or less, we could conceivably drink our way around the world for free. The big question confronting us was could we live through M5? And would we—at the end of this segment, when *QE2* finally pulled into Los Angeles—still be talking to each other?

QE2 assigned us the late eating shift in Mauretania Restaurant. We saw why. The first-sitting people looked like they averaged seventy-five years old. People that old had to hit the hay early.

Seeing so many elderly people surprised me. But I saw a fair sprinkling of young folks and another fair sprinkling of gentlemen and ladies who were noncommittal as to age, like us, being neither old nor absolutely young. These Mauretania passengers had more than their share of money and of accumulated damage inflicted by life long lived: sagging skin, spotted hands (like my own), knotty legs (like my own), rheumy eyes (not yet), wispy hair (yes), and quavering voices (no). In short, I could easily shake their hands and call them Mom and Pop—but not brother and sister, not yet.

That first dinner, Ethel ate the spa selection, and I had a steak. Surprisingly, there were six choices of appetizers, two soups, a lime sherbet (which they call "sorbet," pronounced "saw-bit" because, after all, they're British), four regular entrees, a vegetarian entree, fourteen different desserts, and assorted wines, coffees, and teas. It was a high-style dining experience, an era of romance shimmering in revival. Thank God we're part of it.

"Pinch me," said Ethel. "This tastes like heaven when we have only supposedly entered hell."

"Hurry up and finish dinner," I said. "We might miss the midnight buffet."

"I wonder what P.J. is doing," said Ethel. "Maybe we can get a homing device, attach it to her, and see where she goes at night. Can Vince and Lennie fax us a picture?"

From my wallet, I pulled out a color picture of P.J. and handed it across the table. Ethel seemed consoled while I took my own consolation in a single malt scotch, a MaCallan, eighteen years old, priced very reasonably at (can this be?) $4.

After dinner, Ethel didn't want to dance, but she reluctantly agreed when they announced a dance contest for champagne. Lucky us. We won a bottle of Henkell Trocken Dry Sec white sparkling wine, *QE2*'s pour champagne. Champagne for nightcaps! We are setting a personal record: champagne for breakfast, lunch, dinner, and nightcaps. Are we overdoing it? "Too much of a good thing," said Mae West, "can be wonderful."

Tipsy, Ethel and I stumbled back onto Boat deck to watch the *Queen* pull out.

The ship's horn sounded a deep A at sixty cycles per second. The loud note reverberated deep into the dark Floridian night.

QE2 began to vibrate and move. The around-the-world adventure was starting. Massive numbers of people in cars, across the way, sounded their horns, which bleat too high pitched and woefully weak compared to *QE2*, our ship. People in the apartments on the channel across the way blinked their lights on and off in tribute to the *Queen*'s departure. Between blinks, when the lights were on, we saw them waving, some of them waving furiously. We waved back more slowly, more regally, more joyously. "We're better off. We are leaving. They are not."

Back in the M5 room, we squeezed into the single bed by the wall, and, while *QE2* bounded briskly forward over the waves, we made love. It was like college when we would jump into one of the single beds in the dorm, kind of cramped, but kinky—and nice.

Nothing could be more absolutely certain than we are enjoying ourselves. One could not do otherwise, speeding over the sparkling waters and breathing the soft atmosphere of the cruising life. Care cannot assail us here. We stand out of its jurisdiction.

Day 2

At Sea in the Florida Straits, Headed toward Yucatán

ROUGH WEATHER HITS

At 11 AM, we passed Havana on our left. The sea was calm and vast, daunting our ideas of infinity. We felt wonderful. Everyone else aboard seemed happy, too.

Well, almost everyone. There were a few cranks around. Most of them took the heritage tour. Wherever we went, they found something wrong. This room was too cold. The next room was too hot. No room was just right. One discontented woman said, "World tour? Humpf! Take away the ship and what have you?"

But they liked Norman Cole, the twenty-five-year-old tour guide.

Two old women, who must have been seventy-five and under the influence of those aphrodisiac sea breezes that stimulate hormone production even among the aged, ogled Norman and cooed, "Isn't he cute! Such a nice smile, too."

Poor Norman. He tried to teach us something while keeping the group's interest. This proved difficult, since they all seemed to have attention spans measured in microseconds. Nevertheless, we did learn some history: Samuel Cunard was not British. And he was not American. He was Canadian, born in Halifax. On July 4, 1840, he set out in the wood-hulled steamer *Britannia* from Liverpool for Halifax with sixty-three passengers and the Royal mail. The rest as they say is history: From that humble beginning, the Cunard line grew to own or manage more than two hundred ships.

During the early years, enclosed cabins and other amenities we have come to expect didn't exist, even for the rich. All passengers ate poorly, slept poorly, and suffered long—usually ten to twelve days—while crossing the Atlantic. Advances occurred rapidly, however: *Persia* (1856) was the first iron-hulled Cunarder; *China* (1862) was the first driven by propeller rather than paddles. *Servia* (1881) had a steel hull and was the first Cunard vessel to have electric lighting. (This permits what Ethel calls our artificial sun, the bright white light in our room, because, without it, our little love nest, Cabin 5178, on Five deck, inside without view, would remain in stygian darkness—in perpetual night.)

Refrigeration came in 1885. Up to then, passengers ate eggs, then freshly killed chickens (after which, naturally, there were no more eggs), and, when the chickens were gone, they ate salted meats and fish. Because the liners carried many children, there hung in a sling amidships a resident cow that gave fresh milk.

In stormy weather, did the cow give buttermilk? I thought. But, instead of asking that stupid question, for some unknown reason, I asked, "Any cats aboard?"

"None now, but in the old days, because rats chewed the leather mail sacks, every ship carried an important and necessary trio of cats."

Wow! P.J. our calico cat should be proud of her species. Wait a second. As all cat owners know, all cats are proud of their species and for no apparent reason.

According to Norman, *Lusitania* and *Mauretania* (1907) outshone all competition and had passenger accommodations comparable to the world's best hotels of their era.

One wag, a tall, bald-headed man in the back of the crowd, cupped his hands over his mouth and shouted, "Did they have air conditioning? Because, Norman, we don't."

Norman smiled that cute smile of his and explained that air conditioning isn't relevant to the heritage tour, but the answer was no, they didn't have air conditioning. Fresh sea air had to be piped in using jerry-rigged contraptions made of soup cans. Norman tried to show with his hands how a soup can brings fresh air into a cabin by diverting the relative wind outside the porthole into the enclosed space of the room, but my mind wandered from Norman to focus on the elderly lady on my left who had fallen asleep standing up. Her sleep breathing sounded like the purring of a cat. Should I wake her?

"With the advent of luxury, by the 1920s, Cunard passenger lists had evolved into a *Who's Who* of distinguished people," said Norman emphasizing the word *distinguished*.

I wondered if we had anyone aboard who was in *Who's Who*. And then I remembered that I'm in *Who's Who*. If I'm in it, it can't be all that special.

In the 1930s, Cunard launched the legendary *Queen Mary* and the first *Queen Elizabeth*, ships that continued to set the standards of the world until the fourth *Queen* came along, the leviathan, our very own *Queen Elizabeth 2*.

Thus: Q1 was *Queen Mary*; Q2, the old *Queen Elizabeth*, Q3 was planned but never built; and Q4 is *QE2*. "Why no Q3?" Mr. Bald Head wanted to know. Norman told us that Cunard had second thoughts about Q3 when airplanes eroded the North Atlantic business. Starting in the 1950s, huge jets of BOAC, Pan Am, and half a dozen European airlines lifted passengers by the thousands away from the cabins of the transatlantic liners. Cunard saw clearly that its future prosperity, and probably even survival, would depend on a successful switch to cruising. What Cunard needed was a ship that could cruise and function part time as a liner.

Enter *QE2*, which is a liner that also cruises.

They designed *QE2* as Panamax, as they say in the cruise business, meaning the ship was the maximum size that could transit the Panama Canal. Marine architects went to the locks and made sure that *QE2* fit. Their measurements led to *QE2*'s present dimensions: 963 feet long, 105 feet wide, thirteen stories high—all that and handling eighteen hundred passengers and a thousand plus crew.

QE2 might not be the longest (the *Norway* is) or the biggest ship, but, since the SS *United States* retired, it is the fastest, fully capable of cruising at twenty-eight knots and actually doing thirty-three knots in sea trials. It is a floating city. In fact, a plaque on Quarter deck, by the Lido, proclaims Baltimore the sister city of *QE2*.

Norman poured on other facts, even though it was clear that the group had more or less reached saturation. "*QE2* has the largest of all libraries afloat: six thousand volumes. It has five restaurants, six bars, a CD-ROM learning center, and a computer facility with thirty-seven terminals. It has kennels, a garage for twenty-five cars, its own print shop, and a playroom called Noah's Ark. There is a flower shop (the only one afloat) and a laundry and dry-cleaning service run by the Chu dynasty."

Norman called them "Chu" because almost everyone there bears that name and "dynasty" because they're rich. But why are they rich? A chill went down my spine. I got a feeling that when we get the Chu laundry bill we'll find out.

In 1987 Cunard refit *QE2* with diesel electric engines at a cost of £100 million, roughly $150 million. The old steam engines got thirty-three feet on a gallon of fuel. (Yes, I said thirty-three feet a gallon.) The new diesels electric get an astounding fifty-three feet per gallon. We burn four hundred tons of fuel every day, about four-hundred fifty pounds of fuel per passenger per day.

Suddenly, the ship tottered. We all shifted forward. Norman's smile became a grimace. His tone became wry. "*QE2* has stabilizer fins to decrease roll, but no ship has an effective way of reducing pitch. You will see what I mean this afternoon when the rough weather hits."

This talk of movement focused attention onto the ship. Some in the group appeared momentarily distracted by the ship's motion. Me, too. I felt a surge of nausea as I looked outside and saw six-foot waves on the mountainous sea. The waves crossed each other and imparted shocks and countershocks that would have crushed a craft less solidly built.

Mr. Bald Head announced that it is lunchtime. Norman agreed and momentarily recaptured our attention by telling us that *QE2* consumes 17 percent of the world's total yearly production of caviar.

My lunch started with marinated baby shrimps in an onion and parsley dressing, then beef consommé with vegetable biscuit, a blueberry sherbet to clear the palate, and then grilled marinated lamb on a skewer with peanut sauce, spring onions, a bed of vegetables, fried rice, and zucchini. The dessert chef must be a genius. For it took, I'm sure, a lot of genius and five thousand years of civilization to produce his masterpiece, a Grand Marnier parfait with blackberry sauce.

Ethel and I agreed that someone, probably the higher classes, must be supplementing our fares. No way could our per diem cost in M5 pay for what we are getting. There must be a hitch. Where is it? What is it?

Captain John Burton-Hall interrupted our conversation to explain over the loudspeaker in crisp British English that the weather situation would soon worsen. There was a possibility that we could not safely dock in Cozumel.

Looking out from our cozy table for two, I concluded that the captain knew whereof he speaks: The sea looked rougher still, and we were experiencing a variety of motions of the ocean: pitch, roll and yaw, also wallow, lurch, quiver, shudder, reel, rock, sway, swing, heave, and pound.

As if obedient to the captain's command, the bow spirit took deadly aim at the sky in midheaven, and at the next instant tried to harpoon a shark in the bottom of the sea. It's a weird but wonderful sensation to feel the stern of a ship sinking swiftly from under you and see the bow climbing high away among the clouds. Clasp a railing and hang on. Don't fight it. You are better off moving with the ship and with the sea rather than trying to fight and move against them.

At three in the afternoon, the clouds fell farther, and, soon thereafter, white caps, which the crew calls, by the British term, sea horses, appeared by the millions among ten-foot swells. *QE2* started to sway gently, and, after fifty minutes, she started to sway not so gently. The stabilizer fins eliminate a lot of roll, but not enough. We were rolling fifteen degrees to either side every few minutes. People walked around as if drunk. One woman complained, "This is ridiculous. I want to go back to Florida. Can't he turn it around and seek better weather?"

Request denied.

At 6 PM, Captain Burton-Hall spoke again. "I should think in gale-force winds, there would be no good reason for a passenger to go out on deck."

But I had a good reason: I wanted to see what it was like.

Out there, I heard no thunder, no noise but the pounding of the bow waves, the keen whistling of the gale through the cordage, and the rush of the seething waters. *QE2* climbed aloft as if she would climb to heaven—then paused an instant that seemed a century and plunged headlong down again, as from a precipice. Sheeted sprays drenched the decks, sprays so ambitious that they coated the windows with thick, white crests of salt. Wind and rain made me feel awake and alive again. I loved it.

But this was the warm water of tropical seas. What about storms in the North Atlantic? My thoughts went out to those men who had served on destroyers' open bridges throughout World War II. They worked thirty feet above the water and must have caught the ocean's cruel daily beating right in the face. I could leave the deck when I wanted, but they couldn't. Their watches lasted four hours before they could return soaked and shivering to their cabins below.

I made my way back to M5 but couldn't get through the watertight doors. I had to go up to Four deck and then descend via F stairway to get closer to our room. All the while, I bounced off the bulkheads like a pinball. It's like the fun house at the amusement park. Sure, you are having a good time, but you are a little scared, too.

Interesting effect: One second I was climbing uphill though going downstairs; the next second, I was running downhill, trying to keep up with my legs, which didn't seem to know where to go. I overshot the cabin and had to retrace a few yards, all the while passing other passengers who were green as cabbages. They were headed to stairway C on Six deck. C-Six! Get it? That's the hospital.

The bad news is that, according to the ship's doctor, the queue of seasick passengers seemed endless. The good news is that there hasn't been a single case of jet lag or, marvel of marvels, car ennui.

Ethel and I sheltered in our M5 cabin, which is below and toward the center of the ship so that it doesn't move as much as the other parts of the ship. That was the advantage of being where we are. The disadvantage was that we had no doubts that if the ship went down, we would drown first. That's what the watertight doors were about. Whenever the ship is in danger of hitting something and springing a leak, the doors close. That way, only part of the ship gets flooded—our part—and the upper decks are spared. We don't like the idea, but I guess it's all for the best. Better a few paupers like us in M5 die than everyone.

In the theater, we got an afternoon lecture on the history of the Maya. I learned that Cozumel means the place of the swallows. Cozumel is part of the state of Quintana Roo, where the Maya worship Ix Chel, the fertility goddess of the rainbow. During all this interesting information, Ethel dozed off. The old woman next to her also fell asleep.

Twenty minutes later, with a sudden snore and a jerk, the old woman woke, just as the lecturer started to cover shopping opportunities in Mexico. The old woman looked around, and, to her great pleasure, she saw Ethel still sleeping. The old woman beamed her contentment. She was proud. She slept less than Ethel did.

I thanked Ix Chel that Ethel remained asleep during the entire spiel about shopping. The less she knows about that subject, the better.

Before dinner, I went to the spa. Ten dollars gets the use of it for the day, sauna and steam room included. Those on the world cruise, however, regardless of class or cabin, get all that free. Another perk—and a good one, too. But you have to check in with the cute blond at the desk. She was in her late twenties and had sapphire blue eyes, a slim, trim figure, and excessively reddened lips. "Would you like a treatment?" she asked.

Reflexly I declined, though if given the choice, I would have elected her Miss Universe. Then, I wondered what kind of treatment she had in mind. That old Camel advertisement went through my head: "Do you want a treat or a treatment?" No treatment for me, but a treat sounded good. Should I ask her? Right now I'm chicken. Maybe later.

I had the spa to myself because the other passengers were under the weather. Well, not entirely to myself. Miss Universe is there. It turned out her name was Kathy, the same name that was embroidered on the white blouse that encased her more than adequate bosom. Kathy came out from behind the desk and moved around the outside circle of the world's largest whirlpool, while I, in that pool, whirled around, following her with my eyes, trying not to look obvious. Every now and then Kathy bent over with her backside toward me. She wore no underpants, so I saw the orbic flexes of her behind clearly outlined against the back of her clean, white skirt. There may be no portholes down there in the spa on the Six and Seven deck, but, nevertheless, the scenery looked fine, fine indeed.

God punished me for ogling. Staring at Miss Universe made me feel seasick. Reluctantly, I closed my eyes. Seasickness results from sensory mismatch, a discord between what comes in through the inner ear and what comes through the eyes. Shutting my eyes should stop the nausea if the mismatch theory is correct.

It did.

After swimming for five minutes with eyes closed, I was fine again. Completely fine, except Miss Universe had disappeared.

I swam around in the ninety-six-degree water, enjoying the way the rough sea reflected itself in the whirlpool and added its kick to the mechanical things that make the water twist. In this microcosm, I felt the raw power of the sea, the sea surge, and the sea foam, and the sea swell, all throwing me about. I felt a part of it, part of the sea, and part of the life of the sea; I felt one with the elemental forces of the ocean and of nature. Just think: If it's this rough in the pool, what would it be like in the ocean itself? And if you really want to get scared, imagine what it would be like with the ocean pouring into your M5 cabin and into *you*. In the sea's dimensions, humans count for naught. The myth of our being in control of this planet is just that—a myth.

Back in M5, I decided to read the Cunard cruise brochure. "Look at this," I said to Ethel. "It says here on page 4 if you have any reason to complain, contact the purser. Does that include weather?"

Before Ethel could answer, another announcement came over the loudspeaker telling us what we already knew. More bad weather was approaching. Weather so bad that we may have to skip Cozumel. And then, for no apparent reason, the second officer of the watch announced that on this day, January 7, in 1536, Catherine of Aragon, first wife of Henry the Eighth, died. But Henry didn't miss her, since he had already married Anne Boleyn.

"Henry planned to marry several others, too," I added.

"You had better not do that to me," said Ethel.

"Do what?" I asked defensively.

"Marry another. It says here in the brochure that passengers with *any* complaint should contact the purser."

"They don't mean complaints about husbands," I stated categorically while wondering if Ethel figured out that I had this very afternoon admired some other woman's backside and committed the Jimmy Carter sin: lust in the heart.

Day 3

At Sea

WE WANTED to CRUISE FOREVER

"Good morning, ladies and gentlemen, this is John Burton-Hall, your captain speaking to you from the bridge. I deeply regret having to annul our call at Cozumel. But I did wish to inform you of the considerations that led to this decision. First and foremost is your safety. Six-foot swells would make transfer to the launches and travel on them hazardous and perhaps even dangerous. Also important is what we call the lee shore. At present, a strong wind at sixteen knots blows on shore from the north. The channel here is among the deepest in the Caribbean, so we cannot anchor. The only way we could manage it would be to drift offshore, but, with the onshore wind and the Gulf Stream current pushing us in the same direction at four to five knots, it might be tricky to maintain an offshore position. We shall therefore proceed directly to Cartagena. Again my apologies and regrets. Good day."

Yes, the captain can do that. Read the fine print on your ticket.

That was it! All that somniferous preparation for shopping in

Cozumel and the lecture on Maya culture down the drain or washed up, so to speak. Another hazard of sea travel besides seasickness had surfaced: water so rough we can't land.

What the captain didn't mention was port fees. Not docking means not paying fees. Therefore, Cunard will save money by not docking. One day in New York, for instance, costs half a million dollars. *QE2* is cost effective at sea but cost ineffective at dock. The more we stay at sea, the more the company earns. Did considerations of cost influence the decision to skip Cozumel? The skeptic in me wondered.

Actually, neither Ethel nor I minded. We liked the ship perfectly well and wanted to stay aboard. Everything we need is here. Why would anyone wish to leave? Besides, the weather cleared.

Yes, every storm subsides. And so dull eyes soon sparkled with pleasure again, pallid faces flushed, and appetites came back. Strength returned with eating. Restored frames weakened by sickness gathered new life from the quickening influence of the bright, fresh morning, calm seas, and great food and drink.

Because of the change in plans, the social director, Elaine Mackay, put together a special program that included another heritage tour, a newlywed game called Mr. and Mrs., and line-dance instructions in addition to the usual bingo, casino, movies, live entertainment, shows, and so forth.

Wow! The range and number of activities left no one out: the health enthusiast, the scholarly bookworm, the arts aficionado, the computer buff, the shrewd business man, the inveterate gambler, and the couch potato who happily stays in the cabin all day watching TV. Because you can't do a third of the activities on the schedule, you must become highly selective.

On the other hand, perhaps I should complain to the captain that we had too much to do. Couldn't we get a day off in view of all the suffering that we endured during the inclement weather?

I decided to take the heritage tour again because, after all, I'm weird. The tour might repeat what I learned yesterday. Then again, it might not. Let's see.

Today's tour met at 11 AM in the midships lounge. Just before it started, I took a look at the computer center on Two deck. It was jammed with a bunch of gray heads seated two each to a terminal. Excess students spilled over into the hallway and limned the walls of the room, waiting their turn. Matt, the instructor, a Christian Brother who teaches high school in the Bronx, explained how to save a file and how to click the Word icon to get the word processing program on the desktop. Very interesting. I made a mental note to buy computer stocks. Computers have a great future because the gray heads want them. And as Generation X knows so well, the gray heads have the money.

Andrew Graham announced that he would lead the tour because Norman Cole had to handle the Mr. and Mrs. game. Not only was the guide different, but the peoplescape had changed, too. There were fewer of them, less than half of the previous day's crowd. They were younger by far, average age in the fifties. They didn't seem to have a need to kibitz or complain. Instead, they just went where Andrew told them, and they listened. Some of them, like myself, took notes. Only one woman, who had a very heavy Scottish accent, complained—she wanted Andrew to speak slower because "'is British accent makes 'im 'ard to understand. Ya knaw all aboot sailin' a ship aroond the world, yet ye canna speak."

I assured her that she'd get used to the accent. I have. But later I learned the reason. Andrew is Australian. Australian English is more like American English.

Some of today's stories differed from yesterday's. For instance, the story about that large silver urn given to Samuel Cunard by the people of Boston.

Norman told us someone stole it from the ship, and, a few years ago, one of the crew members spotted the silver urn in a pawnshop on Fifth Avenue in New York.

As a half-baked writer, I'm always sensitive to story premise. A pawnshop on Fifth Avenue seemed odd, but I didn't interrupt to find out exactly where such a shop might be.

Cunard tried to get the urn back but ended up paying for it. It remained locked in the case that was never opened except by the queen herself, Queen Elizabeth.

Andrew's account reached the same point as Norman's, up to the disappearance, but diverged from there. Andrew told us a fan of Cunard found the silver cup in an antique shop on Eighth Avenue and bought it. The cup now stands in a locked case that is opened only for the Queen.

Other stories remained the same: Both Norman and Andrew experienced the big wave last December where four hundred fifty tons of water hit *QE2* head-on and sunk the steel hull of the forward deck eight inches. Since all passengers had been confined to their cabins, not one of them saw the wave, which measured ninety-three feet before the wave-measuring device broke and washed away. What passengers did experience for many hours of day and night were the effects of numerous waves of fifty and sixty feet.

"What would happen if a wave that big hit the side of the ship?" I asked.

"Lots of trouble," came the reply as Andrew rolled his eyes to heaven, indicating many deaths.

Both Norman and Andrew agreed on the substance of another story but disagreed on the dates—1994 according to Norman, 1988 according to Andrew. At the time, whichever it was, the US Government wanted to punish Colombia for its failure to cooperate on drug controls. Because *QE2* called at Cartagena against the advice of the US government, the customs officers in Los Angeles decided to examine the ship, the crew, and the passengers with painstaking scrutiny. They took fifty people off at a time and searched all baggage, packages, persons, and cabins. The ship had pulled into Los Angeles at 9 AM, and the last passenger got cleared to land at 5 AM the following day.

"What did they find?" a young woman who looked pregnant enough to deliver any minute, asked.

"Twenty-four sets of *QE2* china; seventeen sets of silverware; innumerable *QE2* bathrobes, towels, ashtrays, salt-and-pepper shakers; and four major artworks belonging to the ship that had been cut from their frames. The feds found only one funny cigarette belonging to a passenger, not a crew member," Andrew said proudly.

The group passed the lounge. Sure enough, Norman was there, working the Mr. and Mrs. game. The idea was to see how much you really know about your partner. The contestants compete for a much-coveted Cunard red umbrella.

"What animal does your wife resemble?" Norman asked a young man dressed in a black suit. The husband squirmed in his chair and then said loud and clear, "A dragon."

"Come now, Tom." Norman smiled. "Change that to something nice, or you'll break your marriage."

"Nope," said Tom, shaking his head like a child rejecting the breast. "I'll stick with *dragon*."

Sure enough, Tom's wife admits she's a dragon, so they both win the red umbrella.

I asked a woman who was furiously knitting on the veranda by the library what she was making. "I'm making blankets for the needy," she said.

"Why?"

"So I feel less guilty about making this trip."

I knew what she meant. I had thought that I might feel guilty for being cosseted in such luxury. Frankly, all the comfort bothered me, but not too much. Leisure and opulence are the charms of life, sacred things, really. In America, I believe, we rush too much. And, regretfully, when our work ends, we go on thinking of gains and losses; we plan the morrow; many of us even—not I, of course—carry our cares to bed with us, toss and worry over them when we ought to be restoring our racked bodies and brains with restful sleep. No wonder some die early or too soon drop into a mean old age. Thus, *QE2* teaches important lessons. How to enjoy yourself. How to enjoy life. We grow wise apace. We comprehend what life is for: FUN.

After dinner, Ethel and I had an argument. She didn't want me to play roulette. I thought I was lucky, so why not? I assured her I wouldn't play long. And I didn't. I put one twenty-dollar chip on red, and, twenty seconds later, black 26 came up.

"Next time," Ethel said smugly, "just give me the twenty, and I'll get rid of it for you at Harrods."

"There's a Harrods aboard?"

Ethel nodded her head menacingly yes, "On One deck, amidships."

About gambling on *QE2* or on any ship: Fix the amount you are prepared to lose in advance and stick to it. One woman I met at the roulette wheel had a limit of $200 a night. My limit was a more modest $20. Remember, the more you play, the more you lose as the grim law of averages catches up with you and works to the advantage of the house. You can beat a horse race, but you can't beat horse racing.

Most slots at sea pay less than they do ashore, but the ones by the doors pay more. And watch out for the hustlers and card sharks. They have suites and let you play with them there, beyond the watchful eye of the casino staff. They let you win for quite a while, as they set you up for the kill. Whatever happens, don't play with them after you leave the ship. That's the time you are likely to be taken to the cleaners.

My casino loss aside, I think we are in paradise. Ethel and I agree all the wonders we seek are here on the ship. Like Adam and Eve, we inhabit an enclosed pleasure dome. We felt a kind of addiction growing. We wanted the sea-laden breezes to hit our faces forever. We wanted luxury: fine food, good drink, and dancing under soft lights forever. We wanted to cruise forever.

Day 4

At Sea

SEA WATER— THAT EXPLAINS IT

The ship's abuzz with the talk of the big blizzard—the killer snow-storm, as the papers say—that we escaped. President Bill Clinton and Hillary walked home from church in the snow, and the New York Stock Exchange got off to a late start and closed early because of two feet of that cold, fluffy, white stuff that fell and fell and fell. So add to the list of the advantages of the southern seas another item of importance—no snow.

What's this? But what's wrong? Antonio, our Mauretania waiter, has a long face. "You have to eat in the Lido because you missed breakfast here. You didn't set your watches ahead the way the captain said."

It turns out that most people eat at the Lido, where there's a breakfast buffet.

Ethel and I got in line.

The place looked like a floating senior citizen center. Ahead of me limped one of them, an old lady wrinkled and stooped. She balanced her-self with a cane held in her left hand and picked pieces of British bacon out of the trays with her right. When she got to the end of the serving counters, the staff man there started screaming to beat the band: "Catherine! Christine! Someone! Help!"

Christine swooped in and grabbed the elderly soul just as she and her food were about to topple onto the Lido's teakwood deck.

One has to give the gray heads credit. Time has wounded them, but they are still moving: They have gumption. It takes gumption to leave home. It takes gumption to travel at any age and in any condition. I applaud the gray heads. They are not staying home, wasting their lives watching TV, the bullshit medium whose programs show the least commendable aspects of our culture. Scientific studies have shown that while watching TV all the great powers of the human mind are quiescent. The brain uses less oxygen and less glucose while watching TV than it does while sleeping. TV is junk food for the mind. Take a nap instead.

After breakfast, Ethel and I passed through the Queens Lounge. There we saw elderly people seated doing their chair aerobics. Some can barely lift their arms to their shoulders, but they are trying. That's what counts.

The enclosed deck by the library took on the aspect of a writing school: None of these gray heads, I will wager, would have the pluck, endurance, devotion to duty for duty's sake, and the invincible determination to venture upon so tremendous an enterprise as the keeping of a journal and not sustain a shameful defeat. Or, to speak plainly, although their intentions, at this time, early in the cruise, are good, I doubt that they can sustain the effort that I will. *Someone* had to record this unique adventure. That someone is me.

I joined the writing school and typed my notes into my Tecra portable computer.

An old man accosted me. (I would tell you his name except I don't know it. He didn't know it either. When I asked him his name, he replied somewhat bewildered, "I don't have one of them.") Let's call him Herman. He looked German, a big guy with a broad, shieldlike chest; gray hair; puffy, red lips; blue eyes; and a puzzled look on his face. Herman wanted to know what I was typing on. He said he hadn't heard of a computer. Then, in a flash, I realized he didn't know he was on a ship and didn't know where that ship was going.

When an elderly woman came up to him and asked how he was doing, Herman looked at her blankly and replied, "Hello." Then, in the same breath, he said, "Well, it was nice seeing you. Too bad you have to go so soon."

It wasn't the last I'd see of Herman.

Ethel and I, badly behind the power curve, arrived ten minutes late for Waldemar Hansen's lecture on the next day's stop (we hoped) at Cartagena, Colombia.

I took a seat next to a couple who arrived in the theater before us. The husband had fallen asleep, and his wife soon followed. About midlecture, she began to snore, and the woman next to her poked her in the ribs. At that point, Herman wandered in.

Herman seemed startled to see all those sleeping people assembled in such a big, dark room. Bent over and stooped, Herman limped small steps along the aisle, then he stopped dead. By the expression on his face, I could tell he had thought of something. It was the same expression that he had when he said he had never heard of a computer. But what was Herman thinking of? He probably didn't know himself. He turned and left.

Waldemar Hansen, our port lecturer, called Colombia the land of fire and ice, the same thing that Dante had called the Inferno. "The fire we'll experience tomorrow when we land. Dress in the emperor's new clothes."

Slowly the joke, like a developing Polaroid picture, began to catch on. Small isolated chuckles appeared, scattered here and there in the audience among those few who were still awake.

Hansen, encouraged, told another: "I'm your port lecturer. A port lecturer is like the groom at a wedding. Everyone knows why he's there, but the big question is, can he deliver?"

No response.

Hansen, the professional cruise lecturer with thirty-four years' experience, stepped right over the dead joke and continued talking.

On this day, I swam with two companions in the Quarter deck outdoor pool. One, a Japanese man, a poor swimmer with every stroke a Herculean effort to stay afloat, struggled to get from one end of the pool to the other. His wife shot his performance with a Sony video camera. Sure enough, halfway across one lap, his head sank below the surface. He started flailing about in distress. Before I got to him, a propitious ocean surge pushed him against the guardrail, where he, catching his breath, hung on for dear life. His wife signaled; she got it all on tape.

My other companion was Pierre, from Paris, France. He told me that he ate only the spa menu. I made a mental note to tell Ethel that some other person aboard, some other nut, besides herself, ate rabbit food.

In another respect, Ethel and Pierre were quite different: Pierre said he hoped to complete the trip without having a single alcoholic drink. Just the opposite of one of the Japanese passengers I saw who was so drunk at 11:30 AM. the preceding day that he couldn't sign his Yacht Club bar bill. I tried to tell him about the Friends of Bill W, the Alcoholics Anonymous group that met every once in a while, time and place listed in the daily program. But the drunk had just stared at me blankly, mentally more out of it than Herman.

Pierre said he was traveling first class—but there was no first class. Did he mean Grill class, which was like first class used to be, I suppose, but no longer geographically isolated and freely mixed with us plebeians all over the ship.

Pierre said he took last year's cruise in second class but found the service poor and the food satisfactory. What did he mean? Was he in Caronia last year? Pierre didn't state that exactly, and I didn't ask because I had learned long ago not to interrupt French people when they are speaking French. For some reason, I didn't trust Pierre. Why? Poor eye contact? Deceptive facial expression? Closed body posture? Storyline that didn't make sense? Unlikely premises? I guess I just don't believe a Frenchman who says he doesn't drink. So I forgot Pierre and headed to the hot tub.

Resting in the warm water, I felt a gay contentment, an exhilarating spiral sense of joy. I was at peace admiring the vast introspective expanses of the robin's egg–blue sky above and the green ocean all around.

A large lady hauled herself out of the pool, taking advantage of the tidal flow to assist her exit. A sudden lurch and she fell over the top and into the deck like a stranded whale. She quickly recovered poise, stood up, and came over to enter the hot tub. She was one of those American ladies who had expanded in every dimension that God had given her so that her displacement alone raised the water level in the Jacuzzi a full three inches.

"What kind of water do they use in the pool?" she asked in a squeaky, high-pitched voice.

"Sea water," I replied. "From a hose dipped into sea. I saw them do it."

"Sea water—that explains it," she said.

"Explains what?"

"Why it's so rough."

That night, it was our turn to attend the captain's cocktail party. Grill class (Queens, Princess, and Britannia Grills) got its party two nights before. Caronia cruisers got theirs the previous night, and the lowest of the low, Mauretania, our class, finally got its party.

I asked Captain John Burton-Hall why Cunard ships have names that end in -ia. He explained that the names derive from old Roman provinces and are Latin. *Britannia* is Latin for Britain; *Caledonia*, for Scotland; *Aquitania*, for a province in what is now western France; *Lusitania*, a province in western Spain; and *Mauretania*, in northwestern Africa. Even the word *Asia* denoted an eastern province of the Roman Empire that would now encompass the modern state of Turkey. I had asked a simple question and got a lecture. Captain John Burton-Hall was a man after my own heart.

"And Caronia?" I asked.

John Burton-Hall didn't know.

At dinner, Ethel showed me a letter she had typed at the computer center on Two deck:

Dear [Ethel made six copies and intended to fill in the blank of the salutation with the name of the lucky recipient]:

There's no chance of e-mail and phone calls cost $12.50 a minute so we are pretty much out of communication except for letters and postcards.

Our room although small is very well planned. There are two adequate closets and four roomy drawers to store things and room under the beds for suitcases. The food in the Maure-tania is great. They have spa selections at every meal, which I favor. There are aerobic classes in the gym.

We go to the movies every day, lectures about the ports we'll be visiting, and lots of other planned activities. The library, the largest afloat, is well stocked and has two full-time librarians, Emma Rowley and June Applebee. There are plenty of places to shop with duty-free prices, which makes them quite reasonable. Harrods had a branch here and another store sells Clinique beauty products.

In general it's just like home except we miss P.J.

Among the many things she forgot to mention was something pecu-liar: Every once in a while, a cryptic announcement comes over the loud-speaker. No one seemed to know what these messages mean, but I clas-sify them into three groups: (1) Starlight, starlight; (2) Phoenix, phoenix; and (3) Priority one, priority one.

Each of these announcements is followed by some location on the ship. Starlight usually occurs on the passenger decks. Phoenix and Pri-ority one usually occur in the crew quarters. One doesn't have to be a cryptographer to realize that these coded messages contain important information that the crew wishes to keep secret from the passengers. What is it? Why the secrets?

Before we turned in, Nichola, our room stewardess, arrived with a complimentary one-liter bottle of Grand Marnier. The card read, "Cunard, Queen Elizabeth 2, with the compliments of Cunard Line." We still had a dry sec Henkell Trocken that we haven't opened. If things con-tinue like this we'll have to open our own bar.

What the hell. Ethel and I have a drink. She takes hers with ice; I take mine neat (or is it straight?) What's the correct British English? I'll have to ask the captain.

And after, for a brief moment, I lay in my berth, under the always-cheering influence of the sea, rocked like a baby by the measure swell of waves and lulled by the murmur of distant surf.

I quickly passed out of consciousness and dreamed of Cartagena.

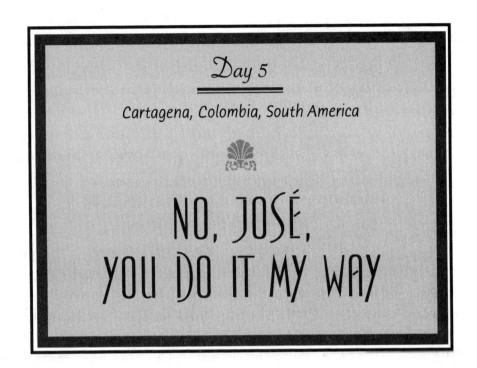

Day 5

Cartagena, Colombia, South America

NO, JOSÉ, YOU DO IT MY WAY

*O*n the map of South America, Colombia looks like ice cream atop a big cone. Let's take a lick.

We arrived by tender at Club Nautico near the center of town. Rough seas delayed things, but we finally did set foot on terra firma. I wanted to bend over and kiss the ground because it didn't roll, pitch, or yaw, but there were too many hawkers at dockside to do anything but move ahead with the crowd. Everything here is for sale, and I mean everything. Of course, for a price, for a price.

In the blinking of the eye, the world became thirty years younger. I saw kids and girls with firm butts and tits. They walked upright and stepped quickly. Marvelous!

But the traffic isn't marvelous. Did Colombia still have hostile Indians? We know it has dictators, corruption, drug lords, wild places, dust, exhaust pollution, and plenty of people. Colombia has the highest birth rate in South America, and I saw why—SEX.

Sex was everywhere. The women looked at me like I'm a sex object. Oh, those languorous Latino eyes! God, do they send me! Especially when they look at me that way.

I saw three colors of people in the crowd: reds, blacks, and whites, and any combination of those three. The reds came first across the Bering Strait twenty-three thousand years ago. The whites came next with Columbus (more or less). The blacks were slaves of the whites, replacing the reds when the reds got sick, or fled to the mountains, or died of syphilis or smallpox.

We decided not to go on the ship's tour. Instead, we hired Luis to drive us around for $30 per hour. Luis wanted payment in American dollars, not Colombian pesos. I don't blame him. The peso was 876 to a dollar yesterday and 956 this morning. You could start the day a millionaire and, because of the inflation, end the day a pauper. Luis was like Trent, my chauffeur at home, only much cheaper. With Luis, as with Trent, we called the shots, stayed or went as we pleased, and didn't get tied down.

Every tour moves as fast as its slowest member, so some of the ship's tours must move mighty slowly, probably according to geological time measured in eons. By the way, shore excursions, invented by the cruise lines to make more money for themselves, do have one distinct advantage: if you are on a ship's tour, rest assured the captain will wait for your group and not sail without you.

Luis asked if I wanted to buy emeralds, for Colombia produces 90 percent of the world's emeralds.

"Nope," I said. "Let's go to the old city."

"Emeralds are a very good buy here, very cheap," Luis explained.

"Old City," I said again and put on my command face, just as I do with Trent. Luckily, I have trained up to dealing with chauffeurs. Otherwise, we would be buying emeralds, most of which were produced yesterday, not from some mine, but from the bottom of a Heineken bottle.

Luis took us to Las Bovedas, an old dungeon now converted into numerous shops selling mainly junk, including thousand-year-old pre-Columbian potteries made yesterday. He wanted us to buy something in a most desperate way, proving that he works on commission.

"Pedro Claver is next, OK, Luis?"

Luis looked dejected, but agreed.

The Convento of San Pedro Claver marks the southern perimeter of El Centro, the old section of Cartagena. Claver (1580–1654), a Jesuit known as the slave of the slaves, devoted his life to the Africans brought in bondage to Cartagena. His skeleton lies there in a glass case under the main altar. We reached it in fifteen minutes driving through narrow, dusty side streets lined with pastel and whitewashed buildings baking in the tropical sun.

A beautiful woman with a tight dress and a good décolletage cleavage lay down next to the skeleton, put her hand behind her head, and preened seductively like Lauren Bacall. Claver didn't respond, and Ethel couldn't get her camera out fast enough to snap the picture.

Religion and sex—that's what South America is about.

In an adjacent room in the same church reside all sorts of zoomorphic and anthropomorphic clay gods. Catholicism is flexible: alternative gods stay here in the church in case the Indians want to hedge their bets.

Directly above the room of the idols, on the second floor, we saw the chambers where Saint Pedro Claver lived. His bed where he lay for the last four years of his life suffering from Parkinson's disease is wider and longer than our beds in M5, and the size of Claver's rooms exceed the size of our cabin by a factor of ten. But I'll bet Claver didn't get a free bottle of Grand Marnier last night, and I know he didn't eat five-course meals in the Mauretania Restaurant.

Luis tagged along looking forlorn, morose. He still has emeralds on his mind. Sure enough, he asked again, but this time I held my hands out toward him palms raised and flat, the international sign indicating stop. Luis was crestfallen. I explained to Luis the size relations between our room on QE2 and Claver's rooms here. Americans who live like that must be poor. Luis won't mention emeralds again.

Next, we toured the Palacio de la Inquisición, where they have a rather interesting collection of torture instruments. The Baroque edifice constructed in the early 1700s for the Holy See has a magnificent carved stone portal consisting of auto- and bus-exhaust-blackened dragons. Over seven hundred heretics died here after undergoing torture with the instruments on display. The Chief Inquisitor had been wont to worm secrets out of the accused and so used villainous machines for crushing thumbs, and stocks where a prisoner sat immovable while water fell drop by drop upon his head until the torture was more than humanity could bear, and a devilish contrivance of iron, which enclosed a prisoner's head like a shell and crushed it slowly by means of a screw.

Holy Mother, the One True Catholic and Apostolic Church, put people in this pleasant Inquisition and pointed to the Blessed Redeemer, who was so gentle and so merciful toward all men, and urged the barbarians to love him; and they did all they could to persuade them to love and honor him, first nipping their flesh with pincers, red hot ones, because they are the most comfortable in cold weather; then by skinning them alive a little; and finally by roasting them in public. That convinced them.

We missed the major exhibit, out on loan: a receipt for a bribe of 10 million pesos signed by Sir Francis Drake, who, in 1586, threatened to burn Cartagena to the ground. But we didn't miss the sign on the wall: *Por favor no haga uso de los intrumentos de tortura—Gracias.*

Part of us wanted to learn all the curious, outlandish ways of all the different people and countries we were to visit so that we could show off and astonish our friends when we got home. But another part of us had reached our culture limit, so we went to lunch and relaxed.

After lunch, while Ethel shopped, I swam in the pool.

Everywhere in the pool and everywhere at poolside I saw young flesh, most of the female components of which wore those special South American bathing suits called *targas* that have merely a small G-string around back between rounded cheeks. Actually, I'm only assuming the string is there because it disappears amid the orbic flexes of their beautiful behinds. I watched with interest as a young woman a yard from me undressed at poolside, put on her G-string, and flashed, in the process, her everything. In Hollywood films, they take it off top down. Here it's bottom up.

One teenager, a mestizo, sports a miniature pink kiss tattoo atop her left breast that attracted me like a magnet. I realized that it is by no means useless to travel if a man wants to see something new. This Lolita had a cigarette in one hand, a drink in the other, and her butt well exposed. Nothing unusual for Colombia. Later, she put down the drink and took a long, sideward glance at me. Had she caught me leering? Was she expressing admiration for the involuntary bulge in my stars-and-stripes Speedo? Lolita uncovered her left breast and flashed a raspberry-sized nipple. My admiration was limitless. We don't get this kind of treat on *QE2*, even in the spa. We have sex objects aboard: the shop girls, the waitresses, the stewardesses, the croupiers, the spa matrons, and the female passengers. But we have nothing like this Lolita.

Incidentally, smoking at poolside or while wading in the pool seemed de rigeur. But cigarettes are not the only things they carry there. Lots of people had portable phones. And lots of men were shouting into those portables, shouting absurd things like, "No, José, you do it my way. Understand?" Were Colombians watching too many Hollywood movies about Colombian drug lords? Was this an instance of life imitating art? Back on the ship, one wag told a story: "My wife got mugged in Cartagena. The guy took all her credit cards. But I decided not to cancel them. Whoever stole them would spend less than she would."

As the sun set, we celebrated leaving our first port of call by dancing on the aft deck.

Those *QE2* pink sail-away rum punches. They don't look like much—they taste like lollipops. But, by God, they pack the wallop of a rocket.

The gentlemen hosts kept the old ladies busy, some of whom dance like they know how, whirling to "You're Unforgettable." Is this their last hurrah? Instantly, other couples flooded the floor. The Americans dance loosely. The British dance stiffly, especially at first. But they catch on. They can learn. They are trainable.

We are all having fun. The whole sight thrills me to my deep heart's core. Men and women dancing together, happy and concordant. Romance blooming all about us like a greenhouse.

Ethel toasts me with her eyes. *QE2* has her under its spell. Some passion catalyst was in the sea air or perhaps in the water—or more likely in the drinks.

We felt a little alcoholic glow. The combined effects of good company and music made the world a wonderful place.

Day 6

Panama Canal

ANOTHER COCKTAIL PARTY— WE CAN HANDLE IT

The crowd on deck massed eight people deep as we entered the Gatun lock. Water pouring in from somewhere lifted the ship rapidly. Even jaded old me was amazed at the mechanical efficiency of 1915 engineering that made the "big ditch" possible.

A Japanese man with a video camera elbowed his way to the front of the crowd. The group eyed him disapprovingly, but no one knew enough Japanese to tell him off. As he darted away, I said aloud, "Next time he pulls that stunt, he goes overboard." The gray heads nodded agreement and turned back to watch the lock.

The woman next to me showed me her right thumb, which had gotten mangled in the garage at home. The thumb was swollen, red, hot, but not tender. The nail had turned eerie white.

"The nail's dead," I said.

"I know, but do I need a doctor? It doesn't hurt."

"Why not see Andrew Eardley? Get some antibiotics to prevent infection of bone."

As soon as the woman disappeared to go to Two deck clinic, the New Yorker on my other side, a retired high school teacher who had an old right facial palsy, started telling me out of the left corner of his mouth, the side that worked, of his ill-fated career. The terminal event was a fight in the gym. While he tried to break it up, a sixteen-year-old girl knifed him in the chest. I listened patiently because I knew he needed to unload. They should have Purple Hearts for the likes of him, people wounded in the line of duty doing civilian combat. Talk it out, friend. It will help your post-traumatic stress disorder. But, remember, you are in the sheltering arms of *QE2*. The students can't hurt you anymore. Just the angst.

Yes, *QE2* is a rest home and a sanatorium in the original sense of the word. Here the walking wounded recover faster and better than they would in the usual hospital and at considerably less expense. I shall write to President Clinton and try to interest him in getting Medicare to pay for around-the-world cruises.

People asked me more questions. Is that the continental divide? Is this Lake Gatun or Miraflores? How far to the Pedro Miguel lock? Naturally, I don't know. I thought of Herman, the master of those who don't know. Where was he? What was he doing? We're all disoriented. We're all ignorant. It's just a matter of how much.

Later in the afternoon, Pierre joined me in the hot tub. Pierre says that he is still on the wagon and counting the days. "No alcohol in forty-two days!" Pierre said proudly.

I told him that Ethel and I drank an excellent bottle of Beaulieu Reserve Cabernet 1982 at dinner last night, taking our last swallows at about 10 PM. "No alcohol in sixteen hours," I said proudly.

Pierre frowned. He thought I was making fun of him. I assured him that I was.

Overheard on deck: "Oh, Mr. Wolff, what do you think of Balzac?"

Wolff, who, at the time, was eating a chicken sandwich, politely ceased to masticate, swallowed, and answered, "I never trade in them Curb stocks!"

While I was swimming in the outside pool, *QE2* entered Miraflores locks, the last locks before we rolled under the Bridge of the Americas and into the Pacific. To celebrate this great event, the crew opened an ice cream stand on the aft deck, and a man in a starched white uniform went around ringing the ice cream bell. Suddenly, the clangor fell off the bell. Several passengers scrambled to find it. After moments of intense anxiety, one passenger reached in a crevice between teakwood planks and came up with it. He held his small trophy on high for all to see and received from the group the acclaim he so richly deserved—everyone lined up for ice cream.

Any time, day or night, they can get the stuff from room service or from the self-serve ice cream machine on One deck. The Panama Canal crossing gave them just another excuse for self-indulgence. Why not? I ate a creamy rum raisin with real rum and real raisins. Delicious! Yes, the canal is a miracle, and so is *QE2*, but rum raisin ice cream remains an even greater miracle. I recalled that poignant scene in García Márquez's book *One Hundred Years of Solitude* where the gypsies arrived in town and sold the privilege of touching ice. In the scheme of human time, it wasn't long ago when people in the tropics never had that chance, the opportunity to touch the crystal form of water called ice.

QE2 started to pass under the Bridge of the Americas. I ran up to Boat deck and ran down the outside promenade, trying to keep the bridge directly overhead. Lots of other passengers tried to do the same, including an old woman limping along on a tripod cane assisted by her paid companion.

Captain John Burton-Hall explained over the loudspeaker that it took over twelve hours to cross the fifty-one miles, whereas it usually took only six hours. "*QE2* can go only as fast as the slowest boat in the canal. You know how that is from your experiences on shore tour yesterday."

A large, rotund man tipping the scales at over three hundred pounds tried to press close to the rail next to me, but his midline got in the way. He used to live across the way in the town under the bridge: "After the Panamanians took over, it became a slum."

Mr. Rotund said that he gained 1.98 pounds per day on the cruise so far. "I'll need a blood transfusion when I get to LA I feel so sluggish."

"Better a week at the Golden Door Spa," I told him. Then I announced that, with all my drinking, I'll need a liver transplant. Perhaps he and I can go to the hospital together.

Crossing the Isthmus of Panama was high drama, especially if you knew history. Columbus would have loved the canal so that he could have made a western passage to India. Think of all the money and lives the French lost when Ferdinand Marie Vicomte de Lesseps's plan to dig a sea-level canal failed. And what about Vasco Núñez de Balboa? It was Balboa who discovered the Pacific. In fact, Balboa had stowed away to flee creditors. Balboa the bankrupt stood across the way in what is now the city of Balboa and, silent on a peak in Darien (the old name for the Isthmus of Panama), named the new ocean he saw, claiming that ocean, and all the lands having shores on it in the name of the King of Spain.

After dinner, Ethel was in a good mood. She let me play roulette. I bet $20 on black and won. Immediately, I cashed in my chips, while the cute croupier pointed to me and announced to the two men in tuxedos and the woman in the green cocktail dress, also seated at the roulette table, that "this gentleman has doubled his money." They know that. They saw it. But they didn't know that I had lost last night. And they don't know that tomorrow I'll play again. I might even bet more because I am now even.

Under the cabin door we found an official-looking Cunard envelope. I picked it up and handed to Ethel. I can't bear to read it because it might be an official notification that henceforth, because I won, I am persona non grata in the casino.

But no, the letter written on thick silky linen and smooth to the touch, merely informs us that we are members of the Samuel Cunard Key Club and can use the special lounge on Boat deck by D stairway as well as the reading and writing lounge on One deck port side by C stairway. Everyone taking the full world cruise gets these benefits plus $2,000 onboard credit for drinks or purchases. And we also got in the envelope an invitation:

Captain John Burton-Hall, R.D., R.N.R.
Cordially invites all
Full World Cruise passengers
and members of
The World Cruise Society
to join him and his officers for cocktails
in the Queen's Room on Friday 12th January 1996
At 7:15 PM
(Please enter via portside by the library)
Dress: Formal.

Relieved, I smiled. "Another cocktail party—we can handle it."

Day 7

At Sea off the Coast of Costa Rica

SNOWSTORMS in NEW YORK CAN'T BE ALL BAD

O n the way to breakfast, we noticed lots of Do Not Disturb signs hanging from cabin doors. Obviously, the passengers have fatigue. But why? And what kind? Could it be canal fatigue? That is possible. A lot of emotional energy went into the crossing. Then again, it could be dance fatigue because they had line dancing last night for passengers aged seventy-five to ninety-five. Those who saw it said that it was amazing, and I'll bet it was. The grays are determined to go down raging into the night. More power to them.

The other cause of fatigue, too much drink, seemed unlikely, since most of the gray heads, and most of the passengers, as far as I could see, drink in moderation. That's how they survived so long already. And that's how they can afford to cruise.

Today I discovered that I liked life at sea better than on shore. At sea I got a chance to relax on my own without having to deal with taxi drivers, surly chauffeurs, lunch, tour guides, and touts trying to sell fake emeralds or phony pre-Columbian pots.

Leisure, pure sea leisure, it's a sacred thing.

Ethel and I got the brochures from the Quarter deck office and started planning next year's cruise. True decadence. Right? We decided to cruise for life or die in the process.

And, speaking of death, rumor has it that we have accumulated our first stiff. What, I wondered, did they do with the body? I know eating people is wrong, so they didn't do that. Did they, as often depicted in the movies, bury the body at sea? Or did they freeze it? Will the decedent's estate get credit for the part of the cruise not taken? I'll try to get the details next time I see Andrew Eardley, the ship's doctor.

The afternoon lecture on tropical reef fish ran over. Impatient elderly others waiting in the wings screamed out, "Was the four o'clock lecture cancelled?" They wanted to hear Michael Law, singer, pianist, composer, and musical director of the Piccadilly Dance Orchestra, present "The Popular Music of the 20s, 30s, and 40s—Part 2." I skipped the music and headed to afternoon tea. On the way, I passed the tail end of the fashion show in the main lounge. Good-looking men and women from the crew modeled the latest clothes, most of which were on sale in the shops on the Royal Promenade, Upper deck. The woman in charge announced a five-minute break before bingo started. She advised the group to stay for bingo so they could win enough to buy two suits or two dresses instead of one. No, thanks. Make mine roulette. It's faster and less boring.

Walking along the deck, I couldn't help notice what people were reading. The majority are still working their way through David McCullough's compendious classic, *The Path between the Seas: The Creation of the Panama Canal, 1870–1914.* They were reading this even though the canal lay 571 miles behind us. Another old man, who looked like he could be 102, slumped in his deck chair facing into the sun, scanned a different book, *How to Be a Success Overnight.* Given his age, I could understand why he was in a hurry.

Three men and one woman assembled on the aft railing for skeet shooting. Gone are the good old days when, in my youth, I used to shoot real shotguns at real clay pigeons off the deck of the *Queen of Bermuda*, the *United States*, or, yes, I'm that old, the old *Queen Elizabeth.* But these guns looked like authentic over and under Beretta twelve-gauge shotguns, and they were not. These guns represented still another dilution of authentic experience. Someone had fitted them with lasers, and, when the trigger was pulled, they made a phony arcade sound. The clay pigeons dropped overboard into the everlasting sea, safe from any harm that might have been inflicted on them by real guns shooting real pellets.

The phony skeet shots were too soft, so the group on the firing line wanted the noise turned up. "Make it more real" is what they said. Norman Cole obliged, but ten decibels higher was still inadequate, and something else went wrong. The woman's gun kept firing even after she put it down on the deck—some sort of electric glitch. And then, as if copying the gun, the watertight doors closed in sector seven, due to some glitch in the electric circuits.

Only a fool doesn't see the real danger here. The energy of machines exceeded that of human beings, making humans objects and not the masters. I couldn't get back to M5 because the doors between the Lido and stairway G closed. Two crew members labored vainly to pry them open. Another stood by with a crowbar. The automatic doors, the loudspeaker explained, closed as if they had a will of their own. No man knew why. My mood was turning sour while I waited for the crew to figure it out. I thought about my twenty-foot 250-horsepower inboard Bayliner boat. It always had something going wrong. A big boat like *QE2* must be like a small boat, only with bigger problems.

Fortunately, my souring attitude got readjusted at the captain's cocktail party.

Wow! What a party—right out of *The Great Gatsby*. A seventeen-piece orchestra played the big band favorites like "Jealousy" and "Temptation," while white-gloved waiters and waitresses circulated with platters overfilled with (real) champagne in crystal fluted glasses. The golden liquid and its bubbles glittered among the shimmering women dressed in metallic red-and-light-blue-spangled evening dresses and men in white dinner jackets and black tuxedos.

Ethel kept going back for caviar—*massosol* naturally, the beaded, less salty, and therefore the more expensive type, with all the trimmings: chopped egg, onion bits, capers (which are nasturtium seeds), and sour cream. I did the same, but also indulged with frequent shots of ice-cold Absolut vodka.

Not bad.

This group knows how to party. They are the World Cruise Society, the club of the crème de la crème of cruise passengers, just as *QE2* is the crème de la crème of cruise ships. These are the people who do the *long cruises*, a technical term meaning more than two weeks. If you have the time, the money, and a love of cruising, you can join them in the long cruise way of life, a way of life that these old salts and old salt substitutes gathered here already enjoy. Why not? Why not have the sea wash off your worries and the sun dry off your tears?

But was the party really that good? Or was it that the champagne and the vodkas had changed the scene before my eyes into something significant, elemental, and profound? No doubt I was enjoying myself. The others were too. I could tell from those vacuous bursts of laughter that rose above the din of the music. The air was alive with chatter, and casual innuendo, and introductions forgotten on the spot, and enthusiastic meetings between people who never knew each other's names. The women, when they danced, put their heads on men's shoulders in a puppyish, convivial manner. I love them when they get that way. That transformation remains one of the great beneficial effects of a real cocktail party with real cocktails.

Captain John Burton-Hall came over and talked to us. He seemed brutally honest and funny when he told us, "Snowstorms in New York can't be all bad. 555 Fifth Avenue [Cunard headquarters] closed down, and, for a while, we had some peace."

Ethel informed the captain of our overarching plan to take the world cruise in progressively increasing better conditions, starting at the bottom and working up. The captain stroked his pepper-and-salt beard. Did I detect a twinkle in his eye? "Actually," he said, "we don't care what class people are in as long as they drink at the bars. That's where the money comes in."

We were hungry, so we left the party and headed to Mauretania for dinner. I'll describe one of the five-course meals there. Let's plan that for on day nine. That way, it is prearranged, and I can't be accused of preselecting the best or the worst meal for review. The movie was *Don Juan DeMarco* where an overweight Marlon Brando looked like he had been on one perpetual cruise without the benefit of the spa, the spa diet, or the *QE2* health club and exercise rooms. After the movie, we made our nightly pilgrimage to the onboard shrine of Fortuna, Roman goddess of fortune.

While I watched, Ethel played out her destiny, losing $5 on the slot machines. This was before she figured out that the electronic poker games play out slower. Notice I said "play out," not "pay out." None of the machines truly pays out for long. With the poker machines, you lose, but it takes longer than with the slots.

Ethel, never a good loser, got really annoyed because everyone around her seemed to be winning. We heard the jingle-jangle of what sounded like hundreds of coins spitting out into the metal trays from machines far from us and nearer the entrance to the casino. Later, one of the croupiers, who shall remain nameless, told me that those machines have the more favorable chips to entice people into the gaming rooms.

Alas, Ethel ran out of coins. She lost her limit of $5 and quit. "Oh, well," she said with a sigh, as she gave me a kiss on the cheek. "Unlucky in chance, lucky in love."

My turn.

At the roulette wheel, I played out my destiny. First, I bet $20 on the last field, numbers 25 to 36, playing two to one, and won. The croupier, a beautiful ebony woman in a striking blue dress, gave me my $40 profit, half of which I gave to Ethel to hold. That's the stake. Now I am playing with profits.

I put $20 on red and won again. I gave that $20 profit to Ethel to hold, knowing I have doubled my money and am now in a position to make a killing. I bet $20 on the first field, 1 to 12, and lost. Because I always quit when ahead, I cashed in. Net profit for the night: $40.

Yes, I doubled my money again. But I have no wish to play anymore because, if I don't play again, the law of averages will never catch up with me, and I shall leave the ship a winner forever.

Day 8

At Sea

OVERNIGHT OUR IN-SIGN-IFICANCE INCREASED

*E*thel and I glide as weightless heavenly bodies, swirling around the stage, moving from dazzling, light-footed quickstep; to graceful, long-striding foxtrot; and on to waltz. I bend her back into an elegant dip and raise her up again to another dazzling array of turns and fancy twists, my black tails flying out behind me, her sequined skirt swirling and shimmering in the spotlights that followed us around the stage. Multitudes watch and applaud and cheer as we, hand in hand, take our final bow. "Encore, encore," they shout. Bouquets of flowers land at Ethel's feet. Mysteriously, years have evaporated from us. We stood young again!

Ethel shook me frantically. "Wake up, sleepy head, or we'll miss breakfast."

As we left our cabin, we noticed that our Do Not Disturb sign had disappeared. Since signs don't walk off by themselves, I assumed someone took it. Taking their own sign as a souvenir would appear too gauche, so they took ours.

Ethel and I are in-sign-ificant, doubly insignificant because we were insignificant before we lost our sign and now we are more so. Talking about significance reminded me of a character in a novel who, when asked about his name, said that it was just a bunch of letters. He was right, of course. But the same may be said for all of the world's literature —just a bunch of letters with some spaces and punctuation thrown in. Can that be insignificant? No way! The significance comes from the structure.

At that moment, Nichola, our stewardess, came down the aisle with her orange life jacket on.

"Going swimming?" I asked.

"No, I've already been," she said.

Because Nichola seemed worried about something (the disappearance of multiple signs? or worse, a complaint from a passenger?), I didn't have the courage to ask her for another sign. Perhaps I can just lift someone else's sign and perpetuate injustice just as it is usually perpetuated in this wide world.

The ship's daily bulletin said the stock market has recovered somewhat in active trading. I didn't realize it was down. I hope I don't get stock-sheet shock when we arrive in Los Angeles. Stock-sheet shock, incidentally, resembles car-sticker shock, except it can be more serious, possibly even fatal for someone like myself.

After breakfast, I tried to read in the library, but the place was jammed and noisy. The gray heads were consulting reference works, trying to get the answers to the daily quiz, a sheet of questions that the librarian hands out each morning.

Oh, no! A fax from home intruded on my tranquil sea happiness. Bad news as usual. *Frontline*, some kind of TV news program, wants to interview me. Why can't they leave me alone?

I put the fax aside. Why should I worry about it? It's just a bunch of letters. Besides, I can't deal with this bullshit now. I'm not in the right mentality. I just want to have fun and smooth sailing, fair weather, and following seas. Meanwhile, the real world continues to enter my life unremittingly, continues to afflict me through the ceaseless ringing of the telephone, the mail in the mailbox, the intrusive newspaper headlines. At least

I'm better off than President Clinton. The paper says he owes several million dollars in legal fees involving Whitewater and sexual harassment.

Yeah. Newspapers are one thing. But TV, that's far worse. Why can't we put a stop to it? Through the TV set we get the unstoppable, incomprehensible penetration of the corrupt commercial, political, and religious practices of contemporary America, hyped, mediated, doped up, born again, and increasingly fundamentalist, iconoclastic, and ignorant. All of which is heading us for trouble, lots of trouble.

I decided to take my mind off *Frontline* by doing some busy work. I changed $20 into pesos at the Travelex on Two deck. I got 130 pesos and considered myself rich. They are new pesos, and they look more beautiful than dollars mainly because of the bright colors, reds and blues. Because of inflation, the old peso was divided by one thousand and got the value of the new one. Next year, if inflation continues, the peso may have to divide again.

At the purser's office, I asked for visitor passes for my son, Craig, and my daughter-in-law, Michelle, whom I have dubbed Michelle the Beautiful, in case they wish to visit when we hit Los Angeles. The purser did the worst thing anybody can ever do to a person. He made me fill out a form. While I worked on the form, a distinguished elderly gentleman came up and complained: "I didn't get an invitation to the captain's party last night."

"You missed a good party," I assured him.

More angry, the man asserted that he was a full world-cruise passenger, a member of the Samuel Cunard Key Club, and a member of the World Cruise Society and therefore had all three reasons to get an invitation. The purser told him the next party will happen on the sixteenth, just out of Acapulco. He'll get invited then. "The party last night wasn't for World Cruise Members [*sic*]."

"It was so," the old guy growled. "You can't fool me."

Last task—I turned in our passports to the manifest office so we can get off the ship in Los Angeles. Herman was two people ahead of me in line. He had a problem. Not only doesn't he have one of those things called a name, but also he doesn't have one of those things called a passport. Claire Evans, the woman running the manifest office, handed

Herman a form for a new passport. Herman just stared at the green form, the look on his face blanker than the form itself.

Since Herman seemed to be too slow, Claire told him to sit down at the nearby table and work on it so she can take care of the others in line. Herman sat and stared, trying to puzzle it out. From my vantage point, I could see that Herman's form was upside down. I didn't set it right. I knew that wouldn't help.

Later I watched *Pocahontas*. I wanted to see this new American icon. The film looked pretty good, a kind of animated operatic romance with definite postmodern leanings, since we never learned whether John Smith lived or died and whether he and Pocahontas ever got together to do the—well, you know. Last Christmas, the Houston Doctors Club party hosted two special guests: Batman and, you guessed it, Pocahontas. Santa didn't show.

When I got out of the movie, everyone was drunk again, or at least looked that way due to the rough seas. I admit a personal failing: I experienced a kind of joy seeing other people, and not me, suffer from the miseries of seasickness.

I went out on deck and was blown by fifty-knot winds. The sea resembled a boiling cauldron with white horses all around. The deck stewards closed the outside pool by hanging a net over it so no one can swim. Even without the net, it wouldn't have been a good idea to try to swim there: the rough sea had sloshed all the water out of the pool.

I had no choice. I had to go back to the spa.

At the reception desk, two other sea nymphets, one brunette and one redhead, have replaced Miss Universe. They have great shapes, and one wonders whether one had to have a great shape to work at the spa or whether working at the spa gives you a great shape. This is the old chicken-and-egg problem in a different form—right? Which came first? Does it matter? Beauty is its own excuse for being and a big calling card on QE2 and in this wide world.

The brunette handed me a towel and smiled as if she wanted to be my trophy wife. She calls herself Elena—Greek for Helen. Like Helen of Troy, she has the face that could launch a thousand ships, and not just rowboats, big ships like *QE2*. Forget Kathy, my former Miss Universe. I want Elena. Her body talked.

In the dry sauna, I met Richard, another M5 passenger who is going around the world as a single. His room is as Spartan as ours, but he didn't mind. He thinks the food in Mauretania is great. He wrote a check for $19,000 (single supplement included) and feels he got the travel bargain of a lifetime. Considering he also got the $2,000 onboard credit, he did get the travel bargain of a lifetime. Of that I have no doubt.

The dry sauna was making me sweat too much, so I left. When I got back to M5, I was really hot in another way. I coaxed Ethel into bed, and we made love. Consequently, we were late for dinner. But what was this? As we came in to the restaurant, I spied Pierre seated in the Mauretania Restaurant. How can that be? Upper-class passengers are not allowed in the lower-class dinning room. But there he was, sitting alone at a table. Closer inspection showed a glass and a bottle of wine. Although those things could be there just for show, the proof that he can't be all that sincere about his health is in his hand—he is smoking a cigarette! Doesn't he know that cigarettes can kill? Too bad cigarettes don't kill reliably or fast enough. From the likes of him, the pretentious liar should be killed unfailingly and quickly.

Pierre caught my eye. With his hand, he tried to cover the cigarette now resting in the ashtray. It's hopeless. He can't hide the smoke. He can't hide the wine. He can't hide himself. He can't hide the truth.

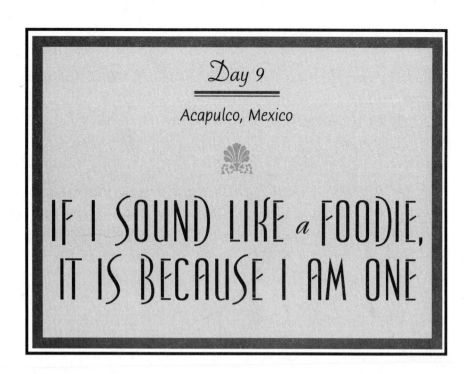

Day 9

Acapulco, Mexico

IF I SOUND LIKE *a* FOODIE, IT IS BECAUSE I AM ONE

*A*capulco Bay shone in the distance. The air smelled fresh and clean and moist after the rain. Shirtsleeve weather. I decided to violate the dress code by wearing shorts to breakfast. Ethel was worried. "No shorts in the dining room. It says so right here in the brochure. They might throw you out."

Roland Ringwald, assistant restaurant manager, didn't mind. He just smiled as usual and bowed as usual, and said as usual, "Good morning, sir."

While others went on the shore excursions, Ethel and I went on our own. First stop: the game room at the Zocalo. It was Sunday. I had to practice my religion, a religion without sin, a religion without God, a religion without menacing punishment, a religion where the only grace is a high score. Many other zealots, mostly teenage boys, were practicing my religion. The game room had literally hundreds of altars, all making noise and lighting numbered lights. Included among the newer machines were some old favorites that you don't see anymore in the United States, like Pacman.

I watched a Mexican boy about twelve years old sit behind the wheel of a drive-a-car game. He selected a yellow Austin Healey, the car of his dreams. Away he went. The scenery moved continuously, making the car appear to speed forever down a marvelous suburban highway, the highway of his dreams. The game represents an allegory of life, for, as the road wound on, obstacles—mainly other cars, some white horses, a garbage truck constantly materialized, menacing the little Austin and its little driver, presenting problems he had to get around or else.

"Hang in there, kid!" I screamed. "It only gets tougher."

The Austin entered the countryside, where sheep, cows, and women with children presented the obstacles now. The boy tried desperately to avoid collisions by cutting the wheel and swerving the car. In furious concentration, he bit his lip. But, as in life, the obstacles kept coming, harder and faster. They wouldn't let up. They wouldn't end. But he does. He crashed and burned. The screen requested another 50 centavos, which the boy fed into the slot. The game showed how it approached the redemptive quality of all great religions. For an offering of only 50 centavos, the boy got to live again. Given enough centavos, he will have as many lives as he needs. He will be immortal.

The cathedral, only eighty-one feet from the arcade, drew our attention with its Byzantine central dome and two cerulean blue domed spires with bright yellow stars. On the inside, the priest was haranguing the standing crowd. What was he saying? Something about birth control. Why was he so angry? Why did they stand there in silence, taking it all in so respectfully? If they were *QE2*ers, they would be shouting back.

Outside by the bust of Juan Álvarez (1790–1867), an Indian woman breast-fed her three-year-old son whose face was covered with impetigo. Her breast, right out there in the open, looked like a muskmelon. The kid ate with relish. I copied the inscription on Álvarez's bust: *Pobre entre a la Presidencia, pobre sali de ella.* Can our politicians truthfully make the same statement?

Ethel and I marched along the Avenida Costera Miguel Alemán, which the signs along the way called "Avenida C. Miguel Alemán" to keep people from referring to it as La Costera (the coast), which most of the locals call it anyway as it follows the coast.

All around people tried to sell us something or tell us where to go so that someone else could sell us something. And, of course, little healthy, smiling children followed us, asking for money. One of these days, I am going to fling loads of money their way just to see what happens.

In some sort of twisted irony that one might find only in fiction, a taxi driver pulled alongside us and tried to buy my beige *QE2* world cruise cap. "How much," he kept asking, and I kept saying that it wasn't for sale. He told me he collects hats. I told him so did I. "But you can get another at the ship."

"I don't think so," I said.

Finally, he peeled off because he wasn't supposed to drive on the beach.

On the dirty brown sand, the pelicans resided in abundance. I counted twenty-seven on one dinghy and counted eight dinghies, each loaded with pelicans. Knowing pelicans and birds in general, I bet they think they own the dinghies, the beach, and everything else, too.

"Pelican, pelican," said Ethel. "Its beak holds more that its belly can."

Here in Acapulco beach burials are popular. We saw lots of people buried in the sand, at least a dozen men and one woman, and three others in the process of getting buried. And one man was trying to bury himself. Those buried looked pretty contented with their faces resting up toward the sun and their whole bodies covered with sand. Mexico went in for perverse pleasures in some respects: one man, with the help of his girl-friend, smoked a cigarette while remaining buried. Between puffs, she delivered wet hungry kisses to his lips that had, only moments before, sucked smoke.

After walking three miles, we got hungry. We got back on La Costera, hailed a cab, and went to the Princess Hotel, Howard Hughes's favorite. Along the way we passed the famous Señor Frog's and Las Brisias, the most expensive hotel in Acapulco. Rooms at Brisias ran $500 (not pesos) a night, meals not included.

The tortilla, a flat, round, unleavened bread, was invented by the ancient Mexicans. Stuff it with meat, chicken, or beans and roll it, and it becomes a taco. Serve it open with a dash of chili sauce, and you have chalupas; sprinkle it with sauce and a little cream, then bake it, and you have enchiladas, what we ate for lunch.

The Princess Hotel wouldn't let us use the pool without paying $21 each, probably to cover liability insurance. And I know why. In 1978, while the famous Acapulco divers leaped into the seething Pacific from the cliffs at La Quebrada and escaped unscathed, Mark Shorrock, one of the *QE2*'s waiters, dove into the Princess Hotel pool, struck his head, and died. He was just twenty years old.

On the way back to El Centro, both of us were under the influence of margaritas, which, incidentally, they really know how to make in Mexico. We passed a theater showing a film titled *Amor de locos.*

"That describes us," I told Ethel while kissing her. We were smooching in the backseat just like kids in high school.

Large numbers of passengers turned out for the sail-away party, ten times the number we had for the Cartagena departure. Ethel pointed out that the word must have gotten around that they serve killer rum punches. That was part of it. The other part was that the group was unwinding. Most of them will leave the ship in two days. Hence, they were on the downward slope of their cruise, and they wanted to have their last fling.

I spotted Pierre.

He turned away and headed in the opposite direction. When a Frenchman loses face, that's an earthquake. I know he lied to me. What punishment does he deserve? Dante punished sinners according to the kind of sin and the intention. Pierre's sin is trivial, telling me he was first class when he actually was, like us, Mauretania, the worst class. His intention was trivial also: to make himself look good. He lied to get me to esteem him more, but since I knew that he lied, I esteemed him less. Isn't that retributive justice? Isn't that punishment enough?

The Mauretania dining room has eight subdivisions, with non-smoking on starboard and smoking on port side, except for our small section on port side aft by the captain's table, which is nonsmoking also. The colors are salmon pink in napkins and tablecloths, and each table has a white vase of pink carnations. Rich, thick smells of roasting meats twitched the nose as Ethel and I greeted the waiters who lined up along the aisles just before we came in. In fact, since we were first in line and closest to the doors, I overheard, just before we entered, Roland Ringwald yell, "Everybody get ready. Look happy!"

Antonio, our Mauretania waiter, and Chris, Antonio's assistant, unfolded our napkins and draped them over our laps while a soft classical violin concerto played in the background. I turned over the plate and read "Royal Doulton, Bone China." Then I lifted one of the spoons and made out "Wm. A. Rogers Hotel Plate Oneida, Ltd." stamped on the back.

Soon we settled down to the serious business of eating.

For me, the meal started with Atlantic and Pacific seafood terrine with peppered sour cream. At the center, this masterpiece had a white fish surrounded by a thin layer of caviar and a salmon mousse around that. I didn't have much time to admire the colors—white, black, and pink— because, alas, the whole thing disappeared in the blink of an eye.

Other hors d'oeuvres included a crisp Waldorf salad with walnuts and hearts of iceberg lettuce, an exotic fruit platter topped with lime sherbet, and *cucuk* (a cucumber, mint, and garlic salad with plain yogurt, tossed romaine, and feta and oregano dressings).

Next, I savored a thick cream of onion soup. Other soups included chilled banana and coconut and chicken broth flavored with lemon grass and shiitake mushrooms. That's typical, three soups—one cream, one broth, and one chilled. We cleared our palates with kiwi sherbet with stone-fruit coulis. A stone fruit is one that has a stone (pit) at its center. A stone-fruit coulis consists of a purée of bits of apricot, plum, and peach.

The main course arrived next: a whole glazed roast duck with brandied orange duck sauce, braised red cabbage, croquette potatoes, carrots, asparagus, and steamed cauliflower. I thought the duck overcooked because I like my duck European style, which is to say, rare. Those who didn't choose the duck could have had broiled fresh swordfish with bush tomato chutney, yam chips, and roasted root vegetables in olive oil.

Ethel let me taste her swordfish.

"Goddamn! I made a mistake. I should have ordered the swordfish," I told Chris, who told me that he would get me a swordfish if I wanted to eat two entrées.

Other choices included a roast leg of pork glazed in honey with mashed yams and braised vegetable casserole or a gravy roast prime rib or beef with horseradish gravy, Yorkshire pudding (a kind of puff pastry popular in England), roasted potatoes, Brussels sprouts, and carrots. And last but not least was the vegetarian dish that always ended the list. Tonight's selection: baked golden vegetable and lentil purse on a carrot coulis with snap peas and potatoes.

A tossed salad with choice of dressings followed, and after that came dessert. I ate parfait au marron glacé (chestnut parfait) with brandied apples, but I could have selected kiwi sherbet, pear of mascarpone (stuffed pear with mascarpone and chocolate pistachio sauce), fresh blueberry pie with whipped cream, or ice cream with three dessert sauces: chocolate fudge, vanilla, and raspberry. After that, one could enjoy assorted international cheeses, chilled whole fruits, Ceylon and China tea, coffees (regular and decaffeinated), cappuccino, espresso, hot chocolate, coffee hag, iced tea, and iced coffee, and any of hundreds of after-dinner drinks.

In every respect, this meal resembled all the others we experienced at Mauretania, with well-presented, colorful, tasty food of great variety.

Oh, yes, how could I forget? Our wine for the night was a robust Château Montelena 1991, Cabernet Sauvignon, an excellent bargain at, I kid you not, $34 a bottle. It was even a greater bargain considering that we paid for it with our onboard credit, and thus the true cost to us was nothing, zero.

Hinano Yeo (Yo-Yo), our assistant manager, filled us in on some Mauretania details. Over six hundred meals were served tonight in two sittings. About forty bottles of wine were drunk, but only one glass of Macallan eighteen-year-old scotch whisky (mine at $4).

Our praise for the food and drink of *QE2* remains unlimited. If I sound like a foodie, it is because I am one.

Day 10

At Sea

WE SCREW OUR WAY ACROSS the OCEAN

*O*pen ocean: the spell of fascination is there. Especially today, a day of faultless beauty. A cloudless sky; a refreshing summer wind; a radiant sunshine that glinted and glistened cheerily on the Pacific surface like millions of finely cut diamonds, flashing from dancing wavelets instead of crested mountains of water; a sea beneath us that was so wonderfully blue—so richly, brilliantly blue—that it overcame the dullest sensibilities with the spell of its fascination. I love you blue, I love you blue.

Off portside dolphins amused the group outside the library, and a few of the gray heads interrupted their intense quest for answers to the daily quiz to admire the dolphins. The ship passed the tip of Baja California, where a seal breeding ground existed, and the first officer announced that a seal had been spotted off starboard. The seal population had been hurt by oversealing, the first mate explains, but now, under protection, the seals are multiplying. And that was good news—but not for the fish.

Today's agenda lists thirty-seven activities, not including Kathryn

Morris the vocalist, the Lynn Hi-Fi, the tea dance with the Glenn Miller Orchestra, the close-up magic show in the Lion Pub, and three movies (*Something to Talk About, Pocahontas,* and *Now and Then*). For some events I don't qualify, like the get-together at the Grand Lounge for grandparents. Bring your pictures, the invitation said. I didn't have grandchildren, and, without pictures, my fraud would have soon been exposed. I do carry in my wallet a picture of P.J., but I know P.J. looks much more like a calico cat than a grandchild. Some of the gray heads would know the difference. And some events sound too decadent even for me to attend, like Captain John Burton-Hall's cocktail party for Cunard World Club members in the Queens Room starting at 11:30 AM.

I decided to set limits. No drinking before noon and only three formal activities per day. No more. After that, I'm free to roam, swim, and lounge around, soaking up the sun and sea. Activity one: I attended Waldemar Hansen's lecture on Los Angeles. This was my chance to find out if Waldemar knows whereof he speaks. Since I know Los Angeles, I can figure out whether Hansen is a hack or not.

Waldemar surprised me by starting out quoting from *The Day of the Locust* (1939), Nathanael West's best book, usually and inevitably compared with F. Scott Fitzgerald's *The Last Tycoon* (1941), since both the Hollywood novels were written about the same time, from similar experiences of working as a screenwriter. Waldemar reads from the beginning, at the fantasy's heart, on the studio sets with their illusions and their stars, but the story quickly moves out into the equally fantastic world of Los Angeles and beyond—exposing a world of sensations and sports, cults and sects, clowns and circuses, narcissistic promises and passions, excesses and extras, flaunted lifestyles. Los Angeles, the City of the Angels, ironically is fed by a daily news–diet of murder, sex crimes, explosions, wrecks, love nests, fires, miracles all of them somewhere between actuality and sensational dream. The citizens are lost and bizarre. In fact, *The Day of the Locust* is a basic work of American black humor, a gothic comedy of a world that, driven to frenzy by extreme desires, seeks solace in absurd and apocalyptic dreams. Waldemar even mentioned that West died in a car accident. Waldemar considered that appropriate for someone who lived in Los Angeles, but Waldemar didn't mention the year (1940) and the place (near El Centro, California). Nor does Waldemar mention West's real name: Nathan Weinstein.

Nevertheless, my esteem for Hansen goes up log numbers. He penetrated the surface and understands things from the perspective of literature. Bravo. I will attend every lecture Hansen gives on this world cruise from now until April 6th from here to eternity via Hong Kong, Sydney, Mombasa, and Rio.

Waldemar goes on praising and vilifying Los Angeles. He quotes Fred Allen, "California is fine if you are an orange." He tells us that more people are in psychoanalysis in Los Angeles than in any other city: "Anyone who goes to a psychiatrist needs to have his head examined."

After lunch, Michael Lindberg, our Mauretania wine steward, takes us below to see the hotel store room and the connoisseur wines, which are kept locked away in an air-conditioned vault. With Michael in the lead, Ethel and I pass through narrow corridors, down metal stairs painted green and white (our footfalls echoing with metallic thuds). We pass through locked doors that Michael unlocked and into the inner sanctum, where, on Seven deck amidships, the great wines rest in air-conditioned comfort and free of roll, yaw, pitch, thrust, or swing. Michael and I admire the great bottles of Château Pavie, Lafite-Rothschild, La Tache, and so forth.

The same room contains the premium cigars, hundreds of boxes of them, including Cuban Romeo y Julietas. Curse our silly government's policy that says we Americans can't have them.

Nick Tanner, the quartermaster, joined us and took us further below to Eight deck, where the ship narrowed to about thirty feet and we can, looking up and to the sides, actually see the three-fourth-inch steel plate that keeps the sea out and protects our lives. Few passengers dare to tread here. In contrast to the opulent decor of the passenger areas of the ship, the grimy working alleyway, with lengths of steel pipe to step over and oil patches to avoid, did not foster a feeling of festivity. Below deck, the area, where almost as many souls toiled to maintain the upstairs opulence as there were passengers to enjoy that opulence, is Spartan and utilitarian but not depressing. The grimy faces we passed showed smiles. They were comrades at sea.

I sniff the air, twitching my nose. Nick assured me that's garbage. Why not? They compact it next door where they used to shelve five thousand packs of cigarettes. "The garbage gets off in LA, along with hundreds of passengers," Nick says facetiously. "Hundreds of other passengers will take their places. They will in turn create new garbage."

We see cases and cases of Henkell Trocken, the pour champagne for all the *QE2*'s three classes. Cases and cases of Heineken beer, as well as loads of soft drinks, loom overhead and could crush us if the ship hit another ninety-foot wave. Strangely, Nick assigns undue importance to the soft drinks. I myself can't even imagine drinking a Diet Coke, for instance; I go for the more interesting drinks. But Nick assures me they are more popular than wine. Oh well, it takes all kinds to make a cruise, just as it takes all kinds to make a world. If they don't want to drink wine, let them drink Coke. Everyone to his or her own taste. And I know mine.

Nick assured us that the same foodstuffs are served in all the *QE2* restaurants. He said the Mauretania chefs don't have as much time as the grill chefs, so the final product doesn't come out as fancy, but it's the exact same chicken, pork, duck, cheese, and so forth. I asked how they handle special diets, and poor Nick tells us about his nightmares. All those never-ending special diets: low salt, low fat, low cholesterol. They seem to invent a new diet every segment. "Will they never end?" Nick wondered. Two years ago the *QE2* solved the kosher problem (they used to have two kosher chefs and two inspectors onboard at all times) by simply buying kosher T.V. dinners and heating them for the people who eat them.

I pointed to my watch and express regret that I was pressed for time, since I wanted to hear Captain John Burton-Hall being interviewed by Elaine Mackay, the social director.

I arrived in the Grand Lounge just in time to catch the tail end of the *What's My Line* game where some young woman with brown hair and a pixie face explains that she operated a bungee jumping apparatus before she became a hair stylist.

Want to know the difference between a fairy tale and a sea story? One starts, "Once upon a time," and the other starts, "Listen up—I shit you not." Captain John Burton-Hall tells his story. It's a sea story, all right, but it sounds true.

He started at age thirteen, apprenticed to learn to sail, and has been at it ever since. His mother burst into tears as he, in his cadet naval uniform, marched off into the mists. His initial pay was £5 a month paid twice yearly, but he makes more now (amount unstated). He got his master mariner's certificate at age twenty-six and was a diver in the Royal Navy. Soon he noticed that he never met an admiral who had been a diver, so he quit the navy and became a commercial captain working mainly out of Asian ports for lines from Singapore.

Captain John Burton-Hall continued his brutal honesty by admitting that he loves the seat he now sits on (he has commanded since 1990) but doesn't like the "Hyde face" (as in Robert Louis Balfour Stevenson's novel *Strange Case of Doctor Jekyll and Mr. Hyde*) he puts on each night to entertain. The captain has another complaint: he doesn't like his diet. He eats only two courses and watches with envy while the guests he entertains eat eight: "It's a kind of torture."

In his spare time, Captain John Burton-Hall stays far away from the sea and repairs his TR3A Triumph and an Austin Healey, regretting as he does so the demise of the British automotive industry.

QE2 is a small town, the captain says in closing, eighteen hundred passengers (two-thirds women) and a thousand crew members (one-third women). Like every small town, it never entirely shuts down. He, as the mayor, stays up a lot.

Elaine Mackay opened the questions to the audience. The usual torrent of complaints followed. One fellow wants to know why they haven't constructed a bubble to run along the outside of the ship so his handicapped wife could more easily move fore and aft. The gaunt, pathetic women at the man's side looks like a ghost and doesn't participate in the debate because she is sleeping. Captain John Burton-Hall replied that putting anything on the side of the ship might risk having it blown off. The voice returns like an insistent out-of-tune violin on an August afternoon: "I have constructed billions of dollars' worth of things like this and will make a plan. You could remove and store the bubble when the weather becomes inclement."

This guy is too much. I pass the fellow a note saying that he should get his wife a motorized wheelchair or an Amigo. Other passengers have them, and they took the heritage tour, frequently arriving at the next spot before the rest of us.

Another malcontent wants to know why the 'round-the-world tour keeps going to the same places over and over again. Captain John Burton-Hall doesn't explain that ships don't go out of this world into space or to the moon, not yet. Instead, he paused, stroked his beard, smirked, scratched his right ear, and then explained that marketing tells him where to go and where to stop and that the US government has several strange regulations that make certain other stops necessary. For instance, the ABC port rule requires that a foreign ship must go to a foreign port before redocking in the United States. That is why, after we leave Los Angeles, we shall call at Ensenada, Mexico. Whenever something doesn't make sense, you can bet the government is involved.

The questioner rejects the answer. These people don't want to be baffled with some kind of government bullshit. And they certainly don't want to hear or consider the captain's problems. They just want the ship to go where *they* want to go. The questioner suggested Aruba.

I asked what the letters after Captain John Burton-Hall's name meant, the "RD" and the "RNR."

He replied, "RNR" means Royal Navy Retired and that is why this ship flies a blue and not a red ensign. The other means my crimes have been undetected for thirty years."

Crimes? The audience laughs with a kind of nervous insecurity. They don't understand. Nor do I. Is it part of the captain's sea mystique?

Elaine signals by shifting her posture in the chair that the questioning will soon end. I know it will because it's four minutes to four, when bingo starts at four. Another gray head in the back with a sincere concerned face stands up and shouts in a raspy, nervous voice that he has been worried about the propellers. He thinks cavitation occurs and this endangers the ship and compromises fuel efficiency as well. The other passengers nod their heads, indicating they share the concern, any concern that deals with inefficiency and danger, though not a one of them, I wager, knows what the hell this guy means when he says *cavitation*. I don't. The *Oxford English Dictionary* says it's a kind of propeller slippage, a failure to fully contact the water.

But Captain John Burton-Hall knows about cavitation. I can tell. He scratches his head, then pulls at his pepper-and-salt beard. "Our propellers turn too slowly for cavitation to occur. We screw our way through the ocean."

Should I raise my hand and tell John Burton-Hall that Ethel and I are doing the same, screwing our way through the ocean, sometimes twice a day? I decide not to. Discretion is the better part of valor. Besides, someone might think I was bragging. Others might think I was being modest. And some, the majority, might not think at all.

I issue myself an hour in the outside pool to have pure, unadulterated fun. We are headed north (the wrong direction; whenever you are headed north or east, it's the wrong direction). The pool water had gotten cooler. But nothing's all bad. The number of people in the pool inversely relates to the temperature of the water, so I almost have the pool to myself.

Something new happened at dinner. They hung flags all about the Mauretania. It looks like a meeting of the League of Nations. Ethel and I sit under a white flag with a big red cross on it.

"What flag is it?" I asked Chris, who replies, "Switzerland, the country where nothing ever happens."

Yo-Yo comes by to explain that we shouldn't miss the midnight buffet in the Lido, which they always have just before a major embarkation. We hurry up eating so we won't be late for the buffet. As we are about to leave, the Mauretania lights go out. Loud thunder noises fill the dining room, and then we see lots of lightning (artificial high-intensity strobe lights) followed by the singing of "Auld Lang Syne."

The passengers and crew join in and sing along. Then, from the forward kitchen, waiters stride out carrying individual baked Alaskas in the center of which stand silver cylindrical tubes squirting fountains of brilliant white sparks. The room fills with light and sparks, some smoke, music, and human voices laughing, shouting, and singing. I sense a true peak moment in my life, an epiphany of happiness.

The mood lasts ten minutes more, while our baked Alaska disappeared too fast. Ethel jokes that we are eating a baked Alaskan. Chris, who is from Cyprus and speaks Greek, even though Ethel's joke plays on a subtle difference in one English word, seems to get it. He laughs. We are being silly. But happy.

Later, I bet $20 at roulette and lost. Despite the loss, my expansive Irish mood doesn't change. In the theater, we see *Now and Then* because the sign said the movie starred Demi Moore. At the end, I'm convinced that I have seen a postmodern movie. The French philosopher Jean-François Lyotard saw the postmodern condition as marked by the collapse of all the great metanarratives (Christianity, Marxism) that presumed to truth and their replacement by essentially provisional and indeterminate forms of narrative. Others argued that the world outside was overwritten and overplotted (still is), so the postmodern novel could do nothing other than rewrite or deconstruct it. And so we get movies like *Now and Then* that abandon familiar ways of thinking about films, that have no plot, characters, or theme. Like every postmodern work, *Now and Then* raised and dropped story questions in the blinking of an eye. I know I'm bored because I notice the black dots in the upper right of the screen that signal the projectionist to change reels.

The film ends, as I thought it would, without a moral or resolution. The postmodern movie, I suppose, is like a captain's party or a travel book: a field of desire and dream ever dissolving and reforming, filled with pratfalls and interrupted fornications, sudden redirections, group activity without closure, and weird rituals all typifying life and all signifying nothing. At least I got to see Demi Moore.

Ethel and I went to the midnight buffet. Amazing ice statues of giant eagles guard trays and trays of food, and around them hundreds of eager worshipers of leisure and pleasure eat and eat and eat.

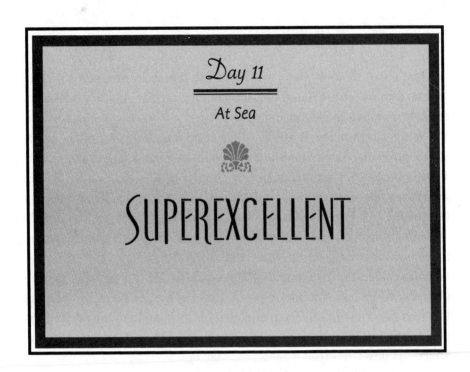

Day 11

At Sea

SUPEREXCELLENT

*S*ince this is our last day in M5, I shall summarize the experience.

But first I have to pay for the next segment, Los Angeles to Hong Kong via Hawaii, nineteen days. The purser accepted my vouchers for $14,844 and the $2,000 onboard credit that Cunard gave us. It's amazing what paper pieces that look so insignificant can do for you. Little pieces of paper, more so than guns, control the world, enslave us all with paper chains.

I think the onboard credit is a great idea because it's free money, and there should be even less attention paid to spending it. My family motto, in case you had any doubt, is: spend it as fast as you can. The $2,000 could be used for just about anything, including bar bills, laundry, telephone calls, purchases in the Royal Promenade, and massages in the spa. This might be my chance to get a treatment from Venus of the seashell, the blond goddess whose demesne resides in the spa, except it might show on the bill and Ethel might raise an eyebrow or two.

Just about the only thing you can't use the onboard credit for is the casino. I know why. Cunard doesn't want me at the roulette wheel using their own money to clean them out.

While at the purser's office, I picked up the sheet on tipping advice and some dollar-sized small white envelopes with a large blue Cunard written on them. Tipping advice is simple: give what you wish. The guidelines are simple, too. As expected, class structure determines the size of the tip. For Mauretania class, $4 per passenger per day for the stewardess and the same for the waiters. If there are several people involved, then they should share and share alike. Thus, the official tip amounts suggested by Cunard would come to $88 for Nichola and the same for Chris and Antonio together. Ethel and I decide to tip more for two reasons: true gratitude and affection for the people involved. It's irrational, I know, but who can explain gratitude? Who can explain how our affections flow?

We tipped as follows (somehow this sounds like a last will and testament). To Nichola, our beloved room stewardess, we leave $200 to be hers now and forever. To Chris and Antonio, our Mauretania waiters, $200, share and share alike. To Michael, the wine steward, and Andrew, our sometime waiter who was always funny, $80, share and share alike. To Hinano Yeo, the assistant restaurant manager who we affectionately called Yo-Yo, $100. That brought the total in tips to $580. Add that to the cost of our tickets ($3,607), and we get $4,187. Add the ten bucks I paid before the brown goddess at the spa, Elena, figured out that as a Samuel Cunard Key Club Member I use the spa free and we get a grand total for this segment, Fort Lauderdale to Los Angeles, of $4,197, a travel bargain that amounts to an average cost of $190 per day per person. How in the world Cunard could deliver such a service at that price is beyond me.

Our final appraisal of M5 is:

♣ Room. Small but comfortable. Adequate for our needs, a cozy love nest. The narrow beds made switching positions difficult when we both occupied the same bunk (your place or mine?) without pinching the partner's arms and legs.

🐙 Food. Excellent in every way: colorful, fresh, clean, tasty, and well presented.

🐙 Service. Fast and efficient. This may have been due to our being in the second sitting, where Chris and Antonio had only seven passengers to take care of, whereas, during the first sitting, they had seventeen.

🐙 Entertainment. We didn't go in for the bingo and the Mr. and Mrs. games and so on, but the movies and the other experiences— including the heritage trail, the port lecturers, and the interviews— were wonderful. The Smithsonian lecturer this segment seemed a little stiff and nervous, but relaxed later. We know the more intellectual part of the trip starts tomorrow with lessons in music history and Chinese and Asian art.

🐙 Total value. Superexcellent. Try to match it anywhere, even for triple what we paid. And don't forget that price included room, gourmet meals, fine entertainment, and the recreational atmosphere of the ship itself. You couldn't match it anywhere, and you can't beat it.

Finally, on this day, I did get a chance to start reading Dante's *Divine Comedy*. The work has great applications to cruising, which I may (if I don't get too lazy) discuss later. For the moment, I concentrate on lines 8 and 9 of canto I in the *Inferno*: "But if I would show the good that came of it I must talk about things other than the good."

Ethel and I have for decades taken baths together in our home tub, which is by design large enough for two. We missed that tub, and we missed the luxury of a full-immersion bath. We won't get a tub for two on *QE2*, but somewhere along our upward journey, we'll get a tub.

The darkness, or rather the lack of natural light (just like hell in the *Inferno*), also bothered us. I tried to make up for it by playing God each morning, switching on the light and saying rather solemnly, as God did in the Bible, *"Fiat lux."* And Ethel would reply, *"Et lux in tenebris lucet."* Cabin 5178 had no plug for our Water Pik, so our gums and teeth suffered. The Grundig color TV couldn't play videotapes, so we couldn't catch up on old movies. At times noises from other cabins near us filtered through the walls, especially the clang of doors slamming; the short, snappy gush of toilet flushes; and, strangely, the on and off clicks of light switches. Vibrations, engine-oil smells, and all those other things we expected to experience in M5, the things we thought we would suffer, didn't happen.

The twin mirrors of cabin 5178 made the room appear larger than it is and the Miro on the wall, with its colored dots, gave a modern look to the scene. Everything is relative. Let's measure 5178 by comparison with what Charles Dickens got when he crossed the ocean sea. Dickens's cabin was a "preposterous little box" that measured eight by six feet, with two chamber pots and two washbasins. There was no bulkhead. The wall came up high enough so that the neighbors couldn't see in, but they could certainly hear. The lights were candles and had to go out at midnight. If you didn't put them out, the steward came around and did that for you.

All of which leads me to offer the following advice about that paradigmatic perquisite, the cruise cabin. Experience cabins in every configuration possible, as we will, or experience just one. It matters not. Each cabin shares without exception a unique and cozy ingenuity lacking in even the most palatial accommodation ashore. Select your room in advance as I did (unlike your hotel room, which they assign to you when you arrive). Select it carefully after a sober evaluation of checkbook and deck plan. Stay toward ship's center and away from public rooms. Avoid cabins where the portholes face an open deck. Examine your conscience. If you need a tub, get one instead of the space-economical shower.

With a touch of sadness, Ethel and I sat on the beds of M5. (We had no chairs.) We wondered whether we shouldn't just spend the rest of the trip there. We'd been happy. We wanted that happiness to continue. Perhaps it would. Perhaps it won't.

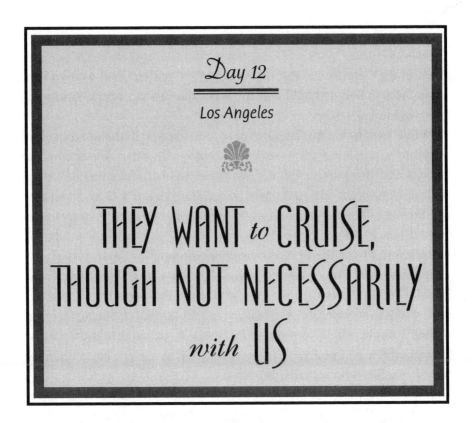

THEY WANT *to* CRUISE, THOUGH NOT NECESSARILY *with* US

*W*e arrived under the green and white Vincent Thomas suspension bridge, both ends of which connect to freeways. Freeways? You bet. This is Los Angeles. Fireboats greeted the *QE2* with streams and spouts and sprays of water in the air, a kind of celebration. Anyway, that's what we were told. You wouldn't catch Ethel and me getting up at 6 AM to watch *QE2* go under a bridge and dock at the San Pedro pier 93 A-B. We had better things to do, like sleep.

After routine morning cuddles, I, on unsteady feet and still-sleepy legs, approached the light switch ready to play God for the last time, pronouncing the words of incantation: *"Fiat lux!"* And there was light. And it was good. And it stung our eyes for the moment. And it bathed cabin 5178 in brilliant incandescence.

The big day arrived, the day of our promotion to cabin 4164, the lowest of the Caronia classes, C4. What will it be like? Will we find happiness there? (This is beginning to sound like a soap opera. And what about Naomi?)

While waiting for the late-dining section to open in the Mauretania, I overheard a man about thirty-seven years old, with a dark-black crew cut and a small earring in his left ear, announce to his friends that he visited the bridge last night. He assured his friends that he knew more about running the ship than the captain did. "I asked what this red button was on the wall. They told me they didn't know. They didn't even know that you should warm up the diesel electric engines slowly!"

Imagine that! I love people like him. They are sometimes in error but never in doubt. The young man reminded me of Professor Rothschild, my teacher of contemporary civilization at Columbia College, a great teacher, I might add. Every class, Professor Rothschild told us specific ways in which he knew how to run the US government better than the elected officials who actually did run it.

Passengers we never saw before now jammed Mauretania, trying to eat breakfast. Chris and Andrew explained. Those people ate in the Lido the whole trip. Since this is their last chance before they get off, they want to check out the Mauretania to see what they missed.

Ethel and I checked the weather outside and then returned to the room to pack. Helen, our new stewardess from four deck, miraculously appeared from nowhere and started piling our bags into the elevator. Service, it's wonderful. Helen told us that she is Filipino and a mother of a four-year-old whom she had not seen in nine months. She hoped they would let her off the boat in Manila so that she could visit her family, but she thinks they might not. "Half the staff is Filipino," she told us proudly. "Without Filipinos, they couldn't run the ship."

As Helen struggled with my last bag (the one with the forty-two books), Ethel and I bid a solemn farewell to our cozy cabin: "Cabin 5178, palace abode of M5 class, you have known us intimately, but we must leave you now."

The joy of our new home quickly relieved the pain of departure. Cabin 4164 astonished us. Quantum jumps exist not only in the physics of subatomic particles but also on the *QE2*. Cabin 4164 doubled our living space, our closets, and our drawers; enlarged our bathroom; and multiplied our comfort twofold. In addition, wonders of wonders, we now have a porthole. Transfixed, Ethel and I gazed out of this aperture to the world beyond, the Vincent Thomas Bridge and the sun and the sea.

"Why not cruise the rest of the world in this room?" Ethel asked. "We have entered heaven. I expected this room would be better than 5178, but this is better than I expected."

"But we still can't plug in the Water Pik, and worse, we still have no tub and no videocassette player. Oh, well, *c'est la vie*," said I philosophically.

What to do? I called our son, Craig, and his wife, Michelle the Beautiful, who live in San Diego. I invited them to visit the ship and have lunch with us. Passes to visitors come through the purser's office, even though the official papers we previously received said for security reasons no passes would be issued. I assured the purser that Craig and Michelle meant no harm. I know Michelle is not a terrorist. About Craig I had no definite information.

An officer explained to me that the restrictions started in May 1972 after some nut phoned in a bomb threat and tried to extort $350,000 from Cunard. The FBI caught the guy, a shoe worker from upstate New York. The judge sentenced him to twenty years in prison, saying: "Your actions were reprehensible and unforgivable. You took deliberate advantage of a reign of terror for very substantial gain."

The passes illustrate one of the endearing features of Cunard and the world cruise staff: They refuse no reasonable request.

While awaiting Craig and Michelle, I bit the bullet, called Boston, and spoke with another Michelle, Michelle Nicholasen, associate producer for *Frontline*, some kind of public broadcasting program that originated at WGBH-TV. I tried to answer the questions on breast implants and their complications, my research. I sensed that Michelle, like every reporter, had her own slant. Reporters are in the media business. They want to sell their product. They have to make things interesting.

TV already broke down many boundaries between public and private information in its confessional talk shows so that they could exhibit human oddities and social outcasts and follow the examples set by the old circus sideshows. Not satisfied with that, to keep the audiences amused, they make up stories or they stage events like those cars bursting into flames. Oh, well, reality is nice to visit, but most Americans can't live there, and wouldn't want to live there even if they could.

Craig and Michelle arrive just in time for a five-course lunch in the Caronia Restaurant. After lunch, I gave my own heritage tour. I explained the decor, the green colors (*Caronia* the ship was painted green and was called the green goddess). I pointed out the center sculptures in the dining room: three large aluminium 'orses rising out of the sea foam. I decoded the iconography: "In British English sea horses are the American white caps. Aluminium is British English for aluminum. And for them the *h* is silent in horses."

Michelle beams her approval. I was making a good impression on one Michelle, my daughter-in-law, the Michelle that counts, even if I hadn't made a good impression on the other Michelle, Michelle the Nasty, the TV Michelle who didn't count.

After lunch, we toured the ship, and, in a moment of sudden illumination, I understood the ship's structure in Dantesque terms. The ship has an intricate geographical structure just like hell, purgatory, and paradise. The ship has a front, a back, and two sides, and it has a top and a bottom. The front stairwells start at A and work back to H. They call the right side the starboard and the left side the port. Remember: Port is left because both words, left and port, have four letters. Furthermore, port wine is red. That's the way to tell what side of a ship or airplane you are looking at at night. The red light is on the portside.

Decks present some difficulties. Dante numbered the circles in hell, purgatory, and heaven, and the ship does the same, starting at the bottom and lowest deck, called Eight deck, and working up to One deck. Notice when they talk of decks, the number comes first. Thus, deck one is called One deck, and the signs on deck say the same: One deck, not deck one. No passengers live on Eight deck, and, in fact, the lowest of the low as far as passengers are concerned is Five deck (I almost said deck five).

Above One deck we find unnumbered decks that have names. This disturbs the logic, destroys some of the organization, and makes it hard to remember things. To impose order on the chaos, I invented a mnemonic based on the first letter of the named decks: SSBUQ, or, if you will, Steam Ship BUQ. Starting from top and working down, we get Signal deck before Sun deck, followed by Boat deck, Upper deck and Quarter deck. Below Quarter deck is One deck, and thence the numbers get larger, that is ascend, as the decks descend.

One last thing: the cabin numbers on the numbered decks always start with the deck number and increase in magnitude from fore to aft (front to back). Even-numbered cabins are on portside (easy to remember: port has an even number of letters) and odd on starboard. Thus, cabin 5178 finds itself on portside and aft (behind) of 5174. Cabin 4164 finds itself on portside forward of 5178 and a deck higher. Some cabins on the named decks start with number eight. I haven't figured them out yet since it's obvious they aren't below water. Far from it, in fact—those cabins starting with eight dedicate themselves to the rich and famous and situate themselves in the empyrean realm of heaven known as the penthouse. When we get to heaven, we'll understand it better. Just as Dante's pilgrim, when he got to heaven, understood it better. In Dante's *Paradiso*, the higher you go, the better your accommodation—the same with the ship.

But the structure of the ship doesn't stop there because, after all, a ship is a human institution. It, therefore, reflects human values and the values of the humans who made it. In line with the stratification of the decks we also find a social structure, a stratification of the passengers who inhabit those decks. On *QE2* there exist three classes of passengers who partake of the heavenly bliss according to their station. Mauretania is the lowest and probably represents a highly evolved residua of the previous third class, or steerage class. Caronia probably represents an evolved middle class, and Grill represents upper class. Within Grill class, there are three further subclasses—Princess and Britannia and Queens Grill, the highest. And get this: each class has divisions, all ranked as strictly as a medieval heraldry directory. There are five Mauretania classes (M1–M5), four Caronia (C1–C4), two Princess (P1 and P2), and four Queens (Q1–Q4).

Thus, in an instant you can figure out your place in the hierarchy. Q1 beats all. M5 beats none. The four luxury suites, Queen Mary/Queen Elizabeth and Trafalgar/Queen Anne, remain hors de combat. The price of each of these double-decked luxury suites exceeds that of Q1 by almost fourfold. The luxury suites might be reserved for the Virgin Mary, Saint Lucia, Beatrice herself, or the superrich. They must be enfolded by the celestial rose of heaven. But Q2 or Q1 is within reach of the ordinary wealthy people. (Not that you should think much of money. Aside from its purchasing power, there is no use for it.)

My tour of *QE2* ended in time for champagne and dancing in the main lounge. When that ended, Ethel, Craig, Michelle the Beautiful, and I headed down to the Queens lounge for tea and scones. White-gloved waiters and waitresses served coffees, teas (China, Earl Grey, chamomile, mint, orange pekoe, lapsang souchong, cinnamon-apple, rosehip, darjeeling, decaffeinated, and real), and a selection of freshly made sandwiches, home-baked scones with strawberry preserves and clotted cream, and a choice of pastries and fresh cream cakes, freshly baked aboard ship. Delicious! Forget class and distinction, we're all in heaven.

Craig and Michelle left contented after a good hour in the spa and a five-course dinner in the Caronia. I could tell that *QE2* made a good impression on them. They wanted to cruise, though not necessarily with us.

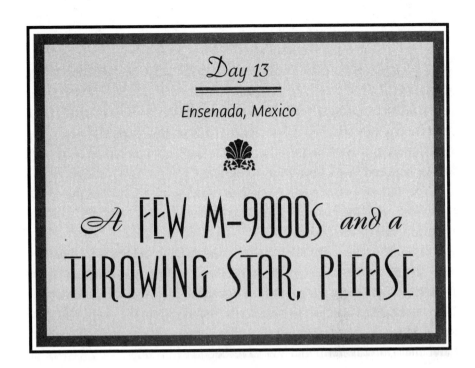

Day 13

Ensenada, Mexico

A FEW M-9000s and a THROWING STAR, PLEASE

*W*hy did we stop here?

Captain Burton-Hall already told us. *QE2* couldn't legally carry American passengers to another American port without stopping at a foreign port in between. We couldn't go directly from Los Angeles to Hawaii. Whenever something stupid like that happens, you can bet government is involved. And so it is: the Jones law, designed to protect Alaskan shipping long ago—and which, by the way, no longer needs protection—required this irrational stop at Ensenada. For the people of this down-and-out seaside town (population 130,000), that is good news. For us, it's bad news.

Ensenada de todos santos (the cove of all saints) did have one claim to fame, La Bufadora—a giant blowhole billed by Enrique, my taxi driver/guide, as the largest in the world. The air trapped in a cave gets compressed by a wave or something coming in, and suddenly wind and water spurted out the top with a roar. The water soars seventy-five feet in the air.

"Hey, Enrique, how is the blowhole formed?"

"Simple, the sea is the land's edge also and attacks that edge when it can. Dunwick, a town on the east coast of England, worked on by the sea for six hundred years, has almost completely gone. Only the graveyard remains, and every once in a while one of the graves falls into the sea. A blowhole forms the same way but from a cave."

"How does a cave form?"

"A crack in the rock. The waves pound the air, and the waves deliver little stones to the crack. Eventually, the crack expands, and the cave appears. When part of the roof of the cave falls in, that makes a blowhole. The water dashes against the cave walls, thunders into the cave. When the waves break in the cave below, the spray spurts up out of the blowhole. Later the roof caves in, and the cave becomes an inlet. Two caves that connect under the headland form an arch, and, when the arch collapses, it leaves a small, tall island called a stack." Enrique looked at me and smiled. "I also can explain why a wave breaks and why waves crash."

"No thanks, Enrique," I said while handing him a twenty. "I do have a question, however. Where did you go to school?"

"Boston University. Majored in oceanography."

After La Bufadora I walked up and down the main street called Avenida López Mateos, generally called Avenida Primera. Multiple shops passed by, but none of the usual stuff in them; the crystal, china, perfumes, cosmetics, or booze impressed me as much as the genuine Mexican handicrafts from Ensenada itself. I picked up one of these, an Indian doll; turned it over; and read a label: "Made in Idaho."

Mexico is another country. They do things differently here. I can tell by the fact that they sell throwing stars. Prohibited weapons in most states, these devilish devices, in all sizes and designs, remain on full display in the shop windows. I admired the primitive beauty of a three-pronged throwing star engineered to slice through anyone it hit. The salesman explained that throwing stars are more deadly than throwing knifes, which don't do anything unless the sharp side hits. But, then again, it takes skill to throw the star without cutting your hand. I decided not to buy a throwing star because I can't imagine getting the thing on the airplane. Besides, what would I use it for? Also I know throwing stars—like brass knuckles, silencers, maces, blackjacks, tomahawks, incendiary bombs, grenades, rockets, mines, dirks, stilettos, poniards, bowie knifes, swords, spears, switchblades, zip guns, armor-piercing ammunition, and machine guns are forbidden in Texas.

Texans may apply for and receive (if they pass the written test and the range test) a license to carry a concealed handgun. Many do. But in Texas you can't have a throwing star. Throwing stars are too dangerous even for Texans.

Another thing I declined, but regretted later, was the M-9000. This looked and felt like a stick of dynamite. A red cylinder, the M-9000 measured a foot long and one inch in diameter—and sold for only $6.75 a piece. The M-grade fireworks work up from M-80. Each time the numbers rise, you get more bang. From experience I know M-80 can blow apart a mailbox. M-200 can demolish a metal garbage can. One can only imagine what M-9000 could do. Probably it could blow apart a garage. I can't reasonably justify carrying an M-9000 on an airplane, but, at the time, I didn't realize that I could have used a few M-9000s on the *QE2*—used them justifiably on another passenger.

Along Avenida Primera I easily fight off the three-foot-tall Indian women who beg for money. Their children seemed dwarfed also, less than half the size expected for age. It can't be all malnutrition. Heredity must play a part because their mothers only come up to my waist. I am a giant among pygmies. I am a king among paupers. I am a white among reds.

The Indian children sneak up on me and put candies in my rear pants pocket. I kept pulling the candies out, smiling, and handing the candies back to them. "No thank you," I said. "Candy is junk food, empty calories of no nutritional value."

Naturally, they didn't understand. But they smiled back.

Hotels that line the strip interested me. The Caribe offered a room and bed for $15. An additional $5 got you a TV. But a sign in Spanish said that Mexicans paid a different rate for the same room—ninety pesos (equivalent to $12.33 at today's rate for the peso) and an additional thirty pesos (US $4.11) for the TV. For the same amount we spent in M5, we could rent a room at the Caribe on the main street in Ensenada in the heart of the downtown area of this fair city and live there for 280 days.

There's a Days Inn, too, called Hotel Villa Fontana, with daily costs a little higher, but the place, with its pink and green jumbled façade, gothic dormers, and multiple gables, looks like an American gothic straight out of Alfred Hitchcock's *Psycho*. Across the street stands the Best Western Motel called El Cid. Its front window displays a honeymoon suite fully equipped with Jacuzzi, champagne in a silver ice bucket, two fluted crystal glasses, and, of course, the king-sized bed. Some things, the world over, remain the same.

At the regional historical museum, I'm the only visitor. The cost of admission was five pesos, or less than a dollar. Two things caught my eye: the jail cells were the same size as our room in M5, and the display cases had lots of female figurines with enlarged butts and breasts, butts much bigger than breasts, and, I imagine, a realistic crotch crease which someone had covered with a miniature white plastic fig leaf. The sign explained that the function of these ceramic figurines was not known, but archaeologists believe they belong to some fertility cult. Ho, ho, ho. I recognized right away some guy's pornography collection. Most men have one. Think about the archaeologists of the future who, two hundred years from now, break into the tomb of some unknown man and find a *Playboy* magazine. The archaeologists, with delicate brushes, open the centerfold and conclude the picture belonged to some fertility cult.

I took a taxi ride back to the tender. Cost a dollar. The tender fought rough seas to get back to *QE2*. Along the way, two pelicans, a big and a small one, did touch-and-goes, part of flying lessons. Mama pelican landed on a piece of green drift palm. Baby tried but crashed into the flotsam. Up they went again and came in for another landing. The small bird tried to keep up with mommy, but fell behind and crashed again.

Two beefy Filipino crewmen carried a paraplegic passenger from our tender onto the ship. Then, the Filipinos brought up the passenger's Amigo, a scooter like a motorized wheelchair but more mobile and handier. This mobility-impaired individual had no need for a plastic bubble that runs from stern to bow. Incidentally, the Americans with Disabilities Act does not apply to ships. *QE2* had only two cabins listed as suitable for wheelchairs. Elevator buttons stand way above chest height, and tendering for the handicapped requires at least two crew members to carry the passenger, like a sack of potatoes, on and off. The blind must have fared worse. I saw no dogs aboard, but one Japanese man hung on to his sighted wife, who led him around.

The outside temperature reads 72 degrees so I know the pool will be empty. I went down and changed into my suit. Sure enough, I own the pool. I own the hot tub (which some merciful crewmember has turned up to 102 degrees) and I own the deck as well. As Captain John Burton-Hall observed, bad weather isn't all that bad.

I would have preferred to draw a curtain over our dinner in the Caronia Restaurant, but Dante said that, in order that you may know the good, you should know what is not so good. Someone stuck us in a crowded subdivision of Caronia probably because we are C4, the worst Caronia class. Tables here press so closely that I have trouble hearing, above the din of other conversations, what Ethel says.

The two waitpeople, Mary from Galway, Ireland, and Eric from Cannes, France, tried hard to keep up, but they kept getting fouled up by Rabbi, who used more of their time than the other fourteen passengers in this subdivision put together. Rabbi, a small, squat, fat man, wore a beard and mustache, said beard having a skunk strip—white up the middle with black edges. Rabbi made statements like: "When I order, I order double. My wife eats the same as I do."

Already I can tell by the gleam in her eye that Ethel wants me to kill this chauvinist pig. I pick up the steak knife. Ethel slowly nods yes.

Nothing pleased Rabbi, so he sent things back. "I want my salads with extra sliced tomatoes and sliced, not chopped, onions. And why did you bring my apple juice that way? I want apple juice with ice. Bring the bagels now. Make sure I know what kind of kosher wines are available for tomorrow. Kosher rules are complex. I don't expect you people to understand them. But try. No butter at the table when we have meat."

At this point, Rabbi disdainfully looks at the butter lying innocently in its silver slaver. Rabbi curled up his nose as if the butter were a smelly piece of shit. Eric quickly whisked the butter away. But soon Eric returned, a concerned expression on his face. "Rabbi, how long will you be with us?"

Rabbi sneers, "Until Singapore." And then Rabbi says while jabbing his index finger at Eric, "I used to be a waiter myself. I can teach you a thing or two."

I pulled from my wallet my Blue Voyage 1033 *QE2* combined security and embarkation card. I wrote on the back and passed the message across the table to Ethel: "Singapore—No way. He goes overboard tonight."

Ethel, grinning, shakes her head a more emphatic *yes*!

Rabbi ordered skim milk and wanted diabetic brownies. Eric explained they don't have diabetic brownies but he can bring regular brownies. The Rabbi agrees to the regular brownies and then drops a bomb. "Send the Caronia manager here. I need to talk with him."

Peter came over promptly.

"We have to talk," Rabbi said ominously. "Tell me when I can come to your office. Also I want to see the ship's stores to see what we can use."

"Yes, Rabbi," says Peter with a bow.

"And where is Mendl?" Rabbi inquired. "When *QE2* had the kosher kitchen, Mendl was my best friend."

Peter replied, "I don't know where he went. Mendl disappeared."

"Too bad," Rabbi said, his head shaking from a familial tremor. "Mendl wasn't a young man. But he wasn't an old man either."

I thought that, hopefully, if Mendl was anything like Rabbi, someone threw Mendl overboard. Should I warn Rabbi that the same fate awaits himself?

Ethel kicked me under the table. I was glaring too much in Rabbi's direction. I concentrated my attention on the finest dessert ever made, Gâteau St. Honoré, a mixture of heavy cream, angel food sponge cake, cherries placed on top of an eclair shell, and topped with a cream-filled baba au rhum. My admiration for St. Honoré knows no limits. For the moment, my mind loses itself among the rich tastes and smells of the sweet, heavy, whipped cream and sumptuous eclair.

When I looked up, I saw that Rabbi and his wife had left. The skim milk and the brownies that they had specially ordered remained forlornly on the china plates, completely untouched.

"I wish we could go back to Ensenada," I told Ethel.

"What for?" she asked.

"I forgot to buy some things. I could use them tomorrow night here in the Caronia."

"Use what?" Ethel asked.

"A few M-9000s and a throwing star."

Day 14

At Sea, Pacific Ocean

THIS HORSERADISH IS
a WASTE of TIME

*M*om and Pop woke us up.

That's what they call themselves in the next room. How do we know about Mom and Pop? Mom and Pop had hearing problems, so they shout at each other, and their shouts come through the bulkheads (the nautical term for walls).

"Feeling OK today, Pop?" screamed Mom at the top of her lungs.

"You bet, Mom," yelled Pop.

Pop always replies less loudly. Does Mom hear better than Pop? Or does Pop hear better than Mom? Does Mom speak louder than Pop because Pop can't hear her or because Mom can't hear herself? I told Ethel that these irksome questions bother me.

"Go over there. Test them. Find out." Ethel says. "And, while you are there, tell Mom and Pop to keep it down in the mornings."

Mom screams again, this time an order: "Pop, close the bathroom door."

Bang! Pop obliged.

I entered Ethel's bed. We rested there cuddling, Ethel with her head on my chest and myself lying on my back listening, in the pauses between Mom and Pop, to the water sounds on the ship's hull. I admired the bright ripples of glistening white light playing on the ceiling overhead. *La vecchia*, that's what the Venetians call it—a dance of marvelously complex and intricate reflected sunlight bounced from the canals to the ceiling of the Palazzo. On *QE2*, la vecchia is even better: It doesn't dance in place; it moves backward as *QE2* ever advances across the Pacific. And la vecchia is best seen while hugging your sweetie while the two of you, at peace with the world, are gently rocked by *QE2* and comfortably nested among soft white sheets. Sea leisure! There is nothing like it. A sacred thing. The moment to enjoy yourself is now. You will be dead a long time! Eternity is now. Remember that!

At breakfast we discovered we're in luck—Rabbi didn't show. We are not the only happy ones. Mary and Eric looked ecstatic. Peter, the assistant restaurant manager, looked relieved. Peter avuncularly placed his arm around Mary, reassuring her that there will be more days like this, days in which the Rabbi doesn't show.

After breakfast, Nichola came up from Five deck to visit. She had never seen this section of the ship. Nichola's admiration shows in her beaming face. "You have so much space! Twice the living room of M5 and a real chair." Nichola caressed the chair as I imagined what her room is like in the crew quarters. I explained that Ethel and I rotated days of the chairmanship. Today is Ethel's day, so she gets to sit on the chair. Tomorrow's my turn.

We told Nichola about Rabbi. Nichola has heard such stories before and often lived through some of her own with similar characters. She had just finished with the likes of two, a woman and a man, a couple, that no matter what Nichola did, she couldn't please. The woman had the nasty habit of keeping the curling iron (Nichola calls them thongs, which is the British for curling iron) on, even when the woman was not in the room. Strictly speaking, such devices are not permitted aboard because of the fire hazard. They are certainly not allowed to remain turned on and unattended in the cabins. When Nichola pulled the thong plug, trouble started.

Nichola got hell for preserving the ship and our lives. Got hell from the two passengers, that is. Not from the head steward, who knows aboard ship, safety first. The passengers, thus rebuked for safety violations, began to complain about all sorts of unrelated, trivial things. And so, they left without saying good-bye. And worse, they left no tip. And, even worse, they left a written complaint with the hotel manager. Nichola got called in again and had to explain.

"Anyone in contact with the public suffers," I told Nichola. You can't please all the people all the time, said President Lincoln, and that's true. About 5 percent of the customers cause 95 percent of the trouble. I was speaking from the vast experience of having practiced medicine for several decades.

The Cunard University of the Pacific started today. Waldemar Hansen led off with Hawaiian history in his lecture "The Sandwich Isles, Aloha, At Your Service," which I can't repeat here due to lack of space except to say *aloha* represents an all-purpose word meaning hello, good-bye, and love.

The next lecture, by Jan Stuart of the Smithsonian Institution, interested me even more, since it covered one of my favorite subjects: "Famous Collectors and Collections of Chinese Art." Jan showed works from the Freer and Sackler Galleries of Asian Art and gave a history of James Smithson and the institutions he founded. She said that Smithson gave the money to the United States because he felt that America was a classless society. (James Smithson had never visited the United States. Otherwise, he would have known differently.)

About Chinese art, Jan made an important point that I learned long ago: Chinese calligraphy stands in China as a much more respected art form than painting. Calligraphers, usually old men, spend three hours a day practicing. Jan even illustrated the tremendous control needed just to write the Chinese word *er*, meaning "number one," which, to the Western eye, looks like a short horizontal line. I myself have practiced writing *Er* over five thousand times in order to get the proper "bone structure" in the sign so that the two ends of the horizontal line are larger than the center.

Rabbi came for dinner.

Ethel and I looked on, wondering what was going to happen as Eric served the free kosher wine supplied by the ship. How come we don't get free wine? The squeaky wheel gets the grease, that's why. But the ship was about to learn a lesson: never appease a tyrant.

Rabbi took a sip and made a poison face. Clearly, the wine doesn't meet Rabbi's expectations. Rabbi shakes his nugatory head and tells his wife, "You won't like this." And, of course, he gives her none.

She replies (facetiously?), "Just as well, I might get drunk."

Amazing! She can speak. This is the first time we have heard her say anything. All the communications at that table have been one way, from Rabbi to her, to Eric, to Mary, or to Peter, all seasoned with complaints, too (sometimes nothing but complaints). Mary has had it. She takes herself out of the loop; she refused to listen or talk to Rabbi. (Those Irish are stubborn, aren't they? No wonder the Romans never conquered Hibernia, and the British never conquered and will never conquer Ireland.)

Mary hales from Galway in western Ireland, where the real toughs hang out. My thoughts fly to the Galway Brigade and Michael Collins, the Irish Free Stater and his original Irish Republican Brotherhood (IRB). The Galway Brigade of irregulars that Collins led held off and eventually defeated the British. Only after the treaty was signed did it become generally known that the Galway Brigade had but twenty members and only twelve rifles. Brigade members rotated the rifles among themselves in shifts. By sheer stubbornness, the Irish won the war.

Using the wine as an excuse, Rabbi started riding his high horse. He asked for horseradish. Mary refused to get it for him, so Eric had to go. After about twenty minutes, the horseradish appeared. Rabbi tasted it and frowned. "This horseradish is a waste of time."

Rabbi crunched his matzos, while Ethel and I got up to leave. I said in Gaelic, "*Erin go bragh* [Ireland forever]," to Mary. She smiled, and her eyes started to shine brightly. How do the Irish girls do that? Make them shine? It is not the effect of makeup since Mary wears none. Eric, hearing the *bragh* (which rhymes with *-oir*), thinks I have said, "Au revoir," and, with a Cheshire cat grin, bids us "Au revoir." Next time, we'll make Eric happy; we'll speak French.

Where would Dante have put Rabbi? What part of hell? Probably
Caina, one of the four divisions of Cocytus, the lowest part of the Inferno,
wherein are tormented those souls who treacherously betrayed their kin,
for that is his main, but not his only, sin. I need to know more before
passing sentence. Everything depends on everything, especially on the
type of sin, the intention of the sinner, and, more important, the degree of
repentance. Too bad we have no Minos aboard who would tell us to what
place in hell this soul belonged by the number of times Minos wrapped
his tail around himself. For each turn, the sinner must descend one circle
(deck?) in hell.

Ethel and I end the evening attending "A Pacific Symphony" with the
Philharmonia Virtuosi, featuring Julianne Baird, soprano; Mela Tenenbaum, viola d'amore; with Richard Kapp, music director. Before each
piece—which included Vivaldi's Concerto in D Minor and Handel's Airs
(British for aria) for Soprano—Richard Kapp gave a short talk on the history attached to the piece, excellent reviews of music history.

Entertainment by artists in the flesh exceeds the experience of
watching them on TV by fourteen-hundred fold. Here they are real: real
people, real size, in real color, in three real dimensions. Many of us have
become so accustomed to the fake we fail to appreciate the real. To us
tonight's experience will be an enchanted memory a year hence—a
memory which money could not buy from us. Can you say the same thing
about any TV program that you watched last night?

Whoever thought up the idea of having musicians on a boat? Perhaps
we have Cleopatra to thank. She sailed on pleasure excursions, in galleys
with silver oars and perfumed sails, and with companies of beautiful girls
to serve her and actors and musicians to keep her amused in days that
seem almost modern.

The stage spotlights vanished, and the overhead lighting dimmed into
a subtle mixture of pinks and reds and a hint of blue, bathing the room in
a soft, warming glow. The music program ended. Ethel and I rushed to
the theater to see *Ties That Bind*, an amazing collection of movie cliches.
I decide this movie program will enable me to catalogue movie cliches,
and I start taking notes. For instance, the "Kevin Kline mustache prin-
ciple" is clearly illustrated because the pathological killer in *Ties* sports

facial hair and plays an eccentric, offbeat goofball. The hero is clean shaven. Come to think on it, maybe there is something to cliches. I am clean shaven. So are Eric and Peter. Rabbi is not.

As we head back to the cabin, I tell Ethel, "You know, the rabbi would have liked the kosher wine even less if I, instead of Eric, had served it."

"How's that?" asked Ethel.

"I would have poured it, with deliberate care, over his head."

"Not me. I would have done nothing of the kind," said Ethel. "I would have splashed it carelessly over his crotch."

Day 15

At Sea, Pacific Ocean

HOPE *to* SEE YOU SOON—
YOU'VE GOT *a* NICE BUTT

$\mathcal{W}$e are still cruising the Pacific Ocean at twenty-seven knots. I see from the porthole the white-capped sea flash by, receding into history as we skip forward into our future.

Two days and we are not more than halfway to Hawaii, and Hawaii is not more than halfway across the Pacific Ocean to Japan. The Pacific, enormous as it is, looms ever larger in our minds as we experience it first-hand, crossing on its surface. We tend to forget that the Pacific is twice the size of the Atlantic and actually belongs to the original and only ocean. The landmasses of the original continents (Gondwana and Laurasia) grouped themselves together in what subsequently became the Atlantic section. The vast primitive unnamed sea, what subsequently became the Pacific, occupied the other side of Earth, away from the land. As the continental plates separated, they drifted apart at rates of inches per year. The sea that filled in the separation became the Atlantic Ocean.

Recall that Phileas Fogg (from Jules Verne's masterpiece *Around the*

World in Eighty Days) allotted twenty-two days to cross the Pacific from Yokohama to San Francisco, but only nine days to go from New York to London. Fogg, incidentally, resembled some of our present *QE2* passengers. He would never take a tour. And he never showed in the dining room, for he sat down quietly to eat in his cabin, never once thinking of inspecting any town, being one of those Englishmen who are apt to see foreign countries through the eyes of their servants. Furthermore, Fogg did not care to recognize the historic towns and villages that raised their picturesque outlines against the sky. They were of no interest. He ignored them.

"Do you think there's too much water on this planet?" I asked Ethel.

"It sure looks that way. There is nothing out there, just water, water, everywhere, and not a drop to drink."

Waldemar Hansen briefed the troops in preparation for *QE2*'s invasion of Lahaina, an old whaling port on the island of Maui. Our *QE2* commandos will hit the beach at 0700, forty-eight hours hence. Poet Rupert Brooke wrote in 1913 that Hawaii was distressingly tainted with tourists and the Americanization of the natives. We will do our part to continue that tradition.

Actually there are two Hawaiis: The (real) Hawaii and the Hawaii of the mind. The real Hawaii probably disappeared long ago or maybe never existed. The Hawaii of our imaginations was shaped—no! the grand illusion was deliberately created by Tin Pan Alley songs—and, most of all, by the movies. Remember those films? The chief's beautiful daughter always wore a red hibiscus in her hair, and she had a golden flower lei around her neck. She would recline on the white coral sand, calling conspicuous attention to her rather ample breasts. Eventually, the princess married the hero white man. And, in that last happy scene, the two lovers playfully swim out to the blue lagoon as their native friends frolicked in the surf or happily danced on the shore to the insistent beat of native drums. Sure, those movies, for dramatic effect to sustain the narrative and keep the audience interested, had villains—someone who ordered the natives to work in the phosphate mines or dive for pearls until they got the bends or the sharks ate them. But, in the conclusion, there was always the happy ending, confirming Hawaii and all Polynesia as an innocent, happy island paradise.

Ethel and I don't watch Hawaiian movies, and, worse for us, we have already been to Hawaii. We have known the fake luaus, the "traditional" Hawaiian banquet where tourists were herded on to finely manicured lawns and fed some overcooked pig and tasteless poi. The dancers give you a free lei, all right. But both the dancers and the leis come from Tahiti. Tahitians end up showing us a Hawaiian culture that never was because full-blooded Hawaiians are so rare they keep them in cages. Hawaii—it's a fantasy world constructed for the tourists. But what the hell, I've lived in reality occasionally, and it ain't all that great. And who knows—maybe this was an island paradise before the fatal impact of the white man, before Dr. Judd.

Each morning, the daily schedule arrived under our door, and Ethel read it out loud. All those activities! As Dante says in canto IV, "I cannot tell about them all in full. My theme is long and urges me ahead, often I must omit things I have seen." Me too. In fact, Dante, when he wrote those words, must have had a world cruise in mind. Deciding what to leave out, not talk about in the narrative is easy, but deciding what to leave out of my day's activities is hard. The whole situation proves the existentialist notions of free will. We choose; therefore, we know we can choose.

Today I choose to follow the intellectual trail. Four lectures, each an hour long. I hoped it will resemble college. It does—only more fun. I started with a preview of the wonders that await us on the world cruise. Time spent in reconnaissance rarely is wasted. The world is wondrous large, as Rudyard Kipling observed. Waldemar Hansen concentrated on the fractured English he has seen, trying to brace us for the diversity of races, nations, and customs that approached. In Japan: "We serve five o'clock tea all day long." In Hong Kong: "Teeth pulled by the latest Methodists." In India: "All vegetables have been washed in water carefully passed by the manager." Hansen whets our appetites with pictures of Hong Kong, Bali, Singapore, Mombasa, and Seychelles, where there is the double coconut, a fruit that looks curiously pornographic. They call it the *Coco de mer*. I can't wait.

At lunch it's Rabbi again. He complained, so they have given him a table for four set for two. No one else in the Caronia has that much space. Rabbi tells Mrs. Rabbi, "This is better."

We all have flaws, faults, and failings, but this guy has more than any of us. I am beginning to experience a perverse pleasure in recording Rabbi's nefarious acts. Part of the joy of writing this chapter derives from abusing that accomplished knave and partly to show how ugly people can be. His is a personal failing. The treacherous miscreant!

I see by his command a new bottle of kosher wine stands on the table already opened. Rabbi, with trembling hands, stood up and poured the wine himself. Has he familial tremor or some defect of the cerebellum in the dentatorubral thalamic connections? Or is he just nervous? If I had fifteen people, two waiters, and a restaurant manager all out to kill me, I guess I would be nervous too.

Because of the shaking, the wine spills over Rabbi's hands and onto his plate and the tablecloth. Rabbi knows he is making a mess, but he just shrugs his shoulders and mutters some prayer, while Mary, who must have received a talking to, stands by with pen and paper in hand, ready to immediately receive Rabbi's orders.

Then, Rabbi made a fatal mistake.

He tells Mary in a somewhat snotty tone, "We're not ready for you yet."

Without a word, Mary glanced toward heaven, begging God for mercy. Then, she made a kiss-pout with her Irish face. Slowly, Mary put away the pen and paper. Thereafter, Mary proceeded to busy herself with everything else under the sun that ever could be done for any and all of the other passengers in our subdivision.

Twenty minutes later, Mary returned to Rabbi, who, I can see, is fuming.

"Ready now?" Mary said with that impish Irish smile.

"Yes, I am," Rabbi roared back, glaring at her with furious blue eyes that stare out of dark malignant skeletal sockets, a stare right out of Balzac, strong as death.

Rabbi placed the same convoluted order of off-menu items prepared to his exact unusual and idiosyncratic specifications, including the extra sliced tomatoes, the salad dressing dropped on two places on the plate— one aside the salad, the other on a section of lettuce but (careful now!) not spread all the way through.

Mary seems to be thinking the same malignant Irish thought that I am thinking: This guy has to go. It's him or me.

In the afternoon, I attended a lecture on the origin of the Hawaiian islands. All the islands come from the same active volcanic source on the southeast side of the island chain. The volcano through a fault (hole) in the Earth's crust deposits the lava into the seabed. The lava eventually builds up and forms an island. The created islands then drift northwest with the Pacific plate at the rate of two inches per year. The first and oldest island is Midway in the far northwest, and the last island is still underwater, under construction. That island won't surface for another twenty million years, a time frame that I personally find too long for any serious real-estate speculation.

After the geology lecture, I sat with Jan Stuart in the Lion's Pub and learned what she did to organize exhibits and what it was like to be a museum curator. Significantly, she had to put together a new exhibit every nine months. Thinking about that symbolism overwhelmed me. (Maybe I'm reading and writing too many novels.) Nine months represents the normal gestation period for a human infant. Jan makes a new one every nine months. The whole thing is pregnant with meaning, so to speak. The venue fees impressed me, too, $25,000 to $200,000 for one exhibit. That's the fee other museums pay to get the exhibit premade for them by the Smithsonian. And the insurance fees (usually paid, for some reason, by the US government) impressed me even more, $250,000. Where but on *QE2* did I ever get to sit with a museum director face-to-face, learning about her job?

The pool temperature prevents anyone from swimming, myself excepted. In contrast to the pool, the hot tub is full. The hot tub turns out to be my most important communication tool and the most important source for new characters and information. In the tub, two fathers discussed the nursery. They like the nannies who are young and cute— "gorgeous"—says one man with a wink, but the men don't like that the nursery closes for lunch. They would prefer the kids stay away all day. The fathers got out. Two land whales got in. A true couple, wifey tips the scales at 270, I estimate, and husband the same, maybe a little less. The land whales displace a massive amount of water from the tub as they ease in, proving the laws of displacement physics still operate out here in the Pacific Ocean in the middle of nowhere.

The land whales lost their bags in Los Angeles—or, rather, someone lost their bags for them. The bags won't join them until we land at Lahaina. Mrs. Whale didn't mind. Because they have only the clothes they wore when they boarded in Los Angeles they spend most of their time in their cabin, lounging around in the nude. Mrs. Whale liked this because her nudity stimulated her husband's passion. Yesterday, they even "did it" for the first time in years.

Mr. Whale proudly confirmed all this while leering. He added, "Didn't you feel the ship lurch yesterday about four o'clock? When we come, you can imagine what happens."

I tried to imagine these two in bed. How do they, during intercourse, manage to stay there? And what about all those arms and legs and necks that get tangled when switching positions? Lots of questions here. And no answers. Mr. and Mrs. Whale looked at each other with *that* look. They climbed out of the tub. Instantly, the water level fell six inches.

Next, a middle-aged blonde wearing a sheer bathing suit slipped into the hot tub. She flashed her breasts my way so that I can easily see her nipples erect under the cloth. The ratio is two to one women passengers to men, so I am always something special among the ladies.

"Do these bother you?" she asked, looking down at her breasts. I said no and proved it by staring long and hard.

Big mistake.

She proceeded to tell me that she is married, but traveling alone. She has her own room on Four deck. She likes men, and she likes to make men happy. Further, she likes the men to pay, though that is not required.

This woman is either crazy, or Prince Charles is her marriage counselor.

I can't think of anything intelligent to say, so I just excuse myself and exit the tub. As I put on my sweatshirt, she waved to me and smiled. "Hope to see you soon. You've got a nice butt."

Tonight we get to go to another captain's party. The floor fills with a bunch of what I think are rather improbable couples. But Ethel points out that there are no couples dancing, only gentlemen hosts with passengers.

By God, she's right. You can tell because the gentlemen hosts have name tags. This Caronia party exactly duplicates the Mauretania party, except the canapés are a little better, and there are more of them and a greater variety.

Monsignor Foley, the Catholic chaplain, showed up in sartorial splendor: he wore his white robe and red sash. Foley is expansive—too expansive. Has he too much of the drink taken? Or is he just ecstatic about cruising? I tell him that there is a rabbi aboard, and I am waiting to see who is the better dressed, him or Rabbi. Foley smiled, surveyed the crowd, and said definitively, "As far as clothes are concerned, it's hard to beat the Vatican."

At that moment, as if on cue, Rabbi entered the room and proved Foley right. Foley won hands down because Rabbi sported a rather dull dark suit, not even a tux.

The Caronia Restaurant shone this night, for it's Gala British dinner night.

Ethel and I enjoyed more chilled caviar with traditional condiments (chopped onion, capers, sour cream, chopped egg yolks, but no ice-cold vodka), followed by fillet of beef, Duke of Wellington style. This marvelous creation, one of my favorites, consists of a filet mignon surrounded by a puff pastry, with goose liver baked in an oven with duxelles (finely chopped mushrooms, parsley, and shallots, put together and used for flavoring). Ethel favored the Maine lobster. We ended the meal with individually prepared soufflés.

As we exited, I read the golden plate award on the entrance of the Caronia: "Epitomizing Epicurean Excellence and Expertise." This alliteration remains true, not only for the food, but also for the whole of *QE2*.

No time to gamble tonight, for we must hurry to the theatre for another night of opera. Ethel and I take seats front row, center, and the singers stand not ten feet away as members of the San Francisco Opera Center present selections from grand operas, including Verdi's *La Traviata*, Bizet's "Toreador Song" from *Carmen*, and also from *Carmen*, "Habanera." Excellent! The French from this last song warned, *"Prends guarde de toi* [watch out]." Carmen is warning her man not to fall in love. Does that go for the *QE2*? If so, Ethel and I are in for trouble. For we have fallen in love, in love with *QE2*. Unlike Carmen's lovers, I hope not fatally.

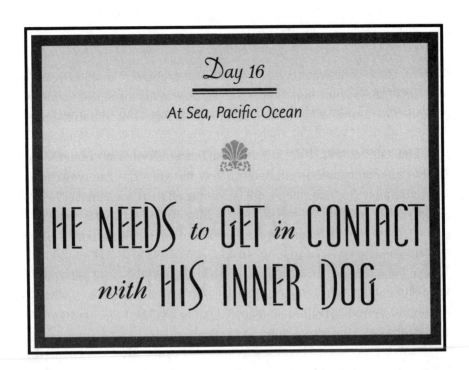

Day 16

At Sea, Pacific Ocean

HE NEEDS *to* GET *in* CONTACT *with* HIS INNER DOG

I have reached the conclusion that *The Inferno* doesn't apply to *QE2* for two reasons: There's too much pleasure here and too little punishment.

Perhaps *QE2* really is purgatory and heaven put together in one place. Mauretania and Caronia constitute the purgatories, and Princess, Britannia, and Queens Grill constitute the heaven. Still, hell does have some onboard applications: where to put Rabbi, for instance.

Rereading *The Inferno*, I find Dante put the wrathful in Circle Five. But, get this: Circle Five had three divisions according to the type of wrath and its seriousness. Division one concerns (and this is not original with Dante but follows Thomistic philosophy from the *Summa Theologicae*) the actively wrathful. Active wrath (what we would call anger), because it is open and usually short lived, is punished least. Division two concerns the passively wrathful, including the sullen (those whom we would call unhappy, boring, or depressed). And division three houses the difficult (those whom we would call pains in the ass). This type of wrath, interestingly enough, the ancient authors considered the worst type of wrath because it is covert, long lived, and seething. Thus the ancients recognized difficult people as sinners who commit the worst kind of wrath. They punished those sinners accordingly. The information the ancients didn't have was voluminous, but they sure did understand human nature.

Because he is so difficult, Rabbi obviously merits Circle Five, third division. The analysis doesn't end there. A more serious type of sin would place Rabbi still lower in hell. Consider this: Does he merit more punishment than Circle Five because he has betrayed the Jews, his kin? Dante, the strict moralist that he is, would place Rabbi, I'm sure, in the depths of the inner hell, in the city of Dis, below the well of the giants and among the traitors to their kindred, next door to the traitors of their country, guests, and lords, because Rabbi, by his misbehavior, made Jews look bad.

Rabbi's behavior at breakfast proves this again. He complained that his grapefruit was not cut. Imagine that! He had to cut his grapefruit himself. Outrageous! After the brouhaha over grapefruit, Rabbi examined the menu for tonight. He frowns. He discovered something: the fish scheduled tonight wouldn't do because it didn't have scales or fins or something like that. "It's not kosher!" he screams.

Peter assured Rabbi that the chef would substitute some other fish for them. "Good, we'll have salmon," the Rabbi decided without consulting Mrs. Rabbi.

Heard on deck today: "I'm confused. Are we going to Maui or to Lahaina or both?" one gray head woman said to another. "We go to both. They're separate islands."

Someone else beside Herman is confused. Incidentally, Herman appeared on deck also. He has started talking to himself. Nothing much except trite social phrases like "Nice to meet you" and "It was good talking to you." Herman will be well prepared for the next captain's party. The captain and the others will consider Herman quite normal.

Cunard University is in full swing, so I attended a lecture by Jan Stuart on Chinese porcelain. Doctor Stuart doesn't talk down and the result amazes me, because the information density is quite high. I learned lots, including the Chinese emperor alone could only use or wear the color yellow. Anyone else who wore yellow or put yellow tiles on his house lost his life. I learned that there were nine orders of concubines. The color scheme of their bowls told where the concubine stood in the hierarchy—yellow on the outside and white within the bowl meant very high, in the top five. Each concubine who produced a son for the emperor advanced in the hierarchy, so the girls worked hard and prayed hard for that to happen. The emperor liked the number nine because it signified perfection. The royal palace had exactly 9,999 rooms and the emperor's main insignia was the nine dragons.

Jan also decoded the pictures on the Chinese vases. They are rebuses. You need to know Chinese to understand them. Chinese has lots of homonyms so that when you say one thing in Mandarin it is possible to think something else, or have it suggested, anyway. For instance, a picture of a red bat on a vase means vast good fortune because the Chinese words for red bat sound the same as the words for vast fortune. This explains the gold fish (abundance of jade) or wasp and lantern together (bumper crops) and so many other things in Chinese art that never made sense to my Western mind. What else don't I know? The sad answer is plenty.

I don't know what's happening to me. I'm hungry all the time and gaining weight, probably twelve pounds since we started. Ethel says it's the fresh sea air, the quality of the food, and the vacation atmosphere. Maybe I should cut back on my food intake. I'll consider the problem later. After lunch.

Rabbi left lunch early today before I finished my charlotte russe at the end of my usual five courses. Joe and Joyce, the couple seated next to us, mentioned (referring to Rabbi) that some people have lots of demands. Eric and we agreed. Eric added that a few special requests are OK, but specials all the time are really reserved for Queens grill. At this point, I showed Eric and Joe and Joyce my note: "Singapore. No way! He goes overboard tonight." Eric rolled and told Mary about it. Eric wanted the note for himself, but since I wrote it on the back of my embarkation card, the card I need to get on and off the ship, I can't give it to him.

New gifts arrived today from Cunard, including another cap for me. This one is gray-green and says in blue letters "1996 World Cruise" under a yellow lion rampant wearing a red crown. Below that, as in a heraldic shield, appears the embroidered words: "Queen Elizabeth 2." I regret not selling my other hat to that taxi driver in Acapulco. He was right. I would get another hat. How did he know? The other gift is a red carrying case for Ethel. The steward who delivers these things is Greek, from Crete. He explained they are for being part of the Samuel Cunard Key Club. Do I fear the Greeks and their bearing gifts? Not at all. It's fun.

At dinner, Ethel and I drank champagne. We selected a Moët (mispriced at $28) from the rather large collection of champagnes on the menu, which included a Brut Rose and seven other vintage champagnes, including our favorites: Crystal 1988 by Louis Roederer, Dom Pérignon, Moët, and Chandon. We skipped over and didn't even consider any of the seven nonvintage champagnes on the list. Although we are in Caronia and should have been slumming it, I am in a spendthrift mood. Besides, we haven't even put a dent in our $2,000 credit.

That reminds me: On the original Cunard ship, *Britannia*, there was only one class. The fare for that one-class (quoted at 34 guineas to Halifax from Liverpool) included all wine and liquor. But after nine months the company literature stated that all wine and liquor would be extra. Can you think of a reason for the change? I can.

Rabbi sinned again. This time at the end of dinner.

Eric and Mary brought over a birthday cake for Mrs. Rabbi. The poor woman huffed and puffed, but she couldn't blow out the one single pathetic candle. (Does she have emphysema? The single candle test used to be the old medical test for emphysema.) Just as well that she couldn't blow it out. You are supposed to wait until they sing for you before you blow out the candle. Many other waiters come, gather round, and join Eric and Mary as they sing Happy Birthday. Mrs. Rabbi is touched, but she still can't get enough wind to extinguish that one burning candle. Mrs. Rabbi gives up and Eric blows it out. Mrs. Rabbi took off her glasses and patted her eyes with the Caronia napkin (Yes, she is crying), and, for the second time this trip, she spoke—spoke with a Bronx accent: "I made it."

So what's the sin?

Despite the occasion, Rabbi, with wrinkled lip and sneer of cold command, without consulting his wife, the birthday child of the day, shouted, "Take it back! It's not kosher!"

Thus did the birthday cake return to the kitchen uneaten—uneaten, that is, by the passenger couple, Rabbi and his wife. I'm sure the staff members ate their fill.

Rabbi needs to get in contact with his inner child. Or, if he doesn't have an inner child, as appears likely, then he needs to get in contact with his inner dog.

After dinner, Ethel and I attended the close-up magic in the Lion Pub. While I sip my gin martini straight up with a twist, Gino, the magician, stuffs a lit cigarette into the pin-striped jacket of my $1,500 custom-made suit. Having recently come under the perniciously bad influence of Rabbi, I shouted, "Hey, watch it! That's a $1,500 suit!" A shake of the hand and puff! The lit cigarette disappeared into the cloth. Gino gives me back my jacket. No hole and no cigarette. Amazing!

More amazing is that my winning streak in roulette continued. I bet the first field and won $40. Then I bet red and won another $20. In two minutes I tripled my money. True to form, I cashed in my $60 profit and quit for the night. Ethel apologized to the croupier and promised she will make me return some other night to bet again. "I'll see to it that you get another chance," she said.

The croupier, the ebony beauty, looked puzzled. She smiled and spun the wheel.

Before we hit the hay, we hit the chamber music concert in the theater, an all Mozart concert with the Philharmonia Virtuosi featuring Richard Ormrod on the piano, Mela Tenenbaum—she doesn't look like much with that poorly dyed red hair but can she play—on viola d'amore, and Richard Kapp as the music director. It was chamber music played the way it should be played in a small chamber to a small audience. We must be in heaven for we hear the music of the spheres. Let the curtain fall, tonight to great music. Music that whirls me farther than Uranus flies; that thrills me more than the climax of my love grip. Well, the music thrills me, but not that much. Cunard entertainment is as great as sex—almost.

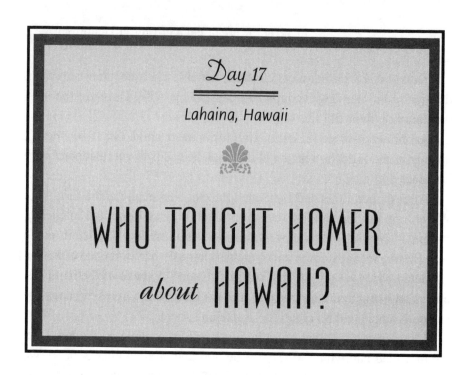

Day 17

Lahaina, Hawaii

WHO TAUGHT HOMER
about HAWAII?

A harpooned sperm whale turned and came back toward us with monstrous rage, carrying twenty tons of fat, muscle, and a tail four yards wide, capable of disintegrating our frail wood boat with a single blow. The gigantic snout rose slightly, then slipped below the boat. This whale had thirty teeth each weighing ten pounds. No one expected those teeth to surge from the water and clamp onto the boat's rim but they did, just a yard away from where I cowered. In went the harpoon and then the whale surged and splashed. The water turned red. The whale came right at us. It seemed enormous. Our boat broke in three, and when we took the final count, three men were dead.

That was the old days when Lahaina was the whaling capital of the world. Now the whales come down here not to kill or get killed, but to spend the winter, mate, and calve.

Strangely, the whales don't eat anything here. They stocked up on shrimp and made lots of blubber up in Alaska, but in Hawaii they go on a strict no-calorie diet. I guess whales don't like Hawaiian food.

Other tourists rent boats to go out and take a look at the whales. The law prescribes that the boats and whales can't get within one hundred feet of each other, but the whales don't seem to know the law. The whales are as curious about the tourists as the tourists are about them. So the whales just swim right up and take a close look. Police should arrest those law-breaking whales, but they don't.

QE2's biologist informed us that the whales have a specific pattern on their tails. Scientists take a picture of the tails, digitalize the image, print it out, and use it to trace the whale's activities. The tail print is to whales what fingerprints are to humans. Evidently, whales have no constitutional right to privacy. One whale, recently sighted off the coast of Alaska, showed up in Lahaina (a trip of over three thousand miles) thirty days later—not as fast as the *QE2,* but pretty fast for a single animal to cross a vast section of ocean.

The *QE2* biologist is full of information about the whales. People working for scientists had permission to shoot some of the whales with darts, and while the whales were sleeping off the tranquilizers, they biopsied their skin. (To a whale this is like a mosquito bite would be to us). The scientists studied the skin biopsies and measured the mitochondrial DNA, the inherited material in the subcellular organelle called the mitochondrion, which is the powerhouse of the individual mammalian cell. Since a whale's mitochondrial DNA comes entirely from the mother and the drift of base pairs is uniform through time, the migration of the whales from northern seas to Hawaii can be traced. Guess what? The whole population of humpbacks derived from a single female! Eve of the svelte leviathans! But her name, this mother of all whales, wasn't Eve. It probably was some unpronounceable whale sound that only the whales themselves can say or understand.

Rabbi was in his usual form: they didn't cut his grapefruits again. He had to do it himself. He asked for the dinner menu, looked it over, and told Mrs. Rabbi, "The menu contains nothing we can eat."

Rabbi called over Kevin Sullivan, the manager of the entire Caronia Restaurant, and complained. Peter is gone, exiled to the Lido with Mary.

Rabbi scowled as he handed the menu to Kevin. "This menu does nothing for us. That's OK, though. We'll eat bread and water."

Isn't it great the way sinners suggest their own punishment? If I were Kevin, I would give them bread and water, but Kevin tells the Rabbi they might have salmon. Rabbi's eyes brighten. He throws the menu down on the table since it's clear Kevin is not going to take it out of Rabbi's hands. "OK, we'll have salmon."

If things continue this way, Rabbi and Mrs. Rabbi will set the record for eating the most salmon on the *QE2*.

Ethel and I went on the tender into Lahaina, the oldest city on Maui and the former capital of Hawaii. We explored the cute Pioneer Inn that once was the only hotel in the city, then we headed to the Great Banyan tree. Over one hundred years ago a sheriff planted it. Originally eight feet high and imported from India, it grew and now covers the best part of an acre outside the court house.

Along Front Street Ethel and I stopped at the Baldwin House, a typical New England–Polynesian with broad up and down verandas or *lanais*. The place, preserved as a museum, was the 1834 home of the American medical missionary Rev. Dwight Baldwin.

Ethel and I love old homes so we go to work exploring. Of interest, they have on display a certificate issued to native doctors. It says: "The Big Kahuna authorizes the native doctor to charge $50 for a grave illness if the patient survives and $10 for a minor illness if a cure is affected." Notice even in the old days writers had trouble with *affected* versus *effected*.

How did one get to be a Kahuna? That's what I wanted to know because I wished to apply. Understand, I don't want to be the *Big* Kahuna, just an ordinary average everyday kahuna. That's good enough for me.

We continued walking along Front Street. A pig in front of one store was digging intensely under a mat. "Just like P.J.!" Ethel exclaims.

I pet the pig but he/she keeps digging. "I wonder how P.J. is? We miss P.J., but not that much."

The stores were peppered with native folk wisdom: "Never judge a day by the weather," "No Rain No Rainbow," and the one I like the best —a lesson for us all—says, "He who dies with the most toys, still dies."

Ethel's friend Isabel, one of the Caronia waitresses, came walking along Front Street from the other direction. Isabel told us she had just come from whale watching and loved it. One of the big whales came right up to the boat and scared everyone.

Someone handed us a flyer about Maui real estate. "Now is the time to buy," it says. The firm specializes in representing buyers and sellers. But get this: The realtors are extremely aggressive in assisting clients with every facet of the buying process, from finding the right property to ratcheting down the numbers to fit a budget. Also, when they represent a seller, they court buyers domestically and internationally. They win both ways. On the back of the flyer they show a two-year-old, four bedroom, three bath ranch in a quiet subdivision priced $550,000. Who would pay such an amount for such a home when, for the same money, they could, in Mauretania class on *QE2*, sail around the world twenty-nine times?

The housing prices here make no sense; someone (the Japanese?) had inflated the market.

Ethel and I celebrate being on terra firma again by walking three miles to the other side of the island, the Kaanapali coast, where the surf is three feet and the coral sharp. We find a real newspaper, the Sunday *New York Times*. I tried to buy the paper but met with considerable opposition because it's a day old. "Why buy it? It's old news," the store manager asked.

"I haven't seen a newspaper in weeks."

The Hyatt Hotel recreates the Hawaiian paradise that never was complete with tropical gardens, multicolored birds and waterfalls. It's glitzy, but I like it.

As night approached, we headed back to the ship. Several people stopped us, coveting our *New York Times* and asking where we bought it. I promised to donate it to the ship's library tomorrow after I have checked the financial pages. I have already checked Amgen, of course, up 2⅞. Not bad. I'm $149,500 richer this week. There were three great inventions, the wheel, fire, and the stock market. Of the three the greatest is the stock market, especially those biotechnology stocks, but only when they go up.

Seven hundred people turn out for the Bill Cosby show at the Grand Lounge. I asked Ethel why are we going to see Cosby? If he were playing in Houston we wouldn't bother and if he were on TV we wouldn't bother. Ethel agrees but thinks we should check it out.

Cosby really did show up and the crowd went wild. He started telling jokes about wives and mothers-in-law. I feel uncomfortable. I don't laugh. Why should I? I love my wife. I love my mother-in-law. When I hear that old one about the two drunks who wake up marooned in the dark on the ice, I decided to duck out. One drunk tried to cut a hole in the ice for fish. A big voice cried out: "There are no fish under that ice!" The drunk with the ice pick says, "The voice of God!" But the voice responds, "This is not God. This is the owner of the skating rink. There are no fish under that ice."

At 11 PM, *QE2* pulled out of Lahaina. I recalled what Homer said about Elysium: "Situated at the world's end where no snow falls, no strong wind blows—only a soft refreshing breeze from the ocean."

Who taught these ancient writers their simplicity of language, their felicity of expression, their pathos, and, above all, their faculty of sinking themselves entirely out of sight of the reader, making the narrative stand out alone and tell itself?

And who taught Homer about Hawaii?

Day 18

Honolulu, Hawaii

MAL de TERRE

We docked in Honolulu.

Mom and Pop next door had a big row. Their screaming came right through the bulkhead walls, which are as thin as those in the single-walled houses in old Hawaii.

Should I go over and play peacemaker? When I heard Pop yell, "Sixty-one years, Mom, I have had to put up with this," I decided I had better not.

Any marriage that has survived that long will likely continue through today. Argument might be a kind of recreation for them. Argument might give Mom and Pop something to live for, something to make their otherwise dull lives, less dull.

Pop ended the argument, as usual, by exiting into the bathroom. Bang! Pop slammed the door. Later, I saw bags outside their room. Mom and Pop are leaving. Their departure explains everything. They have disembarkation angst, a bad case of it. Hart Crane, the great American poet, may have had the same problem when he returned to New York harbor at the end of his cruise. He solved his angst by jumping overboard. They never found his body. Water makes many graves for those who yearn to sleep. All life derives from the sea. Perhaps that is why some people like Crane wish to return to it. One thing's for sure: when Mom and Pop leave, quiet will arrive.

Ethel and I avoided shore tours, but because we love homes and gardens, we can't resist go on our first tour of the homes and gardens of Hawaii.

The bus left late. We had to wait for some old codgers. That's the beginning. Every tour moves as slowly as its slowest participant, and some of the people on this tour move in geological time. At least it feels that way when they try to get them off the bus first while the rest of us wait and wait and wait. Finally, Susan, the Cunard representative on the bus, gets fed up and declares that the able bodied shall get off first. The handicapped shall wait.

We saw three homes. The first, spic and span and lived in by a widow, sits right on the beach facing the rolling surf and flies two flags: the American and the peculiar Hawaiian flag, which has red, white, and blue stripes with a British Union Jack in the upper left-hand corner, reminding us of Cook's visit in 1778 and the subsequent British occupation of these fair islands, which Cook named after the Earl of Sandwich, the same Earl who invented a handy way of snacking so he didn't have to interrupt his gambling.

The fresh sea breezes carry the scent of fish (mahi-mahi, the fish dolphin?) and also have a breath of perfume in them. Our guide, Browny Welch, a member of the local garden club, explains the perfume smell comes from white plumerias. She says as ships approach the islands, the smell becomes more and more intense. Even Captain Cook noticed the perfume when he first arrived.

The owner of the house, a little old woman with a big happy smile and clean white teeth, told me of the day some time ago (she thinks it was in 1985 or was it 1986) when the Japanese invaded. Men arrived with paper bags full of money and offered her on the spot three million dollars in cash for her home, but she refused. Many of her neighbors didn't. Those neighbors left and built new homes on the mountain, our next stop.

On the way up we heard about the Hawaiian language. Like all languages it was first spoken and not written. So there must have been a time in Hawaii, a time out of mind, a time older than the time of chronometers, when there were no forms and no red tape. That must have been the real Polynesian paradise. That bucolic time has forever departed.

The two main features of the Hawaiian language are the guttural stop, which I have been practicing, and the plentitude of *k* sounds. There aren't any *l*'s or *s*'s or *t*'s, and there are only five long and five short vowels and seven consonants.

Browny Welch said something in Hawaiian, which of course no one understands. She said the state flower is the red hibiscus. I tell her it's the anthurium, but it turns out that both of us are wrong. The state flower is the yellow hibiscus, because it is an indigenous flower. The red hibiscus is not.

Ethel and I sipped orange-pink punch while standing on the veranda of home number two, built into the slope of the mountain. Beautiful wind-warped Norfolk pines, trapped in color and dazzled by the light loom in front of us somewhat blocking our view of the sea and the backside of Diamond Head Crater. Nearby, a screech owl called for a mate and in the distance I heard a reply. This lush green pali (*pali*, n. In Hawaii: a steep cliff) with steep falling cliffs reminds me of the Garden of Eden. But a kind of gray-yellow mist obscures our distant vision and gives everything a surreal appearance. Browny explains the mist is *vog*, a combination of fog and volcano smoke. Vog? Volcano smoke? Wait a second. Nobody told us about the volcano. Was it still active? Yes. It is.

Browny pointed out the eyesore next door, a large yellow house falling apart and boarded up. The Japanese bought houses like crazy without negotiating the prices. When Japan's economy took a dive, people couldn't handle the payments and the banks got stuck with the properties. The banks can't handle the repairs. What happens next? No one knows.

The last home sits in Nuluanu Pali, adjacent to a waterfall. The owners, the McGrafts, have a library with a larger than usual collection of books on Ireland. Why not? But the home seems dark to us, and the gentle rain falling makes it appear somewhat dreary. The home has no swimming pool, no vegetable garden, but it does have a redeeming cat that we petted while wishing for P.J.

Upstairs in McGraft's bathroom I weighed myself. Bad news. Up fourteen pounds since the start of the cruise. Starting today I shall not eat dessert at lunch.

Back on *QE2* for lunch. Mary is still in exile in the Lido. Eric doesn't think it's fair. Neither do we.

I glared at the Rabbi. He knows I know that he hurt an Irish maiden. He knows the Irish stick together—always. His face shows his fear. He is wondering how and when I will have my Irish revenge. I am wondering the same thing. Never give an Irishman a good excuse for revenge.

Perhaps I should start the revenge by stealing his blue reserved table sign. It's the only reserved sign in the Caronia Restaurant. How come he gets it and we don't?

In a crisis of conscience, I order lemon parfait for dessert. Tomorrow is plenty time to start the deprivations to get my weight in line. Today, I'm going to feed my inner dog to get me in a better mentality in preparation for this afternoon and the third-degree media encounter with Michelle the Nasty from WGBH Boston.

Meanwhile, I kept Rabbi under close scrutiny. He gets more and more absurd. He rejected the menu again. "There's nothing on this." Then in quick succession: "Bring more mayonnaise. We'll make our own salads. If we need more than that, we'll whistle. Send Robert, the Mauretania chef, here. I need to talk with him. Do you know what sardines are? Get us some."

Then I figured it out. Rabbi and the jerk next to me are duking it out to see who can be the most obnoxious. This other man, who sports a black Hitler type mustache, constantly rolled the Rolex on his left wrist, thus calling conspicuous attention to it. His wife, as they sit down, usually says, "Remember, watch your diet. No meat, only fish."

Mr. Rolex shook his head yes and ordered a pan-fried fish. His wife beamed her approval at his healthy-for-the-heart choice, but she ordered the breaded fried chicken. When the fish came, Mr. Rolex turned up his nose. His wife smacking and licking her lips rubbed things in by telling

Mr. Rolex the chicken is delicious. So Mr. Rolex points to the now much despised fish and tells Eric to take it away. "Bring me what she has," says Rolex. And that, sad to say, is what Eric did.

Why talk about this guy?

To show the gentle reader what a consummate ass one can become when one goes aboard the *QE2*. I speak now of course in the supposition that the gentle reader has not been abroad, and therefore is not already a consummate ass. Or that the reader has an innate desire, as do I, to try not to become a consummate ass.

I asked Ethel, "Who's the bigger jerk, Rolex or Rabbi?"

"The Rabbi is *jerkus maximus*," came her reply.

Ethel doesn't feel well. She looks pale too. Nothing specific, but it started after we docked. Could she have mal de terre, a disease like mal de mer except it occurs on land, and not on the sea? Claire, the waitress who substituted for Mary, says she had a grandfather who got sick whenever he came into port and recovered when he returned to the sea. Peter, now back from exile, said the same, and made the same diagnosis: Ethel suffers mal de terre.

Time for me to make a journey downtown.

Time wounds us humans, wounds us with a fatal wound. And time wounded Honolulu, also fatally. Here the American dream turned into a nightmare. Downtown looked like any other crowded American city. The Hilton Hawaiian Village where we stayed twenty-five years ago resembled a busy airport with people checking in bags and rushing about. It did not resemble the haven of leisure that we once knew and loved. In the hotel's lobby opposite the American Express travel desk and the local events desk (now selling luau tickets), I pushed through the crowd looking for Mike Day, the cameraman who was supposed to meet me here. The tourists were supposed to be on vacation relaxing, but they seem frenetic.

After the third hour of the *Frontline* interview (interrogation would be a better word) in a makeshift studio, Mike Day dropped me back at the Hilton where I milled around until I was sure he didn't follow me. I didn't want him to know that I'm on the *QE2*. I didn't want WGBH to know that I was on the world cruise.

The coast seemed clear, so I tried to hail a taxi. The next in line was a white limousine.

I explained to the driver that I'm not Japanese so I can't afford a limo, at least not on this island. "Get in," he said. "I bought this limo six days ago and I want to break it in." He explained that the law required he charge the same as a taxi and he was happy to take me back to the *QE2*. I got in. Not bad. I'm at home.

Because we are in a limo, they don't didn't stop us at the gate where they stop the regular taxis. Instead, they flag us right up to the gangway where I make a dramatic entrance with several passengers and crew looking on. Thank God the TV cameramen are nowhere in sight. *Wait a second! What the deuce!* They are here. They're filming me as I get out. I waved to them and screamed, "TV—It's junk food for the mind." They won't air that. But it made me feel good.

Ethel fell asleep, still sick with mal de terre. I ate alone. Between courses I read Dante. Mr. Rolex, because he sent back his fish, belongs in circle four of hell for the sin of the unreasonable misuse of material resources. I know Michelle the Nasty from WGBH belongs in hell, too. She and *Frontline*. But I can't figure out how far down into the abyss they should go.

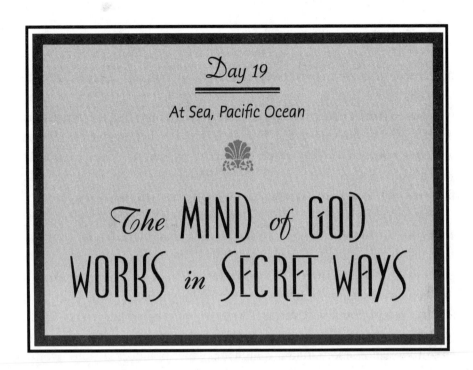

Day 19

At Sea, Pacific Ocean

The MIND of GOD WORKS in SECRET WAYS

*Q*E2 plunges through the blue Pacific headed from here to eternity on the longest and, according to the Rabbi, the weakest leg of the world tour. Weakest leg or not, Ethel and I love the fresh air, the sea breeze, the briny salt taste in our mouth, the fresh smells of ocean teeming with life. Long sea legs thrill us because we can enjoy the ship which is a destination too and we can enjoy the sea which proves as a sanctuary for meditation worth a kingdom. We are beginning to think that the best islands of leisure and the best resorts of happiness have propellers.

It was a relief to drop all anxiety whatsoever—all questions as to where we should go; how long we should stay; whether it worthwhile to go or not; all anxieties about the conditions of the natives; all such questions as shall we ever get to drinks or lunch. We felt the temporary contentment that is born of the banishment of all care and responsibility. We did not look at the compass. We did not care where the ship went, as long as she went out of sight of land as quickly as possible. When I travel again, I wish to go in a pleasure ship. No amount of money could have purchased for us, in a strange vessel and among unfamiliar faces, the perfect satisfaction and the sense of being at home that we experienced when we stepped back onboard the *QE2*, our own ship, after this the wearisome pilgrimage that was our visit to Honolulu. It is a something we felt always when we returned to *QE2*, and a something we had no desire to sell. As Ralph Waldo Emerson said in his poem "Woodnotes": "Go where he will, the wise man is at home/His hearth the earth, his hall the azure dome."

Under that gentle blue dome, I walked about the Signal deck, forward, aft, starboard, and port. Nothing but water stretched to the horizon. I see the surface only. It glistens and glints in the early morning sun while *QE2*, the svelte leviathan, the world's fastest ship, probably the world's most luxurious ship, becomes minuscule next to the sea, a tin cup, merely, floating on a vast surface. And, if you really want to feel small, think of the mass of water under that vast surface. From here to the bottom measures more than a mile. Our planet is indeed a water world. We knew that before we started, but we didn't feel it or didn't understand it emotionally until we started to cross the Pacific.

Ethel read out the daily program. Today I decided to dig out from the ship's museum or library some of the programs from other world cruises and compare and contrast. How did those travelers handle the plenitude of things to do? I also decided to set limits: Only two lectures—Jan Stuart's on Japanese wood-block color prints and Waldemar Hansen's talk on Japan. After those, I intended to remain free, except, if I'm in the right mood, I might go to the French opera tonight.

Rumor has it the ship will sponsor a murder mystery tomorrow. If Brian Price, the cruise director, is looking for a victim, I can supply one—the Rabbi. Such a murder might provoke a lot of sleuthing. There would be many suspects, including Robert, the Caronia chef; Kevin O'Sullivan, the Caronia Restaurant manager; Peter, the section head (now exiled again); Mary and Eric, the waitpersons; Ethel and myself; and even (probably) Mrs. Rabbi.

In real murder, my father, the chief homicide prosecutor of Queens for twenty-two years, taught me the scales of justice tilt only slightly in favor of the victim. If we understood the situation all in all, through and through, many of us would have committed the same crime as the perpetrator.

Ethel folded down the schedule and cocked her head to listen. Only the sea wind, howl and yelp, and an occasional creak when the ship rolls heavily to port, protruded on the silence. Both of us realized that Mom and Pop left yesterday. Today we miss them. But not that much.

Yes, we missed Mom and Pop the way cockney children in London were restless when the Nazi bombing stopped and disturbed a pattern to which those children had grown accustomed.

A fax arrived under the door.

It's from Lennie and Vince, our travel agents. Cunard gave us a courtesy upgrade from C4 to P1, from cabin 3045 on three deck that we were scheduled to move to on February 5 while in Hong Kong to cabin 2047 on Two deck.

Hot Dog!

This promotion, if true, means a merciful God exists, for with the upgrade we must switch dining rooms, from the Caronia to Princess Grill, and thereby forever lose the Rabbi. The Rabbi might be getting more mayonnaise and occasional off-menu salmons, but Ethel and I will get something much more valuable: peace at mealtime. Thus, does God reward the Just, the meek, the humble, and the patient, by elevating lowly sinners like us out of purgatory to Heaven. God does this whenever God's infinite mercy deems it necessary.

Talking about the Rabbi reminds me: At lunch, once again, nothing on the menu pleased him. He asked Eric, "Do you know what chicken soup is?" No response. "Let's have some."

Eric brought the soup. "If we need more, we'll whistle," said the Rabbi.

Rabbi tasted the soup. Then he waved a finger for Eric. "Take it back. It doesn't taste right. It tastes like chicken. I'm sure it's OK but we're not used to chicken soup like this and we're not going to start now."

The three furies—Tisiphone, Megaera, and Alecto—traditional avengers of crime in classical mythology, are too good for the likes of him. I felt the need to take things in my own hands.

Glaring at the Rabbi, slowly I rose, grabbed the steak knife, and with one quick blow stabbed him in the heart. The crimson blood soaked his white shirt as he keeled over and landed face first into his uneaten salmon cake.

And so, our life, a bed of roses, our happy happy life on board *QE2*, would have continued had I not killed the Rabbi. Only kidding of course, but that's the way events were headed.

The folks at Cunard must have figured it out. They wanted to prevent a murder by getting me out of Caronia and away from Rabbi. They didn't want me to spoil my rich and happy life on *QE2* for the temporary pleasure of killing a fellow passenger. Cunard had a good reason for the upgrade.

What about poor Mary? Cunard planned her departure from Caronia, I firmly believe, for the same reason. Mary probably hit the confessional everyday with Monsignor Foley to confess her desire to murder the Rabbi. Catholics believe a sin in the heart is as serious as a sin in fact. But a sin in fact starts in the heart. Foley may have seen what was coming and may have dropped some hints to the captain while still maintaining the seal of the confessional.

I asked Mary about this. She wouldn't say anything more than the usual cryptic Irish way of responding to a question by asking another. "Now wouldn't it be usual that sometimes the waiters are reassigned?"

At dinner the Rabbi tells Eric that they are having rib-eye steaks. Mrs. Rabbi sat up, surprised. "I didn't know we were having steak!"

"Of course, you didn't know. I didn't tell you," said Rabbi with a smirk.

Rabbi waved the index finger of accusation at Claire, calling her over. "You might want to know how we want our steaks cooked."

Claire and I held our breaths in anticipation of this great command, while Ethel silently mouthed the words "well done." And, by God, that's what Rabbi said.

This evening's program consists of French opera from Meyer Beer ("Nobles Seigneurs") to Massenet (Saint Sulpice duet). Nicolle Foland and Kathryn Krasovec sang the Barcarolle from the *Tales of Hoffmann* by Offenbach. Their voices become transcendent, approaching the redemptive quality of art. When they have finished, the audience remained silent, mesmerized by the evocative beauty of this love duet. Then it broke into applause and bravos. Another standing ovation.

Is that life? A few moments of beauty and bliss before the curtain comes down.

Another present arrived from Cunard. This one from John E. Duffy, the hotel manager. Two certificates for $150 each to use for shore excursions, a gift to the members of the Samuel Cunard Key Club.

Ethel pulled out the list of excursions. I want to pet a koala bear and so does she. We'll take the excursion to the Loney Pine Koala Sanctuary. Ethel and I were happy but we were tired. We knew then what we had known before—that it is worthwhile to get tired because, afterwards, one so enjoys sleeping.

Day 20

At Sea, Pacific Ocean

IF WE CAN'T MAKE TIME STAND STILL, LET'S MAKE IT RUN

*R*abbi didn't show for breakfast.

I found I could completely ignore him when he isn't around. This means the upgrade will solve his problem and mine. Getting me out of Caronia will prevent my inner dog from taking a bite out of him.

Ethel returned to the world of the living and remained fully recovered from her mal de terre. If her mysterious illness returns again when we dock in Japan, then we'll know that Ethel has a problem.

Waldemar Hansen, in his morning lecture, warned the group that Friday, January 26, 1996, would not exist because we will cross the International Date Line. The whole day will get swallowed up into the maw of time.

I have significant objections to losing a whole day of life, but no one else seemed to care. We could turn back. We could cancel the rest of the trip. But who wants to do that? That would solve the missing day problem, but would cancel the fun to come. The whole morbid thing raises important questions about time, its nature, and its significance. Any fool with a watch can tell you what time it is, but who can tell you what time *is*?

Time flies on the ship anyway, so what should I care if one day flies by faster than the others? It's all relative. Besides, I know time doesn't exist. Time is just an imaginary human concept. Past time certainly doesn't exist. It might have existed, but no longer exists since it's gone. And future time doesn't exist either since it hasn't happened yet. So if time exists, it exists only in the present and only in the instantaneous fleeting moment of experience, a moment so short most of us couldn't detect its passing.

Come to think on it, crossing the date line has advantages. Hillary Clinton would love to miss tomorrow because she must testify before the Senate about Whitewater. And if tomorrow doesn't happen, then I don't need to get my hair cut. I have a haircut phobia like most men, but my phobia is based on reality.

Long years ago, never mind how many, when I was still practicing medicine, I looked out into the waiting room and saw a familiar face. It was Joyce, the woman who cut my hair for five years. Joyce also cut my son Craig's hair.

"What brings you here?" I asked Joyce.

"When I cut hair the voice of God tells me to stab the scissors into the neck of the customer. I know that isn't right, but the voice is getting louder and more insistent. I'm afraid I might kill someone."

Then I to her (note the influence of Dante on how I indicate who says what to whom, "then I to her" is Dante's construction): "Joyce, does the voice say the same thing when you cut my hair or Craig's hair?"

"All the time."

We locked Joyce up where she belonged in Rusk State Hospital for the Criminally Insane. Thank God, part of her was sane enough to know the voice made an unreasonable request. The State of Texas took away Joyce's license to cut hair. Someone could have gotten hurt. How many other Joyces are out there?

Except for the normal ship's creak and the wind howl, both natural sounds, our room today remains eerily silent now that Mom and Pop have departed. That's what makes this narrative postmodern: the characters inexplicably keep drifting in and drifting out of the story just as they do in life. But some characters, at least for the moment, remain, like Herman.

I saw Herman on Boat deck leaning over the side rail. He looked like a baffled man searching for direction from side to side while shaking his head. His mouth was wide open and he hunched over the rail, short of breath. Emphysema? Anxiety? Heart failure? How does he get along? Where is his caretaker? One thing is for sure: Herman won't miss tomorrow. He doesn't miss today. Herman probably doesn't even know today exists. Even if he did know he wouldn't care. Watching him lean over that rail made me think Herman might someday become a man overboard. It's happened before.

On October 24, 1979, *QE2* was in the harbor of Las Palmas when an elderly passenger fell into the water. Four crewmembers, including cruise director Brian Price, showed no hesitation in jumping to the rescue. *QE2* has more than her share of heroes, but, despite the heroes, the passenger died.

Like any city, a ship the size of *QE2* cannot be without the occasional mystery.

A British vacationer was reported missing by his wife when he had not returned to his cabin by 8 PM on October 29, 1985. Captain Lawrence Portet ordered a thorough search of the ship and, when convinced that the man was not onboard, had the ship turned around and the course retraced. Although searchlights were used in the approaching darkness, the search was abandoned when the captain considered that there was no chance of ever finding anyone in the choppy sea.

In his excellent book *Captain of the Queen*, Robert Harry Arnott told of another mystery. As *QE2* surged through the dark waters of the Pacific on the night of Easter, March 26, 1978, the cruise of a fabulously wealthy Swiss widow named Iris Bodmer ended. Why or how we still don't know, but Captain Arnott believed that Mrs. Bodmer, who was sixty-nine, simply jumped into the sea and vanished into the ocean depths. It's impossible to fall off the *QE2* accidentally unless you're fooling around climbing the handrails, which is hardly the exploit of an elderly lady. Mrs. Bodmer had been a lonely old soul who seldom mixed with the other passengers. She was due to leave the ship the next day in Honolulu, but Captain Arnott is sure she decided to opt out of life before the warmth of the alohas had the opportunity to melt her melancholia. It was a strange decision for Mrs. Bodmer to make because the old lady left behind, in the ship's safe, jewelry (British for jewelry) worth more than $3 million.

Incidentally, Cunard's safety record over its entire history is little short of phenomenal. Not a single passenger's life has been lost through the company's fault at sea during peacetime.

War is a different story. *Lusitania* (1907, 31,550 tons) remains one of the most famous of all Cunarders lost at war. After eight years of commercial service, she was torpedoed on May 7, 1915, off the Irish coast and went down in twenty minutes with 1,198 souls. Incidentally, only a ship has souls on board. Planes and cars don't. Souls on board is the sum of passengers and crew.

On deck, a young couple had an argument I overheard: "You haven't kissed me since we got engaged." Also on deck I see one of the philharmonic virtuosos. He settles down in the deck chair and pulls out a Walkman, hooks it up, and listens to music.

Today's lectures: Jan Stuart told us about Chinese art and the symbolism and quest for longevity. The Chinese, I realize, want to live forever, but, as for me, it makes more sense just to want to cruise forever.

Waldemar Hansen covers some history and culture of Japan. Although I have attended several medical meetings in Japan and lectured there also, Hansen convinced me I never visited the place and don't know it. Nor do I understand Japan's people. Japan seems to be the only third-world country with a modern industrial economy. It's nice to have someone objective like Waldemar calling a spade a spade. I travel to learn, but I still recall that they picture no French defeats in the battle galleries of Versailles. Shintoism fascinates me and so does Taoism. I can't decide which religion to embrace. How about both?

Between lectures a woman strikes up a conversation with us. She is from Florida and is taking the world cruise. She is amazed that she hasn't met us before. The trouble is she has. In fact, we had the same conversation yesterday in the same place, the theater, in the same context (Waldemar Hansen's lecture). The great thing about Alzheimer's disease is that you keep meeting new people.

Rabbi didn't show for lunch.

He probably picked up on the negative vibes from all of us in the section. Poor Rabbi! He wouldn't know his inner dog if it bit him in the butt. His failure to show and the beautiful clear blue day, the calm sea, and the five-course lunch complete with Grand Marnier parfait for dessert put me in an expansive mood. Immortality may dominate the psyche of the Chinese and of mankind in general, but only because they have not experienced cruising on the *QE2*. I came up with some ideas.

I decided to tell Captain Burton-Hall to keep cruising around here forever in this perfect spot of the Pacific Ocean. In fact, forget Shintoism. Forget Taoism. Follow my religion. A new religion based on cruising as the eternal reward. Except for one sin, the sin of being difficult, it will be a religion without sin, a religion without God, a religion where the rewards are a good meal, a good screw, a good drink, a good sleep, plenty of good entertainment, and interesting lectures. In short, the Cruise Religion. Shall we call it Cruisism? No matter. The cult has many devotees, including the already five million who cruised last year, people who make no bones about their interest in fun and pleasure. They are not crass materialists. They're just humans having fun, Homo Ludens, the next evolutionary step in the development of mankind.

At lunch, I told Eric that if I need anything I'll whistle. Eric looked at me, worried, his expression pale. He thought I might have caught the complaint virus. Then Eric realized it's a joke. Eric smiled and laughed out loud.

The pool temperature rose to above 82 degrees, so the mystical Germans (four of them) returned to dominate the scene. Each German weighs twice what I do. How did they lose the war? One English boy, about twelve years old, tries to swim with them and me, but it's hard. The Germans pay no attention to him and just splash away, swamping the kid. The English boy periodically yells at them to stop. The Germans keep splashing.

In the ship's museum on Two deck, I located the papers from the sailing days of eld. I focused attention on a schedule for August 21, 1939, aboard the voyage of the SS *Lancastria*, and quote directly:

The radio installed aft lounge is available 10 AM to midnight. Please turn off the current when through. Gymnasium and outdoor pools function throughout the day. 7.30 Mass, 10.15 Parade of the Day and Sing Song, 10.30 Sports 11.00 Dance class, 11.30 Totalisator 12.15 Deck Buffet (weather permitting) 1.00 Luncheon. Correct attire will be insisted upon at all sittings. 2.30 Treasure Hunt 3.15 Informal talk: What to do, see, and buy in Nassau by Watterson Work 4.00 Bridge Form and Afternoon Tea 5.00 Gulf Stream Races 6.30 Dinner (1st sitting) 7.00 Cocktail Hour 7.40 Dinner (2nd sitting) 8.30 Movies *Stanley and Livingston* (Romantic-Drama) featuring Spencer Tracy 6.00 After dinner music 11.35 Put your timepiece back 30 minutes 12 MN Lucky Dance number 1.30 AM Night Hawks meet in Main Smoke Room Tomorrow movies feature *Charlie Chan, Treasure Island* with Cesar Romero and Pauline Moore.

Wow! That generation had its fun, its happiness, and even its moments of intense pleasure, but they didn't have half the choice of events we do. The past is a different country. They do things differently there. Note the archaic, old-fashioned, and antiquated expressions like luncheon, gymnasium, bridge form, and timepiece. Their cocktail menu interested me. I recognized only two cocktails that we would know, Cuba Libre, and Tom Collins. The dinner menu looks adequate with five courses, but the choices are limited to less than half the selections we enjoyed even in Mauretania.

On the way back from the museum I hear chanting. It sounds strange, ancient, with a sad plaintive timbre. It comes from the synagogue. I look in and see the rows are packed with men and women holding white cards in front of their faces and singing. On a table outside, plastic cups, most of which are a quarter filled with red wine, line up. Do they drink these later? Because Friday, the Sabbath, won't come for this group (we're skipping it tomorrow), they have decided to celebrate tonight.

Rabbi Roth, a happy-looking man, leads the group. Our Rabbi appears nowhere. Are the Caronia Rabbi and Rabbi Roth on the outs?

I hurried. I didn't want to be late for the next treat: the poetry workshop.

Fourteen serious poets gathered in the Golden Lion Pub.

Kate Light, the teacher, starts off with a serious discussion of sonnet structures and rhyme schemes Shakespearean, Spencerian, and Petrarchan. Then we read poems and discussed the poets, including ee cummings, the Bard, Paul Goodman, Edmund Spenser, Elizabeth Barrett Browning, Gerard Manley Hopkins, and Edna St. Vincent Millay. The group has the most trouble with Hopkins, the Jesuit who developed his own meters. The poem I like the best is Goodman's, who asks "Is life worth it as it is?" Kate ended the poetry workshop with an assignment. We should each write a sonnet and hand it in.

No thanks. I can't. I left my rhyming dictionary at home (it's probably the only book I didn't bring). Besides, I'm having too much fun doing other things. Writing poems is work.

The night closed with a large gathering in the Golden Lion Pub for the musical murder mystery. The clues are titles to songs and the group goes wild, after each tune played, identifying the titles and writing them down.

Ethel and I get the easy ones like "Yellow Ribbon," "Michelle," and "Baby Face," but we miss the difficult ones, scoring seven out of the twenty-five. Alas, we didn't win the champagne. But our performance achieved merit especially by comparison. The woman next to me got only one right. Well, she almost got one right. She had "Bring in the Clowns" instead of "Send in the Clowns."

We returned to cabin 4164, contented and amused. Our happiness increased when we found waiting there another gift from the Samuel Cunard Key Club: a white porcelain dish depicting in red, green, and blue the appointed course of this year's cruise of the *QE2* around the world.

I placed my index finger on the extreme right side of the plate where a small blue arrow marked our place just east of the International Date Line.

"Forget it," said Ethel. "If we can't make time stand still, let's make it run."

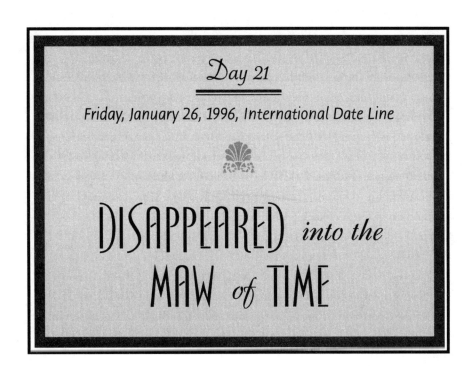

Day 21

Friday, January 26, 1996, International Date Line

DISAPPEARED *into the* MAW *of* TIME

*D*ue to lack of interest, today, January 26, 1996, has been canceled.

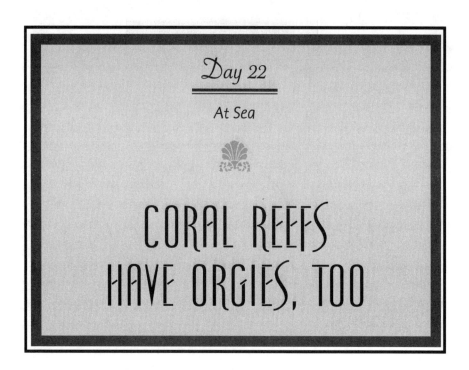

Day 22

At Sea

CORAL REEFS HAVE ORGIES, TOO

*I*t happened.

Yesterday disappeared into the maw of time. Where did it go?

I asked Waldemar Hansen. He tried to construct an answer.

At the end of the eighteenth century, for the sake of marine navigation, someone decided to divide the world into theoretical parallels and meridians. These became our current lines of latitude and longitude measured in degrees and minutes. The parallels, concentric circles running parallel to the equator, use the north-south axis of the globe as their center. Thus, we have 90 degrees north and 90 degrees south latitude with 0 degrees at the equator. But parallels have nothing to do with time since the earth rotates not north to south, but west to east. The sun appears to rise in the east because the earth is rotating from west to east. Earth takes twenty-four hours to completely turn from one side to the other, making a complete day. This period of rotation, for reasons I don't understand, is divided into twenty-four hours. It could have just as well been divided into one hundred units or five hundred or ten or even thirteen. Since there are 360 degrees in a circle, there are 15 degrees of longitude per hour (360 degrees / 24 hours = 15 degrees of longitude per hour). Thus, every time we move east 15 degrees, we must advance our clocks since we are actually going in the direction of the earth's rotation. If you don't understand this, stop right here and think about it. If, after thinking about it for five minutes, you still don't get it, continue anyway. Chances are you're never going to get it.

Every time we move west 15 degrees, we must set back our clocks since we are moving in the direction opposite to the earth's rotation. So to summarize, for every 15 degrees going west to east you set your clock ahead and lose an hour. For every 15 degrees going from east to the west you set the clock back an hour, thereby gaining an hour. This situation causes us to gain twenty four hours going west and lose twenty four hours going east if we completely circled the globe. To correct for this, we must have an arbitrary date line which compensates for the twenty-four-hour differential, a date line that adds a day when you go from west to east, and subtracts a day when you go from east to west.

Ships that passed *QE2* going the opposite direction from the Eastern Hemisphere to the Western Hemisphere had to repeat January 26, whereas we, who traveled from the Western Hemisphere to the Eastern Hemisphere, skipped January 26 altogether.

Somewhat puzzled, I said to Waldemar, "I still don't get it."

A twinkle appeared in Waldemar's eyes. He shrugged his shoulders. "Neither do I. The thing that bugs me is that the day really did disappear."

Next time I'll ask Waldemar why the same system doesn't apply to astronauts orbiting the earth, whom it appears neither gain or lose time but merely accept the same time of whatever place they set down on.

Waldemar continued his lecture series on Asia, whetting our appetites with tales of Shinto creation myths that trace the Japanese emperors directly back to the sun goddess Amaterasu. After World War II, MacArthur made the emperor renounce his divine origin, but MacArthur let the emperor keep his palace.

The classic novel *The Tale of Genji* by Lady Murasaki tells about the regal Heian splendor of the eleventh to twelfth centuries. The story unrolls like a magnificent Japanese scroll, revealing a myriad of characters and events, a panoply including perfume-smelling contests, servants passing notes to potential lovers, concubines in special palaces and closed gardens, firefly lanterns, days spent admiring chrysanthemums, and entire nights spent looking at the moon. All this resembles cruise life, but is actually about court life in ancient Japan. In the end, the prince dies, the scroll gets rolled up, the grass creeps in, the palaces crumble, and the Heian splendor with all that idle beauty, disappears forever.

Talking about disappearing beauty reminded Waldemar of the Golden Pavilion (*Kinkakuji* in Japanese) in Kyoto. A monk burned down the Golden Pavilion, a wood structure built in a garden over a pond. When asked why he destroyed one of Japan's great national treasures, the monk explained, "Because I couldn't stand seeing all that beauty."

That monk had serious problems with his inner dog. Doesn't he know that art is only pure when you don't interfere with it? Because of violence against art, Dante would place the monk in one of the lowest circles of hell, probably in circle eight, Malabolgia, reserved for those who violently created injustice to others through malice or wrong intention. The injustice obviously is that tourists can't see the original Golden Pavilion because the monk burned it down. The monk deprived us of beauty. However, the carefully reconstructed pavilion stands there for our viewing on the Kyoto tour.

Waldemar closed with a Japanese poem: "I am never to grow old. Alas, the New Year's bell."

Waldemar entertained us, but I liked the next lecture better, Professor George Losey on "The Symbiotic Relationships on the Coral Reefs."

It turns out, corals are violent one-celled animals who have some human characteristics. If two closely related species of coral come together, they will meld together, but; if they are unrelated, they will war. Each coral has special miniature weapons, which have toxins—like poisoned arrows—and whole colonies at war will release their poisoned arrows at once, sending them over to the opposite side to kill the enemy.

Coral reefs have orgies too. Each month, usually on the fifth day after a full moon but sometimes when the tides are relatively still, half of the corals will excrete sperms into the water, and the other half will excrete ova into the water. Professor Losey showed aerial photographs of reefs with miles and miles of post-orgy creamy white fertility stuff floating in the water. Mass mating like this produces results in massive reproduction. The little corals swim around for days or months until they settle down on some rock and grow into a reef.

Next we learn about Professor Losey's own research on cleaner fish, cute little fish that clean bigger fish. Pretty cool! The more I learn the more I realize I don't know much. But all that talk of fish made me hungry so we headed to the Caronia for dinner. Rabbi beat us there. Gently touching his black yarmulke, rimmed with embroidered gold thread and held on his head with two black bobby pins, he said, "Can we have hard-boiled eggs with the salad?" But he said this to Mrs. Rabbi because "I don't see any waiters here." And indeed, no one seems to notice Rabbi. He has become persona non grata.

Claire caught the same disease as Mary.

Finally, after much ado from the Rabbi, Claire appeared from the kitchen. Rabbi hits her hard with his special requests: "Tonight on the gefilte fish we want red horseradish, not white. And bring challah. What are potato skins?"

Claire dutifully explains potato skins and Rabbi tells her, "We'll try them." But lo and behold, in her first act of open defiance, Mrs. Rabbi says, "You can have them. Not for me." Rabbi is dumbfounded.

Tonight Ethel and I celebrated three weeks of togetherness and the fact that we are still talking to each other. I order a Château Latour Premier Cru 1976 for $178, a bargain. Sylvan, the wine steward, goes crazy. He decants the bottle lovingly and continued to expound on the great superiority of the French bordeaux over California wines. I knew he would fuss because, after all, he is French. Sylvan fussed about the wine throughout the meal.

With the wine I ate penne pasta, mulligatawny soup, coffee sorbet, and sirloin steak cooked rare. The creamy strawberry ice cream loaded with strawberries ended the perfect meal as I overheard Rabbi tell Mrs. Rabbi, who was taken aback by all the fuss about our wine, "There are all kinds of wine." Rabbi then ordered applesauce for their off-menu lamb chops.

We returned to cabin 4164 contented and found more gifts—a certificate from Captain John Burton-Hall stating that we crossed the International Date Line and a silver medallion larger than a silver dollar that has "1996 World Cruise Voyage to Distant Empires" embossed on its front and on its back all the ports of call we will make. Reading down the list thrills me with the idea of the new wonders to come.

Comfortable in my warm clear smooth soft bed, gently cradled and rocked by the pitching and rolling of the ship, I think as we approach mysterious Asia of the only Zen statement I know:

MASTER: What about a sleeping cat among the peonies?
STUDENT: I would have nothing to do with it.

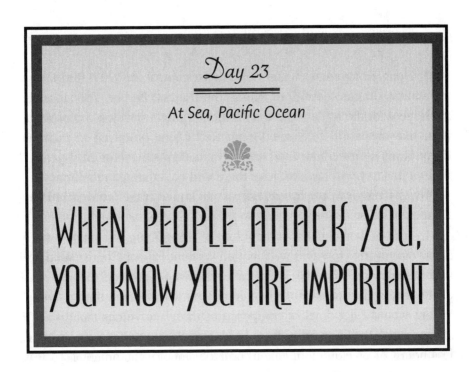

Day 23

At Sea, Pacific Ocean

WHEN PEOPLE ATTACK YOU, YOU KNOW YOU ARE IMPORTANT

*B*y the fourth grade every Japanese school child learns to sing the song about the turtle and the hare. You know the story. The turtle goes slowly and wins the race. Many morals derive from this strange tale, but the one I take is to travel slowly and enjoy the trip. Getting there is half the fun.

I realize what the trouble was with the other cruises that I took including crossing the Atlantic on the SS *America*, SS *United States*, and the *QE2*, and the various trips I took with my family in my youth to Bermuda on the *Queen of Bermuda* or to Nassau: too short. They were too short. They all lasted but a few days. By the time we got settled and started to enjoy the rich benefits of at-sea routine, the cruise ended.

Today's lectures continue to get us ready for Asian ports, with Hansen covering "Hong Kong in Your Future" and Jan Stuart telling us about Chinese gardens.

In 1997, with the expiration of the ninety-nine-year lease signed in

1898, Hong Kong comes under communist control. In 1997, Red China, the restless dragon, gets Hong Kong, the fragrant harbor. This arranged marriage with the bride more than reluctant might develop a plot somewhat like the world of Suzie Wong. Red China promised to maintain Hong Kong's free trade, free speech, and democracy for fifty years. I believe it. They will have to. Else there will be an armed rebellion.

Hong Kong is in our future, but no one knows if the future is in Hong Kong.

Instead of worrying about the future of Hong Kong, Ethel and I worry about our future. How will we function without Eric or Claire? Who will squeeze our fresh orange juice for breakfast or provide the plates of exotic fruits like passion fruit and guavas when we returned home? Where would I get omelets composed of those marvelous small Pacific shrimps with the crisp briny fresh sea taste? Where will we get the skinless breast of chicken with baked tomatoes, one of the breakfasts I love so well. And what about Helen? Who, when we get home, will come and make our beds and clean our rooms every day? Just thinking about the idea that our paradise might end someday brings tears to our eyes. Yes, someday we will have to return home. But how in the world will we get our home to bob up and down and periodically shake to and fro like a children's carousel?

We cheer up. We have over two months more to go. Maybe by that time we'll think of something.

Today I have a dilemma. The Interdenominational Divine Service of Morning Worship, run by Captain John Burton-Hall, conflicts with an interview of Jonathan Wicks, the executive chef, who will discuss "Breakfast, Lunch, and Dinner: The Feeding of the 2,500."

When it comes to religion or food, I always choose food. Besides, Christ fed only six hundred with those multiplying loaves and fishes. Wicks gets out more, and much more varied dishes.

Brian Price introduced the program by saying that the two most important people on board a ship are the doctor and the chef. I don't know about the doctor, because I never think about him unless I'm sick and then he becomes important only temporarily, to fade back to insignificance when I'm well again. So the chef remains my main man, a kind of personal hero since he provides us with so much pleasure. The crowd, more than five hundred strong assembled in the Grand Lounge, agrees. They skipped church, too.

Wicks starts out saying that you are what you eat. That reminds me of Dag in Douglas Coupland's novel *Generation X* who considers himself a lesbian trapped in a man's body and who, believing you are what you eat, liked to gobble down fifty-dollar bills.

Wicks told us that he supervises the preparation of over eight thousand meals daily, using fourteen kitchens and two-hundred-and-thirty cooks and assistants. He can make, and does make, two hundred roast beefs or six hundred ducks at a go (the British for "at the same time"). *QE2* has five head chefs, one for each restaurant: Queens Grill, Princess Grill, Caronia, Mauretania, and the Lido. Wicks plans meals two weeks in advance, has guest chefs come on for special meals, and will try not to repeat a single menu during the whole world cruise. Buying stores occurs in massive amounts. For instance, in Los Angeles they took on 425 tons of produce. When they buy lobsters they buy thirteen hundred at a time! Cooking for the crew presents problems since there are thirty-two nationalities represented onboard. Wicks thinks keeping the crew happy one of his most important missions since an unhappy crew means unhappy passengers. Wicks says that not everyone is happy with the food. Wicks heard about the Rabbi, I know. The reasons for this unhappiness are as legion as the numbers of passengers. Some passengers just have a single bad meal and dislike it because they weren't hungry or perhaps the food was poorly cooked. That problem corrects itself quickly. Some passengers seem perpetually unhappy and Wicks will do his best to set things right, but he knows sometimes there is no pleasing them. They are just difficult people. With these chronically dissatisfied customers the only thing Wicks can do is keep trying. That's what he said. But from a strictly logical point of view, that represents an artificial limitation of possible courses of action.

I scribbled a note to Wicks about an alternative solution: "Just throw the bastards overboard."

Wicks reads the note, nods, smiles, folds the note carefully, and puts it in his left front pocket, close to his heart. Wicks closed by telling us something I have heard from other great chefs: he started by burning down his mother's kitchen. She didn't mind.

Brian then announced a lottery for passengers who want to cook with Wicks tomorrow. At that moment, an unusual stir appeared in the crowd. All hands raised in the air. Some, tightly closed, seemed to disappear suddenly in the midst of the cries—an energetic way, no doubt, of casting a vote. The crowd swayed back, then forward. If they had had banners and flags, they would have wavered, disappeared an instant, then reappeared in tatters like some great army in battle. The undulations of the human surge reached the steps, while all the heads floundered on the surface like a sea agitated by a squall. They all want to cook with Wicks. Me too.

We put our names in the hat. Mine doesn't come out. John Taylor, a middle-aged man who looks and acts like he is a straight woman trapped in a man's body, wins.

John Taylor is lucky. Tomorrow he gets to assist the most important man on board.

Incidentally, gay men and lesbians have no special problems on *QE2*. I saw plenty of them. But don't expect a single gay to come aboard and have a romantic fling. The gays were tightly paired when they arrived and stayed that way throughout the trip.

Before I attacked the outdoor pool on Quarter deck, I checked *Debrett's Peerage and Baronetage* to find out what Captain Burton-Hall's RN and RNR means. RNR doesn't mean Royal Navy Reserve. It means Royal Navy Retired. RN received notice among the awards listed. Although not specifically defined, the book says it is an honor awarded to those honorably retired from the Royal Navy. Perhaps it's the equivalent of the American honorable discharge. Further down the list I spot my own honor: FRSM (Fellow of the Royal Society of Medicine), which actually gives me precedent over a few others, including FWS (Fellow of the Watercolor Society). Americans lack official recognition for any nobility or honorific title, of course, because the Constitution of the United States specifically prohibits such things.

Yoko, my Japanese girl friend, can't swim with me today. She and I met in the hot tub, instead. I know she wants to be my friend because she keeps pointing to me and then to herself, and then crosses her index and third finger and pats the index on the third. Try this and you will see what I mean. After which finger signals she always giggles. One has to be careful about cross-cultural hand signals as they may cause misunderstandings. This one seems quite clear.

Yoko finds the pool too cold, even with her wet suit on, and although she can't tell me that in English, I know that's what she means. I wish I could borrow her black wet suit. I know it would fit me because she and I have the same body build (Japanese women have small tits), but I don't know how to say in Japanese "I need your suit."

So, while I swim in the gelid pool water, Yoko, with a big smile on her face (why is she always so happy?) stood in her black wet suit at the side rail of the outdoor pool and flashed me the thumbs-up sign with every lap I finished. The pool water sloshed back and forth in this rough sea, and up and down more than four feet. Sometimes large amounts of water spill out onto the deck and at no time are there not multiple white caps in the pool itself. The temperature has gone down even further as we continued our approach to the northern climes, and I estimate I'm immersed in 68 degree water. I started to shiver, but no problem. Yoko will be there for me with a towel as I emerge.

A gale-force wind then blew the clock off the One deck wall. The clock hung down on deck with the clock face pointed to the bulkhead, so I can't reckon how long I have to go. (Usually, I swim thirty minutes). Yoko helped me out of the pool. Shivering, I risked electrocution to set the clock face right so that it looked out on deck and not toward the wall. Once again I can read the time from the pool. But the wind blows again and inverts the clock. I can't easily correct the clock's upside-down status so I just leave it that way, dangling at the end of two wires. Since we passed the International Date Line, time has gotten quite jangled.

Then it rained on the few passengers still on deck. They scrambled for shelter. They looked droopy and woebegone like so many moulting chickens. Yoko and I don't mind the rain because we are safely immersed in the hot tub. Yoko gives me the fingers together again and then points to the deck door with her thumb. Then she motions down with her index. Again middle and index come together. Yes, Yoko has something in mind. She is inviting me to see her cabin. Reluctantly, I shake my head no.

Ethel and I went to the four o'clock tea in the Samuel Cunard Lounge with the other Key Club members. I rewarded myself for my polar bear feats by eating a big beautiful raisin-filled scone, which I meticulously fill with clotted cream. Delicious! Lots of British newspapers litter the Key Club lounge.

I picked up the *London Times* and read. Holy Cow! Hillary Clinton's problems with the Whitewater grand jury shrink to insignificance compared to the problems of Fergie, the Duchess of York. A certain Mrs. Mahtani, who became friendly with the Duchess, wants her £100,000 back. To make matters worse, Fergie owes over £3 million in massive personal debts. To get into that much debt you would have to take the *QE2* around the world for a century. How did Fergie do it? Another article was about me: It's attacking me and my research. It says that the president of the American Society of Plastic Surgery says that I am a junk scientist. That's bad news, of course. I always wanted to be a real scientist, not a junk scientist. But in a way it's true. I am a junk scientist because I have been studying a piece of junk—that's what the breast implant was and is.

When Ethel and I returned to the cabin, we found more bad news. Our laundry bill for the week is $82. Shirts are $2.20 each, formal shirts $4.50 each. Underwear gets cleaned for $1.30. No wonder the Chus are rich.

"Why don't you go into the laundry business?" Ethel asked.

"Despite the money involved, I would rather be a waiter. Their white uniforms with gold trim look real spiffy."

Day 24

At Sea, Pacific Ocean

A GREAT BIG, LONG PICNIC

*L*ike the second Mrs. de Winter in Daphne Du Maurier's classic novel *Rebecca*, last night I dreamt I went to the Grand Lounge again. The Grand Lounge resembled Manderlay. It seemed to me I stood by an iron gate leading to the entrance, and for a while I could not enter, for the way was barred to me. There was a padlock and a chain upon the gate as in the novel. I called in my dream to the cruise director, heard no answer, and peering closer through the rusted spokes of the gate I saw that the place was uninhabited. Then, like all dreamers, I was possessed of a sudden with supernatural powers and passed like a spirit through the barrier before me. I found myself with Brian Price, the cruise director. Brian had a brown paper bag and said he had to draw out my name, otherwise I could not continue the cruise. Unlike the lottery to cook with Chef Wicks, I won. Ethel and I may cruise.

And so Ethel and I received permission from my unconscious mind to continue our reckless pursuit of pleasure on *QE2*.

Captain John Burton-Hall turned us north, the wrong direction. The captain kept cruising west as long as possible so we could enjoy southern seas. But we must make that right turn to get to Japan. Captain John Burton-Hall explained the situation and apologized for what was about to happen with the weather. My admiration for him increased log numbers. This man completely commanded a large community afloat, but he admitted that he could not command the weather.

As predicted, the seascape deteriorated by the hour, taking on a dull, dark, and dreary color as the skies lowered and the temperature dropped. Rain continued. Out on deck, the droplets in my face stung like ice. I checked the hot tub. It too was cold and, woe is me, the pool is so cold it's unswimmmable. Woe befalls us all, often for no apparent reason especially when you set your course north in a winter month.

One woman looking like the famous Iron Lady herself, Margaret Thatcher, upset with the inclement weather, asked the captain if he should ask the coast guard for assistance. "Madam," he replied. "If they could get this far out to sea, the Coast Guard would be asking for assistance from us."

Me too, I don't like what's happening. I want better weather. God! I am getting fussy! *QE2* does do that to you. It makes you intolerant of inconveniences. Perhaps that's the trouble with the Rabbi: too much cruise experience.

At lunch Rabbi seemed more intolerant than usual.

"Let me ask you a question," Rabbi said to Claire. But then he changed his mind. "No, get Peter. This is an important problem for him to handle."

Peter arrived with the usual pained and solicitous look on his face.

Ethel and I are all ears, wondering what absurd request is coming. We are not disappointed.

"Is it possible to get plain spaghetti on this ship?" asked the Rabbi.

Even Mrs. Rabbi knows this is crazy and she tells him so: "Dear, we had spaghetti two nights ago."

Rabbi shakes his head slowly, acknowledging with a kind of kiss pout that, indeed, he now recalls they did order and get off-menu spaghetti. "This time I want it with ketchup," Rabbi assures Peter. "See if you can get us some."

Peter says that he will have to discuss this special request with the chef, and that he may have to order it for tonight since it is probably too late to prepare it for lunch. Peter assured the Rabbi that if, in the future, he could let them know ahead of time of their special needs, the staff would do its best to comply.

After Peter departed, Rabbi tells Mrs. Rabbi, "You win some and you lose some."

Claire deposits the usual bagel on Rabbi's table. Rabbi frowned and said, "What happened? Yesterday, you gave me a whole bagel!"

"I'll get you another half," said Claire.

"Never mind. I'm not hungry."

Peter returned faster than expected. He has a spring in his step and is standing up straight, so I know he has secured the much-needed emergency spaghetti.

"I have good news for you," Peter said with a grin. "We can get plain spaghetti today for lunch. And ketchup, too."

Rabbi replied in that low-pitched whiny voice we loved to hate, "I don't know if we can eat it."

Undaunted, Peter makes a short bow. "I ordered small portions. It's coming up."

Of course, most of the spaghetti remained on their plates, uneaten. For that alone, Rabbi deserves a hellish punishment. His multifarious sins include wasting material resources in addition to his usual passive-aggressive behavior and covert hostility. But more important, we now saw the fraud of his pretending he wanted spaghetti to eat when he just wanted spaghetti to bug Peter and the staff. Fraud puts Rabbi in the lowest of the lower circles of hell, just above the traitors.

Overheard on deck between two women who had just attended the Steiner Spa people's lecture on weight reduction without pills: "Would you like to take a pill to make you thin?"

The other woman crossed her eyes and shook her head, "No, to get thin, I would rather take a piece of cake."

Today's lectures interested me, including Jan Stuart's discussion of traditional Chinese ancestral portraiture. She told us how to tell the real from the fake and how to approximate the dates of creation by the degree of shadowing and perspective (western influences) present in the pictures. Most of the pictures consisted of severe-looking matriarchs seated on authoritative, high-backed chairs, receiving cups of tea from obeisant youthful servants, sort of like high tea in the Queen's Lounge on *QE2*.

Professor Losey tells us about what it's like to be a fish. He started off his lecture with a Freudian slip, saying "When my fish were growing up, they used to ask me what I did for a living."

Losey told us amazing things about fish. Fish see in the ultraviolet, for instance, and have all sorts of weird ways of traveling. Some go in schools like Japanese school children and get nervous when separated from the group, even for a few seconds. Others are loners. Except on the rare occasion that when they mate, they spent their lives alone, that is single without a mate. Some fish disguise themselves as rocks and others as seaweed. Still others have lights on the sides of their bodies, which they can dim or brighten and also they control the shade of blue.

The sex life of fishes remains more complicated than that of humans. Fish have no sex chromosomes. Their sex and their gender is controlled by environmental and, believe it or not, social factors.

Losey proves his point showing an orange fish with big eyes sitting in a patch of sea anemones. That female has a harem of males (how come there is no word in English for a group of male sexual servants?). When the female gets weak, the top male fish changes into a female and takes over, pushing the female, his former mate, out of the patch.

And yes, there is another kind of fish with the whole situation reversed. The male has a harem of females and when the male gets weak the chief female turns into a male and pushes the female, his(her) former mate out of the patch.

Losey also shows some slides displaying behavior that could be interpreted as lesbian behavior: a female pretends she is a male and goes through all the motions of spawning, but of course has no sperm so can't fertilize anything. Another slide seems to show a gang bang, where a bunch of males gather around an unprotected and unescorted female, and spawn with her. And yes, fish have orgies just like the corals. Surgeon-fish, for instance, have an orgy off the coast of Egypt twenty minutes after sundown, an orgy every day.

An orgy every day?

In some ways, fish life seems better than ours. In other ways it seems not as good. On considering the matter carefully, I decided it's better to be a human than a fish, because, as a human, you get to travel on the *QE2* alive. Fish that travel on the *QE2* are for the most part, dead.

Dinner tonight makes up for the gloomy weather. I started with a crab-filled giant spring roll that fills my plate. It's just perfect, crunchy and filled with tender crabs and seasoned with ginger and soy and fragrant spices and herbs that I can't name. Following this masterpiece comes the best chicken cacciatore I have ever experienced. Yes, *experienced*, that's the right word for this dish that constitutes a multisensory experience of taste, color, texture, and smell. My admiration knows no limits and I wish I could eat eight of these. Dessert, a banana gâteau, has three strong notes as it enters the mouth: a strong banana flavor and aroma, followed by rich luscious whipped cream, followed by a finish of strong clear rich chocolate flavor and smell.

Champagne was in order and lots of toasts and jokes, all accomplished, I am happy to report, without loss of life.

Ethel and I feel like we are on one great big, long picnic. We feel that way, because we are.

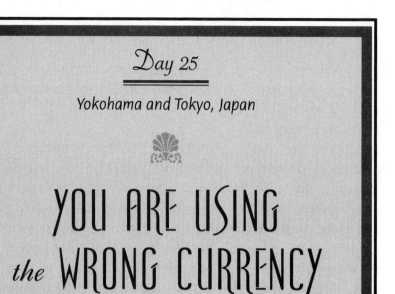

Day 25

Yokohama and Tokyo, Japan

YOU ARE USING
the WRONG CURRENCY

I slept well, but Ethel didn't. She woke when *QE2* slowed to take on the harbor pilot, and she woke again when *QE2* stopped moving and docked.

When the elevated train on the East Side of New York City was torn down, police got calls for weeks from people who woke up at all times of the night. They claimed *something* was wrong. It turned out that the moments of their mysterious discomfort corresponded to the times when the trains would have passed by their apartments. When we left the sea and pulled into port, some people had the missing elevated train syndrome and some didn't. Ethel had it. I didn't. But nothing is all bad. Ethel's disease gave her the advantage after all: she saw the sun rise in the Land of the Rising Sun.

Yokohama, Japan, looked like any other industrial port of the world, reflecting the homogenization of cultures that occurred and will continue to occur. Unlike in Hawaii, the tour bus filled up way before the scheduled departure time. We took off early, bound for Tokyo.

Japan is another country. They do things differently here. And the difference is not just superficial like the tatami mats on the floors, the small claustrophobic rooms, the incredibly high prices, the special floral arrangements that you see in the alcove on the left as you enter a private home. The Japanese call the shrine the *tokono ma*. All tokono ma more or less exhibit the same things—chrysanthemums, a scroll, and a gold fan.

Tatami mats and tokono ma shrines number among the superficial differences. The deep difference involves *yamato damashii,* the "Yamato Japanese spirit." Yamato refers to ancient Japanese culture, before there was contact with China. Hence, it is the old name for Japan.

Those of you who studied history or who lived through World War II may hear an ominous echo in this expression, for it came to take on a dangerous overtone in the earlier half of this century as the battle cry of Japanese soldiers pressing forward in their march of aggression into China.

After the Meiji Restoration in 1868, the Yamato spirit came into play as Meiji politicians used it to unify the people's consciousness in the interests of creating a modern state. In large part, this was done by stressing the absolute nature of the now restored Emperor Meiji as the central figure since he had wrested power from the shogun. From there, it was only a short step for yamato spirit to assume its role as a slogan for imperialist Japan. This sort of absolutism, like any sort of absolutism, showed none of the tolerance and sensitivity that characterizes true humanism, nor an ability to realistically appraise situations. Instead, it led to the fantastic belief that Japan could win a war, World War II specifically, despite trailing far behind in modern weapons and significant items like oil and other natural resources.

And so the Japanese embarked on a war that resulted in disaster for themselves and their Asian neighbors. Consequently, Japan became the only country in the world, so far, to endure atomic attacks.

With the recent drop in real wages in Japan and the collapse of real estate prices, and the failure of so many Japanese banks, the yamato spirit rose again. Japan's peaceful nature, I believe, is as thin as some of those white translucent side-sliding walls on the teahouses. The Japanese Self-Defense Force represents the new Japanese imperialist army, in violation of treaties with the United States and in violation of Japan's own constitution that forbids force as an instrument of national policy and establishes everlasting peace. Allowing Japan to rearm makes as serious an error as reunifying Germany. "Those who don't know history are doomed to repeat it," wrote George Santayana. I won't be around when things go wrong. The politicians who have made these basic errors won't be around, either.

Ueno (pronounced *whe-no*) guides us through Tokyo, the world's largest city, with a population of over eight million. Yokohama, right next to Tokyo, stands second in population. The area we drive through looks pretty dense with people all right.

Ueno briefed us on the economics of living here. The average worker makes about ¥40 million yearly, and after taxes might have ¥20 million left to live on. That translates to about $20,000. It takes ¥50 million to get a two-bedroom apartment and the average home costs about eight years' worth of wages. Salaries have been headed down for three years and prices went up, so most people feel the squeeze. Since the depression started about five years ago, large and small borrowers have defaulted on loans, so the banks are bankrupt. Yesterday the Diet passed a bill that would bail out the banks, just as the United States government bailed out the Savings and Loan Associations. Public money will pay, again, for private greed. It makes no sense, of course, unless you understand who really runs a country.

Ueno further explained the upcoming crisis in social services. The birth rate is only 1.5 children per couple, so the general age of the population has risen dramatically. With less kids entering the workforce, there are fewer people who make tax payments to support the elderly, who now number 25 percent of Japan's population. Who will pay for what? That remains the $64,000 question, only in Japan's case it is the ¥64 trillion question.

We stopped at the Meiji Jingu Gardens and went to the Shinto shrine there. Ueno says no one knows what Shintoism is. Shinto has no great book, no set of dogmas, no organized priesthood. But Shinto does have gods and goddesses—eight million of them, a number less than the 127 million population of Japan, but enough to go around. The main point seems to be to worship the unseen spirits of the emperor, and the mountains, woods, streams, flowers, and all things. I find this convincing and wonder if we could work in my religious leanings toward electronic games and cruising.

Ueno teaches the group how to approach the main altar by bowing twice then clapping hands twice. I do it and feel good, so I decided to buy some Shinto charms. I spent ¥5,600 on assorted objects, including five designed to ward off traffic accidents (there were three deaths in Tokyo yesterday and over ten thousand last year in Japan), small paired white and orange purses to keep a love relation going (of these I buy two, one for Ethel and one for myself), and two charms for a scholarship. One of the scholarship charms costing $8 looks like a miniature Shinto shrine. The counter girl assured me it works and added that I can display the charm on my desk. Naturally, I objected to the orientation. I prefer a charm for scholarship, not one to get a scholarship. There is a world of difference. But the girl at the counter thought my orientation was off. "No one wants scholarship. You want *a* scholarship," she assured me. "In your case, you want two."

"What will I do with my two scholarships when they come in?" I asked.

"Use them both," came her reply.

"What charm sells the most—the scholarship, the safety from traffic accidents, or the love charm?"

"Traffic accidents. Japanese fear those more than they desire love or scholarship."

As I pass out of the gardens under the Ginkgo trees, living fossils left over from the last ice age, I think of the fifteen generations of shoguns that ruled these islands from 1600 to 1868 and isolated Japan from the rest of the world. Those shoguns were pretty effective since the Japanese still remain isolated, socially and mentally. Japan was isolated not only from the West but also from her Asian neighbors. More important, she was isolated from her own true nature.

Ueno points out the closed down geisha houses. Their business is down, he said, because Sony is not as generous as it used to be. Consequently, expense accounts, the main support of the geisha houses, dried up. Also, the subways used to be safe and clean, but then some cult put poison gas in them and killed people. *O tempora! O mores!*

Ueno points forlornly to a government building in back of the Diet (Japanese parliament) and says, "Last year they cleaned the outside of the buildings here. This year they should clean the inside."

While we were stopped in traffic, I saw schoolgirls all dressed in the same blue uniforms marching close together. When one slips slightly out of step or separates a few feet from the mass, they quickly correct. Fish that move in schools: that's Japanese style.

To pass the time until the traffic clears, Ueno tells some sad stories, including the famous one about the wife who gave her husband a kimono every day. He sold these and got drinking money. Despite strict instructions not to look in the wife's room, the husband nevertheless looked in and saw a stork weaving the kimonos. The next day the wife gave him his last kimono, turned into a stork, and flew away.

"Stop it!" one woman yelled from the back of the bus. "We don't want to hear any more sad stories."

Ueno grinned defensively and said, "We live in not-so-happy world. Japan is sad country."

"It is not!" the woman yelled back. "I know. I've been here before."

That woman was one of the old travelers, delightful parrots who have been here before and have done that. They know more about the country than the guides. Ethel and I love to hear them prate and drivel and lie. First, they put out the feelers to see if someone else among the group has also visited and, if not, they brag, sneer, and swell, and soar, and blaspheme the sacred name of truth. The central aim is to put you in your place, a place lower than theirs, make you feel insignificant and humble. I love them for their witless platitudes, for their supernatural ability to bore, for their delightful asinine vanity, for their luxuriant fertility of imagination, for their startlingly brilliant, overwhelming mendacity. As if trained by some TV show, perhaps *Frontline*, they never mind the particulars, go on with the legend, and the good honest lies.

At the Imperial Hotel we got sticker shock. A glass of champagne cost $15 and a bottle of cheap French wine that I could buy at home for $5 cost $38. We drank $6 cups of coffee and inquired at the desk how much a room for two cost for the night—$400. Americans get hit hard here, but it's just as expensive for the Japanese. I can't help thinking that something is wrong. A melon shouldn't cost $45 when you can get the same kind of melon in Thailand, which is only an hour away by plane, for two bucks.

On the way back to the ship we pass through the famous Ginza district. *Ginza* means silver, and at one time silversmith shops were located here. Ginza reminded me of the night I spent in one of those nightclubs. I strictly avoided ordering any wine or drinks because I knew they were expensive. Order a bottle of wine in the Ginza and you might spend the rest of your life paying off your wine debt. My bill for one orange juice came to $40. Nevertheless, I had some fun that night with American sailors who were hanging out in the same place. That year I was on sabbatical in France so just to have some fun I spoke my English with a heavy French accent.

"How do eye zound? Can you un-dee-stand my anglish berry vell?"

"Oh yes," the sailors would say politely. "But, you have a slight French accent."

Then, toward the end of the evening I started speaking in my normal voice and diction. A startled sailor shook himself and exclaimed, "Jesus, just then you sounded like a real American."

Talking about money and sailors in a Tokyo bar reminds me of the story Waldemar Hansen told. An American sailor bellied up to the bar and sat next to the scantily attired Japanese B-girl sitting on the next stool. The sailor took out a hundred-dollar bill and lit a cigar with it. The girl stared at the sailor and then got up to leave. But before she departed she turned and said, "If you are trying to impress me, you are using the wrong currency."

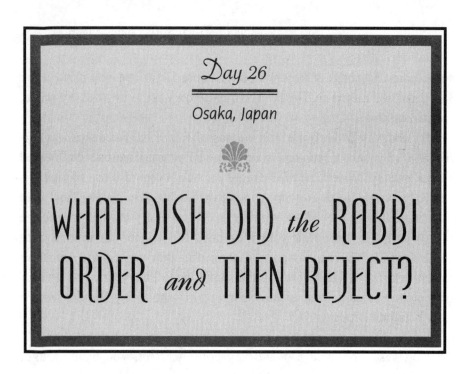

Day 26

Osaka, Japan

WHAT DISH DID *the* RABBI ORDER *and* THEN REJECT?

*O*saka, the main distribution port for Japan, looms in the foreground outside our port window. Looking out, Ethel spies a large, white Japanese ship racing the *QE2*. We know that ship is Japanese because it has a large rising sun painted on it, starting just above the water level and rising six decks. The Japanese ship clips along, gains on us, and wins the race.

Something in me still doesn't feel right about Japan. Sensitive to atmosphere, I detected in Ueno, in the young man and woman who helped Ueno yesterday, and in the bus driver himself, a kind of sullen discontent, an ennui—boredom with life and boredom with their no-account jobs. Theirs is an existentialist depression, occasioned by their loss of meaning in their lives. They feel too much oppressed, too much overworked, have too little hope for advancement, and too little self-esteem.

Why?

These people constitute the generation X of Japan. The generation which by an accident of history will not enjoy a higher standard of living than their parents. All this I detect seething under the surface, for in Japan there is a difference in how the people *are* and how they *wish to appear*. Saving face counts much more with them than with us. Thus this third-world country with $40 melons ultimately needs to face reality.

My advice: In the trade wars, make no concessions whatsoever to Japan. The sooner they confront reality the less traumatic their adjustment will be for them and for us. Don't believe me? Read *Japan, The Ambitious, and Myself* by Kenzaburo Oe who won the 1994 Nobel Prize in Literature.

Significantly, the Japanese greeters showed up late for the welcoming ceremony in the Grand Lounge. Brian Price apologized to the passengers assembled there. Brian knows on *QE2* no one likes to wait for anything. Eventually, a young man who speaks no English welcomes us to Osaka. The staff translator went to work, but the speech sounded better in Japanese. In English it's lifeless, pedestrian, dull, and insipid.

Then kimono-clad little Japanese women, who I thought not especially pretty, took little steps with little feet and gave little bouquets of little white flowers to the captain, the staff captain, the chief engineer, the hotel manager, and the cruise director.

With the welcoming formalities out of the way, we descended the gangway to hit the city of Osaka. In passing, I noticed that in Yokohama they repainted *QE2*'s blue bottom. The ship's hull looks real blue and real good.

Our guide today is Tom, who lives in Kyoto. Tom, middle-aged and balding, has the conspicuous habit of covering his mouth with his hand when he talks, but he is more cheerful than Ueno and more informative. The group likes him all the more because he tells no sad stories, except he did mention that last year he felt a slight tremor when the earthquake hit Kobe, the same earthquake that killed over five thousand people and left over one hundred thousand homeless. Tom speaks enthusiastically about sake, the rice wine they make in Kobe. Tom says, "Sake best medicine."

The Japanese, in one way, resemble Americans because, most of the time, they talk about money. Again we get the economic figures but with a slightly different slant. Tom says the Japanese are not workaholics. They just need to work long and hard to keep up. They would rather rest and have fun, just like the rest of us. Tom, however, does admit that making money is the major goal here in Osaka. In fact, instead of saying hello or good morning, people here greet each other with "Are you making money?"

"They yearn for yen," Tom said, but most of the *QE2*ers don't get the joke.

Tom asked if there were any questions.

Along the aisle and two seats up from us, an old man with his gray hair cut in a close-cropped crew asked, "Where can I buy some beer?"

Tom explained beer was available from the ubiquitous vending machines we see on the streets. And from the looks of it, anything else is available too from those machines, including knives, nail clippers, combs, shoehorns, condoms, and of course cigarettes. The cigarettes differ from the popular brands in the United States. Here they favor Lark, a big brand, and Mild Seven next. Brands Peace and Cabin follow. I am having trouble visualizing some actor or actress on Japanese TV looking sincerely into the camera and recommending that you smoke Cabins. Oh well, we smoke Camels. So what's the difference?

Only people age twenty (not twenty-one) and older can legally smoke and drink here, but the vending machines make it easy for underaged kids to get whatever they need whenever they need it.

Old Mr. Crew Cut then repeated, as if he hadn't asked it before, the exact same question, "Where can I buy beer?"

The few of us on the bus who are still awake realize something is wrong. But with true oriental patience Tom explained again, but, before Tom finished, Mr. Crew Cut started talking to himself and continued talking to himself, mumbling sometimes in Italian, sometimes in English, sometimes in some other language, probably Portuguese.

Ethel and I both know this guy is actively hallucinating, talking to an invisible traveling companion. He is psychotic. We wondered how he got on board, and how he got on the tour.

"There's a difference between the psychotics in the state hospitals and the psychotics on the *QE2*," I told Ethel. "The latter have money."

Our first stop, the Shitennoji Temple, said to be the oldest Buddhist temple in Japan. Founded in 593 BCE, the temple had its ups and downs over and over again, but like the phoenix, rose again from its own ashes. I patted my head with the sacred smoke for good luck as crazy Mr. Crew

Cut continues to mutter in what now sounds like Mandarin. The other passengers clear a wide area for him just in case he goes postal.

Ethel spotted homeless people on the temple grounds. Tom assured us that they are in fact homeless. I asked Tom about all the people I saw wearing white cotton hospital masks over their mouths. Tom explained they have a common cold and don't wish to spread it to others. Not a bad idea.

On the way to Osaka Castle, Tom gives us information about the school system. Despite the complicated Japanese language system with forty-eight phonemic letters (the *kana*) and with thousands of idiographic characters of Chinese origin (the *kanji*), most people in Japan can read and write. Everyone goes to school for free until the ninth grade, then almost 95 percent go on to high school, but only 35 percent proceed beyond that. The examinations they face are very difficult and hence the pressure to achieve.

Tom gives himself away when he explains the parental anxiety to get children more and more educated. "It's not to have better, more intellectually aware people. It's to get a job."

The orientation's off. They want a scholarship, but they don't want scholarship. A scholarship is nice, but scholarship is better because the progress of the world depends on scholarship and not on a scholarship.

A loudspeaker from the street sounds off in Japanese. Tom's face wrinkles, clearly expressing disapproval. He points out the window to several white vans headed slowly in the opposite direction. Loud political-sounding noises issue from the vans. It's all Japanese. We don't understand.

Tom explained, "Right-wingers."

When they heard "right-wingers," some QE2ers in the back of the bus start to applaud, but Tom held his hands out, palms flat and facing them, signaling them to stop.

"They want the emperor back," he says disapprovingly. "The (Tom meant they) wish we could stop them, but we can't stop them because of free speech." For the first time I see Tom speaking without covering his mouth.

The Osaka Castle represents a gigantic monument to the stupidity of the right-wingers and the militarism they represent. It's filled with paintings of battle scenes where one shogun and his many followers tried to hack apart another shogun and his many followers. Japan's history so closely resembled that of war-torn, blood-soaked Europe that I realized in a flash that the Western military tradition was not started by Homer with his book on the Trojan War, nor was it perpetuated by Virgil in the *Aeneid,* which you recall begins *"Arma virumque cano . . ."* (Of arms and the heroes I sing . . .). Nope, poetry didn't start militarism, it just reflected something dark within the human spirit that goes in for such things and goes far, far back to the primitive origin of our species.

A letter in the museum case on the fourth floor catches my eye. Signed by Shume-no-kami, it's a receipt and acknowledgment for 3,369 noses of enemy soldiers that had been hacked off and sent to the commander to prove military valor. Ugh! And double ugh when we find out most of the fighting involved feudal competitions for the right to wear one of two military crests on their clothes, the Paulownia crest or the Chrysanthemum crest. Was it worth it? Was it worth it to fight so much for so little? History teaches some pretty grim lessons.

At dinner we find the Japanese have not only invaded but also occupy more than half the seats of the Caronia Restaurant. I like the idea of a filled restaurant. It means the pleasure dome we know as the *QE2* is likely to continue. For weeks the crew prepared for this day by taking Japanese lessons.

Because the Japanese like to travel in groups, line up in groups, and eat in groups, each table of eight has a group leader who translates the menus, already written in Japanese, into understanding, for some of the Japanese, especially the women, don't know what Western food is all about. Eric said the Japanese sail with us until Hong Kong.

"With them, Captain John Burton-Hall has his hands full because the Japanese feel their tickets entitle them to be photographed with the *QE2's* master throughout the day and night, to have constant access to his services as a signer of autographs, to shake his hand whenever they cornered him in public rooms, companionways, or even in the ship's lifts (British for elevators). At this moment Captain John Burton-Hall is probably praying for relief," said Eric, who himself looked like he was working harder than usual and also praying for relief.

I hoped the captain's prayers would be answered, just as our prayers about Ravel's *Boléro,* which has been playing morning, noon, and night in Caronia, appear to have been answered. The piped *Boléro* music is off. A group of minstrels who wandered from table to table playing mainly Italian songs, replacing Ravel. But the minstrels avoided our subdivision. Have they heard about Rabbi?

Talking about Rabbi reminds me. Just after I took my seat, something curious struck me. Rabbi has taken his plate, and placed it on the edge of his table, and called Claire over.

Rabbi said, "I tried my best. You tried your best. But we can't eat this. I don't know what it is. I haven't eaten this before. I can't start now." Mrs. Rabbi hands in her plate, also uneaten, but she, unlike Rabbi, offers no explanation.

I couldn't see what the plate entrée was that they turned back because Ethel was kicking me under the table.

Rabbi felt guilty. I could tell by the way he kept calling Claire over and reexplaining why he sent the dish back. "The food must be OK, Claire, it's just that we came to the table and found we were not hungry. It's a funny thing, but that's what happened."

Rabbi then ordered two ice creams for dessert, one strawberry and one chocolate, and by eating both invalidated his entire argument. Any conclusion based on a false premise does not follow. If he were not hungry, then why did he eat the ice cream?

After Ethel's kick, my attention focused away from the Rabbi and onto my own meal, which is delicious as usual, especially the remarkable entrée called salmon koulibiac (Russian fish pie), which came in a puff pastry made from foie gras and looks and tastes tasted like beef Wellington, only instead of beef at the center they have placed salmon. This masterpiece melts in my mouth, and I regret eating it so fast. The delicate yellow sauce lingered in my mouth as I decided, after Rabbi left, to ask Claire a crucial question.

"Claire, what dish did the Rabbi order and then reject?"

"The salmon, sir, the same like you had!"

I slammed my fist into the open palm of my left hand with a smack, "Goddamn."

Eric turned around and said the same thing, only with a French accent so it sounded more like "good doom."

Day 27

At Sea

WATER, WATER EVERYWHERE and ALL the BOARDS DID SHRINK/ WATER, WATER EVERYWHERE and NOT a DROP to DRINK

*A*t sea again and it feels fine. The sea proves a sanctuary for medi-tation. It puts me in a poetic mood. The Ancient Mariner could have experienced the same peace had he not shot the albatross and had he known about reverse osmosis and evaporation chambers. Using such devices, *QE2* makes, from seawater, over a thousand tons of fresh water per day. That water is used for drinking and bathing. The water in the toilet, which for some reason the crew calls "the personal waste disposal facility" comes directly from the sea and will change drastically when we get into certain ports, especially Bombay.

Ethel reminded me that our stay in C4, the lowest Caronia class, draws to a close. I should talk about the Caronia Restaurant and do my review. To be objective and to avoid preselection bias I'll review dinner on Saturday night, two days hence. It wouldn't be fair to eat a meal I like and to review that.

Breakfasts in Caronia deserve a mention because I consider it a key meal. Today, for instance, I drank fresh-squeezed orange juice and ate a plateful of exotic fruits including passion fruits, pineapples, watermelon slices, blueberries, strawberries, mandarin orange slices, and kiwis. After that came a skinned breast of chicken with baked tomato, followed by coffee. The raisin Danish pastry melted in my mouth and probably is the freshest Danish I will ever eat, since they start baking at 4 AM. The Danish could not have been older than four hours. Delicious!

Ethel and I realized the linear development of our trip, with our gradual promotion to higher and still higher levels of pleasure, won't last. Someday we must return, after going full circle, to our point of departure. We must loop around back to where we started. In fact, if all goes well, we will return to the same dock at Fort Lauderdale.

But will we be the same travelers who left? This line of thinking focused my attention on some lines from T. S. Eliot's poem "Little Gidding," from his *Four Quartets*, displayed on the wall of the Chart Room bar. He wrote that when our ceaseless exploring ceased, we would be back where we started, and would "know the place for the first time."

Talking about poetry reminds me of Dante. I got through canto XXXII and realized every journey has a spiritual, poetic, intellectual, and a physical component. The pilgrim, the alter ego of the poet, made progress in all fields. His spiritual development showed in his greater understanding of divine will and intellect; his poetical development showed in his better control of metaphor, imagery, and action; and his intellectual development showed his anticipation of what his guide, Virgil, would say and do. The physical progression of the journey displaced Dante and Virgil into Cocytus, the icy mass in the lowest circle where the worst sinners received their just punishments. Rabbi might have belonged there, especially in circle one of Cocytus, called Caine, where Dante placed those who did violence against kindred. Then again, Rabbi might not belong there. In fact, I'm beginning to look at Rabbi from the point of view of a humanist poet. Isn't Rabbi a sad character? Aren't his self-imposed restrictions limiting his fun and pleasure? Isn't that punishment enough? Isn't his life a kind of hell on earth, a hell that he makes for himself every day? Isn't that Dante's real message that sinners make their own hell and their own punishments?

Waldemar Hansen tried to help me make more progress by rising from his flu bed, where he spent the last two days, to give the lecture on Taiwan. Because he is too weak to stand, he gave the lecture sitting down.

Waldemar went over the history of the emigration of over one million Chinese nationalists to the island, also known as *Ilha Formosa*, (Portuguese for the beautiful island), a history I recall talking about in the fifth grade. I will get to see and feel the history I reported on back then, but only knew in the abstract. Taiwan (Mandarin for terraced land) has come a long way since 1951 and now stands as one of the top ten economies in the world. Taiwan's development not only continued but also accelerated when, in 1965, the United States switched its status from aid to trade.

This morning, as we exit the Caronia Restaurant and pass through the portside casino, Ethel and I noticed lots of Japanese playing the slots. I consider gambling (the ship calls it "gaming") this early equivalent to drinking before noon. Nothing is wrong with it, really, if that's what you need. But, why do the Japanese need it? Why do they like losing their money? I think I know. Gambling gives them a chance at establishing a meaning in life, a chance against the essentially indeterminacy that afflicts them, the indeterminacy of life.

Just for kicks, I decided to attend the self-improvement lecture given by Dr. Lillian Glass. As I entered the theatre someone handed me a brochure with the doctor's qualifications. Dr. Glass boasted of having coached Dustin Hoffman, for his movie *Tootsie,* on how to speak and act like a woman. Do I need that? Ethel wouldn't go for it. Furthermore, the brochure lists other clients like Sean Connery, Billy Crystal, and Melanie Griffith, but doesn't tell what they were taught. Sean and Billy talk like men, as far as I know, and Melanie doesn't need training to talk like a woman. Also, I see through the analogy and recognize the logical defect. In fact, it haunts me.

Premise—What's good for Hollywood stars is good for you.
Refutation—I am not a Hollywood star. Therefore, this doesn't apply to
me.

I stayed in the theatre anyway. About fifty other passengers stayed too. Dr. Glass started her presentation by asking questions.

"How many here like the sound of their own voice?"

My hand shot up, but it is the only hand raised. This is amazing! The others don't like the sound of their voice!

Dr. Glass smiled. "Only one of you likes his own voice!" She has done this before. This and the audience gave her the response she expected.

"How many here feel socially at ease at the captain's parties?"

Once again I raised my hand, but no one else did. Dr. Glass surveyed the group and concluded, "All but one feel ill at ease at the captain's parties."

Holy Cow! Is this a group of neurotics or what?

Doctor Dr. Glass continued, "How many think they are a good person?"

All hands but mine went up!

I know I am not a good person, but that doesn't mean I don't like myself. In fact, I can't think of anyone else I would rather be, even though I can see that I am distinctly out of sync with these other passengers.

Dr. Glass then told us, "It's all about winning friends and influencing people." I have heard that somewhere before. Then Dr. Glass proceeded to tell us how to stand, talk, greet people, shake hands, and do all those things I thought everyone knew how to do.

To demonstrate my interpersonal skills, I stood up, made eye contact, smiled, and apologized to the doctor that I must leave to attend Mandarin class, which starts at 3 PM. I liked the way my voice sounded, and when I said this, I liked the open way my arms moved while I asked to be excused. Eye contact, smile, open body posture—that's the ticket.

Mandarin, you don't speak it. You sing it. There exist four tones that the speaker applies to a rather limited vocabulary of monosyllabic words. And that's OK. Having suffered through the complexities of high school and college Latin, with the ablative absolute and the active periphrastic conjugation, I can handle four tones. Besides, that isn't as bad as Cantonese, where there are eight (some say nine) tones.

Mandarin turned me on. I liked the way the Chinese outlook on life reflects itself in the language. For instance, the Chinese character for "house" is a roof sheltering a pig. But the character for "home" seems to be a roof sheltering a woman who has a broom in her hand. The character for discord is a roof with two women under it. No question about it, I have a talent for Mandarin, and in the hour I master (more or less) two pages of common expressions including "how are you?" (pronounced *ni-hau-ma?*) and "good night" (pronounced *wan-an*), which actually means "night peace." When I say this with the proper tone, it sounds so strange and unusual—more than foreign, really otherworldly.

In the sauna I met a different Hoffman—Leonard Hoffman, a typical Brit, who hales from London. This is his second world cruise. He has been aboard eight weeks. He, started on *QE2*'s Caribbean cruise and then sailed back to Southampton to start his world cruise. He's been aboard long enough to drink his way through his $1,750 credit. His per person credit is more than ours (Ethel and I got $1,000 each) because Leonard travels alone. Well, Leonard is not alone, not really alone. No one is alone on *QE2*. Passengers are sociable, through they are not garrulous. Leonard has me and the rest of the passengers with him. He just doesn't have a companion to share his room so he has to pay a singles supplement, and, because of that, he gets a little higher proportional credit. He did the same thing last year. Leonard has already checked the prices for next year and reports that they are 25 percent higher. Part of that increase is because next year tips are included. "But you know how that works," Leonard says. "You have to tip anyway."

Leonard travels in Princess Grill (P1 class). He doesn't like Queen's Grill, even though the food is the same, because the atmosphere is "pretentious." When I ask him why he took the cruise, since he took it last year, Leonard replied, in that crisp British accent we learned to respect so much, "To get away from the *bloody* winter."

I reminded Leonard that one could get away by airplane and even go around the world that way. Leonard smiled and said, "I tried that and spent most of my time in *bloody* airports. On *QE2,* one relaxes in the spa while the countries come to you."

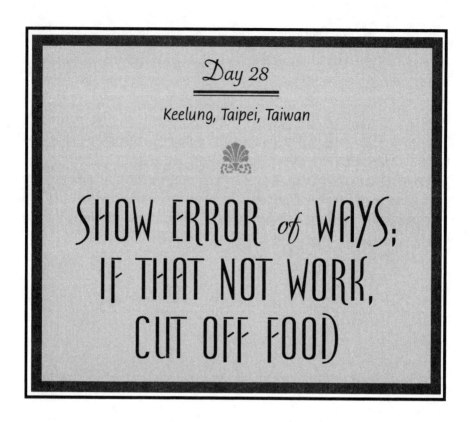

Day 28

Keelung, Taipei, Taiwan

SHOW ERROR of WAYS; IF THAT NOT WORK, CUT OFF FOOD

*C*laire set the tone for the day by telling us at breakfast that the sea looks sinister and evil. I had to agree, but considering Professor Losey's lecture, I informed Claire that if she thought the surface of the sea was evil, she should have considered what was going on underneath —nothing good.

Actually, the sea isn't evil. Nor is it nice. It's just natural. In fiction, attributing human emotions to natural forces, landscapes, and weather conditions is called the pathetic fallacy. Recall that Captain Ahab in *Moby Dick* subscribed to this fallacy. The whale had no evil intent. It is just an innocent creature of God. The whale didn't mean to bite off Ahab's leg. But Ahab doesn't buy that. He says you must look behind the mask. If God lurks behind the mask, then God must be punished. Eventually, they harpooned the whale, but the rope jerked Ahab out of the long boat and down to his death. The whale destroys the ship. Ishmael alone survived in a casket that drifts three days and three nights before being rescued by the *Rachel*.

Wow! Why can't I write something like *Moby Dick*? Why can't we have that kind of adventure? Simple—there exists a profound difference between fiction and fact. The sea looks ominous today but I myself feel great, expansive, happy, hopeful, and supremely contented as I participate in a kind of heavenly bliss. If the sea looks evil, it has no effect whatsoever on my mentality.

Then, as if on cue to prove something, a break appeared in the clouds and beams of celestial light shone through, bleaching the somber dark waves bright green. Nature adjusted itself to suit my mood. Claire, Ethel, and I watched this transformation. Ethel thinks the Virgin Mary will pop out of that cloud, riding the sunbeams earthward, or, if not the holy mother, then an angel. As for me, I would prefer Demi Moore.

Today's cruise news comes under the door, accompanied by a cruise list. Naturally, I looked up Ethel and myself. We are there. But what's this? Sandwiched in between pages I find a letter from J. D. Todhunter, the senior assistant purser. It's official. Cunard has promoted us to Two-deck cabin 2047 starting February 5. This means we leave Coronia. We'll miss our friends—Joe, and Joyce, and Nathan, and Evelyn—but we won't miss the Rabbi. Since the next segment lasts twelve days, I try to calculate the dollar value of this courtesy promotion. It comes to about $154 a day per person. Ethel was right. That brilliant slant of light descending from heaven carried an angel who distributed heavenly grace. Not that we are unhappy in cabin 4064. Who would be? But we had to move anyway, so why not move up faster than expected? Why not skip Three deck and Cl, the highest Caronia class, and advance directly to Two deck and Princess class? Only fools reject heavenly grace. Only fools fail to take advantage of the divine mercy.

Dr. Lillian Glass started today's lecture called "He Says, She Says" by telling us about her credentials. She got her PhD at the University of Michigan. The patient she did her thesis on had had a sex change, but Dr. Glass called this a sex reassignment, probably the politically correct term. Her job was to advise him? her? on how to sound more like a woman and less like a man. Her main advice was to speak with a higher-pitched voice. From this humble beginning there was only one big step to advising Dustin Hoffman on *Tootsie*. From there, Dr. Glass's career blossomed into a consulting service for men who wanted to be more like women. (See! You can make a living at almost anything.) The things Dr. Glass learned advising the transsexuals and cross cross-dressers soon developed into the practical study of male-female communication, leading directly to today's lecture.

Yes, that's the way this lecture started, in peace. Even looking back on it, I still believe no one could have possibly imagined that this lecture would have developed into such a disaster, with multiple passengers almost coming to blows with the good doctor. But it did.

Dr. Glass looked more relaxed today, more natural, and more sincere than she did yesterday. I still felt uneasy listening to her because she seemed to be trying too hard to please, trying too hard to make us like her, trying too hard to look sincere, which only made me doubt her sincerity. To make matters worse, Dr. Glass has dressed in a light-pink suit, complete with thick military-style shoulders with thick padding, but she sported black panty hose that show her legs to advantage since her ultra short (mini? micromini?) skirt doesn't drop anywhere near her knees. Why does she look so tarty? I noted she has no wedding ring.

Yesterday was about making friends and influencing people and today it's about "Talking to win" in the context of male-female communications. I feel ill at ease, as if we are being programmed to be insincere. Far too much dissimulation takes place in this world. We don't need more. But that's what we're taught. Some of it is practical advice. For instance, Dr. Glass quickly teaches me how to ask for a beer. If I am home watching the TV and hear Ethel opening the refrigerator door, I should not say, "Get me a beer." That will likely get me an argument, starting with, "Get it yourself. I'm not your slave."

Rather, I should say, "Honey or some such term of endearment, please would you mind getting me a beer?" That will likely get both a beer, and a foot massage, and anything else I want.

For a moment, I consider this and then realize it doesn't apply to me because I never watch TV (too boring) and I never drink beer (too weak).

Wine is more my drink, or single-malt scotch whiskey, or Bas Armagnac, a delicious brandy produced in France. But I'm being concrete. I understand Dr. Glass's point—be nice.

I get the next point too. Glass said, "Men don't like to ask for directions." That's why Moses got lost in the desert for forty years.

In the next example, she reads from a *Newsweek* report of 1981, giving a supposedly verbatim conversation between Diana and Charles. I paraphrase here because I couldn't take notes fast enough, but it went something like this:

> DIANA: Oh, Charles, I wish I could be with you more. I love you so.
> CHARLES: We probably wouldn't have anything to talk about.
> DIANA: You could tell me about the blondes that are always pursuing you.
> CHARLES: Yes.
> DIANA: I'm jealous of all those people who get next to you who can be with you when I can't.
> CHARLES: I know.

Dr. Glass makes some comments about kings and queens and princes and princesses not living happily ever after. Then she picks up the portable mike and walks through the audience, making a beeline for me. She holds the mike under my mouth, while saying over her shoulder to the rest of the audience, "You, sir, you look pretty well put together. What do you think of that conversation?"

Deep in my heart, I know she has used this example successfully before with multiple audiences, but I just can't go along with it, so I just say what I think. "The conversation sounds too bizarre to be true. If it were true, I would have to know a whole lot more about the parties to comment intelligently."

Doctor Lillian jerks the mike away and goes to a big, fat, gray-headed man, spread out on two seats about ten feet from me. He gives Dr. Glass the correct answer. "Sounds like they don't communicate."

I raised my hand and got the mike back. "Actually, I should have thought that Diana and Charles are communicating very well. He told her he was a stuck-up jackass and she told him that she didn't care. Diana told him that she wanted him anyway."

No comment from the good doctor. She went back to the fat man and asked him, "Do you think that the failure of communication might have played a role in the breakup and the divorce?"

Yep! The fat man does think that way, as Dr. Glass suggested he should. And with those fatal words, the war began.

The Brits in the audience think it's unfair to use tabloid reporting of the royal family. Another Brit complained that the untruthful tabloid reports led to the breakup. Before long, pandemonium broke out. People stood, and shouted, and shook their fists at Dr. Glass.

Dr. Glass tried to make a cowardly amends for all that she has said. But no matter how much she apologized (and the Lady did apologize too much, methinks), the Brits don't relent. Instead, they shouted threats. They yelled that such stuff shouldn't be allowed on the *QE2*. One big beefy man with a big red nose shouted down from the balcony the words that scared Dr. Glass more than any others: "You are an insult to the royals! You shouldn't be permitted to lecture on *QE2*. Go home."

Out of the blue, some man wearing a yarmulke and a black suit stood up and said, "While we're at it, I think, that joke about men, Moses, and the Jews was way out of line."

After time was up, some of us went up and tried to console Dr. Glass. I told her I would have come to her defense but she was handling everything satisfactorily herself. Without thanking me, she turned to shake someone else's hand and apologized again.

Ethel and I are lucky. We got bus Eight for the afternoon tour. Eight means luck because in Mandarin the word for eight (pronounced *ban*) slightly mispronounced can mean "great good fortune obtained quickly." You get the idea. In fact, eights in special vanity license plates are quite the thing in Hong Kong, with the most recent plate of "888888" costing its proud owner one million dollars.

Our guide, Helen, tells us we are in the lucky bus. I tell her that I know that, and I tell her that, if eight is lucky, I know what is not lucky. Helen stares at me, surprised. But before she spoke I said, "Four."

Helen smiled and said, "You berry smart! Four in Chinese sound like death. Not good number! Hotel not have number four floor. Power plant in Hong Kong need only four smoke stack. They put five, otherwise bad luck."

Helen speaks English like it's Chinese. She not conjugate verbs because they no do that in Chinese. She said, "I MIT—Made In Taiwan."

Helen also thinks like the Chinese. I can tell by the way she explained the reason for the tollbooths placed every forty kilometers on the highway. "Men get sleepy. Need stop. See beautiful girl. Every forty kilometers. Wake up."

That reminded me of a Chinese friend in Houston who one day explained why the Chinese army fought America in Korea. "Chinese love America. But Chinese army need practice." (This last word comes out sounding more like 'pract-tiss').

Helen continued to show her cultural origins, her MIT. "Taiwan weather change like woman's heart. Possible, experience four season, same day." She pointed out the numerous motorcycles, but called them "murder cycles." At home we called them "donor cycles" for the same reason. That's where we get most of our donated organs.

The group doesn't like the Chiang Kai-shek Memorial Hall, our first stop. I can't figure out why. Perhaps the crowds bothered those who had gotten so used to being pampered and catered to, who now suddenly were not. This discontent came out in all sorts of petty concerns: "I'm walking too much!" "Do I have to climb these stairs?" "Why is the garden so long?" "The other guide talks longer than you do, Helen." "I expected more than that. Why are we here?"

Yet, Helen kept cool, remained self-possessed. She is probably thinking that this type of boat people, the *QE2* type, don't know anything about hardship. I myself am ashamed of my fellow passengers. Sometimes we can look simply silly, a source of innocent amusement for the guides when they get home and talk. And sometimes we can look terrible.

But the next stop pleased the group. It was the National Palace Museum, the undisputed main attraction of Taiwan. Opened in 1965, this treasure house contains the world's greatest collection of Chinese art. I passed through the jade collection to see the beautifully carved white jade cabbage with a green grasshopper on top, all carved from a single solid piece by three generations of artisans. Great! But the passenger at the glass with me says, "Rather disappointing!" I stared at him, speechless.

I focused on the special calligraphy exhibit on the second floor. Calligraphy, the sign explains, is the highest art form in China, way above painting, porcelain, music, and poetry. The art form is unique because of the flexible brush employed and because of the Chinese characters themselves, with each having its own meaning. I stood before these scrolls enthralled, as if a great power and untamable strength, like that of a dragon leaping through the heavenly gate, had seized me. Some of the Chinese characters I recognized from my *QE2* lessons, but others I don't. Nevertheless, I feel the marvels of drops of water, sudden thunders, falling rocks. I saw in the characters figures resembling black swans, frightened animals, dancing phoenixes, or startled snakes, the violent force of a crumbling oak, or dangerous edge. The aesthetic pleases me to the nth power. Why? Who knows? But it does.

Calligraphy must possess spirit, life force, bone, flesh, and blood. If one element is missing, it is not calligraphy. I find myself especially attracted to seal style calligraphy. It's strong, broad symmetrical strokes thrill me. Perhaps I am a reincarnated calligrapher who lived and worked when the style achieved its peak two thousand years ago. To celebrate my newfound love, I buy two calligraphy brushes in the museum store. Each costs $35.

At dinner, Rabbi pulled a Rabbi. When Peter asked, "How are you tonight?" The Rabbi replied, "We're here."

What would Dr. Glass say about the Rabbi's communication skills? More important, what would Dr. Glass do? Probably recommend therapy, intensive therapy. Perhaps Rabbi would do better if he were more like a woman. Or maybe we should use Helen's Chinese methods of persuasion: "First show him error of ways. If that not work, cut off food."

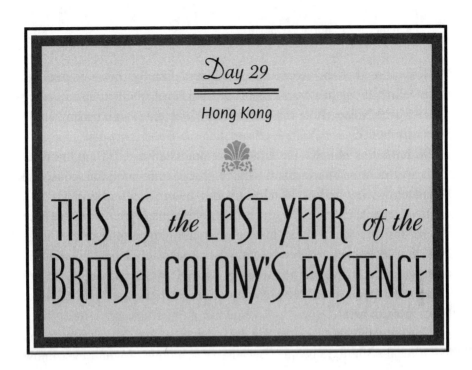

Day 29

Hong Kong

THIS IS *the* LAST YEAR *of the* BRITISH COLONY'S EXISTENCE

What adventures awaited us in Hong Kong, in this the last year of the British colony's existence? That was the question the cruise news asked. Someone had slipped the cruise news under our door. It had good news too with the Dow Jones up to 5404 and the biotech index up 10 percent since we started the world cruise. No word on specific stocks, but it would be unusual for Amgen not to participate in such a rally especially since the fat gene (owed by Amgen) figured large in the news. Hot dog!

Today's schedule staggers me, but I decided to bite the bullet and learn to use Windows. The lesson started at 9:30 and went to 11 AM. The computer center on Two deck filled with gray heads trying to learn. If they succeed, and I see no reason why they wouldn't as they seem so intense, the market for computers will blossom.

The gray heads spotted a hitch right away, though, and they all lost faith in the computer because on the screen it listed the date as February 2. Someone forgot to tell it we lost a day crossing the International Date Line.

Mike, the teacher, seemed puzzled, too. Finally, he reassured the group, telling them the computer aboard British ships tells time according to Greenwich Mean Time. If you can't convince them with reason, baffle them with bullshit.

Within a few minutes the gray heads outdistance me. They know all about graphic user interfaces, GUI, and group icons, program icons, and the anatomy of a window. Windows is fun, even though I think it's kind of slow compared to DOS, (the disk operating system) where you remember the codes in letters instead of pointing to pictures to get things done. For a while we played with the mouse, clicking and double-clicking, and then we learned to drag. I loved paintbrush and filled my screen with Chinese calligraphy in red, green, blue, and yellow. Mike thinks it looks great.

Unfortunately, because of Windows I missed Dr. Glass's lecture on how to deal with toxic people. Because of Windows, I won't ever know how to handle toxic persons. But I do know how to handle a toxic person, the Rabbi. By leaving him, that's how.

We will land in Hong Kong (Hong Kong is the Tokkan dialect word for fragrant harbor) tonight at six. Already the shopping mania has seized the group. They all are talking about what to buy. Waldemar Hansen estimates *QE2* passengers will leave over $2 million in Hong Kong. I know I'll spend some too, though, perhaps not that much. I'm looking for silk scrolls to do calligraphy on and I want to get some more brushes and at least one calligraphy inkstone.

At lunch, Nathan at the next table and I traded war stories. He used to teach at the Columbia (second division) at Bellevue hospital in New York City. I probably had him as a teacher. In fact, I vaguely remember him teaching me how to read electrocardiograms, but I don't tell him that. He might quiz me.

Nathan reminded me of Spike and Dome anemia, a peculiar disease of the Bowery bums. The bums would sell their blood to a company named Spike and Dome, and then come to the hospital for a blood transfusion so they could go sell their blood again to Spike and Dome. Good business!

Nathan was a waiter once, like the Rabbi. One day, Nathan dropped a steak on the floor of the kitchen. The chef told him to pick it right up and put it right back on the plate. Nathan did. The customer, later, told Nathan that was the best steak he ever ate.

"Nathan, do you think such things happen to steaks on *QE2*?" I asked.

Nathan smiled and, like an impish little child, rolled his eyes toward the Rabbi's vacant table, "You bet, especially to some people."

After lunch I weighed myself in the fitness center on Seven deck.

By now, the fitness people are used to the ritual and cheer me on. They know, according to my self-imposed rule, that as long as I hit 160 pounds or less, I can continue to eat desserts at lunch. Today I tip the scale at 159.7 pounds.

"Lots of room left for self-indulgence," I told Ethel.

Diana Preston—author, broadcaster, and freelance journalist—gave a lecture on Hong Kong's history. Diana is British, but she doesn't spare the British. She tells us about the opium trade, and the Boxer Rebellion, and all those other things you learned in high school but forgot. The net result that lingers after the lecture is that the British "turned greedy eyes on Cathay," a name Marco Polo first gave to the region, and took Hong Kong by force and now must return it to China.

I raised my hand and asked why Britain is leaving, when according to the Convention of Peking, signed in 1898, only the New Territories would be leased to Britain, not Hong Kong proper. The New Territories revert to the Chinese at midnight, June 30, 1997. Diana answered that, strictly speaking, the legal situation only required the return of the New Territories, but the political situation indicates the return of all of Hong Kong. This sounds like double-talk, but I said nothing.

As I exited, the projectionist jumped out of the projection box and ran toward me. Breathless, he pulled my right shoulder and turned me around. He explained that the real reason is water. Hong Kong's water comes via the New Territories. Without that water the colony couldn't function. The British have no choice because Red China would simply cut the water until it got what it wanted. The Chinese once cut the water supply in 1839, so I guess the British didn't want to chance going to war again over the same issue.

Avoid war. I think that's a good idea. It's clear history is on our side. Communism fell apart in Russia and will probably fall apart in Cuba. Why should it not fall apart in China?

From the hot tub on One deck, I viewed our entrance into Hong Kong harbor. Macau stands across from HK just as it did when I was here last in 1979. Funny how geography doesn't change much in seventeen years. The Pearl River still flows to the north and beyond that the city once known as Canton stands, but is now called Kwangchou. The harbor reflects the crowded conditions of Hong Kong itself, with every kind of boat crisscrossing hither and thither, sometimes just missing each other. I spotted a flotilla of sampans, tankas, junks, motor boats, utilities, tankers, hydrofoils, the Star Ferry carrying people over to Hong Kong Island, and of course the tugs that are now pushing *QE2* into dock. Lots of ships. I never met a ship I didn't like. Jesus, I sound like Will Rogers.

I got out of the hot tub, and I looked over the side, and read the tug's name: *Tung Lung Tug*. Pretty good poetry. It has alliteration and rhythm both. Before I finished swimming my 150 laps in the gelid 52 degree water of the outdoor pool, night fell enshrouding everything in a haze as mysterious as the Orient itself.

I forgot to review the dinner last night so I will do the review tonight. I started with orange duck terrine with mesclun salad, while Ethel ate fried shrimp balls. There followed a thick sweet and sour seafood pot soup fragrant with jasmine and the other pungent Oriental spices. After that came jasmine tea sorbet, which unfortunately had too subtle a flavor and some hard chunks of ice in it. The sorbet did clear my palate and cooled my mouth. After that appeared medallions of beef that melted in my mouth. They served the beef in a dark brown reduction sauce that had just the right amount of soy. Thin, fresh, tender French green beans; long turnip strips; cubed carrots; stewed tomatoes, and deep-fried new potatoes accompanied the beef. *Remarkable*, I thought as I savored the rich cream of a classical Pavlova, named after the famous ballerina, which had the required kiwi attached. Our wine, and you won't respect us for this, but you must remember Ethel and I were celebrating four weeks aboard ship and the fact that we were still talking to each other, was Château Lafite-Rothschild 1976, which not only is a premier cru classé but has just reached its peak. The bottle cost only $195. But, you know what, we can't buy such a bottle in Houston for less than $1,200. As I sat there, beaming my approval and thanking God for the rich mineral essences of the earth that one can experience in really great wines like Château Lafite-Rothschild, my attention drifted onto the Rabbi, who was about to leave.

Rabbi had the usual frown on his face. He told Peter that "nothing worked out for us tonight."

When a dejected Peter came around to our table, I smacked my lips, rubbed my stomach, and said, "Everything worked out for us tonight."

Peter burst out laughing. But because of professional propriety, Peter wouldn't tell us what went wrong at table 216, the Rabbi's table. I'll try to pry the gory details from Claire or Eric tomorrow. Meanwhile, Ethel and I are too busy getting to Grand Lounge for the show.

The entertainment never ends on *QE2*. Ethel and I didn't want to leave the ship to go to Hong Kong, so Hong Kong came to us in the form of a Chinese show with acrobats, magicians, and dancers. The thing I liked the most was those young girls with streamers flashing their bright colors, red and blue, in the air to the rhythm of ancient Chinese music. It looked like my favorite Olympic event, rhythmic gymnastics, only better.

Four young women dressed in red tunics gracefully took positions stage front. They carried in their right hands a short pole, from the end of which extended two streamers, red and blue. Their left hands remained pressed with stylized palms out against their posterior left waists. They had nicely contoured butts. New music sent them into a marvelous dance of grace and style and beauty that enthralled me to my very core. I began to think that maybe I should have married someone of Chinese origin. Or how about a dancer? The only problem is that that it is out of the question, as I am already married. Ethel would have strong objections.

The Chinese girls started their finale. They seemed to be skating in place, banners flying overhead, streamers faultlessly coordinated and synchronous with the beat of the exotic music. The Chinese girls took their final bows. The show ended. No matter how much I shouted my praises in Chinese, the Chinese appeared to be very ignorant of their own language, Mandarin. My ardor for them faded. Then I asked myself why, when I am within orbit of these women, or any women, can I not escape their gravitational attraction? Is the romantic atmosphere of *QE2* doing this to me? Only when the women leave could I, *would I*, float free.

Ethel and I held hands as we went back to our cabin. Before I turned in for the night, instead of floating free, I locked into her orbit.

IT'S LIKE ATTENDING *the* WAKE *of* YOUR LAST SURVIVING PARENT— YOU KNOW YOU'RE NEXT

*H*ong Kong harbor, busy as ever, doesn't make noise. Therefore we slept well, even though the ship is berthed next to the ocean terminal at the center of Kowloon Peninsula. On deck we saw so many boats crisscrossing each other it looked like the Battle of Trafalgar. The wonder is they don't crash into one another. I guess Chinese captains, from their shoreline experiences, are used to dealing with crowds.

Ethel and I took the early tour of Hong Kong side streets to get the flavor of the old city. The major industry here remains the same as it was fifty years ago—selling on the street, and I'm not referring to sex or to the world of Suzie Wong. But talking about Suzie, Roger, our guide, tells us there used to be eight hundred bars and brothels in HK. Now there are three. Prostitution is not illegal in Hong Kong but just about everything connected with it is illegal. Thus a private contract between a woman and a man exchanging money for sex is OK. But if a third party gets in there with some sort of procurement fee, or if there is advertising involved, the cops jump in and make arrests. Anyway, the prostitution business died a natural death after the Americans left Vietnam.

Roger explained that Hong Kong has the greatest population density of the world. Looking out the bus window at the people-packed streets, I believe it. In fact, on the average, twenty people pack into each square meter of space. Lack of space also makes it difficult to own washing machines or stoves: just no place to put them.

At the first stop I special ordered a personal seal, which the Chinese call a chop, from Lee Yip Man Chop and Printing Press. They charged me two hundred Hong Kong dollars ($28) and promised to deliver to the *QE2* today. Ethel is skeptical and says I'll never see the chop or my money again. But I like the idea of having my own seal to stamp my Chinese name with. But what is my Chinese name? The shop will make one up on the spot for you. But I have a better idea. I wrote the name I liked in Chinese characters. This amazes the Chinese man who runs the shop. He read it right away: *dai-fu-hau*. Translated, this means "big doctor fine" which converted to English comes out "the fine big doctor," but if you pronounce it a little differently, saying the hau as if it were *ho*, then it means "the big spendthrift doctor." This is my little joke. The men at the chop shop get it right away. They laugh. The Chinese love this kind of play on words. Interestingly, they write me a receipt in red ink, the lucky color for the Chinese, a color so lucky that red is the color brides wear at their weddings. Lee Yip Man listed the date as the "second moon, fourth sun," which come to think on it is their way of saying February 4. Only moons and days seem more in harmony with nature and the basic elements of time reckoning on this planet.

The next stop shows us the old part of town where the many stores sell dried fish. One shark skin, an equilateral triangle two feet on each side and a quarter-inch thick, sells for over $2,000, proving that things don't have an intrinsic value. They are worth only what people are willing to pay for them. We admire the dried shrimps of all sizes, sniff the pungent shrimp paste—their universal condiment—and feel the crispy white chunks of dehydrated fish stomachs. I inspected the twenty-year-old ducks that hang forlornly on large hooks, exposed to the open air. Roger informs me the ducks are for sale wholesale only. Looks like I'll have to settle for three-year-old sea scallops.

Somehow this gets Roger into a diatribe about Chinese food in the West. "Chop suey. Can't get here," he said. "Only in West. Chop suey phony Chinese food. What we Chinese call Western Chinese food." Roger shakes his index finger at our group sternly, "If you in restaurant that serve chop suey, not Chinese restaurant." Fortunately, Roger got a call on his portable phone, otherwise we would have not heard the end of this.

Roger went over some Chinese proverbs, the distilled wisdom of the ages: "Why you kill chicken with cow knife?" "Plant bean get bean, plant melon get melon." "Rat know rat way." The one I liked the best: "Who serve powerful, sleep with tiger."

The last stop takes us through the Man Mo Temple. Man Mo was not put here for the tourists. Crowds of real Chinese jam in. The air thickened with the smoke from burning punks. Every once in a while the gong sounded and someone set a basket on fire in the middle of the hallway. When you light a fire, you report to the gods. Bright flames lashed dangerously close to the temple's wooden beams. No one cares. The Chinese are too busy praying for good luck, jade, gold, protection from the communists, etc.

Smoke filled the air, delivering the messages to the gods and ancient ancestors. Roger explained that the punk sticks are painted red because red blinds the evil spirits. The smoke from punks and the incense carries the prayers to the gods and the gong deafens the evil spirits so they can't interfere. The usual thing is to carry three burning punks to the altar. One punk represents the present, one the past, and one—you guessed it—the future.

I prayed to Kuan Yin, the Chinese goddess of compassion. Bring us good fortune. "Let our new room and new restaurant be great," I prayed. "Make my Amgen stock rise. Help me buy, at a favorable price, some good calligraphy inkstones. Watch over me as I negotiate price. Don't let me get gypped."

After temple, I walked down Cat Street and found a small shop selling antiques. It had two inkstones that pleased me. A third remarkable piece pleased me even more, but it cost $3,800, as much as the other two combined. The stones are the size of large paperweights, only they're black and cool to the touch. One has engraved Chinese garden scenes etched on its elevated edge. I spot the ponds, and the stylized lyrical trees that so often populate Chinese landscapes, and realize the elevated lip of the inkstone also functions as the enclosing wall of the garden. The stone recapitulates, in a microcosm, the aesthetic of the Chinese garden. After some haggling I agree to buy an inkstone for $1,800. The salesgirl interrupts her eating a mandarin orange and knocks an additional $300 off the price. Everything is in Hong Kong dollars, thank Kuan Yin.

The price is down $300, but there is a snag. She won't take American Express, but she will take Visa. No problem. She wrapped everything up and gave it to me. She's distracted. I see why. Behind the curtain, a man is waiting. Her eyes tell everything. Eyes of desire! She's in a hurry to get me out. Right after I left, she locked up. No wonder there are so many Chinese.

I finger the inkstones through the brown paper. *Stones? Wait a second.* I have two. I check the sales slip. She charged me $1,500, the agreed price for the one I bought. I unwrap them. Oh, God, she wrapped the antique stone costing $3,800 that I admired and she didn't charge me for it. I went back and pounded and pounded. No answer. I know she and her boyfriend are in the back there behind the black curtain, but they are probably too interlocked in intimate embrace to come to the door.

At lunch, Eric briefed me on what happened last night with the Rabbi. Rabbi ordered special off-menu items and there was a big delay getting the stuff prepared. Finally, when it came, Rabbi said that the sweet potato was burned on one side, and so was the baked potato, and the bagel wasn't crisp enough, but the french fries were OK.

I told Eric the Rabbi never finishes his meals, usually leaving half uneaten.

"What do you expect?" asked Eric. "It is impossible to eat as much as he orders. And three different kinds of potatoes. *C'est un homme absurde*."

Ethel said trying to please the Rabbi is Sisyphean. And I said, "Yes, and uselessly repetitive as well."

This is Sunday, so I seek out and find a game room to practice my religion. I don't have to go far, for a large game room situates itself on the ground floor of the Ocean Center. The game room calls itself Fun Fun World. Toys "R" Us (Hong Kong branch) stood next door. The Chinese turned out in massive numbers to practice this religion. In fact, the density in the game room exceeded by far the density of people in the Man Mo Temple. Amazingly, the atmosphere remains free of smoke. But not free of noise and flashing lights. The din exceeds a hundred decibels. Impossible hear person speak. No matter. Must play game. Not talk. (Without much effort, see how I can sound Chinese?)

Joe and Joyce Gibson, our dining neighbors in Caronia, exhibit the sad dejected behavior of the visage indicating reactive depression. I don't blame them, for tomorrow they will suffer the ultimate demotion. Tomorrow they leave *QE2*, they become nonpassengers. I tried to cheer them up. "Take my advice. Book passage for the next segment." Ethel and I know in two months' time the fate of Joe and Joyce will become our fate, as well. It's like attending the wake of your last surviving parent. You know you're next.

We decided to console ourselves with good wine, so we ordered Le Montrachet 1990 for $280. The sad mood lifted almost immediately. Wine, said Benjamin Franklin, is the proof that God loves us and wants us to be happy.

I decided to spread some cheer by distributing the tips for this segment. Since we are in Caronia class, the recommended tip was $5 per day per passenger for the waiters, and the same amount for the stewardess. Since this segment lasted 19 days, that made $190 ($5 \times 19 \times 2 = 190$) due to Eric and his helpers, and $190 due to Helen and hers. I gave Helen $200 and offered her another $60 to help move us tomorrow to our new cabin, 2047. Helen refused the additional $60, telling me I had tipped her enough.

But somehow Ethel and I still think we are undertipping. We decided the recommended amounts for the waiters, who have given such good service and became such good friends, are too small. So I gave Eric $200, Claire $150, Isabel $50, and Peter $100. That brought the tip amounts for this segment to $700, and since our fare was $14,844, the total price came to $15,544. This amounted to $409 per day per person, compared to the $191 per day per person in Mauretania.

I asked Ethel the big question, "Was it worth it?"

She answered a resounding, "Yes!"

Ethel is right, of course. We got more than double the space in the room, plus a porthole and a chair. The food and service in the Caronia top Mauretania by twofold. The change in dining room pleased us, but not as much as the change in cabins. Sure, Caronia had white tablecloths instead of the salmon pink of Mauretania, and Caronia had additional entrées that didn't get on the Mauretania menu, but the food and service were great in both restaurants. The similarities of the two restaurants outweigh the differences.

Tonight's entertainment of Chinese music closed with a singer who wore a *cheongsam*, a Chinese female costume with a high collar, side slits, and made of silk. Hers had a rich embroidery of peonies, lotuses, dragons, and phoenixes on the collar, sleeves, and sides. Made exactly formfitting in soft red silk, its front, back, and side views add up to a startling panorama of the entire landscape of the female form.

Incidentally, the singing was not a catfight as one wag predicted. The woman thrilled me as she sang high pitched and strange in that strange Oriental tone, with a melody that to my Western ear strived but never quite reached conclusion. Utterly different, utterly unique, utterly Chinese, and utterly beautiful.

Here comes our final appraisal of this segment and Caronia class:

Room: small but comfortable. Adequate for our needs, a cozy nest. This cabin exceeded M5 by a factor of two, directly related to the increase in price.

Food: excellent in every way—colorful, fresh, clean, tasty, and well presented. Steaks came out more cooked than ordered, but this problem solved itself by my ordering slightly different than usual. If I wished my steak medium rare, I simply called for rare or, as Eric understood in French, *"pas a point, sanglant."*

Service: fast and efficient. Sometimes there was a delay in bringing things out, but never so much that we felt we were wasting our time. Eric said the dishes are not "plated," a technical term in the waiting profession, meaning that he had to put things on the plate, not the cooks.

Drinks: cheap and great. We sampled some of the great French wines of the world, which at home would have cost five times what we paid on *QE2*. The gin martinis I drank (and I had my share) met and exceeded international standards, an unusual thing, for usually once you have left the United States, as far as cocktails are concerned, you are camping out. Next segment, I plan to branch out to different wines and other cocktails.

Entertainment: We didn't go in for bingo and the Mr. and Mrs. games, but the movies, the lectures, and the other experiences including the symphony, and the operas were first class. The Smithsonian lecturer Jan Stuart, a real scholar, had masterful delivery. She presented her material with insight and organized it so we could grasp the main points without much effort. When the exposition required nuance and complexity, she gave us that, as well.

But following Dante, if I am to tell you of the good, I must tell you of the things that are not so good. We still lacked a bathtub and a video-tape player. The narrow beds presented some (surmountable) problems with intimacy. The Caronia Restaurant seemed crowded and the tables a little too small to comfortably put everything needed on them. In rough seas those tables moved. On the other hand, the close quarters helped us form close relationships with our eating neighbors, Joe, Joyce, Nathan, and Estelle, an advantage. The same closeness put us in contact with some of the unsavory passengers, like the Rabbi, a disadvantage.

Total Value—superexcellent. Try to match it anywhere. You can't.

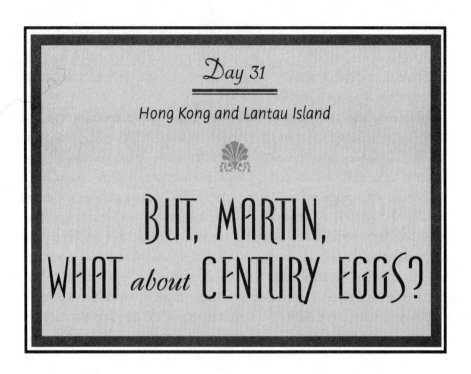

Day 31

Hong Kong and Lantau Island

BUT, MARTIN, WHAT *about* CENTURY EGGS?

We took a boatman's holiday and rode a junk to Lantau Island. The trip took over an hour. All the way we battled wind, sea, tide, and the myriad of other boats in Hong Kong harbor; especially we battled those container ships, some of which have railroad cars piled several stories high. One container ship arrives every two minutes, twice as fast as babies, who arrive in Hong Kong every four minutes.

Ethel can't stand dry land for long. She didn't sleep well and considers the lack of rock and roll part of the cause. She had mal de terre and wanted to get to sea as fast as possible.

This is transfer day. We decided to leave everything to the crew. We won't be on *QE2* to supervise getting all the bags and stuff from 4164 to 2047. If we are away, it will be less work for us and more for them.

Lantau Island, the largest of about 235 outlying islands comprising the British territory of Hong Kong (until midnight, June 30, 1997), measures twice the size of Hong Kong Island, but has far less people. This island constitutes the holiday place for the younger Hong Kong citizens who want to get away to the countryside for a weekend or for some holidays. They come out here, rent an apartment at some absurd price (over $200 American per night for a room the size of a M5 cabin), and enjoy the fine beaches.

We didn't come for the beaches. We came for the fabulous Buddhist temple and to see the world's tallest outdoor bronze Buddha statue, situated high on the top of Mok Yue Hill at Ngong Ping. Our guide, Martin, a professional cook on Lantau who speaks Chinese well enough to have persuaded a Chinese woman to marry him, pointed out along the way two penal colonies. The men there—murderers, rapists, drug dealers, and Triad members (Triad is the Chinese equivalent of the Mafia) await their fate when Hong Kong transfers to China next year. The British don't know what to do with these men, so they decided to leave everything up to the communists.

"The British have decided to wait for a lot of things to happen," Martin explained. "Civil servants are retiring in droves. Nobody seems to want to learn Chinese anymore. What's the point?"

In Tai O, a fishing village, Martin picked up a live crab from a small container, next to some shop on a side alley. While holding the crab over his head for everyone to see, he explains why he thinks Asians live longer than Westerners. "They eat fresh food."

The *QE2*ers got nervous watching the crab squirm in Martin's hand. The crab can't pinch because its claws have been conveniently tied down with small ropes made of seaweed.

"In the West they use preservatives. No one could get away with that here. That's why when they die, Western bodies last so long, all those preservatives. Asian bodies rot right away."

Knowing about the twenty-year-old ducks and the dried shrimp, I decided to pull Martin's leg. "What about century eggs?"

Martin doesn't get it, or else he has decided to avoid admitting that the Chinese sometimes eat preserved foods. Martin put down the crab. He gave us key information about century eggs, as if he were reading it out of his cooking textbook: "Century eggs, preserved in ammonia, gives them that distinctive black color, overpowering urine smell, and a taste so putrescent that even the most intrepid century egg eaters seek gustatory relief by munching pickled ginger."

Martin then opened a jar and ate what appeared to be a goldfish.

"Ever see that movie *A Fish Called Wanda*? Well here's what he ate. Have some."

Martin handed me a sliver of golden orange material. Since I trusted him explicitly and implicitly, I ate it. The sliver didn't taste like a fish. It tasted sweet and had a nice pulp. I know it's not a fish, but I can't say what it is.

Martin beamed that wry smile of his, "Sundried mango."

Martin showed us some shark fins for sale. The soup made from it is a way to show your wealth. As a cook, he would know. "Shark fin soup does about as much for you nutritionally as eating your toenails. But if you need to show off, it's the ticket. When I married I had to pay for seventy-two tables of people, twelve to a table, eating shark fin soup. The Chinese menu had twenty courses and one main course. That's it—the main course was the shark fin soup! It cost more than all of the other courses put together!"

Martin told us about his religion, Buddhism. He likes it and I can see why. It's more flexible than most religions.

Martin pointed to Carole, a young stewardess in the front of the bus. "You don't want to give up sex?"

Carole shook her head emphatically no.

"That's OK," Martin assured her. "They have a branch of Buddhism where you don't have to do that."

"You don't want to give up meat," Martin pointed to the back of the bus at me. "That's OK. They have a branch for that. In Buddhism, the emphasis is on what you learned, not on how you have sinned or why you should be punished. Suppose I speed through the village and run someone over. I come to the temple and tell the master. After he has listened to me he would ask, 'What have you learned?' And if I reply: 'Not to speed,' he would send me away with his blessing."

At Po Lin Monastery, under the blue, yellow, red, white, and orange Buddhist umbrellas, we ate a vegetarian lunch consisting of thickened sweet and sour cabbage soup, juicy noodles, fried rice with steamed vegetables, mushrooms, bean curd, fried taro, celery, broccoli, and carrots. All this looks, tastes, and smells so great and has such a fine textures that it tempted me to abandon electronic games in favor of Martin's religion. Martin assured me that electronic games and all other religions are compatible with Buddhism, including his religion, Church of England Anglican.

Before we left the temple, I tried my luck with the joysticks. There are ninety-nine in a cup. I shook the cup as long as needed to cause one of the sticks to pop out. Then I took the stick over to the lady and paid an offering fee to get a print out. The poem on the stick is supposed to relate to your situation. Mine read, "Change your life now. Do it flamboyantly. And don't look back."

On the bus going back, Martin gave a quiz. He asked, "What three groups of people, besides the Nazis, used the symbol that looks like a backward swastika?"

My hand shot up. "American Indians, Hindus, and [I paused to increase the suspense] Buddhists."

Martin awarded me a picture of the Po Lin Bronze Tian Tan Buddha, the world's largest outdoor sculpture of Buddha. The Buddha sports a paunch. The Chinese equate eating with prosperity. The large male belly means food excess and benefits running over to benefit others. It became a general symbol of happiness, peace, and well-being.

The Royal Hong Kong Police Band entertained tonight.

Herman wandered in and took a seat. He looked bewildered and then started to cry when the bagpipes started to play. Herman appears better, physically, than he had been. He has a healthy glow to his face and I detect no shortness of breath. Sea travel as tonic is an old Victorian cliché that in Herman's case looks true.

The leader of the band, Superintendent Parkinson, selected passengers to do guest conducting. An American named White conducted the "Stars and Stripes Forever," and a Brit did the theme from *Bridge on the*

River Kwai. Both did an excellent job, proving that a well-trained band doesn't didn't need a conductor. The crowd begged for more. But the Royal Hong Kong Police Band marched out in style to the tune of "The Highland Cathedral March." That's the way to leave, while they are begging for more.

And that's the way these Royal Hong Kong Police will march into history next year. The Chinese have trained their own elite police force, which will stream across the border at midnight, June 30, 1997. The special troops are a division of the PLA, People's Liberation Army, the same that "liberated" Shanghai in 1949 and provided the muscle to force private businesses to "merge" with state enterprises. Hopefully, Superintendent Parkinson will by then have returned to England to his tranquil estate in Surrey and won't be around to watch the things he gave his life to broken.

Day 32

Hong Kong

LEONARD BECAME IRATE

*S*ailing away from Hong Kong, Captain John Burton-Hall tried to leave intact the small motorboats that kept annoyingly crisscrossing our path. We also maneuvered between bat-winged junks, moored tankas, cradlelike sampans bustling about the teeming waterway, the Star Ferries, the hydrofoils, and jet boats that go to Macau. As we exit the Fragrant Harbor I can't help but think of *The World of Suzie Wong*.

It's been thirty-seven years since Richard Mason's classic story made its entrance. (Mason was still alive at the time of our trip, living in Rome until he died the following year of throat cancer.) Would he have recognized Hong Kong now? I doubt it. Today little remains of Mason's British colony, the old Hong Kong, inhabited back in 1957 by fictional Suzie, the pretty Wan Chai bar girl. Her story, woefully neglected and out of print, seems destined to be buried and lost. The Star Ferry still runs its endless shuttles from Kowloon waterfront, opposite Hong Kong Island. But today there are two classes, one on top and one on the bottom, sort of like the *QE2* only simpler. Lomax might not meet Suzie since she might have ridden second class and he might have ridden first.

Right now, Suzie and Lomax, on the ferry during that initial meeting, wouldn't have had much time to talk either. Their time on the ferry would be shorter today for the journey is shorter, not because the ferry travels faster, but because the land is closer. Relentless land reclamation has brought the Hong Kong shore out to meet the boat. The new land, reclaimed from the sea, sprouted yet another generation of high-rise apartments, hotels, and the ubiquitous office buildings, sweeping away the old colony atmosphere.with its tide. Gone with the old city is the charming original Luk Kwok Hotel, the model for Mason's Nam Kok Hotel as the haunt of Suzie Wong and her fellow bar girls. New buildings block the view Lomax would have enjoyed from his hotel room from Hong Kong Island across the harbor to Kowloon and the modernized and expanded Peninsula Hotel.

Back in the 1950s Hong Kong was a small, sleepy town. Traffic, if you can believe Mason, as I do, was minimal, and there were no back alleys with neon signs or red taxis charging exorbitant fares. The barefoot rickshaw drivers, harnessed to their two-wheeled carts, still ran their cargoes of humans around town the hard way. Now the one rickshaw driver I saw spends most of his time posing for tourist pictures and charging five Hong Kong dollars a shot.

In Wan Chai, the trams that Suzie took still work their way through the jammed streets, past smoke-filled pickup bars. One even bears the name Suzie Wong in honor of the character. The bars remain here but the girls are not Chinese. The girls come in from Burma, Thailand, Cambodia, and the Philippines. The old business of "No money, No talk" still holds. Only the prices have changed. The hostesses of modern times probably don't even know Suzie or the book. But they too would cheer her story, the way the hostesses of the '50s did, championing Suzie's cause to become "a respectable girl."

The book was followed in 1958 by a successful stage play that ran for two years on Broadway starring France Nuyen as Suzie and Star Trek's William Shatner as Robert Lomax. In 1960 a popular film version was released starring Nancy Kwan and William Holden. In a way, the Suzie

Wong story helped bring Hong Kong before the world's gaze and played a part in the popular recognition of the territory and in that way made a contribution to its development.

Oh yes, before we leave, let's talk about Red China. Once someone asked Princess Di what she thought of Red China. She replied, "I like it, especially against a blue tablecloth."

I like that kind of red china, too, for the same reason. It's the other Red China that bothers me. I fear the real Red China almost as much as I fear cancer or a lawsuit. Ethel and I have traveled there. The people smile whenever we spoke to them. Everyone seemed cheerful, but there's an awful sameness about the smiles and the people. They all seem to think in the same way, behave in the same way. Yet they know they are going places. They believe in themselves. The real danger comes because they think they are right.

Two hours out of Hong Kong, a monsoon about to become a typhoon pushed us along the South China Sea as we headed to Manila. The wind caused gigantic sea swells. I remained unperturbed as ominous natural forces gathered.

Captain John Burton-Hall announced gloomily that this trailing sea, as he called it, will continue for the day and that the weather will soon worsen. Trailing sea? What does he mean? I don't know. But as for the weather, he was right. By noon, the sky grew even more foul, and the storms had long since blown away the tattered remnants of any of our pseudoromantic notions of life at sea.

Passengers on deck moved along like drunks, lurching from one side to the other, but unlike drunks they also rose and fell every ten seconds. I liked the effect. It's like the fun house at the amusement park, with the difference that you can't get out of the house. We were all under the weather.

Under the weather. You would be amazed just how many of our everyday terms come straight from sailor talk. Most of them are pretty obvious, such as "under the weather," "high and dry," and "taking the wind out of somebody's sails." But did you know "carry on" drew from that part of the mentionable portion of bosun's language on the old square-riggers. In those days, when a spanking wind that powered clippers across the oceans was all-important, "carry on" was a specific order not to shorten sail, but to use, or "carry," as much canvas as the vessel could safely bear. And how about the "logbook"? In olden days, sailors used a log and a length of rope in order to measure the distance that their boat had covered, as well as the speed at which it was advancing. The day's result was duly entered in the logbook. Of course, the distance traveled was conveniently measured in, you guessed it, the knots on the rope.

And what about "he let the cat out of the bag"? I didn't know where that expression came from until the *QE2* first mate explained it. Onboard a square-rigger 150 years ago, the expression would have sent shudders through a sailor's spine, for it meant that a sailor had committed an offense serious enough to have the cat o'nine tails extracted from its bag. The "cat" was a whip made of nine lengths of cord, each about 18 inches long with three knots at the end, all fixed to a rope handle. The cat caused serious injury, even death upon the victim. It is no longer carried on today's tall ships. The US Congress outlawed its use in 1850, and the British Royal Navy outlawed it in 1879. Now instead of the cat, *QE2* uses more subtle methods of discipline, such as exile to the Lido or exile to room service. Which is worse? I'll have to ask Mary.

As I made my way back to the room, I spotted one of the crew—a short, small, but happy Filipino—distributing barf bags on the trash cans by the elevators. We have a full ship for this segment—1,500 passengers or more—but you can't tell it by the public rooms. Everything is vacant. Because of the bad weather, most programs have been canceled and no one was about except for the innocents abroad who have never heard the cry "Faites vos jeux." They got a talk in the casino entitled, "Introduction to Gaming." I didn't go. I need a swim more.

Lo and behold, the Seven deck indoor pool is closed. Someone drained it. A red sign there announced that passengers are not permitted to use the pool. I gathered that. With no water, it's impossible to swim. I decided to go to the spa pool but found the same thing pertained there. It's closed and drained.

In the dry sauna, Leonard told me that they closed the Lido because "too many guests were falling. Too much stuff was spilling." Leonard said that they won't allow red wine at dinner for the same reason. No question about it. English humor is subtle. Leonard thought the sea is rough, but as an old salt, he has seen it much rougher.

Talk of wine reminded me of dinner, which reminded me of Rabbi. I gave Leonard a thumbnail sketch of Rabbi. The effect was electric. Leonard's face reddened. Leonard became irate. Leonard shook his fist and said, "Doesn't he realize there are starving people in this world? I never waste anything. It's a sin. It's our duty as passengers to tell people like him off. The crew can't do it. The crew remains restrained by their position. So WE MUST!"

Leonard seems liberated and enslaved by unexpected emotion. This was the first time I have seen any Brit expressing anger. They were capable of rage, I now realized, when the issue is big enough. Leonard comes from London and says all of his anti-Rabbi diatribe in a crisp very British accent, which makes it all sound extremely official, especially since we have gotten used to getting our daily instructions and orders from the bridge in the same stiff British accent.

I liked Leonard. But I know our friendship has a provisional quality, like so many friendships these days. People might buy another condominium and move to it, or else die, or more likely among *QE2*ers leave the ship when we all come home from the sea. The final test of a novel is our affection for it, as it is the test of our friends, and of anything else we can't define.

Leonard was right, of course. We, the passengers, must police our own. The crew can't do it. In a way, I'm sorry I didn't say anything to the Rabbi before we left the Caronia Restaurant. But I'm sure Rabbi sensed the negative vibes coming from my table to his. Wait a second! There is still time. Rabbi is still aboard. Next time I see him, I'll tell him off.

Day 33

Manila, the Philippines

NO GUTS, NO GLORY

oday started off with a lecture on the oceans, given by Dr. David Pawson, acting director of the National Museum of Natural History. Dr. Pawson has had made more than two hundred dives in research submarines. Waxing philosophically, Pawson told us there has always been a mysterious attraction between the oceans and our species. People who have noticed this suggest that there may have been a time when humans tried to be marine mammals, or at least lived much closer to the sea than we do now. This could explain our almost unconscious need to swim and play with water and the joy that such sport brings to us. On the other hand, our species remains curious about anything and everything, so I think it would be unlikely for that curiosity to neglect such a big part of our planet, the oceans.

What Pawson is probably getting at is that all life derives from the sea. Perhaps that is why we wish to return to it. We all carry our little seas around with us with our blood, because blood contains the exact mineral content of the Precambrian Ocean. Early oceans were freshwater. Later they got salty. Our skeletons are made of calcium carbonate, like coral rocks. Some land animals returned to the sea such as the turtle and the cetaceans, the whale and the seal. But we have not, not entirely and not like them.

Yes, the sea is our original mother. That makes *QE2* is our mother substitute. The oceans cover 75 percent of the Earth's surface. Sunlight penetrates to four hundred feet in the temperate zones, but goes down further in the tropics where the water is clear due to the absence of microscopic plants called plankton. David tells us he had read a newspaper a thousand feet under. I wonder where he got it, because we sure don't have them here on *QE2*. I sure would like to get some stock quotes, especially on Amgen. Ethel would love to read the *New York Times*.

The depth of the oceans averages 12,566 feet, and the water temperature varies usually in a narrow range from 30 to 38 degrees F. Below four hundred feet, it ranges pretty close to freezing. Animals exist deep down there, under tremendous pressure exceeding three tons per square inch. The pressure doesn't bother them because they have adapted to the environment and have become mostly water with very little flesh, a reason, David informed us, that most deep-sea animals are not good to eat. The orange ruffe stands as a remarkable exception, because it handles the pressure in a different way.

Our guide in Manila is Geraldine, a short, stocky brown-skinned woman with black hair and a blue dress. Geraldine wears dark, black sunglasses and likes to smoke Salem Lights. She looks like she came out of *Terry and the Pirates*, but she doesn't know that she should be using a long, black cigarette holder with a gold band. Geraldine says that Filipino women are like steel magnolias: They don't look like much, but they are strong. They have to be. The sex ratio here in Manila (incidentally the name Manila comes from a word, possibly from the Tagalog word, the Philippines language, meaning the place where the tall marsh grass grows) is three women to one man. Consequently, the ladies have trouble finding husbands to take care of them and they must work.

Geraldine tells us of the struggles of big-city life. A doctor makes only P5,000, or 5,000 pisos (*piso*, Philippines pesos), per month, about $200 in American money. A nurse makes 4,000 pisos. If that's what doctors and nurses earn, you can imagine what the average salary is in this sweltering, air-polluted city.

Our tour bus passed a neighborhood, consisting of small-roomed homes the size of M5 rooms, packed with kids and adults. I see a bent old woman in the street, carrying water in a number ten can. The woman passed some others, also in the street, bent over an open fire cooking soup. Their clothes, tattered and torn, speak for a kind of abject poverty.

The German philosopher Immanuel Kant said two things filled him with breathless awe: "The starry heavens, and the moral law." I can name a third that astonishes me all the more: the patience of the plundered poor.

The *QE2* passengers saw the abject poverty, but as far as I can tell, it didn't bother them. Geraldine noted my interest in the slum on the right and announced proudly that we were passing through a middle-class neighborhood!

Middle class! Neighborhood? I can only imagine what the timeless slums look like. No, change that. I can't imagine what they look like. Yet, despite the poverty, all the Filipinos have a happy, cheerful mood. They prove that riches don't necessarily ensure happiness—a fact proven on the *QE2* every day—and that poverty doesn't guarantee sadness—a fact proven in Manila every day.

A cherished institution, the Filipino jeepney fits in with the happy mood and keeps the happy mood going. The jeepney, a riotously decorated little bus that zips in and out of the chaotic traffic, evolved from the US Army jeeps left at the end of World War II. Geraldine says the name came from the combination of "jeep" and "honey." In the United States, we tend to shorten the word "honey" by saying, "Hon, would you mind getting me a Coors Light?" In the Philippines they shorten the word "honey" by using the last syllable and not the first, as in, "Ney, would you mind getting be me a San Mig [San Miguel, the beer of choice in Manila]?" Hence, a jeepney is a jeep-honey or a honey jeep.

Each of the 44,000 jeep-honeys is decorated similar to and different from one another, but each always has a silver horse on the front, which represents the girlfriend of the driver. Many silver horses indicate several girlfriends, possibly an adaptation to the sex ratio in town, or possibly a reflection of the kind of parallel or serial polygamy of the type we have in the United States, where men have mistresses or divorce one spouse to marry the next. Jeepney interiors have stereo music, handmade cushions, and pictures of Rudolph Valentino, Elvis Presley, and the Pope. Jeepneys, a vital and colorful part of Manila's transport system, are usually driven in a style that reminds me of hostile fairground *dodgem* (British for bumper cars). At least it's better than driving in the United States, which by and large is boring. But that is what we do. Most of American life consists of dully driving somewhere, and then dully driving back, wondering why the hell you went. Here in Manila, they make driving a spine-thrilling adventure.

Geraldine introduced Ernesto, our driver, who has thus far very skillfully avoided collision with at least 38,000 of the 44,000 jeepneys. Ernesto also answered to the name of Speedy, as in "Speedy, watch out on the left." Ernesto swerved right, and then thanked Geraldine. Then he took his eyes away from the road, swiveled his head around, to turn his face directly at us and shouted, "No guts, No glory."

We passed a street lined with hundreds of red-brown roasted pigs, glistening in the afternoon sun. The pigs still have the spit through their bodies. They are *Lechon*, the national dish. After the pigs, we came to the famous Chinese Hospital and Nursing School. Geraldine said that when things don't work out they press a button on the ward that automatically sends the body down a chute to our next stop, the Chinese Cemetery.

The Chinese Cemetery proves you can take it with you, some of it, anyway. The place looks like a village, except most of the residents are dead. Geraldine emphasized the word "most" because some people live in the cemetery. They are the servants that the very wealthy might need in the afterlife, gardeners and caretakers work full time keeping mausoleums the size of my home in shape. How poor and cheap and trivial these gewgaws and stewards for the dead seemed in presence of the solemnity, the grandeur, the awful majesty of Death.

A big sign on one of the streets announces "No practice driving," but Ernesto just keeps going, just missing a roadside chicken by swerving into the wrong lane.

Amazingly, even in the cemetery the pretense of keeping up class distinctions applies. They bury the ashes of the poor in little stone boxes on the edge of the road. The middle-class dead get into a suburban section, with mausoleums the size of the ones we passed roughly equivalent to a Mauretania accommodation. The multimillionaires end up on Millionaire Row, where the more luxurious accommodations for the dead have air-conditioning, running water, and toilets.

The bus stopped in front of a millionaire's villa, complete with kitchen, bedroom, living room, and study. A rather large staff was at work on the grounds. An armed guard rode up on a bicycle to the front gate to stop us from going in. In view of the .357 magnum revolver hanging from his waist holster, we *QE2* tourists decided to explore other places on Millionaire Row. We are curious to see how millionaires live after they are dead. None of us is eager to join them. None of us is eager to buy. Few of us can afford the accommodations. I know I can't.

Chickens and roosters hang out among the mortuary monuments. They are attached to ropes and tied down to stakes in the ground. The roosters crow a lot, giving an eerie feeling that the dead might awake any minute. And that is why they are there. Chinese ghosts, true to the mercantile spirit of their race, would not grant any petition until some return favor was guaranteed, such as a sacrificed chicken or rooster, which, for convenience, is close at hand.

Among the fantastic houses of the dead, the home that struck me belonged to a certain Robert Tan. Robert devoted his life to organizing volunteer firefighters in the area, gave his money to the cause, and even donated a fire truck. He died, as you probably guessed, from an injury sustained in a fire. Something fell on him, but it doesn't say what or where it hit. Like most Chinese cemeteries, they have Robert's picture on the tablet in front of his home. He looks Chinese and serious, with long, dark hair that falls over both shoulders. His black eyes stare out at us from dark skeletal sockets, as if to reproach us. He helped his fellows. Are we doing the same? Next to the picture, I see a mailbox. "That's for the electric and water bills," says Geraldine while puffing pensively on a Salem. "The dead don't read their mail. At least, they haven't yet."

Poor Robert. He is dead for eternity, and by eternity I don't mean for endless time, but for no time whatever. Infinity of time does not mean time without end. It means for time that time has ended, that has ceased to exist. Robert entered a world where event fails to follow event. For him, nothing further happens, nothing at all. Meanwhile, out here in the world of the living, others inconveniently insist on dying and being born and getting sick. Looking down the streets as far as I can see for miles and endless miles there are more and more homes for the dead. With Dante and T. S. Eliot, I had not realized that death had undone so many. Undoubtedly there will be a great terrible muddle when, and if, the resurrection comes.

We headed out to the Manila Cathedral, the only air-conditioned cathedral in the Philippines. But today, says Geraldine, the air-conditioning is not working. Perhaps we should complain to the archbishop. A sign on the inside notifies us that the archbishop is named *Sin*. Knowing a little Mandarin helps. Geraldine explains: Sin means "new" in Chinese. Sin has nothing whatever to do with sin.

Manila's biggest park honors the memory of Dr. José Rizal, the nationalist leader condemned to die before a Spanish firing squad in 1896. Something is always going on in Rizal Park, just as it usually is going on in New York City's Central Park. Much of what is going on will remain unsolved and unpunished.

After Rizal Park, we visited the fort where the Rizal shrine stands. Just in front of the shrine is a large white cross beneath which a plaque states that six hundred Filipinos were burned alive there by the Japanese just before the Japanese surrendered to the Americans and ended World War II. The sign said, "The memories of all these unknown victims of Japanese atrocities will live forever in the hearts and minds of the Filipino people."

The Japanese *QE2*ers walked away. Good thing they did, because Geraldine explained that the Japanese were pretty clever at devising tortures. She showed us the chamber that periodically flooded with the high tide. The victim had a few hours to talk or the incoming tide would gradually inundate him. I tried to image what it would be like to sit crunched in that small chamber as the seawater begins to pour into the room, knowing that soon the tidal action of the moon would induce my doom.

Dr. José Rizal, the Philippines' national hero, was born in Calamba, a province of Laguna, in 1861. He finished his Bachiller en Artes at Ateno Municipal de Manila, earned a degree in philosophy and letters at the University of Santo Tomás, and subsequently studied medicine at the Universidad Central de Madrid. He came back to his island home and practiced medicine, ophthalmology, and dentistry, in addition to writing two novels, *Noli Me Tangere* and *El Filibusterismo*, both depicting the cruelties of the Spanish friars and other defects of the Spanish administration. For the crime of publishing two revolutionary novels, the Spanish arrested him, sentenced him after being tried in a kangaroo court, and shot him in the back, the usual punishment for traitors. Ordinary criminals get shot in the front. During a vigil on the night before his death, he wrote a poem that he concealed in an alcohol lamp, which was then smuggled out by his mother and subsequently read nationwide. The rest of Philippine history, especially in relation to the United States, fascinates me, but as Dante says, "I am constrained by art and about that may speak no more."

For 35 pisos I buy Rizal's poem. Here are the first lines of the untitled poem, which has come to be known as, "Mi Último Adiós," Spanish for "My Last Farewell."

> Land that I love—farewell! O land the sun loves!
> Pearl in the sea of the Orient: Eden lost to your blood!
> Gaily go I to present you this hapless hopeless life;
> Were it more brilliant, has it more freshness, more bloom:
> still for you would I give it—would give it for your good.

After dinner, Ethel and I met Nathan, our friend from the Caronia Restaurant. He had come to the Philippines Cultural Historical Society show in the Grand Lounge. Nathan didn't have a chair, so he asked the Chinese woman next to me to remove her pocketbook and cane from the seat next to her so that he could sit. The Chinese woman said that she was saving the seat for her husband. Nathan jumped up when he heard that. But then Nathan turned on her. She wore no wedding ring. She had no husband. Nathan sat down again. The woman made a huff. As he doesn't exist, her husband never came.

Nathan gave us the report on Caronia. They isolated the Rabbi by putting non-English-speaking passengers all around him. All the English-speaking passengers had requested reassignment after seeing this jerk in action for two days. "The problem seems contained," Nathan said. "Rabbi's surliness is still based on his power to limit experience," Nathan said, but couldn't give me any specifics because he and Estelle had also asked for and got reassigned eight tables' distance from the Rabbi.

I told Nathan how much we liked the Chinese Cemetery, and Nathan told me the story of the wife who wanted a mausoleum for a birthday present. Her husband considered the request rather unusual, but decided to do it. The wife was pleased with the building of white marble, with two large cedar trees in front. The following year, when her birthday came, she got nothing. "Dear," she inquired, "why didn't you get me something for my birthday?" The husband replied, "You didn't use last year's gift."

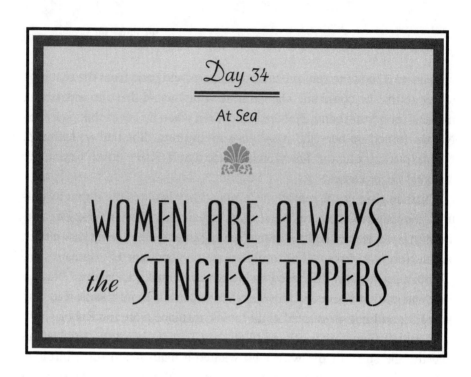

Day 34

At Sea

WOMEN ARE ALWAYS *the* STINGIEST TIPPERS

*Q*E2 entered equatorial waters and the weather is great. Smooth seas, and clear skies, and no wind. Perfect! Ethel and I feel no shake, shimmy, pitch, yaw, or roll, so we don't even know we're moving unless we look outside either of our two portholes and see the sea skipping behind us.

Yes, we have two portholes now and our two beds are together, with each about 20 percent wider and longer than we had on Four deck or Five deck. We also have two chairs, so Ethel and I no longer rotate who sits in the chair. Wonder of wonders, we have a bathtub and the bathroom easily fits the two of us at the same time, and could fit several others, too. Living space more than doubled when we moved to this heaven from cabin 4164. Now we are wondering how we ever got along below.

But into every life a little rain must fall. I still can't plug in the Water Pik.

I started reading *The Innocents Abroad* by Mark Twain. The story concerns the steamship *Quaker City*'s pleasure excursion, starting June 8,

8, 1867, to Europe and the Holy Land. Twain described the countries, nations, incidents, and adventures, as they appeared to him, the author. Mark Twain mentions little about onboard life. All that I found about his cabin was, "Below deck was a square cabin of which the walls bulged out in the form of cots above a circular divan; in the center was a table equipped with a swinging lamp. The accommodation was confined but neat." Twain's information density about his ship and cabin isn't much, but it's enough to conclude that Ethel and I have a better cabin than Mark Twain did. We also have it better, a thousand times better, than those middle-class people we saw in Manila, and a million million times better than the millionaires buried in the Chinese Cemetery.

Another wonder of wonders, we had a videotape player, but it didn't work. Perhaps it is working, but as so often happens these days between us and electrical devices, we can't work it. We'll ask Tracy our room stewardess to help.

While discussing our advancement to Two deck, I should cover the changes in restaurant status. I'll review the food at some later time. I'll cover the restaurant decor now.

Starting with the table and working out, I find the table in Princess Grill measures two hundred square inches larger in surface area than the table in Caronia, a thing that makes it possible for us to have more things on top including an eighteen-inch crystal Christmas tree-shaped center ornament with an overhead light beaming directly on it. This gives off a wondrous bright sparkling mixtures of white and sometimes faint rainbows lights, all glinting and glistening especially during the evening meal. Unlike the Caronia, where the cut flowers on the table are miniature carnations—usually pink but sometimes white or red—the flowers in Princess Grill are small orchids. Here the flowers reside not in glass, but in a fine bone china vase, another touch of elegance.

The Princess table itself has been bolted to the floor, so it moves with the ship and not by itself. The seats are banked sofas, heavily cushioned and much more comfortable and larger than what we sat on in the Caronia. All the glasses we see are fine-cut lead crystal. The fine bone china, by Doulton, heavyweight silverware from EPNS, and the fine thick white tablecloth complete the idea and actuality of luxury. All the changes we detected are small, but biased in the same direction hinted toward luxury and away from the commonplace.

Our two waiters handle our table and two other tables, for a total of fourteen passengers who usually arrive serially. Usually Ethel and I arrived first, and the others followed. The Lus, a nice Chinese family of four, who occupied the table next to ours, sometimes beat us in for breakfast and lunch, but, chowhounds that we are, we always beat them for supper.

Today, our headwaiter, Jon, has a bruise on his right forehead from football practice. His young assistant, Alex, has no bruise and looked like he had never seen or touched a football in his life. Alex sports lots of gold rings and bracelets and things. Both Jon and Alex are formal waiters, but Alex remained a little less formal than Jon. Both are incredibly efficient at anticipating what we want and bring things out as fast or as slowly as we need them. Always they and Robert, the restaurant manager, and Alan, the assistant, check on us each and every meal to inquire if we liked the food and the service, and to see if we need anything. This kind of luxury spoils us rotten, but we have to live with it at least for the next twelve days until we move up to the Queens Grill.

The general layout of the Princess Grill makes for more intimate dining. Tables stand much farther from one another but, despite that, we feel the atmosphere is warmer, cozier. The warm russet colors might create this effect, and the art deco lighting and the marvelous four life-sized statues on the four corners of the sunken dining room. These statues are true works of art, unique. Each of them represents an ancient element: Earth, Fire, Water, Air. And each is constructed entirely of things from the sea, like paua shells, pink corals, sand, and such. Two are male figures and two female. The female that I like the best faces me as I eat. She has a nice face with sweeping hair. She stands nude, with a pixie face, sweeping hair, and small pocket-sized breasts, and so as I enter or leave the dining room by the spiral staircase near the Princess elevator I can't help admiring her beautiful rounded bottom. Her beauty approaches the redemptive quality of art. This is the female form; it attracts with an undeniable attraction. A small golden card at her feet says she is Water by Janine Jane. The female Earth figure on the other side of the dining room, I can't see from my seat, but the two male figures, Fire and Air, are up close with Air made of paua shells glistening over me watching me eat. Air has wings so I assume he is Icarus, the son of Daedalus, who was provided with wings of wax and feathers by his father during their escape from the Labyrinth of Minos.

The other male figure who watches over the Chinese Lu family has a chest of red corals and pantaloons of intricate white reef coral. I wonder how long Fire will last since his pants look so fragile.

Today, I decided to correct my long-term deficiency and went to learn word processing using Microsoft Word and windows. Matt, the instructor, is a serious redheaded man of about thirty-five years with a crew cut. He teaches the course three times today.

I reported at 9:30 AM for the first session, but before we got started, I stumbled onto something important. Passengers have written letters home using the computer. They stored the letters on the hard drive. Margo, a passenger living in London, who is my partner at the computer, and I started to read.

Letter one, written by a young woman named Betty who claims membership in a club called the Mariners, started off by saying that Matt is so handsome she can't keep her eyes off of him and she can't concentrate on the lessons he gives. In Ensenada, Betty invited Matt for a drink, and found, to her disappointment, that Matt is a Christian Brother who has taken the vow of chastity. Matt travels and rooms with another brother, Mark, who Betty complains is always nearby, so she doesn't get a real chance to work on Matt. Betty is convinced Matt needs a woman badly. Betty said she has searched the ship and as yet has not found Luke or John.

"Could this be true?" I asked Margo.

"It sounds true in most particulars. He is a most handsome man," Margo said in that British accent we have come to know so well. "Let's read another."

The next letter is in French, which Margo can't read, but I can. I translated for Margo that this monsieur says that he has had several small affairs so far onboard. "Typically French," says Margo. "Click on another."

But Margo and I can't read any more because Matt has started his lecture and demonstration. He covers the main features and within twenty minutes I found myself writing by word processing. This has to be the greatest advance in the history of writing since the printing press. I can now type away, print, underline, place in bold, italicize, cut, copy, paste, spell-check, use the thesaurus, search, and justify text with ease.

Matt then asked the group to write a short account of some event related to Hong Kong. Margo looked at me and smiled. "Here's your chance."

I began: The World of Suzie Wong has not entirely disappeared I discovered yesterday during my trip to Wan Chai on the upper deck of the Star Ferry. I spotted her when she came through the turnstile. She wore her hair tied behind her head in a ponytail and she wore green jeans, green knee-length denim jeans. That's odd. Why would a Chinese girl wear jeans when the rest had cotton pajama suits? She differed from the rest. I knew because after our eyes met, she stole furtive glances now and then my way. She exchanged a small coin for some exotic red fruit covered with red tentacles which I later learned was called a rambutan. I watched her use scarlet nails to slit the skins and insert the white central fruit between her even white teeth.

Matt then told us to type "love and kisses" and then duplicate it many, many times. I broke off my story and did that. Then for fun I blew up the words "even white teeth" and placed the giant letters of those words in Gothic italics. "Teeth" now stood out on the paper, looking rather ominous. Margo looked at me, disappointed. "What happened next?" she asked.

"I don't know. I haven't thought about it yet. Maybe he'll ask her what that fruit is. But, alas, I know she won't talk with him. Chinese girls don't do that. At least good Chinese girls don't do that."

"Dress her differently. Make her bad," Margo commanded.

Since Margo and I are light-years ahead of the gray heads, we have to wait. So, I amuse Margo with more story. She wore a cheongsam, a Chinese female costume with a high-collared fitting sheath with side slits and usually made of silk. It had rich embroidery of peonies, lotuses, dragons, and phoenixes on its collar, sleeves, and sides. Made exactly formfitting in soft red silk, its front, back, and side views add up to a star-tling panorama of the entire landscape of the female form. She took the trouble to maximize the cheongsam's impact with appurtenances of a pair of stiletto heels, a sequined purse, jade beads, a silk fan, and large silk peonies and orchids for pinning on her shoulder. The color of course is red, the color of happiness, prosperity, and good luck—red, red, red—with small green bamboo patterns and delicate piping of exactly the same shade of green as the collar, sleeves, and hem.

When the lesson ended, Matt came up to me and apologized for going so slowly. He said he could tell I was a fast learner, but he had to keep the pace slow enough for the others to catch on. "What?" I told him. "I learned plenty and I learned it plenty fast." I pointed to my story and the page of printout that showed the words "even white teeth" in 32 point italics. Matt may have thought I have a teeth fetish, but I explained I just wanted to show off for Margo how I could put some teeth into the "teeth."

This afternoon, from the hot tub, I noticed the Rabbi and Mrs. Rabbi on deck, looking out over the eternal sea and admiring the sunset. Unknown to them, Mary had come up behind them. She had a large plastic bottle in her right hand and just stood there behind them with the bottle paused over Rabbi's head. I don't know what Mary was thinking. But I know what I was thinking. I was thinking that the blue liquid was gasoline and that Mary was about to immolate the Rabbi.

Mary bowed her head, lowered the plastic bottle out of sight, turned, and left. Perhaps Mary was thinking that the fire might hurt Mrs. Rabbi and therefore it would not be morally justified since Mrs. Rabbi also numbers among the oppressed.

Mrs. Lonelyhearts, the woman with the beautiful breasts, who prob-ably has Prince Charles as her marriage counselor, joined me in the hot tub. She wore the same see-through bathing suit. This time I noticed her nipples were not erect. Instead, they looked like little miniature hats stuck on some exotic fruits the size of musk mellons. She told me that she could leave her key on the hot tub rail and I could take it and meet her in fifteen minutes in her room. Mrs. Lonelyhearts, I realized, didn't come to *QE2* for concerts, plays, opera, or gambling. She came because she sought an outlet for erotic eagerness. When I refused, Mrs. Lonelyhearts whispered in my ear, "If things work out, I'll tip you one hundred dollars. I do that for the men I like who do it right."

"Jesus! Women are the stingiest tippers," I told her. "Money spooks them."

The episode reminded me of Captain Robert Arnott's story in *Captain of the Queen*, about the wealthy wife who, after dancing on the Mauretania tables, offered $1,000 to any man who was man enough to take her to bed. There were no takers. For her own protection, Captain Arnott had the woman put ashore the next morning. Rich, beautiful wives can be as dangerous as anyone else when jealous passions are aroused.

Mrs. Lonelyhearts got out of the tub and wiggled her beautiful bottom at me as she made her way across the deck to talk with the handsome steward, who, I can tell, is interested. Perhaps the pain of one man's refusal will be buried in the pleasure of the next.

In point of fact, I should be more sympathetic. Lonelyhearts is no more responsible for her behavior than our cat, P.J., when she is in heat. But Lonelyhearts faces fearful odds, with the two-women-to-one-man ratio among passengers. And what's the big deal? She just needs her horns trimmed and she is willing to pay. If I don't do it, someone else will. When you think on it, her drifting toward the crew is as natural as the morning sun. That's where the men are.

Day 35

At Sea

POWERED by POWDERED MEMBRUM VIRILE of TIGER

*W*e crossed the equator today. We are happy that we have left those Chinese seas that are usually boisterous and subject to terrible gales of wind, especially around the equinoxes.

Happy? More than that. We are ecstatic. Traveling slowly unwinds you fast. Ethel and I have totally relaxed. This cruise is a vacation, and a complete change of scenery, environment, and people. It is an antidote to the stresses and strains of contemporary life ashore. It offers a chance to relax and unwind in comfortable surroundings, with attentive service, good food, and a ship that changes the scenery for you as you go. You don't even have to drive. It is virtually a hassle-free, and more important, a crime-free vacation.

Because we crossed the equator, we received a certificate from Captain John Burton-Hall. This was our n^{th} time, but other passengers crossing for the first time got the King Neptune ceremony. The presence of the sea god Neptune hung over the ceremony, requiring a sacrifice. The crew tossed volunteer passengers into the pool with their clothes on. I know a few of the crew who would have liked to do that to Rabbi, but Rabbi did not volunteer.

The equator, zero latitude, which is equally distant from both the North and South poles, marks the Earth at its maximum circumference, like a belt strapped around the midsection of a rather round man. To circumnavigate the globe you would have to travel twenty-five thousand miles. The planet's diameter at zero latitude measures 7,927 miles, so if you dug a hole in order to get to the other side, it would take that many miles. It is a distance I find rather small, especially compared to what we have already traveled. We inhabit a small planet, indeed.

And so QE2 entered the Southern Hemisphere, the antipodes. Aristotle knew the Earth was round and postulated that there was a landmass in the Southern Hemisphere to counterbalance the land in the Northern Hemisphere. Aristotle called the landmass Australia, *austral* meaning southern. Aristotle also said there was a polar ice cap in the southern limit of the Earth, which he called Antarctica, meaning that which is opposite the Arctic.

Because there is little wind at equatorial latitudes, the ship moves along smooth as silk and sunlight reflects on the sea's surface like lozenges of silver. Most times we are under the illusion that we are not moving at all. Thus, the QE2 is a wonderful luxury hotel until we hit the deck and see differently, that we are actually at sea.

During lecture, Dr. Pawson confirmed that the Loch Ness monster is a hoax. The man who photographed the monster confessed on his deathbed that he fabricated the famous photograph showing the beast. Giant sea squids are real, though. Pawson showed us several photos of these monsters and their large body parts. Giant squids grow to over sixty feet, have ten tentacles, and have two eyes the size of dinner plates. Whales like to eat them, and many giant sea squids have beached or been spotted off the coast of Newfoundland where whales hang out. Pawson also showed us pictures of mysterious sea blobs, large masses of formless organic material that, now and then, roll up onto beaches. No one knows what these are, but they definitely derive from some sort of animal life. Pawson showed one blob that might have been the decaying flesh of a very large shark, but the other blobs remain a mystery.

Next lecture: Pilot Foley's story of the *Bounty*. Captain Bligh was commissioned to get breadfruits from Tahiti and then bring them to the West Indies to provide cheap food for the slaves. He set sail from Tahiti and a few days out to sea the crew mutinied. Bligh and his loyal seamen were put to sea in a small boat. Amazingly, that boat and Bligh made it over three thousand miles to Timor, the easternmost island of the Lesser Sundas, between the Timor Sea, Savu, and the southern part of the Malay Archipelago, in a trip that took seven weeks. From Timor, Bligh returned to England. People blamed Bligh for the trouble, but an English court cleared him of all charges and subsequently he was promoted. Eventually, Bligh became a governor of Queensland, one of the largest states in Australia. Fletcher Christian and the mutineers returned to Tahiti, and after a few months there, they set out again to find a safe place to hide. They rested at Pitcairn Island, where their descendents still live. They burned the *Bounty* there.

The British admiralty sent another ship, the *Pandora*, to arrest the mutineers. Captain Edwards, a cruel man much more like the fictional Bligh of the movies, captured some of them on Tahiti and placed seventeen men in a deck prison no larger than our M5 cabin. Edwards and the *Pandora* then set out again for Fletcher Christian, who eluded capture. During the search, the *Pandora* hit a reef in the Torres Strait and sank. Four of the prisoners died and the other thirteen made it back to England. Three of them were hanged and the other ten got off. Finally, another ship was sent to get the breadfruit and this time it arrived in the West Indies. The trees grew well, but the slaves refused to eat breadfruit because the slaves said it tasted bad. Actually, they meant it had no taste, for it is an insipid fruit.

Of greater interest is what happened to Fletcher Christian and his colony on Pitcairn. The Tahitian men killed all the British men except for two, who then killed the Tahitians. When the colony was eventually discovered, only Allen, the last survivor, a bunch of native women, and lots of half-caste children remained. Allen never told the details of what happened, who killed whom and why. Something went seriously awry, but we will never know what.

In the pool, I spotted Matt, the debonair Christian Brother who teaches computer class. I swam with him and told him about the letters I read from the hard disks, including the one from Betty, who is in love with him. Appalled, Matt told me he would erase the letters today.

Matt had a theory about Rabbi. He thinks Rabbi needs psychotherapy, and, in fact, he was undergoing psychotherapy prior to the cruise, but the psychiatrist couldn't take Rabbi anymore. The psychiatrist needed a rest. So the psychiatrist told Rabbi to take a cruise. "Not a bad theory," I told Matt.

On the way to dinner, Ethel and I took the same elevator as the *QE2* tourist who talked to himself while we were in Taiwan and Japan. He's still hard at it. Neither Ethel nor I can fathom what he is saying. This time we can't even identify the language. He seemed to be saying "Yumkee, Yumkee."

We passed by a box marked "Litter" by the elevator door. Ethel read the sign and said, "Lots of litter, but no cats. I wonder how P.J. is doing?" I tried to cheer Ethel up by saying, "P.J. never taught us anything of importance beyond a few pointers on the art of relaxation. We're learning much more from the onboard lecturers."

Ethel stared at me. For a moment we both felt sad, but later at dinner in the Princess Grill we cheered up. The Four Elements, the statues I love, surround us as we eat. The four elements constitute a Western idea, whereas the Eastern nations have five elements, the fifth element being Heaven.

My dining room mission of waist expansion is interrupted by our Chinese dining neighbors. The Chinese, I've noticed around the world, seem to be born with an inherent gift for sheer hard work. But these Chinese, the Lus, also like to eat.

The Lus told us that they are here for a segment, Hong Kong to Australia. The ultimate classic voyage for any experienced traveler is a world cruise, but segmenting, or traveling for only part of the total world cruise, is ideal for those who wish to be a part of a world cruise but have neither the time nor the money for the prolonged extravagance of a three- to-four month vacation.

The older son, Jack Lu, came over and sat with me. He wants to go into medicine and study in the United States. I advised him where to inquire and then I spoke Chinese to him. He had lots of trouble understanding his own language, but he finally realized that I was speaking Chinese.

We ended the night watching *Miami Rhapsody* with Mia Farrow and Antonio Banderas. There is no credit line for the screenplay, but I know Mia wrote it because it sounds and looks like a Woody Allen film. Mia probably wanted to prove that she, not Woody, writes the stuff for the many films Mia and Woody did together. Like most of Woody's films, the topic covered is relationships between the sexes. I liked the part where Mia's tired but still loving husband says apologetically, "I'm getting old. When you are my age, it takes a volcano to light a match."

The Chinese have solutions to this rather common problem: ginseng-soaked snake wine, powdered rhinoceros horn mixed with spit of swallow and dried, and powdered membrum virile of tiger.

Forget the powdered tiger penis. I have a better solution—cruise on *QE2*.

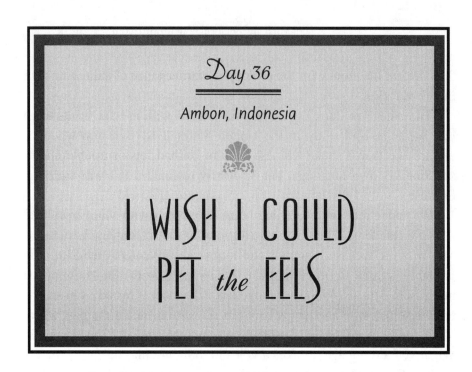

Day 36

Ambon, Indonesia

I WISH I COULD PET *the* EELS

*W*e awoke to exotic music in a foreign key that wafted into the cabin from the dock. We looked out our porthole. A *gamelan* orchestra, an ensemble of metallophones, xylophones, drums, and gongs, played on the dock, circling and circling with melody. My Western ear awaits a conclusion that never comes. This type of music has a melody supported by rhythm in the background, but harmonics don't exist. The note scale differs from our own, too, and unlike a Western orchestra, I can clearly hear each individual instrument. Indonesian music was never written down, and people just learned it from one generation to the next, an out-of-tune gift from prehistory.

I had a nightmare last night. I dreamed *QE2* struck a barrier reef and the alarm bells sounded, seven short blasts followed by a long one, meaning the ship was sinking. I managed to save my floppy disk from the computer before the ship started listing.

"But what about me?" Ethel asked about my dream.

"You were sleeping so soundly, I didn't want to disturb you," I replied, shrugging my shoulders.

"You're tired of cruising," Ethel said. "Else, you wouldn't have sunk the ship!"

"I don't think it's that. It's just an anxiety dream about sinking, based on Pilot Foley's lecture that told us that thousands of ships have sunk in these waters. What happened to them could happen to us."

Beyond the Ambon docks stretched a tired worn-out little town of about two hundred thousand people. It was bombed to pieces during World War II and rebuilt in a hurry in modern third-world slum style, with small stucco-walled homes and roofs of rusted corrugated tin. Beyond the Indonesian town hangs the vastly contoured mountains and hills covered with dense, lush green. The rainfall averages 3,450 mm, or 136 inches, per year, making Ambon four times rainier than drizzly Seattle. Rain also makes the flowers grow in abundance, so the air here smells fresh, with a breath of perfume in it. The average wage here is 2,000 rupiahs a month, or one American dollar. Could that be right? With what I have in my wallet right now I could feed a whole village for ten years.

Spices from Ambon used to be in great demand, because of their ability to help make spoiled food taste better. With refrigeration, preservatives, and ultrahigh-temperature pasteurization, spices are not in great demand. Ambon suffered accordingly. Looking around, it's hard to believe that Maluku, once called the Moluccas, had been fought over. And what was the fighting for? Spices, mainly cloves and nutmeg. The cloves are the flowers of a special tree that grows here in abundance, and the nutmeg also comes from a tree. The volcanic island of Ternate to the north claims the oldest clove tree in the world. After four hundred years, this tree still produces half a ton of cloves every year.

In Ambon Town there is a statue of Thomas Pattimura, shown brandishing a cutlass. He led a failed nineteenth-century rebellion against the Dutch. Just before his execution, the unruffled Pattimura is reputed to have told his captors, "Have a pleasant stay here, gentlemen."

Another startling statue in front of Ambon's Roman Catholic cathedral shows Saint Francis Xavier, who once visited Ambon. The statue depicts the saint upholding a cross while a giant crab at his feet offers him a small crucifix. Xavier, the first Jesuit missionary, touched base in the Moluccas in the 1540s on his way to try to convert the Japanese to Catholicism. Being granted sainthood is not a recognition of an earthy honor; it is a recognition of the fact of God's will that the person in question has been admitted into heaven.

On the opposite side of town, the ANZAC War Cemetery provides a resting place for more than two thousand troops from New Zealand, Australia, India, and the Netherlands killed during the Japanese invasion and occupation. Waldemar got choked up when he tried to explain what happened to over seventy men there. I don't blame Waldemar. The thing is so terrible, so horribly bizarre, that even I can't talk about it. It surpasses the immolation of the six hundred Allied prisoners in Manila. The evil deeds of the evil Japanese will remain long in the local memory. Add Ambon to the list of places, including China, Korea, and the Philippines, where the Japanese have few friends.

We descended the gangway. Dancing maidens greeted us with red roses. We climbed into the coaches for sightseeing and shopping. Our time was limited, so we got only a small taste of the country, but it was enough time to arouse our appetite, or in the case of Ambon, to extinguish it.

Mael, our guide for today, has trouble with English, so things come out rather strangely. For instance, Mael told us the present government has a policy to "overcome the poor." Sounds like the Republicans must be in charge. The bus made way through tropical jungles and mud-covered roads, proof that we are in a third-world country in which there are a lot of poor to overcome. It's bad, but I've seen worse in Kenya and Cambodia.

About thirty kilometers northeast of Ambon Town, on the Hitu peninsula, stands a weird sight—a pool of eels at the village of Waai, a hive of huts one story high and as square as dried goods boxes. All over the town one finds melancholy young boys shouting, "*Baksheesh!*" Such boys didn't really expect a cent, but they had learned to say that before they learned to say mother. *Baksheesh* has no English equivalent. It means something for nothing. One of these days I am going to surprise them and toss lots of money their way and see what they do.

The eel keeper, standing in the ice-cold clear water, invites the eels out of the small caves that line the pool. If the eels don't want to come out, he bribes them with a raw chicken egg, a great delicacy as far as the eels are concerned. The eels are treated with the greatest deference, because they are thought to embody the spirits of island ancestors. An entrenched superstition says that any time the eels go away, something terrible will happen to the villagers. I believe it, because any pollution will ruin the freshwater supply for the village. Downstream we see women washing clothes in the water. It seems a shame to ruin such a beautiful stream with soap suds.

There are two kinds of sacred eels, black and white. The black are more common and therefore less esteemed, considered only half holy. The white eels, of which I see two coaxed out of their lairs by the keeper, are larger, measuring over four feet. They have bigger, meaner mouths with more prominent teeth. The keeper pets the eels on the bellies and then caresses their backs. I'm jealous. I wish I could pet the eels.

Before getting back on *QE2*, I bought a collection of flag pins, one pin for each country that the world cruise will visit. I'll wear the flag of the country we're visiting on my jacket for dinner, starting with Indonesia, working to Australia, and, after that, around the world.

In the hot tub, I got to talk with the two men and two women who annoyed most of us today by repeatedly diving into the pool and splashing water all about. The signs that hang poolside all say no diving, but these rogues and rowdies paid no attention. They are two couples, one from New Zealand and the other from Australia. The New Zealanders are unmarried and traveling together, something we have seen a lot of on *QE2*, and the other couple hails from a small mining town west of Perth, Australia.

The larger man from the second couple, the Australian, whispered something in my ear that I couldn't understand. I explained that I understood English, or at least I thought I did. "Could you speak slower?" I asked. He spoke slowly in English, but mispronounced in the Australian way. The rogue complained that the deck steward had words with him and had told them not to dive in the pool. They might have hurt themselves because the pool in one area was only five feet deep.

The woman from New Zealand winked at me, as the Australian suddenly gave the unsettling smile of a con man. "Tomorrow," he said, "I shall defy the ban by diving off the top deck railing and descend twenty-two feet into the pool. That will teach them!"

"Get real drunk before you do it," I advised.

"Drunk? What on earth for?"

"When you break your neck, it won't hurt as much," I explained. "And if you're drunk, people will blame the alcohol and not your stupidity."

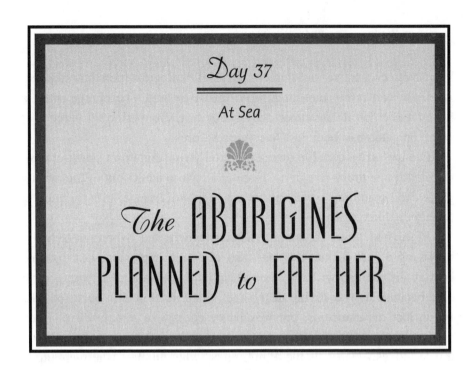

Day 37

At Sea

The ABORIGINES PLANNED to EAT HER

The sea remains so calm and smooth that Ethel and I keep forgetting we are sailing along on top of an ocean over two miles deep. That ocean reminds me of Dr. Pawson's lecture "The Sea Provides, But for How Much Longer?"

The news isn't good. Fishery yields, unlike the American stock market, have declined enormously. Take that blue-finned tuna, for instance. They fetch lots of money, especially in Japan, where one seven-hundred-pounder the previous year had sold for $67,000. With that kind of money at stake, the hunting becomes fierce and uses all the tools of modern technology, such as sonar, air surveillance, large nets (some twenty miles long), and fishing boats that are factories, capable of processing 550 tons of fish per day. The numbers of lobsters, oysters, and scallops are dropping fast as well. Halibut fishing is so far down that the law allows fishing for halibut only two days a year. In the days of colonial America, cod swam in abundance and measured six to eight feet long. Now cod are so rare that commercial fishing for them has stopped. A caught cod rarely measures more than two feet. The orange ruffe, a fleshy, tasty fish unlike other deep-water fish, dropped to 50 percent of what the catch had been just five years before.

Orange ruffes can live over a hundred years, and don't start to reproduce until age thirty-five or so. Fishing all those adults out of the mating game can do nothing but devastate the supply of orange ruffe for another twenty or thirty years.

More bad news. Dynamite fishing, where the fisherman actually blows up a reef to harvest dead fish after the explosion, destroys the habitat and the fish with the same blast. One of Pawson's friends almost died because he was diving near a reef when a detonation occurred. His friend lost his eardrums, but was lucky enough to remain alive. Even more worrisome is cyanide poisoning, popular in waters north of Australia and especially in the Philippines, wherein the fishermen piped cyanide into the reef to stun or kill the fish. The process also killed the coral, since they are only one-celled animals.

Further bad news: the hunting of whales has prevented the natural deaths of these gigantic animals. The whale carcasses used to fall to the sea bottom and remained there, preserved by the near freezing temperatures. Thus, the preserved whale flesh kept millions of small fish in food for decades.

Pawson's voice remains calm, matter-of-fact, and scientific. That makes the facts even more disquieting, because I realize what he said is true and not media hype.

"Think on it," Pawson tells us. "No one believed the passenger pigeon would become extinct. In fact, there was a time when the skies in the United States blackened with passenger pigeons. A time when people chopped down oak trees to get to ten thousand nests in that one tree to eat the squabs. Passenger pigeons—once there were billions and now there are none. The same almost was the weary fate of the American buffalo. Once there were fifteen million. Now there are a few thousand."

What was the solution?

Dr. Pawson doesn't know, but he does think the problem needs to be addressed intelligently. Salmon management has worked in the northwestern United States. Perhaps the same approach could be applied to the deep-sea fish. Aquaculture had a future for freshwater fish, but so far hadn't worked for deep-ocean fish. They need too much space to roam and feed, and they have very special mating requirements. Obviously, dynamite and cyanide fishing must stop.

I tried to comprehend the bigger picture, to think of what all this means in terms of the world economy. Since China and Japan use most of the world's fish supplies and are fairly dependent on them, a reduction in fish must impact those two countries the most. That spells trouble for them and trouble for the rest of us.

"What does it mean for you?" I asked Ethel.

"While there is still time, I should order halibut for dinner," she replied.

QE2 entered Torres Strait, the small neck of water that stands between Papua New Guinea on the north and Queensland, Australia, on the south. This strait was once a land bridge connecting Asia with the Australian continent. Then the sea rose, or the land sank—scientists haven't decided which—and the land bridge disappeared. The submerged mountains, granite rocks, and other land features that lie under the sea provide an ideal nesting place for coral. Coral is found here in abundance. The Great Barrier Reef that hugs the eastern shore of Australia has a similar history that provides the same continental underpinnings for its coral. To the east of the reef lies the great Coral Sea, which figured large in the sea battles of World War II.

Some of the rock and granite islands we pass on our starboard side are inhabited and some are not. All look bleak, old, worn out, and desolate, just like the Australian continent that lies behind them. Pilot Foley reminded us that the natives of Torres Strait hunted heads not long ago, and, in fact, traded human heads and shells for dugout canoes. The stark evidence shows that many ships that went aground here discharged passengers into the hands of the natives, who kept the passengers alive, tethered or caged like farm animals, until they were ready for the pot. That sounds like a most inauspicious ending for a cruise.

Sometimes a cruise passenger so discharged might find luck, as in the case of Barbara Thompson, who lost her husband when her ship sank and who was captured by Aborigines. They planned to eat her, but the chief of the tribe recognized Barbara as the reincarnated spirit of his daughter. Barbara lived among the natives for four years until she was rescued by another ship. By the time the rescuers arrived, she was as tan as the tribespeople, but unlike the others she cried out in proper English that she felt ashamed she was naked.

A famous cruise ship, the *Quiter*, which had its own following like *QE2*, sank in these waters in 1890. At Cape York, the ship hit a submerged rock, which tore a large hole in its bottom. Within three minutes the *Quiter* quit, falling under the waves. Only five women survived because the women were down below tending the children, while the men were on the upper decks smoking, drinking, and playing cards.

One teenaged girl survived, swimming thirty-six hours in the water. She was asleep, but still doing the Australian crawl when the rescue ship found her. If people can walk in their sleep (like Ethel), I don't see why they can't crawl.

When the head-hunting business fell off, the people of the Torres Strait made a good living selling mother-of-pearl, but with the arrival of plastics, the mother-of-pearl business went bust. The major industry here abouts has become the welfare check.

Although I hate getting my hair cut, I went to Steiner's. The stylist, Oila from Dublin, likes to talk and has the gift of gab. She explained the system to me. They must clear $500 per month and after that they earn commissions. The money isn't great and she could make more in Dublin, but the fun is the traveling. She bunks with Alice, another stylist, in a cabin so small that one of them has to leave so the other can dress. Sometimes they may move into passenger cabins when those are not occupied. Oila wanted to backpack in Nepal, but her mother nixed that idea (Irish girls still obey their mothers), so she settled for a much safer form of world travel aboard *QE2*. Oila says the crew socializes in their own private club and they have their own pub and parties. The crew food doesn't approach the passenger food in refinement or delicacy, but it is good, basic food.

After Oila finished, I told her the story of Joyce, my former hair stylist who heard the voice of God tell her to ram scissors into her customers' necks. Now Oila knows why I don't like getting my hair cut, but Oila didn't laugh. She just nodded her head. "God never said that to me, but I know the feeling," she said.

I forgot this was the night I was to review the Princess Grill's dinner. I got so busy eating it I didn't take notes. The memory lingers, however, that this was one of the best meals of my life. I had the most perfect châteaubriand. Soft and tender, the flavors melting in my mouth, accompanied by the lightest, freshest, most subtle béarnaise sauce I had ever experienced. Yes, experienced a multisensory event with just the right smells, tastes, and tactile sensations in my mouth. Always a hearty *trencherman*, British for chowhound, I enjoyed munching through all of that. A strolling group of two musicians played favorites "As Time Goes By" and "La Vie En Rose," while I gazed around the room, enthralled. Robert, the Princess Grill manager, cooked up flambéed peaches for us, and I recall clearly the wine we drank: Château Batailley, grand cru classé 1966 from Pauillac, one of the wines of the world great enough to complement a great châteaubriand.

Forget eternity. Give me the instantaneous moment when I sip a vintage wine with my eyes closed. I asked Alex to give me the night's menu so I could remember the list and do a complete analysis. He will try to get it for me. While he searched for the menu, I continued to indulge myself by ordering another pony of Armagnac.

Yes, cruising had come alive for me. I looked out over the dining room and realized cruising, formerly dominated by the affluent and retired, was now dominated by the affluent and retired.

At the theater we saw a movie called *Nina Takes a Lover*.

After the film ended, the man in front of me turned around and smiled. He is short and wearing glasses, but has a happy face. The middle finger of his left hand is missing.

"What did you think of that movie?" he asked.

"It's nice to know some other people lead duller lives than our own," I said.

For some reason, maybe the Amagnac, I was in an expansive mood so I expatiate further, "Most people would agree the predominant art form of modern times is film. Film consumes more money, more time, and more interest than all the other art forms put together. But how does film do it? By pandering to the popular taste. By producing an insipid film such as the one we just saw in which no true human emotions appear, no intelligent dialog passes from one character to another, and no story is told."

The stranger's face became animated. "Isn't that the truth. I don't know how they can make crap like that. I write films. I can't get my good stuff filmed. Nobody can."

Marty Brill then introduced himself. He will give the comedy show tomorrow in the Grand Lounge. Marty used to be a concert pianist but accidentally got his finger cut off. He holds that hand up to show us the missing finger. I nodded. No question about it. His finger's gone. That missing finger stopped Marty's music career, so he started writing for a living.

"Hey, I'm a writer, too," I told Marty.

I showed him my notes for today. He stepped back, saying he isn't going to read them, but that he will tell me his secret: "The secret of all good writing is rewriting."

When Ethel and I got back to cabin 2047, we found another gift from Cunard, a blue satin valet bag to carry my suits in. Not bad. Not bad at all.

Ethel looked at me, soft and doe-eyed. Without speaking, we welded together in a spiritual glow, in our private form of personal communion. Soon, together, it felt like we were not even there.

Day 38

At Sea along the Great Barrier Reef, Eastern Coast of Australia

IT TURNED OUT IT WASN'T PLUGGED IN

*T*his morning, a helicopter landed on *QE2*. Medics tried to evacuate a sick passenger, but decided his condition was too poor to allow him to travel by air. The helicopter left without the patient, who will get off in Brisbane and to go to the hospital there, if he makes it that long.

John Foley, our Australian pilot for the Torres Strait, slowed *QE2* because at a faster speed the ship was squatting, that is, its tail was sitting lower in the water. We have but thirty-feet clearance, and keeping that at the maximum possible sounds like a good idea, in view of all the ships that have met their demise in this region.

Thinking of sunken ships reminds me of the most famous sunken ship of them all, *Titanic*.

Titanic represents a titanic reason to avoid maiden voyages. What troubled people especially was not just the tragedy, or even its needlessness, but the element of fate in it all. If *Titanic* had heeded any of the six iceberg warnings on that fateful Sunday, April 14, 1912 . . . If the ice conditions had been normal . . . If the night sea had been rough or moonlit . . . If she had seen the iceberg fifteen seconds sooner or fifteen seconds later . . . If she had hit the ice any other way . . . If her watertight bulkheads had been one deck higher . . . If she had carried enough lifeboats . . . If the *Californian* had only come—If any one of these Ifs turned out right, every life might have been saved. But they all went against her—a classic Greek tragedy.

Even more mysterious is the fact that the tragedy was predicted in 1898 by a struggling author named Morgan Robertson, who concocted a novel about a fabulous Atlantic liner, far larger than any that had ever been built. Robertson loaded his ship with rich and complacent people, and then wrecked it one cold April night on an iceberg. This somehow showed the futility of everything, and, in fact, the book was called *Futility* when it appeared that year. Fourteen years later, a British shipping company named the White Star Line built a steamer remarkably like the one in Robertson's novel. The real liner was 66,000 tons, and Robertson's was 70,000 tons. The real ship was 882.6 feet long, the fictional one was 800 feet. Both vessels were triple screw and could make twenty-four to twenty-five knots. Both could carry about three thousand people, and both had enough lifeboats for only a fraction of that number.

On April 10, 1912, the real ship left Southampton on her maiden voyage for New York. Her cargo included a priceless copy of *Rubaiyat of Omar Khayyam* and a list of passengers collectively worth $250 million. On her way over, she, too, struck an iceberg and went down only a few miles from where Robertson's fictional ship sank. Robertson called his ship the *Titan*. The White Star Line called its ship the *Titanic*. Pretty close! That raised the question, did the fictional *Titan* carry a *Rubaiyat*? The answer is yes, a priceless jeweled copy from Persia. Even more amazing is the fact that Robertson checked himself into the psych ward at Belleview, claiming that a person from the future was dictating his writing to him. After weeks of observation, the doctors concluded that he was sane, just working under a harmless belief that an imaginary person from the future was dictating to him.

Later, in another novel, Robertson depicted Japanese airplanes bombing an American navy base in the Pacific. That was prescient, considering that the airplane had not been invented yet. The imaginary person from the future who gave Robertson his story ideas also dictated the design to the periscope. Robertson built the periscope, according to the specifications, and sold it to the US Navy for a pile of very real money.

Australia, Waldemar Hansen told us, would be the highlight of our trip. "Is it a continent or an island?" he asked.

"Both," the group shouted out.

Naturally, I expect marching bands playing "Waltzing Matilda,"Australia's most widely known song. No band appears. All I see is a few deserted islands on our left, and a few larger, but also deserted, islands on our right. Even the great seaman Captain Cook didn't realize there is a great continent out there, beyond the reef and beyond the western islands, though Cook did land on the continent in Botany Bay, so named because of the abundance of flowers.

It's more than a little scary to realize that just beyond the reef, further to the east, lies the Coral Sea, where the Battle of the Coral Sea took place, the turning point of the war in the Pacific. There, on May 5 and 6, 1942, opposing carrier groups sought each other, and on the morning of May 7, Japanese planes sank a US destroyer and an oiler. The next day, Japanese aircraft sank the US carrier *Lexington* and damaged the carrier *Yorktown*, while US planes crippled *Shokaku*, the lead ship of her class. So many Japanese planes were lost that the invasion force bound to attack Port Moresby, without adequate air cover and harassed by Allied land-based bombers, turned back to Rabaul. The four-day engagement was a strategic victory for the Allies, whose naval forces, employing only aircraft, never got within gunshot range of Japanese vessels. Thus, the Battle of the Coral Sea was an air battle, not a sea battle, in which the US fleet prevented the invasion of Australia. Think about how that made the Australians feel about us.

Australia is similar to and different from America. Australia and America have the same colonial roots, having both belonged once to England and they both, more or less, share the same language, English. Using her Australian dialect, the woman whose husband planned to dive off the rail into the pool thanked me for saving his life. Actually, it wasn't me. It was the deck steward who solved the whole problem by draining the pool and putting a large net over the empty pool. When the Aussies get off, the deck steward will fill the pool again. This action illustrates a general rule I've found true: The real power on *QE2* remains in the hands of the crew. The power of the passengers is more illusory than real, and quite limited. When a passenger steps out of line, the crew will do something to get things back in order. Closing the pool was the solution to the Aussie problem. Isolating Rabbi was the solution to managing his surliness.

Waldemar Hansen said that Australia had grown up when we weren't looking. Like the United States, Australia had a love for personal freedom and a strong sense of optimism. The essential difference seems to be in Australia, the people are not as ambitious as Americans. The Australians are not subservient to the Bitch Goddess of Success.

When the sea rose and the land bridge to the Australian continent sank, it was a lucky day for the animals of Australia. They could survive in that kind of isolation. They couldn't have survived with common Asian predators, like the tiger. Thus, the animals here are unique, not found any other place on Earth. Australia has wombats, kangaroos, emus, koala bears, and parakeets. All black swans, except the ones from Russia, come from Australia. The human animals here are unique also. The Aborigines live in the Stone Age without agriculture, but have a highly developed cultural and aesthetic system.

At weigh-in after lunch, I topped 160 pounds, my personal limit. This means no desserts until I weigh less. But then I thought of something. I removed my sweater and shoes and stepped back on the scale. The gray-headed woman behind me, who is waiting in line, yelled, "You're only fooling yourself."

Pleased because I was under 160 pounds, I stepped off the scale and answered her objection. "That's nothing new. I fool myself all the time. It's fun. Try it."

The old woman then gave me the once-over with leering eyes: "Take off more," she said. "This could be fun!"

In view of my waist expansion and fifteeen-pound weight gain, I told Ethel that I am some kind of eating machine. She said she thinks of me as some kind of other machine, which she can't mention in public and which I cannot in print. I agreed with her appraisal also.

Today I stayed only thirty minutes in the spa. Leonard objected, saying, "You didn't spa enough today, Bernie. You are eating more, spaing less. Not good."

Leonard was right. I didn't spa long enough. There is just too much else to do. I explained to Leonard, "The mark of true intelligence is the absence of a system. A man like me seldom claims a systematic mode of doing anything."

Leonard remained unconvinced. "Make up for it tomorrow," he said.

At 6 PM, *QE2* passed Restouration Island, where Bligh landed and restored his loyal men after the mutiny. This place has an epic history.

Marty Brill told jokes in the Grand Lounge. Some hit my funny bone, like the one where he said he went to synagogue in Ambon and thereby tripled the Jewish population of that town. His joke about O. J. Simpson fell flat with his punchline, "The DNA evidence didn't lie. The police killed Nicole." Marty told the old one about how he carries a bomb on airplanes because the chance of two people carrying a bomb on the same plane is a billion to one.

When we got back to the room, we found another joke, and this one was on us. Tracy, our room stewardess, fixed our videotape player. She had plugged it in.

Ethel and I finally used the player to look at *Gallipoli*, the Australian director Peter Weir's film about two young sprinters who volunteered to join the Australian army in 1915 to fight against the German-allied Turks. Their story interested me because I had just finished *Palace Walk* by the Nobel Prize-winning author Naguib Mahfouz, which covered the same era from the point of view of an Egyptian family.

In *Gallipoli*, two scenes impressed me most. One impressive scene was when the Aussies discovered that they had bought a fake antique for £10. They went back and demanded their money be returned. The poor Egyptian shopkeeper told them that the object was not his. "That is not mine," he repeated. The Aussies tipped over a shelf of pottery, and when that didn't work, they destroyed another shelf. In desperation, the shop-keeper gave them the ten bob. The Aussies passed out into the street, celebrating their great triumph. Suddenly, the Aussie who had made the original purchase realized he had gotten the wrong store. The fake antique had been sold to him by the merchant next door. The Aussie tried to tell the others, but they couldn't wait and didn't listen.

The other impressive scene showed the battle at the Turkish peninsula of Gallipoli, where the Aussies, under British command, received orders to charge the Turk trenches without air cover or loaded rifles, using only bayonets. This was a diversionary attack, allowing the British to land somewhere else while wave upon wave of Aussies were mowed down by Turkish machine guns. Great! One of the greatest antiwar movies ever made.

The prime minister of Australia, as a result of this battle and others similar to it, announced Australia's interests lay more with the United States than with the British Empire. In the future, Australian troops would not support the British in Burma, or elsewhere, as Winston Churchill had requested.

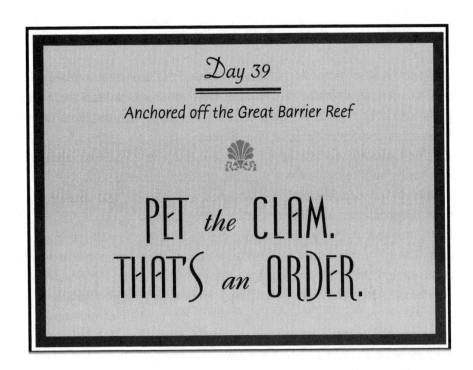

Day 39

Anchored off the Great Barrier Reef

PET the CLAM. THAT'S an ORDER.

This morning, everyone assembled in the Grand Lounge, not for bingo, but to await their number so they could go down to Five deck and board the Quicksilver catamaran.

Today we explore the Great Barrier Reef Marine Park, an area of enormous biological complexity, and, according to my astronaut friends, the largest and only animal-made structure visible from space.

Before we can leave *QE2*, the Australian customs authorities made the passengers deposit on a table at the front of the lounge all the food-stuffs concealed on their persons or in their bags. Fruits and meats and vegetables and candies in addition to Fritos, Cheetos, Oreos, Yodels, Snowcaps, two bottles of Yoo-Hoo, and other assorted junk foods piled up fast. For some reason, nothing like that can go off the ship. The customs officer knows this group. He announced that they might search the passengers, and those found smuggling food could be arrested. Within a few more minutes, the table became piled high with more junk food, as well as tomatoes, oranges, bananas, sandwiches, and even a pineapple. *QE2*ers tried but failed to take enough food with them, in case there was a shipwreck. The *QE2*ers must be dying of hunger. Who can blame them? Most haven't eaten for at least six minutes.

The Quicksilver catamaran traveled at thirty-two knots for about an hour and a half, taking us to a gigantic pontoon moored on the reef. The catamaran traveled so fast that *QE2* quickly got smaller and smaller, and then disappeared under the horizon.

Along the way, Gerhard, my diving instructor, showed me how to dive. The big things are: (1) keep your ears properly pressurized when descending, otherwise your eardrums might rupture, and (2) never hold your breath, especially when ascending, otherwise your lungs might rupture. All of that makes sense according to the physics of handling the pressures, but one passenger in the group, a blond-haired Aussie, wants to know what to do if we meet a shark.

Gerhard said that if a shark is spotted, he will signal us by placing the flat side of his hand on his head. Then we should all form a circle with him in the center, so that he is unlikely to get attacked. "Usually the shark will get only one tourist at a time," Gerhard said. "When that happens, everyone left should reform the circle and tighten it up."

Besides the shark signal, we learned to point to our ears to indicate pain. Thumbs-up meant I want to go up. Thumbs-down meant I want to go down. The international signal for stop still pertained to under the sea, but the signal for an emergency was shaking the palm of your hand back and forth, parallel to the ocean bottom, with the top of the hand toward the surface.

The Quicksilver pontoon, a rectangle measuring 50 meters by 23.5 meters and weighing 230 tons, could support the weight of 500 people. It easily handled our group of 350. Next to the changing and showering facility, the pontoon had a diving facility and snorkeling area on one side, a walk-through underwater observatory, plus three semisubmersible boats for reef viewing. The main attraction for the group, however, remains the open-air cafeteria. The lines queued up right away, but that doesn't matter to me because divers couldn't eat until they finished diving.

The inexperienced divers lined up at 1:15 PM for final inspection and the practical test before we can go under. The fat Russian next to me asked to be excused for five minutes so he can smoke a cigarette. My partner, a tall blond English woman named Clara, claims she is a grandmother. Clara may be a grandma, but she doesn't look it. The men in our diving group got their eyes glued to her bosom. My eyes glued there, too. It turns out Grandma Clara isn't the oldest diver. The oldest is Alex, who admits to being a shade under eighty. Alex, unlike Clara, looked every bit his age, and more. We all wondered if Alex can even carry his tank. He can't. We held the tank on his back while supporting Alex, as he entered the water. The last thing Alex said before he placed his facemask over his mouth was, "It's now or never."

Yes, death approaches. Death stalks us all. If Alex doesn't try today, he will never dive. Will I become as cavalier as he is when I get to eighty? Will I ever get to be eighty? Alex is right. It's now or never.

What's this? Grandma Clara, my partner, pinched my butt. I turned around. It wasn't an accident. She is smiling and giving me the eye. "Just being playful," she says with a wink. I reproved her by making a naughty sign with my fingers.

To make room for my tank, I whipped off my shirt. Grandma Clara said, "Gee, Bernie, you took that shirt off like a male stripper!" Then looking up and down my muscular arms, burly from daily swimming, she said, "You've got muscles like Arnold *Schwarzenigger.*" I correct Clara, explaining that the last part of his name was pronounced *nay-ger*, not *nigger*.

Going down under the surf, my ears gave me lots of trouble, especially the left ear, which hurt like hell. I kept signaling Gerhard and he kept signaling for me to clear my auditory tubes by blowing my nose while pinching my nostrils closed. Finally, I blew as hard and as long as I could, and heard a giant squeaky pop in my right ear. The pain immediately disappeared. Encouraged, I tilted my head back and forth and then bent to my right, blowing my nose with all my might. Sure enough, the left ear pain went down by half its former intensity. It wasn't pleasant, but I could live with it.

Meanwhile, Grandma Clara showed off by doing some somersaults and petting the bright yellow and black striped Sergeant Major fish.

Grandma did a lot better than Alex, the octogenarian, who stopped swimming, and then stopped moving, and then started limply drifting with the current toward the coral. Alex ran out of puff (puff is British for breath), I said to myself.

Some divers helped Alex get control, but Alex's muscles were flabby, weak, and had stopped working. Alex was so tired he couldn't even raise his arms to give the distress signal. But who cares? Alex's collapse is distress enough. The divers carried Alex up.

Some diver came from I know not where and started interfering with my air hose. Most annoying! Why the hell did he do that? I didn't recognize him as part of our group and I couldn't get him to stop. So I punched him hard in the stomach. Too hard! This guy became limp. He started drifting like Alex. They took him away, too.

A passenger named Dave started to show off by taking the air tube from his mouth and pretending to eat a plate-sized slab of sea anemones, not an advisable thing to do since they would sting like hell. Chris, a fellow passenger, tried to outdo Dave by putting the slab on his head, as if it were a toupee. Thus, a few QE2ers found their true personalities underwater. Meanwhile, having gotten my ears under control, I began to relax and look around. Now I know what people are talking about when they mention the grandeur of the deep. The colors, the shapes, the numerous fish: all too beautiful. A school of sea bass, each the size of a Cossack boot, came over to inspect me. They have that stupid inquiring face I had seen on other wild animals, particularly the lions in Kenya, as if to say, "What the hell are you guys doing here? This territory belongs to us."

Then it happened.

You know how psychologists talk about peak experiences in your life. Well, I had one of my own. Gerhard pointed out a large open clam, and I mean large—the size of a big TV set. Gerhard stroked the outside rim of the shell and zoom! the clam clammed up. Gerhard waited a minute, and almost as fast as it closed, the clam sprang open again. Gerhard indicated he wanted me to pet the clam. Naturally, I waved the no signal, but Gerhard pointed at me and then insistently at the clam, as if to say "Pet the clam. That's an order."

I cautiously went over and ever so lightly touched the clam's outside shell. Instantly, the clam closed. You couldn't make a machine that sensitive or that efficient. Books are made by men like me. But only God can make a clam.

After that, Gerhard wanted me to pet a sea anemone that looks like a birthday cake except the sides are deep green and there are too many pink candles on top, hundreds of them. I'm smart enough to pet the clown fish that hides among the candles, luring prey to the sea anemone and then eating the tasty leftover morsels. I didn't pet the candles, though—too dangerous.

Gerhard proved it's safe to pet the green side of the anemone, and following his example, I did the same. I'm thrilled. It felt smooth, like satin. So I started petting everything in sight.

Barrier fish run a colorful gamut: brilliant butterfly fish, demoiselle fish, spotted rays, and stonefish, who are death dealers with their venom. I didn't see any bêche-de-mer (sea cucumbers). At one time they were an economic pylon of the local economy since they were easy to catch and bought for high prices in the Asian markets, particularly in Hong Kong.

I wanted to stay here underwater forever, but Gerhard pointed to his watch and then he pointed to the air hose. Does he really believe I have any need of air when I am having so much fun? I pointed my finger at Gerhard and then gave him thumbs-up and then I pointed to myself and pointed down. That made things clear.

Gerhard became, I believe, quite unnecessarily agitated. He thinks thirty minutes at thirty feet is enough. He wanted me to quit, but he seemed reluctant to touch me because he saw what happened when I punched the other guy. I can't believe that thirty minutes has already gone by in the winking of an eye. But it has. My dial still shows I have plenty of air, because I am thin and used far less than the others.

On the way back up the ropes, my ears started cracking and popping, as all that air began to expand as the surrounding pressure became less. The Russian signaled trouble. The divers went to take care of him. He's a big man and maybe the cigarette he smoked before the dive damaged his oxygen-carrying capacity. Who knew? What they did know was he had run out of air. They gave him some of theirs and escorted him to the surface. I concluded humans, Russians included, cannot survive underwater without air.

Back on the pontoon's deck, I started to shiver to beat the band. Gerhard seemed excessively happy that the dive was over. Wonder why? They got the dive on film and we would see an instant replay on the catamaran's TV on the way back to *QE2*.

The group on the deck started to stagger and sing on the way back. The sea was rough, but not that rough. They were drunk from all the free champagne. I left them and went below to the diving lounge to watch myself, Dave, Grandma Clara, Alex the octogenarian, and Chris on the TV.

I looked so good petting the green birthday cake and doing the somersault and scratching the side of the giant clam that I ordered a tape of it for $55. Grandma Clara thought I looked good, too. "Gee, Bernie, you have nice buns!" She ordered a tape, telling Gerhard, "I want to see Bernie's buns over and over again."

I explained that I was married and that Ethel, my wife, was traveling with me. That usually works. I didn't explain that I thought Grandma was a victim of some kind of passion catalyst carried aboard *QE2* and that she was no more responsible for her behavior than a pheromone-charged moth on a hot, midsummer evening. Grandma and the women aboard like her were just getting into the swing of things, becoming looser, and acting more natural. Back home such statements might have been considered offensive, but on *QE2,* where we all have been traveling together for over a month, we were more closely bonded than strangers. What Grandma said to me sounded perfectly fine, a compliment in fact. Besides, what's so bad?

Sex is necessary. Without sex, our species wouldn't survive. And, since flirting is a necessary prelude to sex, by that direct line of reasoning, I can state that flirting is necessary for the survival of our species. Try this: If flirting from woman to man is OK, then by the universal rules of symmetry, flirting from man to woman must be OK too. Laws to prevent flirting won't work. Flirting on this planet will go on and on until the sun burns out. Most women on *QE2* knew that the world cruise was one-third over, so they were flirting even more than before. Time, that old jade, was running out. It was now or never.

Alas, some loves are never to be. I turned away, and, undaunted, Grandma Clara gave me one of those stiff British upper lips and said, "I can't open your heart, Bernie, but I can dream, can't I?"

Gerhard assured me they'll deliver my tape to our cabin when *QE2* reaches Sydney. Ethel doubts that I'll ever see the tape or my money again. "Why not? You were wrong about the chop I bought in Hong Kong. It arrived. The tape will, too."

Trouble. The Quicksilver catamaran can't get close to *QE2* because of rough seas. Neither Ethel nor I feel the least seasick and from the looks of the others no one else is seasick either. We all had earned our sea legs. The Quicksilver captain announced that, due to the rough seas, they will have to anchor and *QE2* will send tenders to pick us up. That operation lasted over two hours. No one minded. That problem disappeared when viewed rationally, as so many problems do. We just started cocktail time two hours earlier. Champagne flowed freely. *QE2*ers, as a whole, can party any time and in any place. They have trained up to it.

The nondivers left aboard the ship had started with champagne when we left earlier that morning, they certainly didn't mind the delay. I doubt that they even knew we were delayed, or that we were anchored or stuck out on the reef. Back on the ship I saw two rotund men, lying on the aft deck, who certainly didn't care. One of them was fast asleep. He had rapid eye movements, indicating his brain was making those usual short-circuit connections we call dreams. The other, though not asleep, possessed the deck in a kind of dumb torpor.

At dinner, as usual, the two British couples next to us ordered a double helping of off-menu caviar. At first, I thought Ethel unkind because she called them caviar addicts. But now I know Ethel is right. I wonder if they really want or like caviar that much, or are they ordering caviar just because it's expensive? Intent remains important, according to Dante, in evaluating sin.

Ethel and I liked the Chinese family on the other side better. Our admiration for them increased enormously when they invited us to eat at a Chinese restaurant with them in Sydney. I showed off by speaking more Mandarin. Everyone laughed. They have gotten used to my accent. They understood. A little Mandarin goes a long way.

Returning to the room, we found planted on Ethel's bed a heavy, beautiful commemorative lead crystal Waterford clock, another gift from the Samuel Cunard Key Club. When will the manna from heaven stop?

Day 40

At Sea, Cruising through the Whitsunday Islands

ETHEL PROVED HER SLIDE *into* DEGENERACY

Some of you may be wondering what the hell Whitsunday is. I am, too. Captain Cook, the famous navigator, arrived at these islands on what he thought was Whitsunday, or the feast of Pentecost, and named the islands accordingly. We know now that Cook was off a day because he had crossed the International Date Line and forgot to set his calendar a day ahead. I may not know what Whitsunday is, but I do know that today is not Whitsunday. Today is Valentine's Day.

Valentine's Day at sea.

QE2 made a big deal of this secular holiday with special menus and lots of heart-shaped balloons in the Queens Lounge and the Grand Lounge. Someone slipped a card under our cabin door from the captain, senior officers, and the entire crew of *QE2*. The card had a picture of two hearts carved in brown sand next to a starfish and scallop shell. This sort of thing was entirely unnecessary, but nice. With the card Ethel and I received a special box of Neuhaus chocolates. Ethel noted the date on the box, 1857. Any firm that had stayed in business that long must make delicious chocolates. We tasted them and concluded they did. I ate so many I began to fear the next day's noon weigh-in. If I didn't come in under 160 pounds, I would have to go off lunch desserts. Lately, before the weigh-in, I had been taking off my shoes and shirt and sweater. I wasn't wearing anything else that I could take off, so I no longer had any leeway.

From all that work diving the day before I felt stiff and my arm still hurt from punching the diver who interfered with my air supply. The big red abrasions on both my shoulders, made by the air tank straps digging into my skin, still hurt and began to form scabs. My cold, which was clearing before the dive, had come back in force, probably another side effect from the dive. I concluded it would be my first and last dive.

Jon, our Princess Grill waiter, is in a talkative mood. Jon told us he comes from Blackpool where he has a wife and two children, a boy and a girl. Because he goes to sea, he doesn't see them often and laments that he left when they were crawling and returned when they were walking. He had missed the stages in between. Jon said the money on *QE2* wasn't great, but the experience was worth it. He soon intended to get a good recommendation for a job on one of the ferries that crossed the English Channel, so he could be closer to home. Jon missed his children, but what he experienced couldn't match what Captain Cook experienced.

Cook was away most of the time, yet his wife, Beth, conceived three children during his brief times ashore. On Cook's penultimate voyage, Cook returned to find that during his absence a son and a daughter had died. Because of that, Beth made Cook promise that the next voyage would be his last.

It was. On that last trip the Hawaiians cooked Cook and ate him for dinner. He never did return to England or to his wife. According to what I read in the *Encyclopedia Britannica*, Captain Cook is still dead. For a pseudoscholar my research methods remain excellent: when I don't know something, I look it up.

To celebrate Valentine's Day, Ethel couldn't wait to get back to the cabin to show me the new paisley bow tie and cummerbund she had bought for me. I told her I didn't have a gift for her, but actually I did. I had concealed it in my medicine cabinet, which I knew she would never check. I planned to present it that night, when the timing was right. It was an Olympus camera that I bought onboard for $255, duty-free.

Waldemar Hansen lectured on Australia, working up the group's enthusiasm.

To get ready, I bought some Australian money. It looks better than the green and black dollars with the portraits of dead old men that we use in the United States. The Australian fives are especially beautiful with lavender color and a special see-through window. The orange twenty has a window too, and so does the blue ten. Money like this is unique. It's the only money I have ever seen where you can see through part of the bill. How in the world do they do it?

Waldemar told us that although Australia is the size of the United States, it has only eighteen million citizens. That was 7 percent of the US population, making the population density much lower. Maybe the Australians should have sold one of the western territories to the Japanese or to Hong Kong. Waldemar wanted us to try specially brewed Australian billy tea and damper. Billy tea is made by using a special pot to boil the water over a campfire, and then the tea leaves are added and left to steep. Damper is a baking-powder bread formed into flat cakes and usually baked over a campfire.

My freezing experience yesterday at thirty-five feet below the surface made me decide to swim in the indoor pool on Seven deck, where the water temperature is a cozy 87 degrees. A big fat German woman and Joe, her instructor, were working on a swimming lesson while I swam around them. After ten minutes she gave up because she ran out of puff and I had the pool to myself.

In honor of St. Valentine, the Princess Grill tonight has been decked out with balloons and red hearts. The women and men decorated themselves in valentine reds as well. I wear my red and black hand-painted formal shirt, my red and black cummerbund, and red tie. "If they make such a big deal over Valentine's day here, what would Christmas be like? Or how about New Year's?" I asked.

"Let's find out by inviting all our friends to spend New Year's on *QE2*," said Ethel.

"But who will pay?" I asked.

Since it was Valentine's Day, I let Ethel choose the wine. She selected a Dom Pérignon 1985 for $110, proving her slide into degeneracy.

When we get back to the cabin, a bad-news fax from the radio room was under the door. The fax comes from Janet Fife-Yeomans, senior legal writer for the *Australian*, a newspaper. She wants to interview me and have a photographer take my picture. She also wants to do a press conference after my lecture in Sydney.

Lecture? What lecture?

To get my mind off the bad news, I peruse the cruise news and note a headline: "New Retirees in 'Limbo.'" Americans, the article said, were retiring earlier and living longer, creating problems so distinctive that researchers had designated a new life stage to describe the circumstances. "'They call it Limbo,' a Cornell University scientist said. 'People often find they are leaving their careers through planned or forced retirement—in their fifties and will have to deal with as much as thirty years, resulting in problems that society does not have answers for.'"

What?

I don't see the problem. Neither does Ethel, who has been retired longer than I have. But if there is a problem I can suggest a partial solution. Take a cruise.

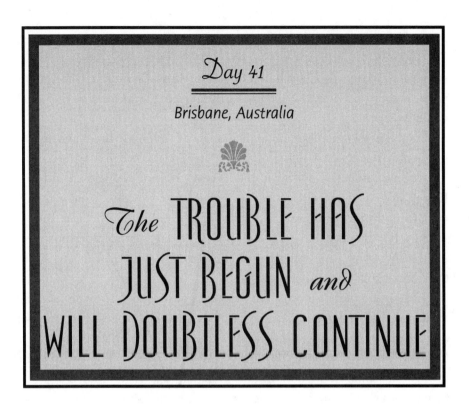

The TROUBLE HAS JUST BEGUN and WILL DOUBTLESS CONTINUE

*F*rom the deck of *QE2*, Brisbane looked like some skyscrapers plopped in the middle of a deserted dry countryside. I spotted an airplane landing at the airport. Who in the world would want to come to Brisbane, and for what? Ethel supplied the answer, "To see koalas. Same as me."

Alex, Jon's assistant, shamelessly encouraged Ethel by telling her that last time he was in Brisbane, he got his picture taken with a koala. "Quite an experience," Alex said with a stiff British accent that sounds so authoritative. Lucky for me I can sound the same way, doing a good simulation of the British accent. I impressed even Ethel. My mother hated it when I did it as a kid because she thought my speech might get locked permanently in that mode.

Putting on my best British accent, I addressed Alex directly, "Pictures are nothing, I say. We should like to hold and pet our own koala. And we want to bring it back to Princess Grill and keep him here at our sides while we eat."

As the passengers line up to disembark, I catalogue the types on this segment.

The Australians constituted the largest group. They got on in Hong Kong. Most of them will get off in Sydney, just like the Chinese family next to us in the Princess Grill, our friends, the Lus. The Lus live in Sydney, but they also have a house in Hong Kong. Mr. Lu does business, mainly importing and exporting clothes, and the little Lus, a girl, four-teen, and a son, sixteen, are students.

Elderly couples comprise the second-largest group. They come in all varieties. The most common is couples that have been together for decades, like Ethel and myself, who silently and relentlessly proclaim the enduring power of marriage and love. Most couples of this group share cabins, but some don't. For instance, Nathan and Estelle have adjacent cabins with a door that opens into the other's room. Margaret and her hus-band, Lewis Soutar from Scotland, have completely separate cabins. In the morning Lewis comes round knocking at Margaret's door to see what she wants to do. Other couples travel together and share the same cabin, but are not married. The ones of this ilk, and there were quite a few that I met in the hot tub, were evidently proud that they were not married because I always got informed of the fact right away, usually by the woman. The unmarried couples function quite well, except the women seem restless. More than one woman from such a pair has hit on me, usually in the hot tub, while her unsuspecting male companion sunned himself on deck or swam in the outdoor pool. Another type of couple shares a cabin, dines together, and are usually seen on deck as a pair, but they hardly ever look at each other, touch each other, or speak to each other. They don't make small talk to each other during dinner. They look the other way and don't seem to know the other sits next to them. Yet, there remains a kind of sullen togetherness. They seem perfectly content. Couples of this type that I met are usually making their third or fourth world cruise. I'll bet *QE2* sees them back again next year. *QE2* must make some contribution to the continuance of their marriage. But what? And how? And why?

Another type of couple, seen quite frequently around the outdoor swimming pool and in the hot tub, consists of an older man, sometimes quite old and quite infirm, hobbling about with a cane while holding onto his younger trophy wife. These couples vary in their age gaps. Some have fifty years between them, others, the ones usually with a child two to four years old, had thirty years between them. This group, I would wager, consisted of a large number of second marriages, perhaps between a boss and a secretary, a doctor and a nurse, or, among the ones with the very old men, between a nurse and a patient. All of this illustrated what Anna Karenina said about love: "There are as many kinds of marriage as there are couples and as many types of love as there are hearts."

Oh yes, I forgot. There are rare couples of men. Some are obviously homosexual, and some are obviously not, like Matt and Mark, the Christian Brothers. Some of these men seem OK and others looked sick. At least one is so thin and weak he must have AIDS. I feel sorry for him, but think he is brave to attempt a trip around the world. I hope he makes it. The homosexuals are overrepresented in the spa, the dry sauna, and the hot tubs, but for some reason, they don't hang out in the steam room. They seem like happy, well-adjusted, peaceful people, and I like them better than I like some of the straights, such as Rabbi. Naturally, some of these men have given me the eye, but that doesn't bother me because I get the eye from the women plenty of times. Men or women, once I brush them off, don't bother me again. Once is OK. Twice is harassment.

The group about which I know the least is the singles. There are men traveling without wives, and many of them have suspiciously latched on to single women onboard. I'm sure they are romancing a little, in a harmless sort of way. Other men are strict loners and eat, drink (usually heavily, with six martinis before dinner), and sit alone. We had one of these men sitting behind us in Mauretania. He remained a morose recluse who sat by himself at every meal, drank upwards of seven and sometimes nine martinis, and looked unhappy at the beginning but happier at the end of the meal. He's handsome, about forty-five years old, well built, and immaculately and formally dressed every evening. What dark past haunts him? Only the shadow knows.

Singles have separate parties and dances, so the social program gears up to help them make contact. The gentlemen hosts also provide some dancing for the single ladies, especially the older ones who might not be able to get a man on their own. What the hell! This is their last hurrah. Let the good times roll.

I told Ethel that after she died I would become a gentleman host.

"But, what if you die first?" she asked.

"In that case I won't become a gentleman host."

The bus driver, Ray, was also our guide to Brisbane, pronounced *Bris ben*, not *Bris bayne*).

On the way into the city, we motored past large oil refineries, and giant grain elevators, one of which spilled tons of yellow-brown material from eight stories high onto a small hill of the same material below. At first, I thought the yellow stuff was sand, but it turned out it was wheat. Next to that mountain of wheat was an even larger mountain of coal. Ray told us that because of the high cost of mining coal in the midlands of England, it was cheaper for them to ship Australian coal to Newcastle. So that's what the Australians did—brought their coal to Newcastle and made a profit.

Australia is a different country, with different ways of saying things. The signs said things like: "Nappy service," Australian for diaper service, and "Takeaway food," Australian for takeout food.

There were lots of homes standing on stilts, Queensland-style, so the air moving under them cooled them and the stilts protected them from flooding.

The city hall, pride of the locals and the focus of community life, displayed a heraldic coat of arms with two supporters of upright griffins, a scroll, and motto underneath showing its British origins. We passed the Fortitude Valley post office, but we didn't drive by the Brisbane cathedral that should have been next to it. We didn't drive by it because it doesn't exist. The Brisbane cathedral doesn't exist because the cardinal, entrusted with £22,000 for construction funds, went "around the corner." Neither the money nor the clergyman has been seen since. Ray said jokingly, "Neither the cardinal nor the blessed money came back."

We admired the five different kinds of frangipani, the purple-colored flowers of the jacaranda and the numerous signs for Castlemaine XXXX, or Four X, the most popular local beer. Hard times arrived in Brisbane during the early 1980s, and according to Ray, many businessmen went to the wall, including the owners of Castlemaine. New Zealanders bought it, but only the ownership, not the taste of the beer, changed.

Ray made us anxious to see the koalas. It turned out the koala is not a bear, although it might look like one to the untutored mind. Up until this moment of enlightenment, I certainly thought the koala was a bear. Now thanks to Ray, I know that the koala, like most of the animals in Australia, is a marsupial, mammals of distinction because of their reproductive traits.

After mating, koala gestation lasts thirty-three to thirty-five days. Then the little koala, roughly the size of a US quarter (fifteen millimeters) and weighing less than a dime (about five hundred milligrams), crawls out of the mother's cloaca (a posterior opening serving as an intestinal, urinary, and genital tract) and heads up the underside of its mother's belly. Eventually it pops into the mother's marsupial pouch, where it attaches to one of two teats and stays there for the next six to seven months, sucking milk. After that, the baby koala gradually exits the marsupial pouch and may travel around for a few months, riding on its mother's back. Somewhere in this time interval, the baby eats the mother's feces. (Yes, that's right—I did say eats the mother's feces.) Eating feces is necessary, so that the baby's two-foot long appendix can become colonized by a special bacteria that helps digest the koala's only food, the eucalyptus leaf.

Most of the time the koala remains a quiet, slothful, thoroughly relaxed animal, except during mating season when the males aggressively compete for territory and the you-know-what that goes within the territory. Once the males have secured a territory, they are an item, which the females actively seek. And then it all begins again.

I inspected Kev, our koala for the day. He seems lively enough and looks at me with adorable brown eyes. He weighs much more than I thought he would, maybe forty pounds or so. Kev has two thumbs and three prehensile fingers with which he firmly and friendly grips my right shoulder as some *QE2*ers prepare to take our picture.

Someone gives us a darling Polaroid photo showing Kev, Ethel, and me as one big happy family. We wanted to take Kev back to *QE2* because we have bonded to him and consider him like a grandchild, but the rangers don't understand. They won't let Kev leave Lone Pine Reserve even though Kev shows them, by hanging around my neck and refusing to let go, that he wants to stay with me. Kev knows a good thing. He wants to go back to *QE2* and eat in Princess Grill. Losing their cool, two rangers shout at me and pull Kev off. Ethel and I wanted to keep Kev forever, but the only thing we get to keep is the photo.

Deep down, Ethel and I knew what we wanted was not possible. Pets are simply not carried by cruise ships, with two exceptions. One is on the regularly scheduled transatlantic services of *QE2*, which has sixteen air-conditioned kennels, a genuine British lamppost, cat containers, and several special cages for birds. The second is on the regularly scheduled south Atlantic service from England to Cape Town and the Ascension Islands aboard the *Saint Helena*.

After leaving Kev, we turned our attention to the other animals, including the kangaroos and wombats. The roos came right up to me seeking food, but when they found none they stuck around for petting. I felt an overwhelming happiness, as I petted a solidly built male roo and then switched my attention to a female who had a small joey in her pouch.

These improbable animals hopped around rather fast. They had surprisingly intelligent and curious faces. When they stood on their two hind feet, their smaller forearms and paws made them look almost human.

The wombat was sleeping in a hollow log. We couldn't wake him. The sign said the wombat ate grasses and fruits, so it was not entirely dependent on one source of food, the way the koala is. The Tasmanian devil was also asleep in a hollow log. Because of its rather bad reputation, we didn't attempt to wake it.

In the Lone Pine Koala Shop I bought three Dr. Stacey's right-handed returning boomerangs, made of Queensland hoop pine, designed by aerospace engineer Conrad Stacey, BE, PhD, and endorsed by three-time Australian boomerang champion Bob Burwell.

"Who are they for?" Ethel asked.

"The two kids and myself," I answered.

Ray told us to wipe our feet free of kangaroo poop before we reenter the bus. His logic is impeccable: "If everyone comes into the bus with poop on their shoes, the whole place will smell like an animal den."

I did what he said, but poop happened anyway.

Multiple faxes came, telling me my lecture was to take place at a medical and scientific conference at the Darling Harbour Convention Center, in Sydney, on Saturday morning. Dr. Mark Donohue, the president of the medical society, told me in his fax of the mounting pressure his organization had been under. The Australian government had continued its support of the conference, but the breast implant companies, including Dow, refused to participate. Dr. Donohue said, "Your story and scarcity have done the predictable thing and created an almost insatiable media demand."

Donohue was starting to get a feel for the pressure. His office had been "invaded" with computer viruses and confidential documents had been viewed, while he also dealt with a boycott from the plastic surgeons who were pressuring the Australian government regulator (Therapeutic Goods Administration, or TGA) to drop its support for, and attendance of, the conference. And, oh great! Dow's PR firm, Comber Consulting, had been faxing around "dirt files" and US newspaper clippings on the US speakers. Donohue said he had been roundly abused and even threatened with legal action by plastic surgeons and a professor of medicine for bringing "these discredited charlatans and turkeys" from the United States.

Conservative medicine closed ranks and although Donohue approached over three thousand doctors with an interest in the field, only about sixty would attend the meeting. Disaster loomed. I could feel it in my bones. The association would be out tens of thousands of dollars if no one attended the conference. On a somewhat better note, Donohue said they had the support of Senator Crowley, who was the Australian minister of health in charge of the TGA. Australia's premier comedienne and beauty myth smasher, Ms. Wendy Harmer, would launch the conference and introduce some of the US speakers. Donohue even had some advice for me: "Show yourself as a flawed hero. That's what the Australians go for. They don't mind charlatans as long as they are heroic."

"How about turkeys?" I asked.

"American slang. No one here knows what it means," he answered.

Flawed hero? No problem. I am flawed. I don't know about the hero part, but I'll just act natural and be myself. I have no other choice. A round man can't fit into a square hole right away. He needs time to change his shape.

The phone rang and I did a phone press conference with the reporter from the *Australian*. She wasn't as nasty as Michelle the Nasty, but she was nasty. She promised she wouldn't tell anyone that I was onboard *QE2*. I thought of that old Celtic saying: Never trust a slave with money or a woman with a secret.

As I put down the phone, I told Ethel that within a few hours everyone will know that I'm on *QE2*. "Get ready."

At 6 AM I received a phone call from the radio officer on the bridge. "Sorry to wake you, sir, but we have a fax here. We don't know who sent it and we don't know where it came from but it says, 'You are bleeding!'"

To Americans, "You are bleeding" doesn't sound like much. To the British, anything concerning blood, bloody, or bleeding is just about the worst swear you can use. That was why the radio officer sounded so jangled by the message.

I thanked the radio officer, told him to expect more like that, and asked him not to bother me with them. Then I rolled over and fell asleep. At home we got anonymous calls, including death threats. At sea we get anonymous faxes, too.

CUNARD

QUEEN ELIZABETH 2

1996 WORLD CRUISE

VOYAGE
to DISTANT
EMPIRES

The official logo for the 1996 World Cruise.
(Cunard Line)

Queen Elizabeth 2
List of Senior Officers

Rank	Name
Captain	John Burton-Hall
Staff Captain	Ray Heath
Chief Officer	Ian McNaught
Chief Radio Officer	Eric Bainger
Chief Engineer	Steve Hare
Staff Chief Engineer	Steve Storey
Ship's Service Manager	Alan Dale
First Engineer	William Robinson
Chief Electrical Engineer	Terry Kearney
Hotel Manager	John Duffy
Asst. Hotel Manager (F&B)	Beat Hofer
Purser	Jamie Luke
Finance Officer	David Luke
Executive Chef	Jonathan Wicks
Accomodation Services Manager	Tracy Jessop
Cruise Director	Brian Price
Deputy Cruise Director	Angela Behrens
Social Director	Andrew Graham
Social Director	Elaine MacKay
Principal Medical Officer	Jon Newstead
Medical Officer	David Cowie

1996 World Cruise Itinerary

Port		Arrive		Depart		Nautical Miles
New York				Thur	JAN 4th	4:45PM	925
Port Everglades	Sat	JAN 6th	7:30AM	Sat	JAN 6th	11:00PM	1,495
PDC/Cozumel	Mon	JAN 8th	8:00AM	Mon	JAN 8th	5:00PM	2,421
Cartagena	Wed	JAN 10th	8:00AM	Wed	JAN 10th	6:00PM	2,687
Panama Canal	Thur	JAN 11th	6:00AM	Thur	JAN 11th	6:00PM	4,117
Acapulco	Sun	JAN 14th	8:00AM	Sun	JAN 14th	6:00PM	5,619
Los Angeles	Wed	JAN 17th	7:00AM	Wed	JAN 17th	11:00PM	5,767
Ensenada	Thur	JAN 18th	8:00AM	Thur	JAN 18th	5:00PM	8,020
La Haina	Mon	JAN 22nd	7:30AM	Mon	JAN 22nd	11:00PM	8,122
Honolulu	Tues	JAN 23rd	7:30AM	Tues	JAN 23rd	12 Mid't	11,512

------- CROSS THE INTERNATIONAL DATELINE LOSE FRIDAY JANUARY 26th ---------

Port		Arrive		Depart		Nautical Miles
Yokohama	Tues	JAN 30th	7:00AM	Tues	JAN 30th	6:00PM	11,512
Osaka	Wed	JAN 31st	11:00AM	Wed	JAN 31st	11:00PM	11,839
Keelung	Fri	FEB 2nd	12:00PM	Fri	FEB 2nd	8:00PM	12,715
Hong Kong	Sat	FEB 3rd	7:00PM	Tues	FEB 6th	9:00AM	13,196
Manila	Wed	FEB 7th	1:00PM	Wed	FEB 7th	12 Mid't	13,831
Ambon	Sat	FEB 10th	8:00AM	Sat	FEB 10th	6:00PM	15,131
Pass Thursday Island	Mon	FEB 12th	9:00AM			--------	16,121
Barrier Reef	Tues	FEB 13th	9:00AM	Tues	FEB 13th	7:00PM	16,651
Pass Holburn Island	Wed	FEB 14th	6:00AM			--------	16,886
Brisbane	Thur	FEB 15th	8:00AM	Thur	FEB 15th	4:00PM	17,429
Sydney	Fri	FEB 16th	5:00PM	Sat	FEB 17th	5:00PM	17,899
Adelaine	Mon	FEB 19th	9:00AM	Mon	FEB 19th	12 Mid't	18,874
Fremantle	Thur	FEB 22nd	8:00AM	Thur	FEB 22nd	6:00PM	20,214
Bali	Sun	FEB 25th	8:00AM	Sun	FEB 25th	7:00PM	21,686
Laem Chabang	Wed	FEB 28th	1:00PM	Thur	FEB 29th	7:00PM	23,366
Singapore	Sat	MAR 2nd	8:00AM	Sun	MAR 3rd	7:00PM	24,152
Port Kelang	Mon	MAR 4th	8:00AM	Mon	MAR 4th	6:00PM	24,347
Bombay	Fri	MAR 8th	7:00AM	Sat	MAR 9th	2:00PM	26,585
Mahe, Seychelles	Tues	MAR 12th	8:00AM	Tues	MAR 12th	6:00PM	28,337
Mombasa	Thur	MAR 14th	8:00AM	Fri	MAR 15th	2:00PM	29,319
Durban	Mon	MAR 18th	8:00AM	Mon	MAR 18th	8:00PM	31,038
Capetown	Wed	MAR 20th	8:00AM	Thur	MAR 21st	2:00PM	31,843
Rio De Janeiro	Tues	MAR 26th	1:00PM	Wed	MAR 27th	7:00PM	35,118
Salvador	Fri	MAR 29th	7:00AM	Fr	MAR 29th	2:00PM	35,913
Barbados	Tues	APR 2nd	7:00AM	Tues	APR 2nd	12 Mid't	38,344
St. Thomas	Thur	APR 4th	7:00AM	Thur	APR 4th	6:00PM	38,782
Port Everglades	Sat	APR 6th	7:30AM	Sat	APR 6th	4:00PM	39,763
New York	Mon	APR 8th	7:30AM	Mon	APR 8th	3:00PM	40,706
Southampton	Sat	APR 13th	6:00PM			--------	43,921

right:
List of the senior officers of *Queen Elizabeth 2* with Captain John Burton-Hall on top and working down. It may surprise you to know that, according to the overwhelming majority of passengers, the most important officer was Executive Chef Jonathan Wicks, who prepares over 8,000 meals daily using 14 kitchens and 230 cooks and assistants. *(Cunard Line)*

left:
The itinerary— Around the World—three months, 22 countries, 43,921 nautical miles. *(Cunard Line)*

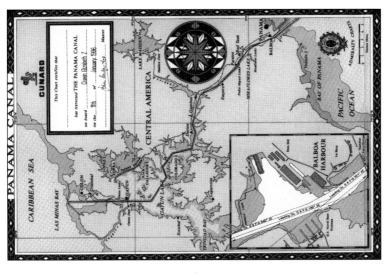

Map and captain's certificate that we had crossed the Panama Canal. Crossing the canal gave the QE2ers just another excuse for self-indulgence. Why not? That's what we're here for. *(Cunard Line)*

Queens Grill with our two waiters Nick (*right*) and Colum. Simon the wine steward is away responding to the slight lift of my finger for an Armagnac. I appointed Nick my factotum because he always knew what I wanted, and when I wanted it. I loved the way he would quickly eye a cleaned bananas Foster dessert plate and nod, "The same again." Cheerful service—there's nothing like it. *(photo by Alex Seymour)*

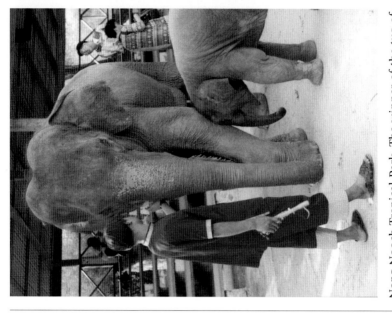

Nong Nooch Tropical Park. The winner of the tug-of-war, the ponderous pachyderm at the center, pulled all the tourists off their feet and across the field, washing them away as if under the overwhelming influence of a gigantic tidal wave. And after, the tourists looked exhausted, but the elephant was as fit as ever.
(Photo by Ethel Patten)

CUNARD

Queen Elizabeth 2

DAILY PROGRAMME

Wednesday, 21st February 1996   *Sunrise: 6.23am Sunset: 8.01pm*   *On Passage To: FREMANTLE*

Dress Code This Evening: FORMAL - TUXEDO OR BUSINESS SUIT REQUIRED

At 11.30am in the Theatre

"EPIC PICTORIAL PREVIEW!

ANOTHER PART OF ASIA, FROM BALI TO BOMBAY"

After Australia, QE2 heads north to complete her Indian Ocean odyssey with exotic splendours of as-yet-unvisited "distant empires" of Asia!

This preview will "orient" you

to the next major segment of your 1996 World Cruise!

An illustrated presentation by World Cruise Port Lecturer

WALDEMAR HANSEN

(This lecture will be repeated on TV Channel 9 beginning at 6.00pm and running continuously)

At 3.15pm in the Grand Lounge
"DICING WITH DEATH"
A 3-Part Question & Answer Session
with World Famous Actor
CHRISTOPHER LEE
(star of "The Mummy", "Man with the Golden Gun" and "Gremlins 2" amongst many others), referring to the number of times he's been 'killed' and the number of times he's nearly been killed really - by accidents on the set

For those of our guests disembarking in Fremantle
CAPTAIN JOHN BURTON-HALL and his ship's company hope that you have enjoyed your voyage on board Queen Elizabeth 2 and that we will have the pleasure of welcoming you back in the not-too-distant future!

⏰ FROM THE NAVIGATOR'S DESK - CLOCKS WILL BE RETARDED ONE HOUR ⏰
AT 4.00AM TOMORROW THURSDAY, 22ND FEBRUARY.

Cruise Director: BRIAN PRICE   *Captain: JOHN BURTON-HALL*   *Deputy Cruise Director: ANGELA BEHRENS*
Social Director: ELAINE MACKAY   *Social Director: ANDREW GRAHAM*

Page one of the daily program. Ethel circled the events she would attend. Poor Christopher Lee. He may have been killed many times in the movies but in real life on QE2 he was hounded to death for his autograph. The nautical signal flags at the right spell out from top down C-U-N-A-R-D. *(Cunard Line)*

Ethel, ready for aerobics class, stands in the worst, smallest, and least expensive class room on the ship—M5, where M indicates Mauretania (the worst class) and 5 indicates the worst division of M. The flowers, the bottle of Grand Marnier, the champagne, and the chocolates that adorn the vanity of this, our little love nest, are gifts from the ship. Like so much of the cruise experience, these handouts are not necessary but nice. *(Photo by Bernard Patten)*

At table in the Mauretania restaurant, the lowest class restaurant of the five restaurants aboard QE2. Here dine the hoi polloi, the majority, the masses. They dine well here, although only in muted luxury. *(Photo courtesy of the author)*

Saint Pedro Claver (1580–1654), a Jesuit known as the "slave of the slaves," devoted his life to the Africans brought in bondage to Cartagena. A beautiful woman with a tight dress and great cleavage lay beside his skeleton to have her picture taken. She is a woman who, we may imagine, knows and loves men and often has power over them. But not this time. Claver did not respond. *(Photo by Ethel Patten, but too late to show the preening woman.)*

Shinto shrine, Meiji Jingu Gardens. The smoke is cupped onto your head to protect you from evil spirits. Shinto has no great book, no set of dogmas, no organized priesthood. But Shinto does have plenty of gods and goddesses, 8 million, a number less than the 127 million people in Japan, but enough to go around. *(Photo by Ethel Patten)*

View of Hong Kong harbor from the hot tub on One deck. Usually the flotilla of sampans, tankas, junks, motorboats, tankers, hydrofoils, sea cats, cruise ships, and tugs reflects, in the microcosm, the chaos and confusion of the fragrant harbor itself. The Star Ferry in the center toward the bottom was the place Lomax met the Wan Chai B girl named Suzie Wong in Richard Mason's classic story *The World of Suzie Wong*. *(Photo by Ethel Patten)*

Quicksilver pontoon at anchor at the Great Barrier Reef, National Australian Park. The author *(center)* is happy to have survived his first and last dive, and so is his instructor, Gerhard *(top, right)*. *(Photo by Ethel Patten)*

Kev, our koala for the day, looks at us with adoring and adorable brown eyes. Kev has two thumbs and three prehensile fingers on the hand with which he firmly grips my right shoulder as the other QE2ers take pictures. Kev bonded to us and wanted to go back to the ship. He knows a good thing. He probably wants to eat eucalyptus leaves (his only food) in Princess Grill. Who can blame him? Losing their cool, two rangers from the Lone Pine Koala Sanctuary pull Kev off. We wanted to keep Kev forever, but the only thing we got to keep was this photo.
(Photo by Alice Pierce)

Sydney, Australia. QE2 is firmly sheltered and embedded in the Sydney landscape. The Coathanger (left, the bridge across the harbor) offers trips over the top for those tourists who have a tendency toward suicide. *(Photo by Ethel Patten)*

Nong Nooch Tropical Park. Some *QE2*ers let the elephant lift them with its trunk, others let the elephant step on them with its foot, some let the elephant do both.
(Photo by Ethel Patten)

Washing ghats, Mahalaxmi Station, Bombay, India. OK. You want something foreign, foreign looking things, and foreign looking people. Something thoroughly and uncompromisingly foreign—foreign from top to bottom, foreign from center to circumference, foreign inside and outside and all around, nothing anywhere about to dilute its foreignness, nothing to remind us of any other people or any other land under the sun. And lo! India!
(Photo by Ethel Patten)

Mahé, Seychelles. While the famous Seychelles turtles enjoyed a postcoital nap (but no cigarette), we tourists visited the coco de mer palm trees. These trees, some of which are over 800 years old, come in male and female varieties. After about 25 years, the female, if fertilized with pollen from the male, starts to bear a large nut, weighing up to 44 pounds, and taking 7 years to mature. The male, not to be outdone, has the largest catkin in the plant world. *(Photo by Ethel Patten)*

Queens Grill. *(left to right)* Alex, Colum, Ethel, Nick, Bernie. Note the crew is much better dressed than the passengers, and for good reason: they are working and we are on vacation. All are happy: The passengers because of the wonderful service. The crew, in part, because they have just received their big tips. *(Photo by Geoffrey Coughtrey)*

Mombasa, Kenya, at Fort Jesus with Ali, a Shiite Muslim who believes in jihad, holy war as the sixth pillar of Islam. Ali sure is one hell of an expensive guide—40,000 US dollars for a 32 minute tour. We paid him $40 and made our escape because the muezzin at that moment, just as Ali and his thug friends were about to make jihad on us, called the faithful to prayer. *(Photo by Ethel Patten)*

Mombasa, Kenya. The famous Black Lady, safely onboard and surrounded by a protective gesture. A native wearing khaki pants and dirty white shirt, stepped protectively between the black lad and me. He whispered, "She's for sale, like so many African women." His voice was low pitched, raspy. The asking price: $1,000. The final price: $300. *(Photo by Ethel Patten)*

Aft on *QE2* showing the author's main social center and source of ship information: two hot tubs and pool. It was in the hot tub portside that Miss Red Bikini, one of those old-time tawdry blondes, first appeared with a scotch in one hand and a cigarette in the other. She announced that she was looking for a new lover, someone more flexible than the deck steward, someone who didn't mind that she liked to make love with her high heels on.
(Cunard Line)

Tiffin Room, Raffles Hotel, Singapore. As usual, they were booked solid in the Tiffin Room. The maître d' shook his head and turned us away. But a waiter who looked familiar pulled us aside, had mercy on our souls, and invited us in the back way, thus bypassing the maître d'. The waiter remembered me from two years before when I left a gigantic tip (usually 30 percent). It's nothing, really, but to waiters a big tip is memorable.
(Photo by Ethel Patten)

The Chinese Cemetery in Manila proves you can take it with you—some of it, anyway. The place looks like a village except most of the residents are dead. I say "most" because some people live in the cemetery. They are the servants that the very wealthy might need in the afterlife and they are the gardeners and caretakers that work full time keeping up mausoleums the size of my home. Still these gewgaws seem poor and cheap and trivial in the presence of the solemnity, the grandeur, the power, and the awful majesty of Death. *(Photos by Ethel Patten)*

Chinese Cemetery

Chinese Cemetery

Japanese children are like fish: they travel in schools and get nervous when separated from the group even for a few seconds. *(Photo by Ethel Patten)*

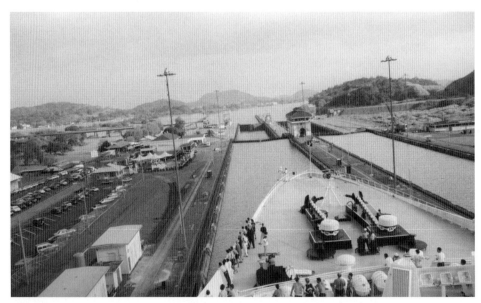

Panama Canal. If it looks like a tight fit, it is because it is. They designed *QE2* as Panamax, as they say in the cruise business, meaning the ship was the maximum size that could transit the Panama Canal. Marine architects went to the locks and made sure that *QE2* fit. Their measurements led to *QE2*'s present dimensions: 963 feet long, 105 feet wide, 13 stories high (201 feet 9-3/4 inches), all that and handling 1,800 passengers and 1,000+ crew. *(Photo by Ethel Patten)*

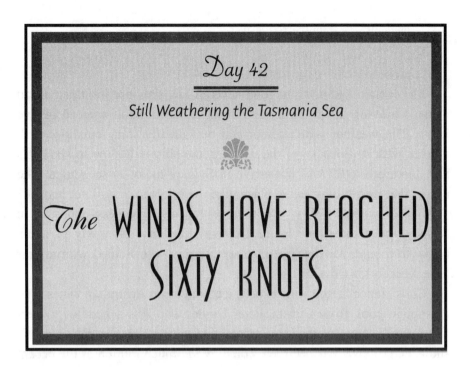

Day 42

Still Weathering the Tasmania Sea

The WINDS HAVE REACHED SIXTY KNOTS

The sea's rough embrace gripped us last night and continues today, holding tight. She won't let go. Ethel and I followed the sea's example and embraced intimately while the ship rose and fell, alternately pressing and releasing us. The rhythm is primitive, primal, and animal. We continued to embrace. It felt good. At least it feels good to me. "How about for you?" I ask Ethel, who replies, "I miss Kev. Wish he were here in bed with us."

I forgive Ethel, for she, no more than any other human, is not responsible for how her feelings flow. But I did say, "You love Kev more than you love me."

"Not really. I love you both the same."

While we are coupled together in intimate embrace, Captain John Burton-Hall comes on the loudspeaker overhead. The speakers are found in each cabin and function to keep passengers informed on what's happening. Still, it feels a little strange having the captain's deep voice bellowing overhead while we are still locked in an animal position.

"Can he see us?" asked Ethel.

The captain had bad and good news. A low-pressure front just ahead of us is moving down the eastern coast of Australia at a speed of five knots. The weather will worsen, and our already sorry condition will worsen with it. Because of the weather, the ship will slow to six knots and, therefore, *QE2* will not arrive in Sydney today as scheduled. The events that would have taken place, like the opera tour, will not happen.

I disconnected. Wow! Good news for me. The less exposure in Sydney, the greater the chance I'll leave the city alive. My paranoia began to mount. Maybe, just maybe, that guy who fiddled with my air hose worked for Dow.

Chris Hancock, the wine expert, lectured us on Australian wines. The Australian cook from Cicada, Peter Doyle, who was scheduled to perform, didn't show for the same reason that most of the passengers didn't show. Peter Doyle has been overcome by too much motion of the ocean. Peter Doyle is seasick.

Chris Hancock started by asking the Aussies to raise their hands. They are the majority. Second comes the Americans, and last, two English couples. There are no Japanese. I guess the Japanese don't want to know how to drink wine.

Chris then explains what we all wanted to know about wine but were afraid to ask. He trained us how to taste wine, something I had learned in high school. First, we smell the wine, because flavor cannot be tasted, only smelled. All of us in the audience tried to hold that smell in our noses and sinuses. What we can smell, when we work on it, amazes us. After the smell, we take a little wine into our mouths and suck in some air with it. The aeration brings out the tastes and augments the flavors. The first taste is sweet, which when added to the smell, comes out fruity.

"Memorize that taste and smell and you'll remember a good chardonnay," Chris told us. "Also remember we're cruising not far from Hunter Valley, the place that gave birth to this fine drink." The crisp clean taste, Chris said, identified with more modern wines and would identify, he believed, with the wines of the future.

The history of wine production in Australia involves King George III and his loss of the American colonies. Because of that, the king needed some other land to send POMEs to. A POME, or pommy, was a Prisoner Of Mother England. George III sent the worst criminals to Australia for safekeeping. At one time, only criminals could live in Brisbane. All other settlers were excluded by law. The original pioneers in Australia were criminals the way the original settlers of America were social outcasts, practitioners of despised religions, and debtors.

Some POMEs tried making wine, succeeded, and Australian wine gained a good reputation. Soon, people knew Australia as the Vineyard of the Empire. In those days, people used wine not to get drunk or to accompany food but for medicinal purposes, a use that has returned full circle recently since we are now told that one or two glasses of wine a day prevents heart disease and strokes.

Jonathan Wicks took over and proceeded to show us how to make crusted tuna, but first he gave away Peter Doyle's secrets for good Australian cooking: Prepare simple dishes using quality products. Mix cold, hot, and different flavors, so the tastes explode in the mouth. This remains somewhat more modern than the traditional *QE2* approach, which has been and will continue to be more classical cuisine.

"Sydney and Australia used to be a culinary wasteland, but in the last five years they have developed. Now they enjoy a culinary reputation worldwide," said Wicks as he patted the crust on the fish.

Following Hancock's example, Jonathan Wicks explained how we should taste food. Wicks took in his hand a small bottle of balsamic vinegar. He read the label with obvious relish and smiled his approval. He can't resist talking about the stuff and waxed eloquent about how the balsamic vinegar tastes so delicate and smooth. "If you come across a bottle of hundred-year-old vinegar, buy it. You'll have no regrets. The balsam matures in sherry oaken casks. . . ." and on and on he went about it for twenty minutes. I never thought anyone could know twenty minutes' worth of lecture about vinegar. The man showed his love. The whole scene reminded me of when they read the will of some Italian patriarch who had recently died. The money, so what! The gold, who cares! The vineyards, forget it! The chairs drew up closer. The inheritors leaned forward on the edges of their seats to hear who would get the vinegar!

Wicks told us how to buy a tuna fish. Get the slice one inch thick. Make sure the fish isn't too young, or else it won't have much flavor, and not too old, because it will have tough meat. Aim for the middle mature, he says. Feel it to make sure it is firm and fresh, and smell it to make sure it smells right. The flesh shouldn't look too dark or too light. Wicks amazes us with how much he knew and how much we didn't know about a stupid thing like tuna fish. In a flash, I understand why *QE2* became a mecca for foodies—it was guys like Wicks. And I like the training I'm getting on becoming a bon vivant, my true vocation. To me, it comes naturally, but we all can use help in developing our natural talents.

At lunch, Ethel and I ordered the crusted tuna.

Jon, our waiter, says he can't figure out why so many people ordered that dish. I explained that the demonstration had whetted our appetites and I showed the detailed directions given to us by Chef Wicks. I alerted Jon and Alex that if the instructions are not followed correctly, we will return the dish. That drastic, nearly Rabbi-like action proved unnecessary. The tuna tasted, smelled, and felt great.

At lunch, Ethel showed the Lus the photo of Kev, our koala. The Lus loved the picture and they loved Kev, too. The British group on our other side conferred their considered praise as well. Then the son, Jacky Lu, took our picture with his family members, as they all squeeze close to us at our table. It's nice to have friends.

At the spa, Leonard warned me again that we won't like Queens Grill because it will seem too pretentious. I promised him I would let him know. Right now that's the least of my problems.

Leonard tells me he can't stand the rough seas and the bad weather. He thinks he will leave *QE2* at Sydney, stay awhile there, and then fly to Perth to catch up with the ship. Edgar, his friend, has a different plan. He wants to leave at Sydney and then hop a train to Perth. So far, he only has been able to book a recliner seat since all the sleeping berths have been previously "engaged," British for reserved. Leonard cautioned Edgar that

the scenery on the way to Perth this time of year will bore him and that
the trip isn't worth making.

When I left the spa, the two of them were still debating the issue on
and on, as if they were in the House of Commons.

Seasickness! What a disease. If the authorities of Sydney had known how
badly we had it, they would have quarantined the ship. Leonard and
Edgar had had enough. They could no longer face an ocean contorting in
spasms of white-topped wrath. In order to deal with the situation that they
couldn't leave, they constructed a fiction, loosening the grip of the reality
of the temporal world on their human spirits. I know and they know that
they are not leaving *QE2*. They will remain as will we all.

At dinner, the Lus surprised Ethel and myself with a bottle of Château
Montrose 1975. I know what it cost because we ordered and drank it
before. Now that we know how to drink wine, how to appreciate it more
fully, Château Montrose tastes even better. The wine expands my mood,
so I briefed the Lus on what they will see and hear about me in the Australian papers and on the TV. The media will try to make me look like
more of an asshole than I really am.

The Lus get the situation right away. They passed me their Hong
Kong and Sydney addresses and invited us to visit. I know this will
happen because we like them too. We have to make up for the Chinese
dinner the bad weather caused us to miss.

Oh no! Back at the cabin, another letter is under the door. What bad
news lies within the envelope?

Surprise! Cunard offers us a courtesy upgrade to Q3 and Queens
Grill. If we wish, we can go to cabin 1041 on One deck instead of our
scheduled room on Two deck. We are really out of sequence, because
Cunard promoted us on the last segment from Caronia and Three deck to
Princess Grill and Two deck. The coming segment from Sydney to Mombasa, Kenya, we were supposed to be in Britannia Grill, so we are skipping ahead two classes. Oh well, a little sunshine must brighten every

life, just as into every life a little rain must fall. This promotion makes up for buckets of rain we experienced these last two days. The upgrade reminds me to calculate the cost of this segment and also appraise the quality and value of this part of the trip, which you recall encompassed Hong Kong to Sydney.

We tip generously because we felt we got excellent attention: Allen got $60, Robert $200, Jon and Alex $300 each, and Tracy $200. The tip sum came to $1,060, which when added to the $12,186 I paid for the segment, gave a total of $13,246, making our daily rate $552 per day per person. Ethel thinks this was well worth it. I do too. It's not the numbers that count, but what you get for them. We more than doubled our space and pleasure for less than double the cost. Therefore, on this segment, a remarkable rapport existed between price and quality. I see it as one of the great travel bargains of all time.

THERE IS NO SUCH THING AS BAD PUBLICITY

*F*rom the Lido, the sight of Sydney right in our backyard astounded us: a giant city close up to the ship, closer than I have ever seen a city come to a great cruise ship. The image was all the more impressive because we had become used to seeing nothing but rain and sea and clouds. We could see close up the famous Sydney Opera House, which stood on the starboard side of *QE2*. The opera house looked like a giant crab surfacing from the ocean depths, up to no good.

Thus, *QE2* was firmly sheltered and embedded in the Sydney landscape. Indeed, the ship had become a part of the city, and not just physically, but emotionally, as well.

The taxi driver knew all about the bad weather and why the ship had arrived late. Last night, he had seen on TV pictures of the ship's interior only, since no one was permitted on deck, and someone, probably me, swimming in the pool. *QE2* had celebrity here in Sydney. So did I.

My talk went well. The doctors caught on right away. I left the podium to thunderous applause. Other papers presented by other physicians confirmed the findings—the silicone breast implant is a piece of junk. We had a panel discussion where I answered questions from the floor.

For a brief moment I felt happy. Then the press conference started.

Right from the beginning, the press conference speakers took on adversarial tones. I tried to keep cool, but the questions obviously focused on me personally and not on my work. For instance, how would you respond to this question?

"A neurologist at the Mayo Clinic says that as far as he is concerned, Dr. Patten is a socially marginal person who has always functioned on the fringe of society."

"Who is this guy who is knocking me down?" I asked.

The reporter looked puzzled. She is supposed to ask the questions. "We don't know. The statement was made anonymously."

"Too bad," said I. "I was just curious to know if that guy had been talking to my wife. If you do find out who it is, let me know. I want to cross him off my Christmas card list."

No response.

Instead, the reporter looked baffled. Next question: "Isn't it true that the *New York Times* reported you used expensive and dangerous treatments on sick women?"

Whenever a question starts with "Isn't it true," the answer that you should give is usually "No, it isn't true." But I was in one of those reckless Irish moods. I didn't care what I said. "Did you want me to let them die?"

The reporter, obviously irritated by my Irish way of answering a question by posing another question, decided to ask another. "Why is the Baylor College of Medicine not affiliated with a university? Isn't that typical of the inferior medical schools?"

This was the first time I had heard that question. It's a good one. I suppose I could have said Baylor is affiliated with Rice University, which it is, loosely, but instead I said, "I don't know."

There followed multiple other questions designed to embarrass me or throw me into disrepute. Much to my chagrin, I heard myself admit to traveling to work in a limousine and I admitted, "That's normal for millionaires."

No question, I shall receive some rather bad publicity here in Sydney. I consoled myself with what Bela Lugosi said when he was arrested for drugs: "There is no such thing as bad publicity."

I could see the story the reporter was shaping. God, I would look awful. Appearances would convict me. On Australian TV I shall definitely look flawed, but would I look like a hero? Finally, when the reporter popped the question I've heard so often from Dow attorneys, I knew Dow had gotten to her. This time, I knew my response would stop things cold. "Isn't it true," she said venomously, "that the president of the European Plastic Society called you a 'shit scientist'?"

If I said yes, people might not know what I was agreeing to—the shit part or the part about the president saying it. If I said no, then I would be stooping to their level and lying. In logic school, we call that a complex question and the way to answer this particular question was: "It wasn't the president of the European Plastic Society that called me a junk scientist. It was the president of the American Society of Plastic Surgery speaking in Europe. But, you know, in a sense, I am a shit scientist. That's what I have been studying this past decade—a piece of shit. That's what the breast implant was, and is—a piece of shit."

No more questions.

They would edit my answer, but that didn't change the good feeling I got from giving it. I knew this would happen. The story line had been prefigured. There was no way to change it. Truth and fiction, as we commonly understand the distinction, don't exist in the media. It's all narrative, narrative, narrative—shaped by bias. And the bias is shaped by money. It could probably be shown by facts and figures that there is no distinct American criminal class except CEOs and, of course, Congress. If the two of them ever get together, we're in for real trouble.

After the conference, I sauntered along the circular quay of wharf five and stopped at Doner Diner to eat a doner kabob. It was good, but not as good as in Istanbul, Turkey.

I passed back toward the ship. Along the quay, I heard Johnny Verbeeck's calliope, worn out, mechanical, and tired, reiterating some worn-out old songs. Things picked up when a little girl, about four years old and wearing a cute brown straw bonnet, started to dance for the crowd in front of the organ to the tune of "Saint Louis Woman." Somehow the music and the child's ecstatic happiness lifted my spirits. I realized what bothered me is that my main message didn't get across because I let them focus on me, rather than the research. But was that my fault? You know when you have won the argument when the other side refuses to show up for the debate, or turns sullen, or starts shouting, particularly when the shouts are personal insults. It was amazing that Dow and Comber Consulting could shift the argument away from their shitty product to a discussion of me as a person. Ad hominem arguments like that are always irrelevant and diversionary.

Hell, I tried. It was time to relax. I dropped a coin in the tray and became an organ donor.

I went back to *QE2* to the new room on One deck. I felt better right away. The space measured thirty-six feet by eighteen feet, a giant room, the details of which I'll describe later. Right now my attention focused onto an object on the table, a bottle of champagne that someone had placed in the room, cooling in a silver container, just waiting for me. It was Perrier-Jouet Grand Brut. Ethel and I had moved up. Ethel showed up and we drank the champagne and ate the fist-sized strawberries that came with it. Where and how did they grow such large strawberries?

My mood brightened. Besides, Ethel and I couldn't be bothered anymore by all the press and TV garbage. We had jobs to do.

We went up on deck and became intensely occupied in supervising the departure. We controlled the letting go of moorings, the making fast of the tugs. Then, as the enormous power of *QE2*'s engines began to throb through to the shafts and spin the propellers, the ship safely breaking away from the tugs toward the unfettered freedom of the seas, we bade Sydney good-bye. We waved to the people. People, people, people—people standing everywhere—above us on the Coathanger (the nickname for the Sydney Harbor Bridge that stretches across the harbor), below us on the quay, to the right and left of us. Not just a few have turned out to send off *QE2*. There are thousands. Myriads of boats accompanied us as we headed to the granite teeth of the headlands at the harbor's entrance. Multiple horns sounded. Two people on jet skis buzzed by the ship. A helicopter with a TV cameraman, his legs hanging out the window, circled us overhead. Two other helicopters hovered dangerously in midair over the ship, close to the aft funnel. Some sailboats tried to keep up with us, but they couldn't. The powerboats do keep up for a while, but, once *QE2* got moving, they fell behind.

The captain piped bagpipe music of Highland Cathedral through the public address system. Men in starched white uniforms distributed rocket-powered glasses of orange planter's punch. Ethel and I danced on the aft upper deck to the music of the *QE2* band. They played "Let's Face the Music and Dance." The words have a certain poignancy: "Before we pay the bill, while we still have the chance, let's face the music and dance."

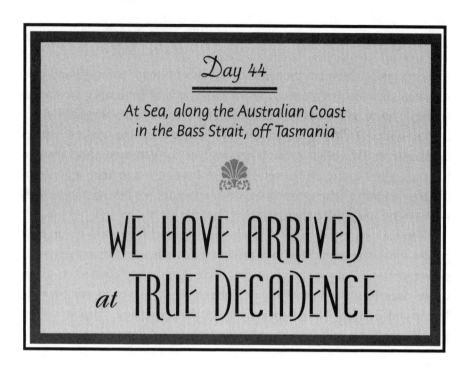

WE HAVE ARRIVED
at TRUE DECADENCE

*Q*ueens Grill. I was confused, but then I figured it out. During the 1994 refit, Mauretania Restaurant became Caronia, Columbia became Mauretania, and Queens Grill kept its name, but was redesigned. Just as before, space, grace, and pace all still resided there. Viva Queens Grill! We had arrived.

Queens Grill. It's the top restaurant on *QE2*, rated five stars, and one of the great restaurants of the world. Ethel and I are here. At last!

Queens Grill. It was here, many years ago, my father taught me how to spot the Americans at the tables. They cut their meat, put down their knives, switch the forks to their right hands, and eat that way. The others—the rest of the world—keep their knives on the right side and balance everything on the slippery side of the fork, which stays put in their left hands.

Queens Grill. It was there that I learned about full place settings that included ten pieces of cutlery. While other restaurants provided the correct cutlery before each course is served, Queens Grill had it all out there to start with. If you find it bewildering or don't know which knife or fork to use for which course, the rule is always start at the outermost pair. Work toward the innermost pair. The knife and fork closest to where the plate is set will be for the main course.

Ethel and I started to settle in. My expectations are high, and having trained up to luxury, I'll tell you what I expected: superb food, superb service, and excellent drink in a gracious, friendly atmosphere. In particular, I expected the caviar would be served with the correct mother-of-pearl or bone (not metal) caviar spoon. The *sommelier*, or wine steward, would serve our wine from the appropriate decanters, with the correct glassware, and would provide a leatherbound wine list. And there would be no supermarket teas.

Queens Grill. The appeal seems universal. To the social historian, Queens Grill is the microcosm of the times. To nautical enthusiasts, it is the ultimate dining room on the ultimate liner. To students of human nature, it is an endlessly fascinating laboratory of behavior. For lovers of nostalgia, it has the allure of yesterday. For me, Queens Grill remains the luxury standard by which all other standards should be measured.

Too bad our waiters, Paul and Colum, don't know this. They are nice, but they don't measure up to Jon and Alex, who spoiled us rotten in Princess Grill.

Ethel and I shall have to train Paul and Colum. It was partially our problem; we, Ethel especially, had gotten fussy. Ethel wanted brown sugar instead of white. She wanted our drained water glasses refilled right away. She didn't like the fact that the Queens Grill menu didn't list the calorie counts, like the spa menu items. Ethel said, "Every item should have calorie counts and salt content, not to influence decisions or to scare people, but simply to make people aware of what they are eating." The corrupting influence of complete luxury continued to work on us. We felt ourselves transforming into foodies, *winees*, and *cruisees*, people skilled in eating, drinking, and cruising. These skills, to a limited extent, are born into your character structure, but they can be developed.

Another fault in Queens Grill is the loudspeakers are muted. We can't hear Captain John Burton-Hall's report from the bridge. We do hear him say the temperatures are dropping because of the wind from the south that blows off the polar ice. Fancy that. In Texas, a south wind would bring a heat wave. In the antipodes, everything made sense, if inverted. Because of the noise and the poor acoustics, we also miss the second officer's noon navigation report. Without the noon navigation report, Ethel felt lost. I made it up to her by making up a report and delivering it in my crisp British accent: "Good afternoon," I said. "This is the second officer of the watch with navigation information for today, Sunday the 18, February. The ship's position at noon today was 40 degrees south latitude, 140 degrees east longitude, a distance of 685 nautical miles from Sydney. Average speed was 27.45 knots. Air temperature is 72 degrees, the sea temperature is the same, and the relative humidity is 43 percent. The barometer is 1,024 millibars and steady. Wind is south-southeast at force-three (nine knots) with a slight sea and low swell."

In Queens Grill, the sounds of creaking and groaning differ from what we heard below in Princess Grill. Each place has its own sound. We just have to adjust to it. How minute my sensitivities have become. Keeping a diary helped develop my observational skills. I started paying attention to things I would have missed.

I was in the ship's library returning a video when Estelle, one of our dining room friends, made the mistake of asking how my day went in Sydney. So I told her. She understood and was sympathetic. Concern showed clearly in her eyes and on her face. "Now you know what it's like to oppose the powers that be," she said. "Personal attacks are not nice and prove the companies are desperate."

I nodded yes.

Libby Tinsley, the chef from Petaluma's Bridgewater Mill restaurant, couldn't give her demonstration today of how to make a mango and passion fruit meringue layer cake, so Jonathan Wicks had to do it. Wicks, you recall, replaced Chef Peter Doyle, who was seasick. Now Wicks replaces Libby Tinsley, who has lost her voice from all that shouting at a cocktail party last night. Australian chefs must be pretty fragile.

First things first. Before we learn about food preparation, we must sample some wine. Brian Closier, a vintner, started off right by telling us to forget everything that Chris Hancock said about wine. Chris, the previous lecturer on Australian wines, came from a rival winery.

As Brian gave his spiel, white-gloved waiters passed out the first wine of the day. I glanced at my watch, 11:22 AM. God, this is decadent. What sacrifices we make to learn about wine. Out of the corner of my eye, I checked around. Sure enough, some passengers looked like this was not their first drink of the day, but, rather, the last drink of last night. Wherever free alcoholic beverages are offered, *QE2* passengers are there.

With everyone's glasses loaded up, some *QE2*ers, by instinct or by compulsion, have started drinking. Brian yelled at them, "Stop! Don't drink that wine until I tell you to!" Most of the drinkers continue gulping, of course. On *QE2*, self-will and the consequent disobedience has become a way of life.

Brian tried to get a feel for the audience. He asked how many think Australian wines are the best in the world. At least half the people raised their hands. Brian surveys the vast sea of hands and shook his head in a nugatory fashion. "Obviously, there are lots of Australians in this audience. Australians like wine. In fact, they embrace anything alcoholic." Brian went on, "How many believe American wines are the best in the world?" Ethel's hand shot up, and my hand followed. "Obviously, Americans are not parochial for there must be more than two Americans here."

"How many believe English wines are the best?" English wines? I had never heard of such a thing, but several hands (all attached to Brits) go up. "Obviously, there are lots of misinformed Englishmen here," said Brian, smiling. "England has no wines."

Brian told us that wine and food have become an important part of modern life and that this is especially true on *QE2*. Really? Holy shit, mate. That shocks me.

Brian pointed to a map on the blackboard. He called it a "professionally drawn depiction of Australia." The audience howls for the map looks more like one of those mysterious sea blobs, an amorphus round nothing. Brian confessed he drew the map himself. A wag from the back yelled out, "How many wines did you sample before you made that, Brian?"

We learned about the formation of the continent of Australia. India broke off from the north and Antarctica from the south. It appears that the continent is the oldest land mass that has not undergone reorganization by volcanic activity, or by the uplifting of the earth's crust, so it has very old slate rock that has been continuously worn down by the wind and weather. Hence, there are few mountains but many rolling hills and flat plains that make up most of Australia. For me, this became a moment of sudden illumination. I realized why Australia looked so primal, so primitive, so basic, and I concluded that made Australians the way they are. That, and the tyranny of distance, the isolation one feels in the great expanses of dry, dead space. They have the land, but the land also has them. The land looks worn out, depleted, silent, and lonely, and so it was for most of the early settlers. There always were too few women compared to the number of men, so the culture grew up with men without women—always a sad thing. Too much roughness, too much drinking, too much self-absorption, and too little tenderness and love. Mars without Venus doesn't work.

June Owen, our onboard lecturer on Australia, illustrated the loneliness of Australia with a story. There is a gap with a large cliff near Sidney where lots of people commit suicide. One day, a policeman came upon a young man who was sitting on the edge. The policeman, who had just finished training in crisis management, said, "Let's talk about this, mate, before you do anything."

The young man told of his business failures, his wife who had left him, his home reverted (reverted is British for foreclosure) to the bank, and so forth. After about forty-five minutes, they both went over.

This sense of keen alienation is felt even more by the older Australians, who feel the immigration of Asians has changed things forever. I overheard two elderly Australians talking about it, and one said, "We don't belong here anymore. It's our turn to vanish like all those extinct animals."

Brian told us about the great ice mass in the southern part of the Southern Ocean. The mass cools southern Australia and permits the cultivation of grapes closer to the equator than is usually possible. He told of the peculiar soil conditions that make for great wines, and he proved that they are great wines by letting us, the few who had been patiently holding our glasses, go ahead and drink. The Riesling tasted fruitier than wine from the Rhineland. It smelled of peaches and had a higher alcohol content, 13.50 percent instead of 10 to 12 percent. It was dry, not sweet, and considering my personal long-held objection to sweeter German Rieslings, it was great.

Brian taught us to taste the varied flavors, including herbaceous (pea pods), tropical passion fruits, citrus, and, after awhile, honey. He told us a fact I learned in high school: a good wine should not taste or smell like kerosene.

As an instructor, Brian must have taken lessons from our computer teacher, Matt. He pursues the subject with the same meticulous attention to detail and coached the students through the material. "The first sensation in the mouth is sweet, and that should be a fruity sweetness. Then appraise and enjoy the balance of acidic and sweet and the other flavors. Then swallow and remember how long the good flavors last in your mouth. The better the flavors and the longer the aftertaste, the better the wine."

Brian then quizzed the group. "How many feel the aftertaste lasts long?" The majority raised their hands. Brian said, "It's uncanny how the consensus usually gets it right. The individual may err, but the majority usually knows the correct answer."

Isn't that the philosophical foundation for democracy?

The group went on through the chardonnay, which seemed better than the American variety: fruitier, less sweet, and, with a 13.5 percent alcohol content, a bigger punch.

We made our way to lunch. Continuing a decadent tradition, Alex Seymour, assistant restaurant manager of Queens Grill, showed us the dinner menu in case we have amendments, meaning in case we want to order something, or order anything. Thus, we have arrived at true decadence: wine before noon and review of dinner before we start lunch. I loved it. So does Ethel.

When we returned to the room we found another present from our travel agents, Vince and Lennie: a bottle of cabernet, Mouton Cadet 1991, made by Baron Philippe de Rothschild in Bordeaux. Not bad. This time we'll know more about how to appreciate it better. This time we'll drink it right.

Lennie and Vince's note read, "We and the cats miss you. Have a great voyage—nice upgrades."

"I wonder if that's true?" Ethel asked.

"What's true?"

"P.J. misses us."

"In her own little selfish cat-centric way, I'll bet she does. And if P.J. knew about all this aimless luxury, she'd be jealous."

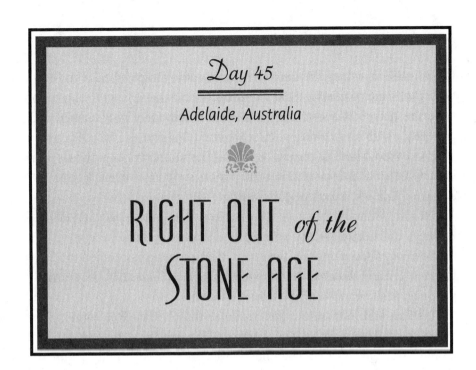

Day 45

Adelaide, Australia

RIGHT OUT *of the*
STONE AGE

*E*scorting tugs dazzled the packed quayside crowds with a colorful display of water jets, which broke into a million rainbow droplets as they fell through the sunlit sky and onto the yachts and motor launches milling around the ship.

The southern waters recalled a memory that occurred to me on *QE2* in 1978. *QE2*'s radio room received a signal prefaced by the letters GBTT—the call sign of the *Queen Mary*. The message had apparently been sent during World War II, had traveled to outer space, and then, some forty years later, had returned to earth to be picked up by the *QE2*'s receivers. The incident surprised the radio officer, but it wasn't totally unique; similar phantom radio messages, plunging back to earth from who-knows-where, are occasionally reported, but never before had one come bearing the royal call signal of RMS *Queen Mary*.

Incidentally, *Queen Mary* is for sale. The price is $30 million. The city of Long Beach had bought the grand old lady of the Atlantic in 1967 for $3 million, when she had been losing an average of $1.8 million a year. Since the purchase, local California critics have been trying to torpedo the *Queen Mary*—something the German navy was unable to do between 1940 and 1946 when *Queen Mary* carried 765,000 troops between the United States and Europe. The detractors say *Queen Mary* isn't worthy of museum status or public support. But as a seaman I believe that's just a load of codswallop.

While I thought about weird messages from outer space, an official-looking, uniformed twenty-seven-piece marching band welcomed *QE2* as the ship pulled alongside the quay. Most passengers seemed too eager to get off. They jammed the midship lounge on Two deck, awaiting the gangway and the captain's permission to exit.

Nathan and Estelle, our friends from the Caronia Restaurant, numbered among them. Ethel and I pushed through the crowd to get with them. Last night, Nathan saw me on Australian TV. "Highly controversial," said Nathan, but he was open-minded. Nathan agreed to read my scientific papers. That's better than Michelle the Nasty, the reporter for *Frontline*, who wouldn't read a blessed thing.

Nathan said the TV newscast was very favorable to me, and, while he avuncularly patted my right shoulder, he told me why: "Australians love flawed heroes, you know, especially those who show lack of respect for authority."

At 9:30 AM, like a giant tidal wave—a human tsunami—the released passengers flowed off *QE2* and into the ocean terminal. Thousands of Australians turned out to meet us. *QE2* is an item here just as if one of the royals had appeared. No, probably better. Most Australians that we have met don't seem as keen on the royals as the British.

Mary Anne Kennedy guided us today. She seemed to speak more clearly than the other Australians, but then again, maybe I was getting used to the accent. I started to speak with an Australian accent to amuse Ethel. "Be careful, your voice might stick in that mode," Ethel admonished me.

Adelaide, designed for the good living, began as the brainchild of the liberal British philanthropist Edward Gibbon Wakefield, who dreamed of an Australian colony inhabited not by convicts but by decent, free, law-abiding men and women, a microcosm of civilized society. The site for the city, ideal in many ways, was chosen in 1836 on rising ground below a range of hills near the sea and named after the British queen Adelaide, consort of King William IV. Thus planned, Colonel William Light—whose statue on Montefiore Hill presides over the city—laid out the symmetrical, square-cut jewel design with Victoria Square as the city center and beyond that spreading out into a planned grid of streets. The carefully planned green spaces, the recreational grounds, the meandering Torrens River, and the warm weather were all good reasons to settle in Adelaide. The original English settlers needed workers, so Germans came and many stayed because they were paid in land. Thus arose a unique collection of different national types, outlooks, varied foods, and wines.

A taxi pulled alongside our bus and started beeping. Two resourceful tourists had missed the bus and wanted to join us. We stopped for them. That's the right way to do things. No reason for the people on time to wait for those who are late. If they are late, make them catch up.

Riding through town we saw familiar and unfamiliar signs. The familiar included McDonald's and Wendy's, the unfamiliar Happy Jack's, which Mary Anne explained was Burger King in disguise. Burger King couldn't use the name because that name had already been taken in Australia. Also unfamiliar were corrals of camels. Mary Anne said the camels there breed disease free. For high prices, the locals sold the camels to the Saudi Arabians. Mary Anne reeled off half a dozen other industries in Adelaide: GM and Mitsubishi made cars, British Aerospace made planes, and lots of people made good food and drink. More restaurants existed in Adelaide per person than in any other part of Australia. I believed it, because on the road all we saw were row upon on row of restaurants. As soon as we approached Barossa Valley, all we would see were row upon row of wineries.

People living in South Australia like to have fun, and that's why the license plates call the place the Festival State without actually mentioning the name of the state of South Australia itself. Mary Anne couldn't resist telling us about opals and Coober Pedy, the small town we didn't have time to visit. Coober Pedy, where daytime temperatures hit 120 degrees F and nights are freezing, has a molelike population of two thousand people who live there in cave homes underground. The people emerge during the day to mine 90 percent of the world's opals! We also heard of Kangaroo Island, which we also didn't have time for and was six and a half hours by ferry and forty minutes by air, south of Adelaide. Kangaroo Island had hundreds of seals, kangaroos, fairy penguins, emus, shy duck-billed platypuses, and koalas. *Koalas?* In a flash, Ethel and I realized that we had signed up for the wrong tour. We should have been headed with the other group to Kangaroo Island to see the koalas.

Our bus passed the Parafield Airfield, whose name was spelled out in trees so it could be read easily from the air by the numerous students, mainly Vietnamese, who went there for flight training. The weather was CAVU: Ceiling And Visibility Unlimited. I could see why it would be a good place to train pilots. One drawback, Mary Anne explained, was flight school cost $120,000. Why pay that, for with the same amount of money or even less, two people could cruise the world on *QE2*?

We entered the countryside and passed along tree-lined roads, some of which were unpaved dirt. Along the roadside stood several pink flowers, about eighteen inches tall and without leaves. Each plant had a single flower that merely sat on top of a single green stalk. They called these flowers naked ladies. Naked ladies were everywhere and almost as beautiful as the flowering gum trees. We rode over the famous Jacob's Creek, whose name applied to the most popular Australian wines, with over fifty-two million liters consumed each year in Australia and another seventeen million liters consumed in New Zealand. We stopped at the Jacob Creek Winery and started drinking.

First came champagne, then Riesling, and then a sauvignon blanc with a bold flavor. The woman poured freely and kept filling my glass faster than I could get the stuff down. She explained the Solero method, pouring old wine into new or new into old or something like that. I was too looped to care and had a grand old time.

On to cahrdonnay, which I could no longer spell. The world began to whirl. I heard myself start to quote Dr. Johnson: "Claret is for boys; port for men; but he who aspires to be a hero must drink brandy." Just as I downed a fruit brandy (pear? plum? who knows?), time was up. Back we stumbled onto the bus and off to the next winery.

We tried to sober up at Angas Park, sampling delicious dried raisins, apricots, and kiwis. The collection of nuts astounded me: cashews, glazed almonds, and peanuts.

Mary Anne suggested we clear our heads by walking into town. I knew it was Australia, but it could well have been an old Wild West Hollywood film set. There was one line of faded, white-painted wooden houses with fenced balconies that hung out over the street. We passed a quaint hotel that could have been for a good place to crash before High Noon. There was a lubritorium, for cars not people; grocery stores selling cabbage by the kilogram; Schultz's "Small Town Small Goods Store; and in the village square a monument to the Clydesdale horse.

Bill, a fellow passenger who owned a sheep farm in New Zealand, had an experience similar to my own with Clydesdales. When the tractor arrived, the Clydesdales went crazy, raging and stamping around. The horses knew they were out of a job.

The next winery was Yalumba. On the lawn, under the lichen-filled branches of white oak trees, we sampled more wine: Rieslings, chardonnays, merlots, and cabernets. By accident, I ran into the guy next to me, spilling wine on him. He didn't mind. In fact, he thought it so funny, he couldn't stop laughing. Something seemed funny to me, too. I couldn't stop laughing, either.

Next, we ate lunch in the wine cellar among the round red-rimmed barrels, which together contained five hundred liters of wine. Thank God the spigots remained closed. I felt like I had enough wine to last me for the century and beyond. I was wined out. I hated wine, all of which may explain why, at this point, I inanely asked the gentle hostess in charge of the winery for a glass of Glenmorangie, a Scotch whisky. Request denied. For some weird reason, I quoted Doctor Johnson again. "He who drinks until he becomes a beast gets away from the pain of being a man," which is hardly funny at all, and yet I kept laughing and laughing.

Back in the bus, Mary Anne suggested that if we wished, the group could sleep. Most QE2ers paid no attention to this excellent advice. They were already out cold.

I woke briefly to see us passing an area fenced off with white corrugated metal, the first nudist colony in Australia. Mary Anne said we couldn't see in unless we had a double-decker bus, which we didn't.

As soon as we got back to *QE2*, I headed aft to the outdoor pool on One deck. The water was ice cold and woke me up. Then I heated myself up in the hot tub. For a brief moment I was happy, happy until three Aussies joined me. They had a grand old time splashing and crashing, yelling and screaming. Oh well, by then I was used to it. Wherever there are Australians, there's noise and sometimes trouble, but you can't really blame people for enjoying themselves. Can you?

You can blame them for what they said about the Japanese. "Japs are on the ship," confided one Australian. "I wouldn't associate with them in my social life. I certainly don't intend to spend my vacation with them. We're getting off in Perth and shall request a refund."

"The Japs aren't so bad. At least they don't act like rowdies in the hot tub."

That's what I should have said, but I didn't. I have come to rather like my nose on my face the way it is now—straight.

Tonight the show featured another kind of Australian, Aborigines, three boys and fourteen girls called the Janbock Mob. Their faces were coated white, and the boys have coated their bodies white to look like skeletons. The boys wore orange-red diapers, which I am sure they don't wear in the bush. Right away I know the outfits are not authentic. The early white settlers reported the Aboriginals didn't wear orange and they didn't wear white. Aboriginals didn't wear anything.

They danced to the complex rhythms of wood sticks, a strange, primitive, and scary beat. I don't have to ask where it comes from. It comes right out of the Stone Age. The Aboriginal leader treated us to a recital with an instrument made of a large hollow branch, called the didgeridoo. It made a collection of weird, almost electrical sounds, like a shortwave radio transmitting nonsense, surprisingly futurific and certainly unlike anything we had heard before, and probably something that we do not wish to hear again.

Day 46

At Sea, on the Great Australian Bight

SICK SQUID SOUNDS LIKE SIX QUID

*E*thel woke me from an erotic dream. I was using the computer and the mouse to do word processing, but I must have been thinking about breakfast, because I was word processing the Queens Grill breakfast menu.

"That's not erotic. It doesn't have to do with love," she said.

"Does too," I replied. "There is no love more sincere than the love of food."

QE2 continued to cruise westward in the Great Australian Bight. We are getting used to setting the clock back an hour and enjoying, on a routine basis, twenty-five-hour days.

A bight, incidentally, is a large body of water that lies in an indentation of land. The bight is calm, but we are too far south. It's cold. We can't stay comfortably outside, nor did I think about swimming in the outside pool. We are cold, but what we are suffering is nothing compared to the record snows reported in the northeastern United States. Up and down the East Coast people dug out from the region's fourth major winter storm that broke records from Connecticut to Virginia. The latest storm dumped nearly five inches on Lynchburg, Virginia, putting the total snowfall for the season at fifty-one inches, which broke the hundred-year-old record. Poor Hartford, Connecticut, a city used to dealing with snow, handled over seven feet.

Cruise news quoted a certain Ben McDonald from Washington, DC, saying, "I'm sick of this."

Right, Ben, but may I suggest next time you solve the problem by cruising on *QE2*. Better to take one cruise than to curse the snow.

"Hecklers Blast Clinton on AIDS in New Hampshire," read one headline. I read the article to find out how he handled the questions. The reporters accused Clinton of not fulfilling his promise to distribute free syringes among drug addicts to try to keep down the spread of AIDS. The president replied, "Would you consider, at a time of declining public spending, a 30 percent increase inaction?"

Think about the answer.

Clinton must have had special training in PR. That was why he didn't even attempt to answer the question directly. First, he defined doing something as spending money on it. Second, he didn't make a definite statement, but asked a question. Third, he doesn't mention the actual amount of money spent because to some it might have appeared too much, and to others, too little. Every politician likes to keep things vague so as not to offend anyone. Clinton should have replied, "Goddamit, I was so busy I completely forgot about it" or "I talked to my advisors. They told me giving out free syringes would increase, not decrease, AIDS" or "As far as I am concerned, the issue is of no real interest. I had more important things to do, like sleep or pet my cat, Socks."

We were having more than the usual conflicts about what to do.

Waldemar Hansen talks about Perth at the same time as the wine and food demonstration. I selected the latter, and from the size of the audience, most proved the existentialist notion of free will by making the same choice.

Jonathan Wicks showed up again. I wondered which Australian chef he was substituting for this time.

The wine expert of the day, David Hohnen, started out with questions, but the group had become more wine aware than ever. Finally, he asked, "How many have had wine within the last twenty-four hours?" All hands went up.

Hohnen taught us about the wines of western Australia: how they started in 1827 and continued to the present, and how they changed from strong alcoholic beverages for hardworking people into the more modern-styled wines with fruity flavors and less alcohol.

The two wines we tasted were actually quite good, even though they were modern and less alcoholic. One was a mixture of sémillon and sauvignon blanc and the other a mixture of merlot and cabernet. In both cases, the harshness of the stronger wines were rounded by the less strong. Not bad. Right away, from all the wine training and experience we had, I could easily tell the wines from Perth were the best in Australia. The crowd agreed, and more important, so did Ethel. The wines had attractive colors and smells, and fruit-driven fresh tastes. Delicious.

Chris Taylor, the Australian guest chef, then made sardine cakes for us, using fresh sardines, pepper, and spices. He covered the layers with a perforated pastry shell. The complexity of construction, the time and skill involved, made me truly appreciate the great food we ate on *QE2*. Even Johnathan Wicks, *QE2*'s executive chef, showed up not to teach, but to learn how to make this extraordinary dish.

Chief, Ethel's boyfriend, an eighty-nine-year-old retired police chief from Rochester, New York, showed up for the next lecture by June Owen, who spoke about the convicts who founded Australia. This is Chief's third trip around the world. One day, he says, his son will receive a telegram and to come to the funeral or not come. Chief wants to die while cruising. He hopes to be buried at sea in his police uniform with his police chief cap, which he wears today and every day.

June Owen's lecture on the convicts explained it all. I understood the boisterous attitude in the pool, the reckless diving from the rails, the loud laughter, the disrespect for authority, and the lopsided sense of humor that I had seen among the Australians. At once I understood why the reports in the papers—I made page one of most, page two of others—are so favorable to me: Australians really did love a flawed hero; it's in their national character.

The first thousand convicts arrived in 1788. The supply ships that were to follow never did. So these forgers, robbers, and murderers were left on their own to work on the great land and form the "Lucky Country." The POMEs were usually given jobs related to their former talents. A forger became the mapmaker, or a doctor sentenced to death became the assistant surgeon. These men laughed at hardship and death. They made up terms of derisive nicknames for their punishments: the Barclay tigers equaled the stripes produced on the back by the lashes. Yes, Jack is as good as his master down under, and when official authorities boycotted my lecture I got the respect of the multitudes. For the Australians the flawed hero is the only hero.

All this applies to Perth, Sydney, and Brisbane. But Adelaide differed. Adelaide was colonized, as told by a highly selected stock of individuals who were not convicts and so, to this day, the people of Adelaide differ somewhat from the people of the rest of Australia. Descendants of convicts brag about their ancestors nowadays because such talk is in fashion. They didn't do that five years ago.

In the dry sauna sat eight men. Three have their bathing suits on while the others wear nothing. One of the men wearing nothing complained about the three who still sport suits. This was addressed to the group, but I know it applied to Leonard, the big Australian, and me. The Big Guy, tugging on his bathing suit, said in a loud, low-pitched, commanding voice, "I have penis anxiety. Want to make anything of it?" That shut them up. That guy could plaster them all. He stood six feet four, weighed more than anyone else, and looked like he lifts weights or fights professionally. And so we just sat for a while, sweating in silence.

To break the silence, I asked Leonard about Max Mygraves, the entertainer scheduled for tonight in the Grand Lounge.

"Don't go, Bernard," Leonard said. "It's the same old patter over and over again. I don't know why people listen. We Brits call him Max Migraine.

By the way, how do you find the Queens Grill?" asked Leonard. "Everyone says the service is pretentious."

"Too soon to tell. We're still training our waiters."

In the whirlpool at the spa I met a seventy-year-old from Sydney who motions me to come closer. He whispered a secret, "You are not supposed to use the spa more than twice a day, but I'm here for my second time." The old guy smiled wickedly. He travels alone, got on in Sydney and will get off in Perth, has a Four-deck cabin, and eats in Mauretania. His fare was about $5,000 because singles paid more, and he had a cabin to himself. He got no discounts because he decided at the last minute to take the trip, and he travels only a short distance, not even a whole segment.

We went to see the show in the Grand Lounge that evening. Leonard was wrong. The crowd loved Max Mygrave and gave him a standing ovation. I loved him, too, but Ethel didn't. She didn't think the jokes funny. Here's a few. See what you think.

A nine-year-old went into the chemist's and said, "Three condoms, please, Miss."

"Don't Miss me," said the woman chemist.

"Right. Make that four condoms."

How about this one?

An eighty-year-old man celebrated his birthday by taking a hot bath, during which he wiggled his toes and said, "Hello toes, happy birthday." After that, he looked at his knees and moved them about and said, "Hello knees, happy birthday." Then he spotted his willy. "Hello Willy, this would have been your birthday, too, if you were alive."

Max told one related to breast implants.

A woman asked her physician for advice about breast enlargement. "Don't get implants," the doctor said. "They might have consequences (consequences is British for side effects)." So the doctor gave her a magic mirror, which she addressed at home, "Mirror, mirror, on the floor, make my breast size a forty-four." Bong! It happened. The woman showed her husband. While she was away to get a larger bra, the husband tried it. "Mirror, mirror, on the wall, make my ding-a-ling hit the floor," whereupon the tires fell off his bicycle.

More?

A doctor gave a woman an external device so that if she pumped her arm up and down, her chest would enlarge to make it look like she had big breasts. So she went to a singles' bar, saw someone she liked, and tries it out. "Do I know you?" she asked the young man. "No, but we have the same doctor," he said, as he pumped his right leg up and down.

There's no stopping me now.

A Catholic priest went to London and walked along the West End. Some ladies of the night came up to him and said, "Try a quickie, Gov'nor, for five quid." Farther down the lane, another lady came up and said, "Five quid for a quickie." The priest refused again, but he realized he didn't know what he was refusing. So when he got back to Dublin, he called the Mother Superior in the convent next door and asked, "Sister, what's a quickie?" "Five quid, same as London," she replied.

The joke I liked the best, Ethel thought terrible.

A shark found a sick giant squid languishing in the Thames River. The shark said, "Mr. Squid, you should be in the Mediterranean, not here. Perhaps that explains your sickness." The sick squid agreed, and the shark offered to carry the squid on his back to the Mediterranean. Just after they passed the Strait of Gibraltar, the two spotted a barracuda. The shark shrugged the squid off his back saying, "Here's the sick squid I owe you."

The Brits roared with laughter, and I not only roared, I fell off my seat. *Sick squid* sounds like *six quid*. Get it?

SEXUAL THERAPIST, STRANGE CASES WELCOME

*A*t breakfast, Colum, our Queens Grill waiter, looked exhausted. He explained they had a special show for the crew last night. The show started at midnight and went to 2 AM, and then there were after-parties. Most of the crew are nursing soreheads (British for hangover). "But worth it," said Colum.

Colum explained that the crew has their own facilities. Ethel and I already knew about Container Beach on the Forward deck, just aft of the spare anchor. Someone took a container box used in container shipping, cut off one side, put that side up, drilled some holes, attached hoses, pumped in seawater, and made a swimming pool. Container Beach didn't operate in the Southern Ocean, though, because the water was too cold.

"We have the Pig and Whistle, the crew's pub, and the Cosmopolitan, the crew's dining room," said Colum. "Usually at dinner there are five types of entrées and there are special cooks for special members of the crew, like the Filipinos."

Colum smiled. He described with satisfaction the crew's gym, the table tennis room, and the crew's library. This is his third world cruise. He likes it.

Christopher Lee, the man with the golden gun, sits two tables from us in Queens Grill. I recognized Lee from the 1974 James Bond movie—actually, I remembered bombshell Britt Ekland better—but out of a decent respect for Lee's privacy, I didn't go over to get an autograph. Besides, I felt sorry for the poor guy. He could barely sit down before crew and passengers would line up at his table for his autograph.

Out of homage to Christopher Lee, I went to the 9:30 AM showing of his classic film *The Mummy*. The story concerns a tomb curse and an undead mummy who, when transported to England, goes on a rampage.

Movies in the morning, wine before noon: decadence has seized us—true decadence and I love it.

Lee will give an interview this afternoon that I shall have to miss because Dr. Clyde Roper of the Smithsonian Institution will talk at the same time about his over thirty-five years of research on cephalopods, including octopodes (he calls them octopuses) and giant squids.

Under our door there appeared two pieces of paper with good and bad news. The first is our bill for the cruise. The good news is that by some accounting quirk, which I shall not question, we received a $4,000 credit instead of $2,000. The bad news is that of our onboard credit, only $881.55 remains. Most of the money was spent on booze. A telephone call cost $335 for 26.48 minutes and the fax I sent cost $23.25 for the minute and a half it took to transmit. Ethel and I decided to ride herd on our most important expenditure, those great wines. We resolved to get—no change that—we resolved to *try* to get wines costing less than $100 a bottle. It's going to require some sacrifice, but I know we can do it. The really bad news came from the medical staff and concerned malaria.

Malaria exists between Bombay and Durban, and the London School of Hygiene and Tropical Medicine recommends that passengers and crew take mefloquine tablets as a prophylactic. Antimalarials should commence March 1 and continue until April 12. No thanks. We decided to skip this. We'll take our chances with the disease rather than with the medicine. We'll avoid the mosquitoes. We don't plan to go out at night.

Besides, my theory was if your blood alcohol level is high enough, the mosquitoes wouldn't bite.

I saw some amazing things during Dr. Roper's talk. Large sea squids washed ashore and their giant, remorseless eyes stared at you. Their giant squid brains surround their upper esophagi. If they ate something too big they would injure their brains. Undoubtedly, mother giant squids continually caution baby squids to chew their food carefully, or else they might suffer brain damage.

Roper believes there are thousands of these creatures in these waters. Starting next year he will try to prove it. The giant squid must exist because of all the evidence, but no one knows where they live or how they mate. *Architeuthis* can be sixty feet or more in length, and the size alone spawned fear and tales of terror for centuries. The mere mention of the giant squid evokes a spine-chilling picture. The squid has eight powerful arms, eyes the size of a human head, two fire hose–sized tentacles covered with barbed suckers used to snatch its prey, and a parrotlike beak. Despite its reputation the giant squid had never been observed alive in its natural habitat until 2004, when biologists snapped pictures of a twenty-six-feet-long squid.

The only known predator of the giant squid is the sperm whale. Using what little information is available about the feeding and migration habits of this huge whale, an area around New Zealand has been targeted as a likely spot to find and study both sperm whales and *Architeuthis*. The idea is to use the sperm whale as a kind of hound dog to lead the scientists to the squids.

In November Dr. Roper planned to man a submersible lowered into the frigid, inky depths where the sperm whales feed. In the protected confines of the submarine, he will dwell for months if need be to get pictures of the giant squids. I would go with him, except the room on the submersible looked smaller and more cramped than an M5 cabin, sort of like a monk's cell. And I see no ensuite bathroom, nor do I believe that vessel capable of carrying great wines or food. More power to Dr. Roper and dedicated scientists like him whose motivation and quest for knowledge I can't really fathom. Count me out of the expedition. I have more important things to do, like play shuffleboard.

In the hot tub I met a dairy farmer from Scotland. He showed me where his fingers got crushed when he tried to deliver a calf. I inquired why he didn't get a vet to do the job. "They bloody cost fifteen quid [I almost wrote 'fifteen squids']. That's more than the bloody doctor, who costs ten bloody quid." The dairy farmer then proceeded to rail against the national health scheme (scheme is British for plan), which he says taxes him each month but won't let him see the doctor. He claimed the doctors have it all sown up tight. "The doctors get paid for doing nothing. The queue is so long unless you have private insurance, nothing happens until you die." The discussion, or rather, his oration, sparked some recognition from our other partner in the hot tub, an Australian man about forty-five years old, with bald top and remaining side hair obviously dyed jet black.

This Australian agreed, "The same problem pertains in Australia." He had arthritis. After months of waiting, he saw the doctor. The doctor wouldn't tell him anything except what he already knew, that the arthritis involved his shoulders and hands. The doctor told him there was no treatment, but a friend suggested cod liver oil. It worked. Within three months of taking one tablespoon a night, the arthritis, which had previously been so bad he couldn't close either hand, went away. He cut the dose of cod to a teaspoon a day and the arthritis remains in remission.

"You have to stop the cod liver oil and see if the arthritis returns," I told him.

"I did. It started to come back. I got scared and restarted. I've taken it for four years."

Then the Australian became garrulous, revealing a deeply negative attitude about the future of the world that was so severe and so extreme, I shall henceforth call him Mr. Doom, or Doom, for short.

Doom took over the conversation. Doom told us about the coming financial crisis, a crash so severe it would be the crash to end all crashes. "Japan can't hold out much longer. The central Bank of Japan, about mid-April, will sell American bonds to get cash. The American bond market will collapse. Then the American stock market will crash. America will no longer pay its army, so the Chinese will invade Russia."

Very interesting.

"Oh, by the way," I asked Doom, "What do you do for a living?"

"For the last twenty-two years I've been giving financial advice to major international corporations."

Negative people don't interest me, so I tried to lose Doom, but he followed me into the pool and swam laps with me, all the while shouting about a world financial collapse. "Even Australia is broke, not just the United States," Doom said as he turned on his back and spurted water on high like a sperm whale. "The only way anything gets done in Australia is by borrowing money from the Japanese."

I left the pool and headed back to the hot tub. Doom, a Cassandra trapped in a man's body, followed me. Finally, Doom had to go to the loo and I used that chance to sneak away to cabin 1041. Thus did I evade Doom.

At Queens Grill, Alex Seymour, the assistant manager, asked me if I am related to the great Patten, the neurologist who recently figured so prominently in the Australian news. I said no. Ethel poked me in the ribs, "Since when are you so humble. You are the great Patten."

I called Alex over and held my index finger over my lips, indicating silence. "Don't tell," I told him. "I don't want them lining up for autographs the way they torture Christopher Lee."

Ethel is riding one of those giant waves of happiness. Her good mood lasted throughout the meal. It's her fifty-fourth birthday. She wanted caviar and she got it. She intended to order it special off-menu, but there was no need since caviar is listed tonight among the many appetizers. We ate blinis and caviar, accompanied by ice-cold vodka and then, what the hell, we celebrated with a bottle of Mouton Cadet, followed by a port for Ethel and a twenty-year-old single-malt scotch for me. Thus did we exhaust our credit.

The scotch reminded me of something. "Which royal personage is said to have been partial to a half-glass of claret topped up with scotch?" I asked Ethel.

"Not impossible to guess. Victoria, she looked the type."

"Right. Her choice of tipple is said to have startled Prime Minister Gladstone, probably because of the violence it did the whiskey. Gladstone was a good friend to scotch, legalizing its importation into England in 1860."

On the way out of Queens Grill, our way was blocked by a slow-moving cripple with severe left hemiparesis, who was hobbling on a cane. There was something printed on the back of his red shirt. We got closer and read: "Doctor Bob, Sexual Therapist. Strange Cases Welcome."

"When the world's financial crisis hits," I told Ethel. "That's what I'll do."

Back in the room we found a card from Captain John Burton-Hall, wishing Ethel a happy birthday. Nice touch!

Day 48

Fremantle (Perth), Australia

The PERFECT PARTNER for MR. DOOM

Our new Do Not Disturb sign has disappeared, undoubtedly lifted by some disembarking Australian tourist, eager to return home with trophy and treasures. Ethel and I are again signless, or in-*sign*-ificant. Yet the purloined sign will not be the only thing to go ashore when the distinguished Australian guests leave *QE2*. According to an unnamed but reliable source, hundreds of salt and pepper sets, wrapped in multitudes of linen table napkins, will also vanish. The experience has been that each of the silver-plated, cylindrical condiment sets, embossed with the Cunard motif and specially designed for *QE2*, has a high probability of departure. Perhaps that's where Cunard made a mistake; maybe they should have supplied something like Woolworth salt and pepper sets instead.

A crowd and a marching band playing Highland songs greeted us in Perth. Why do all those boats and people show up for *QE2*? We are an item, as much as Princess Diana or Prince Charles, an iconic floating funhouse full of crazies.

Perth, our last Australian port, lives exuberantly, buoyed by a booming economy in minerals, cosseted by a leisure lifestyle, and nourished by the Australian zest for living and fun. Perth straddles the beautiful Swan River, where black swan used to breed in abundance, but no longer do, due to the destruction of the reeds that formed their nests. The climate is Mediterranean through and through, the air unsullied by pollution or smog. The streets and buildings sparkled, especially now after the cleaning and restoration they got when Perth won the coveted America's Cup.

QE2 sailed in, as predicted, under blue skies and in brilliant radiant light, better than I have seen anywhere in the world, even in Sicily, where the light also is amazingly pure. Looking over the people waiting on the wharf, I concluded half the population of the town is less than twenty-four years old.

While waiting in the midships lounge on Two deck to disembark, Estelle told me I have a fierce opponent onboard, someone named Welch. "I should talk to him and try to get him to listen to reason," I said.

Estelle advised, "Don't waste your time. Just watch out. He's out for blood."

Estelle and Nathan attended the captain's party last night. During dessert, the man next to Nathan collapsed. Nathan felt a good pulse and the guy came back fast. The ship's doctor said it was a fainting spell, but Nathan suspected carotid artery disease.

While we waited, Nathan and I traded stories about vacation medicine.

Years ago, at the Bright Angel Lodge, just as I was about to sip my Manhattan, a middle-aged man across the room clutched his chest and fell sideways off his chair and onto the floor. His heart had arrested, but Ethel and I got him back.

Nathan and Estelle beat my story with their account of an old man who they took care of on the voyage last year. The old man knew he was dying and that the trip would be his last hurrah. Three nurses took turns taking care of him in eight-hour shifts. The old guy ate and drank himself into oblivion until the very last day of the cruise, when he died.

"I guess he didn't want to pack his bags," I joked.

The tour we selected today takes us to New Norcia, in Western

Australia, a town devoted exclusively to a Benedictine monastery and to music, monks, and mystery.

Why were crass materialists from *QE2*, who are steeped in the pleasures of this world, wishing to visit a Benedictine monastery? Ethel and I heard that if we went, we would see the golden teeth of Bishop Dom Rosendo Salvado, who founded the place in 1846.

Along the route we got to see the outback and heard about bushrangers (Australian for highwaymen) who get caught because they are often found drunk in wine cellars. We learned there is a water shortage unless you have your own bore (Australian for well) that reticulates (waters) your lawn. We heard about Paddy Hannan, an Irishman who discovered gold in Coolgardie in 1892. The reef (Australian for vein) brought thousands seeking wealth and was known as the Golden Mile, the richest vein in all Australia. By the 1950s, more than thirty million ounces of gold came out of the reef, worth $12 billion, American. We learned of Aboriginal cures, including the one where you chew the red gum of the gum tree and your diarrhea stops. But if you chew too much you get paralyzed. "How long?" I asked. Jacqui, our guide, doesn't know. "It makes a difference," I said. She agreed.

The bus stopped in the town of Bindoon for a loo break. Jacqui gave the group only five minutes, but we needed more than that just to get off the bus. The gray head ahead of me at the urinal needed three minutes just to get started. After the loo, many disregard the request to get back on the bus. Instead, they wander about into the store.

History riddles this place with great stories. It's impossible to cover even a tenth of them. I want to share one from Bishop Rosendo Salvado's own book, *Salvado Memoiries*, published in 1854:

> During the oppressive hour of the mid-day heat, we were engaged in teaching catechism, which we regard as a welcome relief from the labours of the fields. One day, a poor native woman came running towards us pursued by her enraged husband brandishing a spear, the deadly "*gitchie*". Neither we nor his friends could prevail against him. In order to prevent an awful crime, we took the unhappy woman to our cottage, the only safe place for her, and locked her inside. Finding him-

self thwarted in his evil intent, the maniac, gesticulating in anger and uttering terrible imprecations, left the mission, whilst we continued our instruction.

At the same time on the following day we saw an inferno of flames devouring grass and trees alike and rapidly spreading towards our crop of corn, which we had partly stacked in sheaves. A high wind was blowing and within a short time a wide area of about a mile was burning furiously. Both we monks and the natives ran to meet this danger to our crop and to the mission. Following the native method, we used green branches to beat down the flames by sweeping back the parched grass, which was growing very thick and three feet high alongside the field where our crop lay. Our hands and faces were burnt, our beards singed, and our habits scorched for the flames were high against us. We realized our helplessness. Unaided, we could not prevent the complete destruction of the mission. In such extreme danger, we had recourse to God's Infinite Mercy through the motherly intercession of the special Patroness of our mission.

We took the beautiful picture of Our Lady which had a place of honour over our altar, and placed it against the standing corn, which seemed about to catch fire at any moment. Then, with confident faith, we besought Her to look with maternal compassion upon our natives and upon ourselves. Merciful Heaven! No sooner was the sacred image of the Queen of Heaven in place in front of the raging fire than the wind blew in the opposite direction, carrying the flames away to where everything was already burnt black. The fire soon died out, and thus did we witness the protection granted by our Holy Mother.

Why Salvado calls it corn Jacqui can't explain. Locals who read the story all agreed it was a wheat field, the first successfully grown wheat field thereabouts. The mad husband had set the fire, all believed, and the Virgin Mary saved them. The wind always shifts 180 degrees during a frontal passage, though, so the Virgin's miracle was probably just good timing.

Still, I believe Salvado's life of devotion to the mission more of a miracle. He went to heaven, if no better place, a true saint.

Ascending the escalator to get back to *QE2*, I saw a new sign, saying that due to industrial disputation, the electricity may cut off. In other words, a strike is brewing.

Heard on deck: "Let's move to Perth. It's just like England, but the weather is better."

In the outside pool I swam with three girls, all about nine or ten years old. They had a complaint, too. The ice cream dispenser on One deck wasn't working. I assured them it works. The crew always shuts it off in port.

A tall, fat Australian woman with obviously dyed red hair stuck her foot in the pool. "Too smart!" she exclaimed, meaning the water was too cold. "Is the indoor pool any bigger?" she asked. I told her it isn't. She wrinkled her face and forehead. "The crew said this was freshwater," she told me. I regretted to inform her differently and tried to assuage the blow by saying seawater is probably healthier. "Too salty!" she yelled. "That's not healthy!" She seated herself on the rail by the hot tub and lit a cigarette. Then she came over and stuck her hand in the hot tub. "Too hot!" she screamed. She took a deep drag and dropped the cigarette onto the deck, crushing it out with her white Cunard slipper.

At last the perfect partner for Mr. Doom. Why not? The mysteries of love are wrapped in doom as that Shakespeare story about two houses both alike in dignity in fair Verona proves.

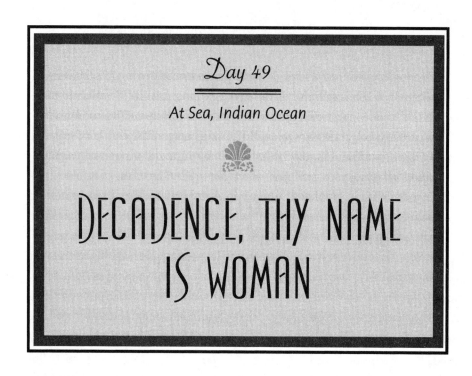

Day 49

At Sea, Indian Ocean

DECADENCE, THY NAME IS WOMAN

*E*thel woke me again from that vast mysterious void called sleep. The sea air knocks me out. Never have I slept so soundly, so close to feeling death. It's scary.

During the night, *QE2* headed north. We noticed the difference already. Warm, moist air lapped over us and the sky remained blue and clear. We will soon leave the Southern Hemisphere, just when I'm beginning to figure out that everything in it is upside down and backward. Here it's summer and the cold winds come from the south. Here, the Man in the Moon looks like the Rabbit in the Moon, and the night sky is inverted.

The cruise news indicated the stock market had inverted, also, dropping 152 points in two days.

"Will we go back to being poor?" Ethel asked.

"I expect so, especially if Doom is right. But we'll have each other."

Ethel looked unhappy. "But what will you do for money?"

"If worse comes to worst, I'll write magazine articles."

In fact, after hearing Dr. Clyde Roper's lecture on bioluminescence, I planned on writing an article on the sex life of fish. I knew about fireflies and glowworms and fluorescent fungi, but no one had prepared me for fish that glow when they wish to have sex.

The glow fish I like best hangs out in the abyssal deep. Yes, hangs is the right word, because this fish spends its time oriented vertically, not horizontally, and it moves vertically as well, rising to warmer water when there is more food at night and descending in the day when there is less food and fewer enemies. The black-colored glow fish has a typical fish shape, except its mouth opens vertically, not horizontally (the mouth is hinged to do that), and just over its mouth it has a small glowing nodule on a projecting piece of tissue the size of a toothpick. The fish turns its light on and off, and jiggles the bait a little and eats anything that comes near its mouth. But that's not all. This fish has a tiny fish, or what looks like a tiny fish, attached to its belly. That tiny fish was once a larger male fish that was once attached to the female with its mouth, but then male and female tissues had fused together. After the fusion, the male's organs, brain included, are absorbed into the female, leaving only a tiny fishlike appendage attached to the female. The appendage's only job is to supply sperm. Guess what else. The male fish takes on body lighting identical to and synchronous with the female. This idea better not get around. Some women might like the arrangement too much.

Another marvel is the flasher fish. It has lots of light organs, which are covered by millions of scales that look like eyelids. When someone irritates the fish, the eyelids open and flash, like taking a picture in a dark room. The idea is that the flash scares the predators. It works.

Do you know that in the inky depths, octopuses gain no advantage by squirting black ink since nothing can see the ink in the dark? By some sort of miraculous adaptation in that dark environment the octopuses squirt an ink loaded with phosphorescent bacteria, which when it hits the oxygen of the water, glows like crazy, giving the octopus the chance to get away.

The last glowing fish looked like some kind of clown fish, for it had plastered on its front a giant white patch shaped like a mouth, but a hundred times larger than its real mouth. We assumed this was some way of pretending that it had a big mouth, and therefore was thought to be a bigger predator than it really was. Nope! The white mouth flashes on and off as a mating signal. All this confirms my thinking that fish do things differently than we do. A mouth should be red as a mating signal, not white. Right? That is why women use lipstick.

Today for lunch Ethel and I headed below into the crew quarters, where Food and Beverage Manager Bert H. Hofer and Executive Chef Jonathan F. Wicks hosted a Frühschoppen, a traditional Bavarian brunch just for Samuel Cunard Key Club Members. On Seven deck, below the water line, a vast array of German food confronted us. They have lined the walls with white Oktoberfest signs and pictures of beer steins hang overhead, suspended by blue cords. The group gulped down excellent bottles of Pilsener Urquell, the world's first golden beer, still made in the town of Pilsen in the Czech Republic. *Urquell* is German for original source.

After the beer, we attacked knockwursts, franks, blood sausages, white pork sausages, sauerbraten, noodles, and potato pancakes, followed by Black Forest cake and apple strudels ladened with apples, cinnamon, nuts, and raisins. I switched from beer to schnapps, starting with kirschwasser, then working through apricot and pear brandy, and finished with raspberry aquavit. By the time one o'clock rolled around, we're potted. In a kind of happy but dumb torpor, Ethel and I danced the polka in the freight elevator next to the hall where we ate.

Too much schnapps caused me to get a jumbled idea of June Owen's lecture on how Englishmen changed into Australians. I did get the message that the transition was not gradual and that Australians differ substantially from the mother race. Australians go for the fast quip, and have a strong oral tradition in song and poetry. I heard what a *drover* is, but I can't tell you what he or she is, nor can I say what they do, except it sounds like there were plenty of them. They appear in Australian tall tales, too, like the one with a drover who keeps bragging about how smart his dog is. Another drover says that if the dog is so smart, why couldn't it come in and have a drink? The braggart drover considers it a while, drinks two more beers, and then replies, "I can't let him drink. That dog has to drive me home." Another one goes: two drovers are in the outback together. The first day, drover one says, "Nice day, though I think it might rain, mate." Drover two nods. The next day, drover one says, "Nice day, though I still say it might rain." Drover two makes no reply, just frowns. The next day drover one wakes to find drover two had left. On the knapsack a note reads: "G'day, mate. You talk too much."

Do you know what "Waltzing Matilda," Australia's most famous tune, is about? A Matilda is actually a hobo's possessions, carried over his back in a sack of some sort, and to waltz Matilda is to be on the road, hitchhiking and begging for handouts. Something like a walkabout, but not quite. A walkabout is a rite of passage for Aborigines in which a person, usually a man, disappears for a year or two, thinking and walking about. Later he might return home, or then again, he might not.

Nathan made me promise to show up for deck games tomorrow. I prefer the lectures, but what the hell. We can't always do everything we want. He rewarded me by telling me about the time he answered a house call for the actor Jason Robards.

Nathan recalled ringing the doorbell to the apartment and Lauren Bacall, Robard's wife at the time, answered. She told Nathan to go into the bedroom where Robards lay in bed. Nathan entered the bedroom and was shocked, for on the wall was a full-length color photograph of Humphrey Bogart, Lauren Bacall's deceased first husband.

"Must be kind of hard to perform with that picture looking at you," said Nathan.

"Yes, Nathan, I agree. But, considering that the object of my performance would be Lauren Bacall, I know that I could handle it."

At dinner, Christopher Lee probably wished he had his golden gun with him. Every few minutes, someone, crew or passenger, showed up requesting an autograph. By the way Lee threw back the signed papers, I know he's disgusted with celebrity. It's nice not to have that kind of stuff to worry about. All I have to worry about is Ethel. *QE2* is spoiling her. Tonight she had Paul cut up her lobster and loosen it from the shell. She also ate two large helpings of caviar. Caviar, twice in the same week!? And double portions!

Decadence, thy name is woman. She will have trouble adjusting to poverty. Me too.

Day 50

At Sea

BOB *and a*

NINETY-ONE-YEAR-OLD WOMAN SLEEP TOGETHER

oday in Queens Grill a ninety-one-year-old woman fell asleep at breakfast, resting her head on the bone china plate in front of her. I'm not making fun of Miss 91. I realized someday I would be falling asleep in my breakfast, too. Alex Seymour, the assistant manager, didn't wake her. She's the one who keeps insisting, "Don't push my chair in until I sit down. You might hurt my legs. I am sorry to have to tell you this, but I don't want my legs hurt." Miss 91 should team up with Bob, I thought, the hemiplegic who advertised that he is a sex therapist. Several tables away from Miss 91, Bob also sleeps. They are sleeping together, in the literal sense.

Alex told us that because Bob falls asleep every dinner, the waiters have instructions to leave the courses on the plates only for a certain amount of time, then they clear them and replace them with the next course. Some nights Bob goes through an entire dinner without having ingested a single calorie.

Alex told us some of the crew's secret code words, too. Starlight meant a death or a near-death event, like a cardiac arrest, has occurred. Priority One is a burst pipe. Phoenix means fire. Phoenix finally had a meaning for us. Each time we heard it over the loudspeakers, it meant fire crews fought and mastered a blaze in the depths of the ship while carefree passengers above dined or watched a cabaret, largely unaware of the white hot drama being played out below.

About the rejection of the chicken soup: The highest number of *QE2* food complaints concern chicken noodle soup. The noodles are too big or too small. The soup doesn't taste the way it did back when, or back home, or both. "The best soup is the one that has no taste. That's the way they really want it," said Alex. Now I know why Rabbi didn't like his chicken soup.

Rabbi. I wonder where he is and I wonder what he is saying. He's probably still in Caronia, saying something absurd like, "Waiter, this vichyssoise is cold."

As I promised Nathan, I showed up on Boat deck for the morning games. It's a real tournament, much more organized than I thought. I hate organization. Another Bob, Bob the supervisor, handed out playing cards, one to a passenger, and then yelled out, "Aces?!" A man and a woman stepped forward. They are the first team.

Bob explained that it works better that way, so that the best players can't team up and leave everyone else feeling like sore losers. Chance and the cards, a four of clubs, match me with a tall German woman named Hildegard.

Before the games began, Nathan took me aside for private lessons. "Listen, Bernie, you haven't played before, so I'll teach you." Nathan took my hand and led me to the starboard shuffleboard area, handed me the stick, and nodded to the yellow disks lying disorganized on the deck.

"Stay away from the Ten Off. That's the killer. Stay in your box and release the disk before you push it over the white line."

I pushed a disk. It didn't make it to the other side.

Nathan shook his head and pouted. "You need practice! Let me show you."

With a smug air of command, Nathan shot a disk into the Eight. He smiled, then handed me the stick. I tried again. Again the disk still didn't make it into the scoring triangle. From the frown on Nathan's face, I realized my cause looked hopeless. "You need practice. Show up a few days in a row and you'll get it. Today, you'll get eliminated in the first round. Then come watch me. I'm a superior player."

Hildegard, my partner, with a firm German will of iron, held up her end beautifully and scored two Eights in the first frame. I beamed my admiration and patted Hilde on her shoulder. I wanted to give her a big fat hug and kiss, but her husband, twice my size, is standing by, looking grim. I went and scored nothing.

Our opponents scored nothing too. After four frames, Hilde and I won by Hilde's sixteen points. Nathan and his partner, Beth, also won. And so I must stick around while the others play out their fates. This annoyed me. I told Bob, "I can't stay beyond 10:30. I must attend the lecture on the sex lives of the deep-sea squids." Bob nodded yes. He understood my need for knowledge, especially since the topic, squid whoopee, is so important.

Bob consulted the tournament list. "Don't worry," Bob assured me. "You're against experts, people who play every day. You'll lose soon."

Seven other couples eventually lost their games. That brought Hilde and me to round two.

I watched as Nathan threw his room key in the air. Just as the key reached its apogee and remained suspended in air, about to reverse trajectory and fall, Nathan yelled out, "Numbers!"

No one carries coins on *QE2,* so they toss up room keys, which have conveniently been made for shuffleboard tosses. The room keys have numbers only on one side of the key. With a heavy heart, Nathan picked his key from the deck and said, "No numbers." Nathan lost the toss. The other side decided to go first.

Nathan, in a stage aside, cupped his hands over my ear and whispered in that low-pitched, gravely voice of his, "Fools! Always elect to go last if you have the choice. The last shot makes all the difference. These people don't know strategy. Watch how we cream them." He was Ahab with a shuffleboard stick.

Nathan's opponents might not know strategy, but they do know how to play. David stands six feet six and Mickey stands a squat four feet four. They are a married couple from Australia who liked to hold hands between sets. Their love was a totally uncritical love, unencumbered by the viciousness of the shuffleboard crowd.

Nathan got gloomy because his team remained behind eleven points going into the last frame of his game. Alas, by one point, Nathan lost.

Now that Nathan was out, he became my private coach and adviser.

Hilde and I, behind twenty-seven points, looked like probable losers. We're up to our last frame and I am up. *Bang! Caroom!* The disks jumped this way and that. When we went to inspect the results we found that I scored two Eights, a Seven, and had knocked our opponent's black disk into the Ten Off. I earned thirty-three points for Hildegard and myself. By a full six points, we won.

I glared at my watch. Ugh! 10:48 AM. The squid sex lecture started without me! I am being deprived of knowledge all for the privilege of sweating bullets under the hot equatorial sun in a shuffleboard tournament.

The thought crossed my mind to throw the next game. But that wouldn't be right for Hilde and it wouldn't be fair for the others, either. If they win, I wanted it to be fair and square. Throwing the game would be the equivalent of cheating the other competitors out of a deserved victory.

Damn the sex life of squids! Damn the lecture! Full speed ahead! The game must go on!

Nathan put his arm around my shoulder in a fatherly embrace. "I must be a good teacher. See how fast you learned," he said.

I nodded and smiled. "That last shot was more luck than anything else," I told him.

"Strategy, the effect of strategy," Nathan said, pointing his index finger at me for emphasis. "These people don't think. I told you that last shot makes all the difference."

In the final round, Hilde and I were pitted against Mickey and Dave, the same team that defeated Nathan and Beth. Poor Hilde choked and ended up scoring a Seven followed by a Ten Off. So going into the final frame, my team has minus three points. The other team has nothing, so we are behind by three points. Everything depended on me.

Dave led off. Poor Dave! He landed his first shot right into the Ten Off. Nathan seemed overjoyed and clapped his hands in a moment of unsportsmanlike joy. He snarled, "Lock him in." By now, of course, I was feeling the pressure; everyone was watching me because this was the championship. Hilde and I, we are the playoff.

Bob chided Nathan, "Oh leave him alone, Nat. Bernie does great without you."

Bob, truly proud of me, turned to pat me on the shoulder. Thank God Bob didn't see Nathan giving Bob the Finger behind his back. I followed Nathan's strategy, and the game ended amid wild cheers and jumping for joy. Hilde and I won. The final score was minus three to minus ten.

Bob handed Hilde a box of *QE2* stationery and handed me a bone china thimble with the picture of *QE2* on it. Nathan wanted to hold the trophy. I let him, but I kept a sharp eye on him, making sure he didn't slip it in his pocket. Instead, Nathan held the trophy on high while telling everyone what they have heard from him before: "Bernie's my student. I'm a great teacher."

After I gestured with my right hand, Nathan handed back the trophy and said, "In the old days, before Cunard started losing money, the prizes were much better. In the old days, champ, you would have won a bottle of scotch."

I admired the thimble, and Hilde, overjoyed, shook my hand. I wanted to show lusty and lively Hilde my gratitude, because men tend to show less gratitude than women. I knew Hilde wanted to hug me and give me a big kiss, but with her disapproving husband there, all Hilde could do was show me the *QE2* stationery. It's nicely embossed on brown linen.

Although I will never know about the sex lives of squids, my victory was worth it. As I turned to leave, Nathan said, "Next time take up paddle tennis, Bernie. Do tennis, a better sport for you. Leave shuffleboard to us elders."

Word spread fast. At lunch in Queens Grill, Colum and Paul both addressed me as Champ. I am a celebrity. Hilde and I were the shuffle-board champions of *QE2*, but strangely, the crew and passengers still line up for Christopher Lee's autograph and not for mine.

This afternoon June Owen ran a writing workshop in the Golden Lion Pub. More than forty writers and would-be writers attended. The woman seated with me at the table told me she is sure that she is a writer for, since the cruise started, she has written 668 postcards. I made her feel good by telling her the truth. As far as postcards were concerned, I had written none.

June Owen asked us to scribble a description of something that happened on deck this morning and gave us two minutes to write. Then she talked about the usual things that make up good writing: details, ideas, individual voice, self-confidence, and clarity. June asked some students to read their compositions and she critiqued them. As a veteran of sixteen years of writing classes, writing workshops, and writing conferences, I recognized the painful process of having to expose yourself to a group of strangers.

When my turn came, I grabbed the mike and read in a full, loud voice: "Nathan arrived ten minutes early eager to start. He wore a white headband and a small gray *QE2* cap. 'When the shuffleboard tournament begins, stick with me. I know what to do,' he said smugly, handing me the stick and nodding toward the yellow disks which lay disorganized on the worn teak wood deck."

"Oh, well," said June. "Obviously, the work of a professional. Notice how he didn't use many adjectives and we can picture this man, Nathan. Hemingway wrote a whole short story without using a single adjective."

I went to the purser's office to buy Indonesian stamps. The usual signs were out: "This segment of *QE2* is fully booked" and "No cabin changes are possible." Despite this, the gray head ahead of me was arguing to have her room changed because of a rattle in the ceiling.

Norman Cole stood at poolside this afternoon with some kind of weird contest to see who could make the largest splash diving into the pool. Some people obviously trained for this event at midnight buffet. When they showed up, I went below to swim because I didn't want to pick up the pieces when someone broke his neck. That plan didn't work too well, for a cripple in a wheelchair showed up in the Seven deck indoor pool down below. The cripple, a middle-aged man, fell out of his wheelchair onto the deck, crawled along the floor, tumbled down the wooden steps, got his stick-thin left leg caught between the railings, extricated that leg with great difficulty, and then crashed and splashed down into the water. After three tense minutes he surfaced, told me the water was nice, and started to swim quite well without the use of his legs.

After swimming fifty laps, I retired to the whirlpool in the spa and relaxed to the German lieder that played overhead. I floated while listening to the trained soprano. Her voice thrilled me to my deep heart's core.

I'm happy. Supremely happy.

Day 51

Bali, Indonesia

THEY HAVE ENTERED RUBBER TIME

Lush green peaks, sharp-edged ridges lined with palms. Storied beaches surrounded by the deep blue sea. Flat terraced rice paddies. We have entered the tropical paradise of Bali.

Ethel and I knew Bali, because we visited here two years ago. The island hasn't changed, but the people have changed. They acquired a money hunger. We saw it right away as the tender docked. Swarms of kids and some adults descended on us, offering woodcarvings, puppets, postcards, junk jewelry, and brightly colored batik sarongs.

In Ambon, Indonesia, when we said no, they went away, but here they don't. They linger and sometimes become more insistent, trying desperately to make a sale. Understand, they don't beg. They offer something for sale. They're not beggars. The difference remains important and commands attention, but when they won't take no for an answer, it becomes tiresome.

The Balinese police moved in. Still, some of the merchants wouldn't stop or move. So the police hit them with clubs. That convinced them.

In Bali time evaporates like the rain puddles after a tropical storm. They have an expression for that phenomena. It's called *Jam Karat*, or rubber time.

Our tour guide, Pantana, is on rubber time, but the *QE2* group is not. They wanted to see everything and get back to the ship as fast as possible. They behaved like a crass band of American consumers, treating Bali like it is just one more item on the menu. Yes, *QE2*ers were in that mood: They had no disposition to examine carefully or think deeply about the foreign land they were in. They only wanted to glance and go, to move, and to keep moving.

God, what must the Balinese have thought of us? We came thousands of miles to see their island and we stayed but a few hours, during which we rushed about. Incidentally, the Balinese call their idyllic island the home of the gods, but we were anything but idyllic tourists.

Bali, best known of the Indonesian islands, has an interesting history. In the fifteenth century, the East Javan Empire fell to Muslim invaders, so the best of the Hindu society—the artists, scholars, and artisans—fled to Bali. Good genes to start with explains why these small-boned brown-skinned Malaysians look so beautiful. The genes also explain why everyone here is an artist. From our last visit, we recalled four things: the Barong dance, the kris, the gamelan orchestra, and the Hindu religion, all of which make this island famous.

The Barong dance depicts the eternal battle of good and evil. The Barong, a kind of mythical animal that looks like a lion, assisted a virtuous king dressed in gold and jewels and fought against the wicked witch Rangda, who wears a frightening mask and costume. In the dance, we saw the male dancers, under Rangda's adverse influence, go into a trance and at the height of the action they stab themselves with their ritual knives, the krises. I liked how in the Barong dance good never entirely conquered evil and the outcome never appears final or simple. This constitutes a great moral lesson. The dance demonstrates evil mutating into different forms and even becoming invisible at times, for during the dance, Rangda disappears, but her evil presence quite palpably persists. Evil does that. And since evil does that, people should know it.

Every Balinese village has its gamelan orchestra of percussion instruments. The gamelan players have undergone years of apprenticeship by ear, for there is no musical notation. The scale is almost pentatonic, with shimmering waves of timeless exotic melodies, a circulating metallic sound that rises and falls seemingly toward a final resolution, which the Western ear always seeks but never gets.

I once heard wind chimes on a gusty day emit sounds resembling the gamelan orchestra. Perhaps gamelan music got started in a time out of mind, before clocks. Once started, this tradition wouldn't stop. The Balinese love it too much. America celebrates change. Bali celebrates tradition.

The kris, more than a knife and more than a defensive weapon, symbolizes the mystical projection, or soul, of the owners. At all official ceremonies, including weddings where even the women sport their krises, one sees these short swords tucked into waistbands. A real kris has a blade, called a *pamor*, which is forged of iron and nickel in alternating layers. Special artistic provisions prescribe the type and ornamentation of the scabbard and the hilt. To the Balinese, the kris is a living entity believed to have witchcraft capabilities that grow in power by drawing blood or by rubbing it in snake entrails. In Bali some krises reside in village shrines as objects of daily worship, which brings me to the subject of religion. In Bali religion means Hinduism.

Waldemar Hansen told us that Hinduism is basically monotheistic.

Hogwash!

He has his Western glasses on and wants to see things his way.

Hinduism has three main gods: Brahma (the creator), Vishnu (the preserver), and Shiva (the destroyer). These gods have individual personalities and represent different projections of the human psyche. They are three distinct gods, not a combination adding up to one, like the Trinity in Christianity.

I like Shiva the best, especially when he appears in his temple in the *lingam* form. The lingam is a symbol used for worship, represented by a giant phallus embedded in the *yoni*, or the vulva. Early in the morning, village ladies come to Shiva's temple and pour cream or melted butter down the top of the phallus, thus creating the image that Shiva's phallus has just had a giant ejaculation. This, indeed, constitutes the worship of the life force, the reproductive potential of the living universe, a worship in its most basic and primitive essence, and no more startling than praying to the bloody image of a man hanging on a cross, his head crowned with thorns.

There also exist on Bali hosts of lesser gods and goddesses that represent the mountains, seas, rivers, and the entire natural world. Every village and house has presiding deities. No one sows a crop without invoking the beneficence of the gods, for the gods protect against evil spirits, which are as omnipresent as the gods themselves. Religion in Bali, as it does in our culture, dictates numerous holidays, ceremonies, observances, offerings, purifications, temple festivals, processions, dances, cremations, and burials. Religion also dictates how children are treated. Children, especially the younger, are deemed closer to the gods. Therefore, no child is ever beaten. The young child is sacred, and the younger they are, the more sacred they are. Part of the religion even requires that the youth get their teeth filed. I consider teeth filing in Bali no more interesting than our own tooth ritual called orthodontics.

From the tour bus window, I saw bare-breasted grandmas and waved to those sacred children lining the road in abundance. Most seemed friendly, but not everyone liked us. One sign read, "FULK YOU ALL." Their spelling is funny here, but we got the message.

The bus passed along small, narrow jungle roads, through dense bamboo forests interspersed with indolent palms, banana trees, and plenty of roadside huts with roofs of corrugated metal. Each home has a temple lined with spiritual houses, like miniature pagodas, into which people had placed flowers, bamboo shoots, and fresh fruits. The houses are lined with yellow streamers and wrapped in black and white checkered sarongs, which represent good and evil mixing, just as good and evil mix in life. Occasionally, temples have the inverted swastika that we have seen in the Buddhist temple in Lantau. Here in Bali they don't have a chicken in every pot or a car in every garage, but they do have a temple in every house and several more public temples outside. In fact, there are over twenty thousand temples in Bali.

We stopped at Tenganan, the home of a secretive community of Bali Aga people, so-called because they resisted outside influence for many centuries, preserving their pre-Hindu customs. What those customs were, we never learned, nor were we allowed into their sacred areas. Hinduism, the world's oldest religion, has its primitive features. One can only imagine what the Bali Aga people have in mind. Hinduism has over seven hundred million worshipers, but the Bali Aga, I doubt, have more than two hundred.

The guide moved us through a red brick portico. I become anxious because we have been warned not to enter the sacred regions, *Pura Batan Cagi,* and I know these people are serious about their religion. We stepped through another gate and opened a red wooden door, carved with intricate floral and plant designs. My fears increased. I saw wood-carved geruda birds playing with that serpent they called *Naga* and thought we had entered a temple. We have, but it was not the Pura Batan Cagi. It's a temple of commerce, a market for the Bali Aga to sell their stuff. The QE2ers go wild. They bargain for wood-carved gods, woven baskets, and sarongs of intricate design and great vivid colors—lavender, purple, red, gold, and orange. The birds in the trees overhead join the negotiations with lots of twittering. Perhaps the birds get a commission when a sale is made. The roosters do. I know from the way they had started to crow.

Our guide, Pantana, explained, "These people have a eunuch culture."

Ethel convulsed with laughter. She loves eunuchs.

Next we headed to Putung, an observation point overlooking the sea. But a fierce storm poured tons of water down, showing us how it rains in the tropics. The kids outside—the sacred kids, I should say—covered their sacred heads with banana leaves. Our group doesn't trust banana leaves and voted not to go out of the bus. So we proceeded directly to the king's palace, Puri Agung Karangasem.

This place, Pantana explained, is also eunuch themed, with eunuch steps going into the eunuch buildings. The palace was previously the seat of the Rajadom before the Balinese independence and reflects the power of the kings in architectural design and layout. We stepped back in time, stepped past the moss-covered gate demons and into groves of lichen-coated trees, vast buildings for retainers, open courtyards, and marble pavilions erected over pea soup–green lily ponds. We walked through the enclosed formal gardens, along paths made from golf ball–sized white stones. In the middle of the path stood a large tree, under which rests a large blue stone. I sat on that large blue stone, a magical stone. The sign over-head promised: "If you sit on me, you will get up refreshed." It worked!

The group lingered among the flirtation dancers, two charming pread-olescent girls. The girls wore sarongs, decorated with gold, and are tightly swathed from neck to waist in gold bands. On their heads are golden crowns loaded with yellow-white flowers. The girls, who retire at puberty, trained from age four to perform the story of a captured princess and her rejected suitor. The dance, stylized and artificial, captivated us. Enthralled, the group remains transfixed, watching two of the world's most beautiful girls dance one of the world's most beautiful dances. We sipped fruit punch and listened to the gamelan in the background do its stuff. The *QE2*ers don't want to go back to the buses. They have entered rubber time.

NOT ONE TIME DID THEY EVER TELL ME I HAD *to* PACK MY OWN BAGS

*Q*E2 entered the Java Sea between Sumatera, or Sumatra, and Kalimantan, the Indonesian portion of the island once called old Borneo. Since *QE2* reflects the last of the imperial and commercial influence that the British had extended during the twentieth century, I see no harm in mentioning the old names. Sumatra and Borneo sound normal to me, proving that I am part of an older generation now fading away. Of course as opposed to the bad new days, those were the good old days when liners were actually liners and not occasional callers. Now the cruising vessels (except for *QE2* on her scheduled North Atlantic runs) are not liners, but floating leisure complexes. Despite the transformation, the new names, the high drama and sense of occasion persists, much of it engendered by the huge size of our ship, its reputation as the last of the great superliners, and, I believe, its presentation colors: bright red, white, and blue. The old superliners, mostly coal burners, didn't make half of the impression we do. They were painted black, or became black from soot.

Today after breakfast, in spite of the tropical rainstorm, Ethel and I walked on deck. The soft, warm tropical rain didn't bother us, but the deck is slippery, so we found ourselves slow and cautious with our legs spread more apart than usual. I like walking in the rain. It wakes me up, makes me feel more alive. Try it.

Val, our cabinkeeper, is still at work cleaning cabin 1041. Actually, this room is so vast I should call it a stateroom, not a cabin. Our cabin days ended when we left Four deck. Rather than distract Val, I went to the library.

The gray heads occupied all the tables and chairs, frenetically working on the morning quiz. Two of them, a man and a woman, undoubtedly in their second childhoods, told me they wished to consult the atlas I was looking over. I stared at the old man and said, "Are you kidding? Can't you see I'm using it!" Realizing one punch from me would kill him, he backed away. It would have been hard to complete the morning quiz with a black eye.

These people have been spoiled rotten. They think because they want something, they must instantly get it. My duty remains to instill some sense of reality before their personality disorders become permanently fixed.

The morning lecture on octopuses was interrupted by a watertight door drill. The persistent drills that the crew has for flooding and fire make me feel uneasy. Is all of that really needed? After over fifty days at sea, I feel nothing can go wrong. Nothing hurt us.

Or can it?

The almost infallible word of mouth among the passengers whispered that something happened to *Sagafjord*, one of two sister ships that has been making a round-the-world cruise, too. What happened? The buzz runs from total loss of *Sagafjord* and all passengers and crew to some sort of crack in the engine, which they quickly repaired. Another rumor has it that *QE2* will alter course to rescue the *Sagafjord* survivors.

Dr. Roper talked about the blue-ringed octopus. This brightly colored little fellow can kill with one sting by injecting maculotoxin, a poison that affects the sodium channels, thus preventing electrical conduction in nerves and muscles. Dr. Roper told us about two soldier pals who went to the beach for R&R. They found a blue-ringed octopus and one fellow slapped it on the other's back. The soldiers walked a little way and the fellow with the octopus felt a little sting. A few minutes later, he died. Another woman thought the blue-ringed octopus looked so neat, she would bring it home. Not having any container, she slipped it in her bathing suit. She felt the sting and then felt faint. They rushed her to a hospital but she arrived too late. She died, too.

I skipped swimming in the outdoor pool because I spotted Doom in the hot tub and knew he would bend my ear about the coming international financial crisis.

In the indoor pool, an old German woman does stretching exercises while I swim my fifty laps. A Japanese couple, the woman about twenty-two and the man about thirty-five, enjoy themselves, splashing in the water. Are they honeymooners? I looked at them curiously because they are the first Japanese I have seen laughing and the first Japanese couple I have seen who are obviously happy with each other. The Japanese man showed off by staying underwater for more than three minutes. His wife or girlfriend appeared more than impressed and she wanted to demonstrate her admiration. She urged him out of the water with that look in her eyes that can mean only one thing—passion. Change that. She is not only in the mood, she is positively a nympho. Did someone slip her something?

As I headed out, I saw her frantically kissing him by the elevator. She saw me and stepped back, embarrassed. She's really hot and she even made a lunge toward me. He pulled her back, pushed her in the elevator. Too bad I can't follow them to their bedroom. No, I would probably be too late. They're probably doing it in the elevator, right there and then.

After my swim, I went to the spa on Seven deck.

Doom was soaking in the whirlpool. Is Doom following me? Doom caught my eye as I entered and yelled, "I told you *Sagafjord* needed repairs! It's adrift now, due to engine fires!" Doom tried to bug me some more, but another passenger interrupted.

There are some who call themselves Muslims, and some who admit to being Christians at heart, and some who say they are rabbinical Jews, but there must be a new religion out there called Complaint. This passenger, a man in his sixties and a devotee of the new religion, has decided to practice his new religion in the spa. He decided to practice it on me. He complained that the tours were too short, the buses too slow, the guides poorly organized. If he were in charge, he would do things differently. I didn't say anything. Instead, I gave him the same blank face and indifferent treatment I give the street hawkers: Don't look at them. Don't show the slightest interest. Maybe they will leave.

Nope, that technique didn't work. Too bad there are no blue-ringed octopuses around. Mr. Complaint could have used one as a nice hat. He raised his voice ten decibels and told me: "I have to start packing my bags two nights before I get off in Thailand. Not one time did they ever tell me I had to pack my own bags. Not once. Do you hear! Not once!"

Oh where, oh where, are those Balinese police when I need them? They could show up and urge this guy away with a swat of their clubs. I opened my eyes. No policemen arrived. But Doom came to my rescue. "Excuse me," Doom told Mr. Complaint. "I was talking with him first. You interrupted." I wanted to rip my ears off and hand one to each of them.

While Doom and Mr. Complaint duked it out for my attention, I snuck out of the whirlpool and headed into the steam sauna. Because of the steam, they can't see in from the spa, so they won't know where I've gone. Most men can't go in the steam room, anyway. It's too hot for them.

Perhaps what we needed onboard is a cruise psychologist to help these people adjust to their situations. This poor soul, Mr. Complaint, undoubtedly doesn't want to leave the ship. Who would? So he has transferred his anger about leaving into a more neutral area that he perhaps knows deep within his unconscious mind he can handle better. Packing has a symbolic significance for him, reflecting the true problem, just like the paranoid projections of real lunatics with real problems. You know? When those voices start calling them homosexuals, that's what they are worried about. Or when they think they are Charles V, it means they lack self-esteem and aspire to become someone important. Complaining about not being told he would have to pack his own bags means he didn't want to pack and certainly doesn't want to waste the little time he has left on *QE2* doing such a mundane task.

Time to review a dinner in Queens Grill. Every meal measures up to five stars, and would measure more if such a measurement existed.

Let's do drinks first.

I started with a dry martini, straight up with a twist of lemon. Most non-Americans don't make cocktails well, and I could tell some stories that would make your hair stand on end. Such worries don't apply to *QE2*, where the cocktails stand in my high regard. This was an A+ martini. Next came our wine for the evening, a Château Pavie premier cru classé 1986, which cost only $76. Those of you who know wine know that this is not a good wine, but a great wine, one of the greatest wines of the world. It smelled and tasted great as well, providing an indescribable experience. . . . Thus did we blissfully partake of the rich mineral essence of the earth, drinking one of the great Bordeaux wines, Château Pavie.

Hor d'oeuvres started with truffled foie gras, *real* truffles and *real* foie gras accompanied by fresh miniature toast, then followed by port wine. Heaven! Next, I consumed a tomato and basil soup with cheese palmiers. This soup can't be praised enough. It had a strong flavor and taste, with a rich, smooth texture. I told Ethel they should can it and label it *QE2* Tomato Soup. It will outsell Campbell's a hundred to one. Next, I cleared my palate with blackberry sorbet. As a sorbet veteran (one at lunch and dinner for fifty-two days makes one hundred and four total, with few repeats), I can appraise them pretty well by now. This had a strong, fruity flavor, but not too sweet. The ice crystals were a mite larger than usual, but the general effect in my mouth was cooling and pleasant. I exhaled rich blackberry fumes, just a little tart. On the whole, a successful effort. I pleased myself because I had become a fussy connoisseur of sorbet.

My entrée also pleased me greatly, a whole roast rack of lamb chops so soft and thin, yet so perfectly cooked they melted in my mouth. The best lamb I had ever tasted, well associated with market vegetables and roasted potatoes.

Ethel ate paupiettes of Pacific sole, stuffed with chopped prawns on a bed of saffron rice and steamed Chinese cabbage, topped with coconut ginger vinaigrette. Perfect, she assured me.

And so we passed to dessert.

Here in Queens Grill, the dessert menu comes separate from the regular menu, a nice little extra. The choices included more blackberry sorbet; golden-baked pear shortcake; cherry parfait; exotic fruit tartlet with raspberries and passion fruit coulis; baked saffron yogurt; Zuppa Inglese with vanilla sponge, marinated in amaretto and berries, then topped with custard and cream; ice cream; frozen yogurt; and three dessert sauces—coconut, orange, and peach.

I chose the Zuppa Inglese and had no regrets, though the pastry chef could have added a touch more amaretto to make the zuppa stand up better. With the assorted international cheeses I indulged myself with an Armagnac, and thus concluded the meal.

How's that?

You would have a hard time duplicating such a meal in any of the great restaurants of the world. The miracle of it all stands out: we are miles from nowhere, floating on the wine dark sea, and yet in the Queens Grill we are eating like royalty.

I hoped our fellow round-the-world cruise passengers on the *Sagafjord* ate as well this night as we did. If the rumors about *Sagafjord* are true, they did not.

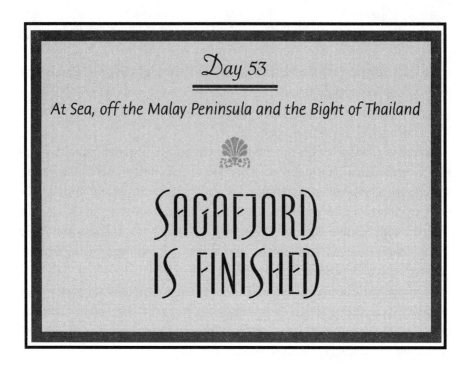

Day 53

At Sea, off the Malay Peninsula and the Bight of Thailand

SAGAFJORD IS FINISHED

"*S*orry to interrupt your repose, but rumors going about the ship make it necessary for me to advise you of the situation of our sister ship, the *Sagafjord*. I have delayed any announcement until I had the facts in hand."

Captain John Burton-Hall didn't interrupt our repose. But he did interrupt our morning stroll, our daily romantic tour about the decks to inspect the weather and the ship while taking in the sea air. No better way to spend time than just messing around, enjoying being aboard.

"*Sagafjord* has suffered fire in the engine room. At present she has no power, no utility water, or fresh water. There have been no casualties, neither among the crew nor among passengers. At present, *Sagafjord* is adrift. The engineers are working to restore power and two tugs have set out from Manila. The first tug is expected to contact *Sagafjord* at about noon today, three hours hence."

"When I have further information in hand I will pass it along to you.

Meanwhile, I thought it necessary to dispel the rumors. Again, my apologies and I wish you all a good day."

OK. Here's the gist: *Sagafjord* left Hong Kong and then suffered a fire in the South China Sea.

We knew exactly where *Sagafjord* was because we followed her progress on the map outside the library, called the World Cruise Route of the Explorers map. With *Sagafjord* disabled, only two ships remain on that map: *World Viking Sun* and *QE2*.

On deck, everyone talked of the tragedy. God! Can you imagine what it would be like without *air-conditioning*? What about not being able to *flush the toilet*?

That happened to us for a few hours when we were on Two deck and for eight hours when we were on Five deck. Quite an unpleasant experience. The others, mostly gray heads, nodded in agreement. Despite the tragedy, the Sports-o-rama must go on.

Bob, the sports supervisor, appointed me his assistant, mainly so I could catch the flack when I exposed the cheaters. I handed out the cards to pick teams and I got matched with Dawn from London. Dawn knows more about the *Sagafjord* because she has been talking to a woman at the Harrods shop onboard *QE2*, whose sister works in the galley on *Sagafjord*. The fire happened last night. The passengers have been deprived of decedance and functional plumbing for over twelve hours, and it will probably be more than a day before they step on dry land. Meanwhile, like the immigrants who came on ships from the slums of Europe to the slums of America, they eat out of cans for breakfast and lunch and barbecue on deck for the evening meal. Many can't sleep in their cabins because of the insufferable heat, so at night they plop down on the open decks. Power is out, so stewards conduct passengers downstairs and to their cabins with flashlights. *Sagafjord* is finished. Passengers will be repatriated. Their world cruise ended.

"Isn't that terrible?" Dawn exclaimed while holding the quoits for the first event.

"In a way, it's lucky. It would have been much worse for them if they had been in an airplane," I said.

Dawn looked puzzled, so I explained. "You know. Loss of power in an airplane and you go down."

"But in the air, you suffer a much shorter time," she replied.

Dawn informed me that she won the quoits championship on a previous world cruise. But that was long ago and, alas, her skill left her long ago. That's the way it is with most of the other contestants. They are used to winning, but with advancing age, they don't win much anymore. They keep playing, however, and they keep cheating.

Dawn's decrepitude showed. She can't get the basketball near the hoop, much less in it, even though Bob has awarded her a handicap and let her and the other women shoot from right under the basket instead of from the foul line. Poor pathetic Dawn can't get the disk past the foul line in shuffleboard, so Bob let her shoot closer up. Still trying, Dawn hit an Eight and then, in the next frame, a Seven. When we were putting golf balls, she missed most and after each shot that went awry, she apologized to me.

"You have to understand the idea of sport. It's not the winning, but the participation, that counts," I assured her, paraphrasing Baron de Coubertin, who founded the modern Olympics.

Bob looked like a harried kindergarten teacher who can't wait until recess, so he can smoke in the teachers' lounge. I couldn't take it anymore, either. So, as the official game assistant, I started pointing out the petty cheating, the fouls, and the incorrect addition of scores. Some gray heads inflated their quoit scores by calling threes fives and ones threes. I deflated those scores right back to where they should have been. The expected effect occurred; I am much despised, but none of my companions seems to understand why I remain so contented. Neither do I. I guess I'm just happy that we're on *QE2* and not on *Sagafjord*.

Since the gray heads got nowhere with me, they started complaining to Bob. Bob doesn't seem to mind. He's been doing this job a long time. He is used to it. Bob's wife had a mastectomy recently, followed by radiation therapy, so he is worried about her, not sore shuffleboard losers. A few days ago she got a puncture wound in her left arm during the surgery. Since then, Bob's worries have doubled. The group knows nothing of this, and Bob, the professional that he is, doesn't tell them. Bob just keeps going. Bob listens, unflinching and genuinely concerned, to their babblative laments.

I noticed that someone took down the sign that announced Hildegarde's and my big shuffleboard win and replaced it with a new sign that announced that Jeff and Jill have won the paddle tennis championship. My reign as shuffleboard champion of *QE2* has not been forgotten, but the new sign indicates that my moment of glory draws quickly to a close. *Sic transit gloria mundi*. Thus passes the glory of the world.

Loss of notoriety doesn't bother me. I prefer to be a nobody. I always have. I want to be left alone, a nameless scholar without public exposure, without a public face. I want to retreat into my cave and stay there a long, long while.

At noon, Captain John Burton-Hall announced there is no further information on *Sagafjord*. Either the captain believes what he told us or he doesn't. I don't know which possibility is more scary. We all know differently. Our sister ship has finished its world cruise. There, but for the grace of God, go we.

"No way," said Mrs. Lonelyhearts. "*QE2*, built like a battleship. That's what they say about it in Germany. We are invulnerable." Mrs. Lonelyhearts scooted her bottom closer to mine in the hot tub. "By the way, Bennie, I'm having fun with the deck steward. But, you know, I'm recyclable. A vagina can be used innumerable times without signs of wear. Want to try?"

How a change of semen can make a woman bloom! Mrs. Lonelyhearts now had the healthy look of a solid animal and lips that had that puffy look, like Michelle Pfeiffer, and a bottom that a man can't forget, a solid fact that was now nudging me underwater. Of course, I wanted to ask Mrs. Lonelyhearts if she was German and I wanted to ask her: Who paid whom? Did she pay the steward or vice versa? From the attention she gets on deck these days, I had a feeling it was vice versa. Deck stewards perform well, but they perform better when tipped.

"You know," I told Ethel. "The same man who told me about the *Sagafjord*'s engines, that they would break down and wouldn't complete the world cruise, told me the *QE2*'s props were about to fall off."

"Who?" asked Ethel.

"Doom."

"The guy who predicts a world financial collapse?"

"The same."

"We had better live it up."

"You bet."

Since I covered dinner at the Queens Grill yesterday, I should cover our room today.

We reside in 1041, a cabin about four times the size of our M5 cabin. The long hallway that leads to the living space is lined by wood-paneled walls and the main living space by yellow cushioned walls which, I imagine, are soundproof because we hear nothing from the outside. The ceilings are lined with varnished wood panels and are higher than in M5 by about two feet. Our beds are longer and wider and together. We sleep like a married couple rather than a pair of monks. This makes lovemaking a lot easier and we take advantage of the new situation at least once, sometimes twice, a day. Something about the cumulative effect of sea air has stimulated our sexual appetites. Who knows why? The room also has a private safe, for which we have made the combination 0627, meaning June 27, the date of our wedding. And there is a bar, a refrigerator, two large easy chairs, two bureaus, and a desk for me to type on the computer. We have two walk-in closets. Ethel's closet measures only a little shorter than the entire size of our M5 cabin. Most remarkable is the marble-lined bathroom, which is just about the size of an entire M5 room, and fits not only a tub larger than myself, but also a bidet. Contributing to the sense of spaciousness is our picture window the size of six portholes. True, two iron bars run vertically down the window, but they cannot detract from the vast vista we see each morning as we rise and each evening as we toast each other with Australian sherry. Of course, we get fresh flowers daily (usually orchids), fresh fruits (usually oranges), apples, pears, and sometimes black grapes. Someone, probably Val, provides fresh ice in a yellow ice bucket, kept handy on the bureau.

Oh, yes, the TV measures forty inches and the videotape player works well, except something happened to the color. We haven't had the time to tell someone about that. *Raging Bull*, the movie that won Robert De Niro an Oscar, didn't look bad without that distracting color. But we found out later that *Raging Bull* was filmed in black and white.

All in all, we found our room a most pleasant place to live. How many passengers actually notice much about their cabin or think of the designers and architects who planned and constructed it? Not one in a thousand, I'll bet. Passengers are too busy living to bother contemplating upon that living.

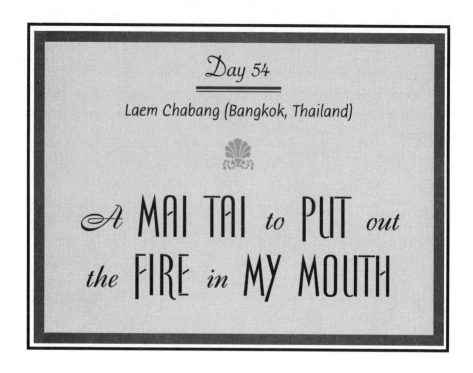

We are still cruising the Bight of Thailand and won't arrive at Laem Chabang until noon. This country used to be called Siam, but in 1939 the name was changed to the more nationalistic Muang Thai, Land of the Thais, a name that itself means free. Hence, Thailand means Land of the Free.

My faith in the ship's quiz was shaken when the reported correct answer to the question "How many cranial nerves are there?" was seven. As a neurologist, I know there are twelve. That number won't change in a million years. It hasn't changed in three million years. In fact, that has been the number since the Devonian fish. If I weren't so busy enjoying myself, I would have written cruise news a correction.

Paul, one of our Queens Grill waiters, leaves today or tomorrow so I decide to tip him today. Since Paul leaves and Colum doesn't, I decided to tip them both so Colum doesn't get jealous. Two hundred dollars each should do it.

Ethel and I visited Thailand several times. We think we know it. The picture of the king on the money had changed over the last ten years. No longer a boy, in fact a Harvard-educated jazz enthusiast, he looks older now and wears glasses, but the rest of Thailand remains the same, including the Thai script that no Westerner, without considerable application and study, can read. Those who want to learn some Thai should pickup *Thai without Tears* in the local bookshops. It helps, but just getting through the alphabet remains a formidable task likely to elicit tears and weeping and gnashing of teeth.

Last time Ethel and I visited, we stayed in the Sangri-La Hotel in Bangkok. The time before we stayed a week at the hotel repeatedly voted the world's best hotel, the Oriental. Both the Sangri-La and the Oriental border on the famous Chao Phya River, the mother of waters. Both hotels are great, but I give the Oriental the nod. I like the string orchestra that plays each night for guests sipping cocktails or sherry in the lobby. And there are two great swimming pools that overlook the Chao Phya. One night we even witnessed the festival of Loy Krathong, an ancient festival honoring water spirits. We and millions of Thais floated little banana-leafed boats, complete with candles, incense sticks, and coins, down the river. During the festival they have a beauty contest called the Noppamas Queen Contest, in honor of the eighth-century princess who invented the festival. The contest proved beauty remains in the eye of the beholder. The woman who won was a preadolescent teenager who stood four feet tall in bare feet and had a thin, weak frame and no breasts. By Western standards, judges wouldn't have even given her a passing glance, but to the Thais, she was a veritable superlative incorporation of absolute feminine pulchritude.

Up river from the Oriental and the Sangri-La, we visited the Grand Place, the fabulous city within a city, and the various *wats* (Buddhist monasteries or temple complexes), including Wat Arun (Temple of the Dawn), Wat Pho with the gilded reclining Buddha, and Wat Benchamabophit, the marble temple. In each temple, anyone wishing to learn about Buddha can and anyone that wishes to gain merit can by liberating birds from their cages.

Ninety percent of the Thais practice Theravada, a conservative branch of Buddhism. To understand Thailand, one needs understand two things: Buddhism and the *Ramayana*, the Indian epic written by Valmiki over two thousand years ago. In Thailand, the *Ramayana* became known as the *Ramkien*. I'll cover it on the way to India. Let's talk about Buddha.

The Buddha, born Siddhartha Gautama, was a prince commanding a kingdom near what today would be called Nepal. He grew up in great luxury, took a wife, and had a son. On a single fatal day, the previously sheltered young prince saw an old man, a sick man, a dead man, and a religious mendicant. Startled by the realization of age, illness, death, and poverty, the prince left home, abandoning wife and child, and set out searching for answers to the human condition and human suffering. Under the sacred Bodhi tree in India, Gautama meditated for forty-nine days, rising only after he had solved the riddle of life. After Gautama achieved enlightenment, he thereafter became known as the Buddha, a term that means the enlightened one.

Buddha traveled for the next forty-five years preaching, teaching, and making converts. Before dying, he said to his gathered disciples, "Be lamps unto yourselves. Work out your salvation with diligence."

So what? you may inquire. What did he teach that makes the Buddha so special, so venerated throughout the East?

Four noble truths stand out: (1) Suffering is universal. (2) The cause of suffering is the mind's craving or desire to grasp an ungraspable reality. Buddhists regard the ever-changing nature of phenomenological reality as proof of its illusory nature (*maya*). (3) The cure for suffering is to get rid of the craving. (4) The way to rid yourself of craving is to follow the Eightfold Way: right knowledge, right intention, right speech, right conduct, right means of livelihood, right effort, right mindfulness, right concentration. Eventually, the faithful followers of the Buddha will achieve inner peace and free themselves of worldly desires, achieving a state called nirvana, a state of blissful oneness with the nonbeing at the heart of being.

Confused? Don't get it? Think of how difficult it would be to explain Christianity or the Hebrew religion in a short space like this. Don't care? Perhaps you watch too much TV. Wipe your hand across your mouth and laugh. The joke's on you. This religion has over four hundred million devotees, more than the entire population of the United States. Yet, it's a religion without a god and instead a religion that venerates a man who did some serious thinking about the serious issues of life.

Bangkok! Called *Krungthep* (City of Angels) by King Rama I, Bangkok is just a big ugly urban village without a central downtown. There are sex shows where women do amazing things with their vaginas; Thai boxing set to martial music with no holds or blows barred; weird iconography including Karura birds (half-man and half-eagle) and women that are half-fish and half-princess; and the ubiquitous Hanuman, the king of the monkeys. And how about kite fighting? Did you ever see people attack each other's kites with such power and passion?

The *klongs*, waterways that have prompted some to call Bangkok the Venice of Asia, are not just there for boat races between James Bond and the Man with the Golden Gun. They are the places of the great produce markets, where people come from far and wide to buy and sell. Take a boat trip and watch as your water boy assists your pilot by diving down every once in a while to liberate the propeller from the twisting, enveloping weeds. What other country in the world bans the *King and I*? Yes, both the book and the movie and anything else concerned with the story of King Rama III, who opened Siam to foreign influences, is banned. The Land of the Free does not include the freedom to read everything.

Incidentally, to the Thais the king's body is so sacred no one can touch it. If the royal barge were to sink, no one could rescue the king. To touch the king would result in the penalty of death. The kings, when they needed to be deposed, were wrapped in a sack and beaten to death with sandalwood bats. Thais can assassinate their king, but they can't touch him.

Thailand made a mistake by siding with the Axis powers during World War II. The Japanese treated the Thais more like a captured people than friends. The United States, wisely for a change, treated the Thais more like friends than enemies, refusing to recognize that Thailand had declared war on the United States and refusing to attack Thailand. The Thais remain bosom friends for good reason.

Ethel and I took the courtesy bus to Pattaya, which the passengers pronounce *Pattay-a*, so I know the correct way of saying it must be *Pat-taya*. In Pattaya, everything is out in the tropical open, even the go-go bars. This used to be a major R&R place for American GIs. It still retains that sin and vice appearance, as evidenced by the names of some of the hotels that rent rooms by the hour: the Porn Hotel, Angle's Place (probably *angel* spelled wrong, it sports pictures of nude women on the walls just in case you have trouble figuring out what all those bargirls are doing hanging around the lobby), Texas Inn, Nipa House, Poteen Still (for the Irish), and Mick's Bar. One hotel is even called the Clinic. I guess it functions as a combination giver-and-curer of VD. There is a special street called Boy's Town, which bears no resemblance to Father Flanagan's Nebraska home for boys. Anything sexual you want you can get for a price, of course, for a price. Just looking around and with no personal experience whatsoever, I would say that Pattaya beats Paris as far as variety, quantity, and price of sexual provender. But in this era of AIDS, you have to be pretty gutsy to try some casual sex here or anywhere. Nevertheless, along the street, I saw some pretty casual couples in every combination: old men with young boys, Thais or Laotian women with middle-aged American men, young men with young women, very old men with girls, and even some women with women. Anything goes.

The street vendors tried to sell me fake Rolex watches. Why would someone buy one? Wearing a Rolex is usually an invitation to getting killed. So wearing a fake Rolex would do the same for you, but with the distinct advantage that you paid less for it, so you would have paid less to get killed. I passed over the fake watches and instead I picked up six pairs of Lacoste socks for 100 bahts, or $4. They're phony, I know that, but even if they only last one day, they are a bargain.

Shopping here is fun because the Thais are never too pushy in promoting their wares. The Thais take the view that the important pastimes in life are fishing, eating, and loving. As for selling things, for most of the time they just can't be bothered.

Ethel and I stopped in a supermarket, which smelled like a backed-up sewer. The locals shop here. While Ethel tried to find a plastic bowl for our Water Pik, I looked at the booze. The labels amazed me. They were fake. Fake Bordeaux wines with white labels announcing *"appellation contrôllée"* but conveniently omitting the *d'origine* of the usual *appellation d'origine contrôllée*. They couldn't even copy a label correctly. The fake Bordeaux comes in a clear glass bottle, not the green we usually see from France. The wine inside the bottle is clear, too, with a sick pink color, not the deep ruby red of a real Bordeaux. No way could that wine have come from Bordeaux. In fact, I wonder if it is even wine. It might be antifreeze.

We headed for the Garden Hotel and the shopping center next to it. All the wonderful Thai things are present: antiques, bronzes, dolls, gems (especially rubies and sapphires), jade (probably imported from Burma), and pentachrome porcelains, the misspelled sign says *"procelain."* I liked the teak woodcarvings of Kuan Yin. This Buddhist goddess of mercy stands serenely with hands in the position of prayer, polychromed, life-sized, beautiful, and available for about $400. Next to Kuan Yin, two other polychrome statues the same height stood, debasing her image. One is Donald Duck and the other, Mickey Mouse. Donald and Mickey I can live without, but I love the goddess. I wanted to possess her, take her home, worship her each morning. But how would I get her home? Kuan Yin is too big and too heavy for me to carry. How about something smaller? The thought crosses my mind about buying an over-sized teak Buddha mask, but exporting of any image of Buddha remains strictly against Thai law. I decided not to chance it. The law is not just a meaningless shadow the way it sometimes is at home, especially when it comes to Buddha images.

I just read in the *Business Post*, the Bangkok paper, about Sandra Gregory, an English teacher in Bangkok, caught trying to smuggle 104 grams of heroin in her vagina. The court sentenced her to death. The paper shows a color picture of her weeping after hearing the court's verdict. Gregory's lawyer said he hoped she might be included in the royal amnesty, expected this year to mark His Majesty the King's fiftieth year on the throne. I doubt it. No mercy for drug dealers has been standard policy here for decades. Singapore also has the same penalty for people caught trafficking drugs—death.

American influence shows with a Ripley's Believe It or Not on the top floor of the Garden Shopping Center, next to a number of amusement rides, a game room, and a theater showing American films. Of course, down below we passed up lots of fast food shops with familiar names, including Popeye's, Sizzler, Kentucky Fried Chicken, McDonald's, and Burger King. Ugh!

We beelined for the real Thai cooking and we have the most fiery experience of our lives. One bowl of spicy Thai shrimp soup required two glasses of orange juice and a mai tai to put out the fire in my mouth. When you have eaten real Thai food, you know you have eaten.

Day 55

Laem Chabang (Bangkok, Thailand)

FINALLY, RED EYE HANDED ME
a TWENTY *and a* FIVE

The Nong Nooch Tropical Garden attracted our interest. We decided to spend the day there. But, guess what? Overnight, taxi prices rose 50 percent. This called for bargaining, so I got the guy to agree to take us to the park, wait for as long as it took us to see the sights, and then take us back to *QE2*, all for $50.

At the Nong Nooch Tropical Garden, our young driver, Noi, looked and sounded shifty. I made sure he understood our contract: He must wait for us in the parking lot and meet us there at 4:15 PM. And, I emphasized, at that time I would give him a tip. Noi smiled. He shook his head yes. Noi understood, but would he do it? I memorized Noi's license plate number—5323.

Before we started the visit, I made an offering at the small shrine of Kuan Yin, the Buddhist goddess of mercy that guards the entrance to the cultural center and the market. Her statue stands between two fresh pink roses. Kuan Yin's countenance looked like that of the Virgin Mary in some pre-Raphaelite pictures.

Modern technology, in evidence everywhere in Thailand, showed in this shrine: the three punks, for past, present, and future, are plastic and emit no smoke. They have electric lights where the fire should have been. Will the absence of smoke confuse the evil spirits? Will the absence of smoke prevent my message from getting to the gods? Next to the electric punks stand two electric candles that look even more phony than the electric punks. The offerings on the altar, however, are real: three soups, vases with yellow orchids, and some oranges.

Kuan Yin have mercy on us, I prayed. Make our taxi driver wait for us. Because if you do not, Ethel and I will be stranded here in Thailand unable to return to our sheltering mother, *QE2*.

Why is it that I like the idea that the god that I am praying to is not a man?

The market exists strictly for the locals, and come to think on it, I see few Westerners in the park or the gardens, but there are hundreds of Thais. I know the market exists for the locals because most of the fruits and vegetables I can't even recognize. I do recognize the dried fish stomachs, the dried skates, and the cuttle fish that we learned about on Lantau. I also recognize some of the easy fruits: banana, pineapple, tapioca, sugarcane, mung bean, durian, mango, rambutan, litchi, mangosteen, and papaya. Melons cost 150 bahts, about $3. Why can't they send those melons across to Japan so the Japanese don't have to pay $40? Some Japanese government regulation gets in the way. That's why. As a general rule, when something makes no sense, some government is involved.

We walked up the hill to see the elephants. I bought several hands of bananas and fed them to the elephant standing closest to the banana stand. It eats the whole handful at once. As an experiment, I buy a whole bunch of bananas and hand them into the elephant's trunk. *Whoosh!* The bunch disappeared in one gulp. I begin to respect elephants even more than before. Any animal who can eat faster than I can commands respect. I then feed the elephant a whole coconut. Without apparent effort, the animal cracked the shell and devoured the fibrous shell and all in three bites!

Tour buses kept arriving, dropping Japanese, Chinese, and mostly Thai tourists off at the cultural center. In the main parking lot, at least thirty-five buses have parked, and in the auxiliary parking were eight other buses, down the hill by the bird sanctuary, the pedal boats, and the duck and geese houses.

I should have made a bigger offering to Kuan Yin. We weren't sure if we could attend the next cultural show, scheduled for three o'clock. If we miss that one, we can't stay for the next. I went back to the cultural show entrance and tried to buy tickets. No deal. We must wait until two o'clock. So we strolled around and enjoyed the grounds.

In the gardens we saw amazing things. Whole sections were devoted to cacti, ferns, bonsai, and, of course, there was an epiphytic orchid wonderland. We enjoyed the quiet stroll through the multiple multicolored flowers and smelled the multiple fragrances of millions of flowers. They even have a European garden here with statues of the Nine Muses, the way the other gardens have statues of Sita, Hanuman, and the other characters from the *Ramayana*.

At lunch I suffered through another Thai spiced shrimp soup, this one hotter than the one in Pattaya. This time I needed three mai tais to put out the fire in my mouth. My lips and tongue continued to burn, long after the food has gone down. I soothe myself with some delicious, delicate fried rice with crab. The waiter told us he comes from Laos, as does the cashier. He told us he knows the United States has a king, just like Thailand. I explained that we don't have a king. He said we were very ignorant of our own country because he had learned of our king in school. "Your king's picture is on the one dollar bill," he assured us.

"Actually, George Washington refused to be crowned king," I explained, but that got nowhere. "George Washington your first king."

Surprisingly the tickets for the cultural show cost only $8 each. I glance down the road to the parking lot where our taxi man was supposed to wait and no one was there. I won't tell Ethel. Besides, maybe he just went for a smoke.

The Thai Cultural Show at the Nong Nooch Tropical Garden turns out to be the highlight of the visit. It started with remarkable Thai music from a three-tiered orchestra, with each tier revealed first by its music and then by the curtain on that tier, raised to display the musicians. Then they brought out the cocks to fight. But the cocks don't want to fight. They pushed the cocks together and nothing happened. They spit some clear fluid over each cock and push them together, but still no fight. Then they got two other cocks, who, from the looks of them, with their lack of feathers in large patches on their heads and bellies and multiple stab wounds, will fight. Sure enough, these two birds fight like they want to kill each other. The boys break it up when they sense the crowd doesn't wish to see any more carnage.

Next came the Thai boxers. Thai boxing doesn't have the Marquis of Queensberry rules. Far from it. Anything goes, and I mean anything: kicking in the head or groin, punching below the belt, kidney shots—anything. The whole show takes place to martial music but not before the two boxers, one in red and the other in blue trunks, pray at each of the four corners of the ring and then kneel and pray together in the center of the ring. Occasionally, I have seen American fighters make a quick sign of the cross before they begin, but I have never seen any fighter pray this extensively. Perhaps Thai boxers need prayer more. Each boxer also has a small paper wrapped around his upper arm containing some Buddhist prayers.

They started. Immediately I felt relieved, for I got the same feeling I get watching American professional wrestling. They are pretending. Everything is scripted. Multiple blows don't seem to connect, yet the boxer gets knocked down, and they alternate who hits whom, how hard, and where. I know the thing is pretend when red trunks misses blue trunks with his left foot and hits a ringside spectator, who promptly falls down unconscious.

The next phony thing, or should I say, demonstration, consists of a fight between two elephants, while human masters on top of the elephants clash with spears. The elephants play along and lock trunks while the humans clink spears and raise some sparks. I wonder what the elephants think of all this music and cheering and noise and stupidity. Whatever their opinion, they keep it to themselves, probably to get some more bananas.

Next, we saw some genuine Thai dancers, with one beauty representing a goddess and the other, an angel. These women train up to this from their youth and each hand movement, each gesture, each eyelid raise, or elevation of eyebrow incorporates a coded message. It's a message I can only guess at, but the Thais in the audience get it right away. It enthralls them. They clap ecstatically. In the United States this dance wouldn't go over, mainly because no one could concentrate on the aesthetic for more than five seconds. TV has damaged our attention spans that badly. The dancing stopped. Everybody filed out to the field in back for everyone's favorite, the elephant show.

This is worth the price of admission ten times over. We will never forget it. The ponderous pachyderms, the gentle giants, the symbols of Siam, perform tricks the likes of which, because of liability considerations, you never will see in the United States. The elephants play soccer, kicking a black and white ball, triple normal size, clear across the field and into the goal. I never realized elephants can kick, but they can, and accurately, too. The goalie, a large gray male, picked up an English tourist with his trunk, ran her across the field, and then put her down on the other side. The elephant then went through the audience, stepping over the benches and getting lots of pets on his trunk and side. I petted him, too. The skin felt dry and hard and thick and tough. It had that wild animal feel and smell. A group of elephants came from nowhere and ran across the field, picking up bottles with their trunks and handing them up to the rider. All this is done without apparent effort and without breaking stride. Magnificent! The elephants proved their point. They must be very intelligent, clever, and well-coordinated animals.

The tourists, especially the Chinese, are wild. They trusted the pachyderms with their lives by lying down on mats on the field while the elephants stepped over them. That one is not for me. I knew history. In India at the Red Fort in Delhi, adulterers, thieves, and murderers were summarily trampled to death by an elephant executioner.

Some tourists volunteer for an elephant massage, wherein the tourist laid on the ground while the elephant rubbed their back or front with a large, flat foot. Suddenly, the elephant got dirty, probably a hidden cue from the handler, and started to massage the genital areas. The crowd roared with laughter. On request of a man who feels his genitals had been manipulated perhaps too roughly, the elephant stopped and then proceeded to remove the guy's shoes with his trunk. That will teach him! The elephant knew it had pleased the crowd and carried the poor guy's shoes away to the end of the field. Then the elephant honked, wiggled his ears for applause, and took some bows before returning the shoes.

Next came the tug-of-war. I volunteered, along with about sixty other tourists. I thought we'd win because, after all, there are sixty of us against one small baby elephant, an animal smaller than I am. When they blew the whistle, we started pulling with all our might and the baby elephant backed up a little, giving ground. We screamed our elation. Easier than I had thought. I knew we'd win.

Nope! The ponderous pachyderm was merely playing with us. Baby Dumbo started to pull effortlessly. All the tourists, myself included, were swept off our feet, dragged helplessly across the field as if under the overwhelming influence of a gigantic tidal wave. We gave up, exhausted, but the baby elephant looked as fit as ever. The elephant glanced back at us. Is he smiling? Don't ever have a tug-of-war with an elephant. You will lose.

The Thais start drumming and the elephants start dancing to the rhythm. Then they play disco and the elephants did some disco dancing. After that, I paid 20 baht to one of the handlers. He told me to hold on to the left tusk and then *swoosh!* with one graceful movement the elephant lifted me with its trunk above its head. I remained there, suspended, experiencing one of those peak moments of happiness that poets and psychologists speak of. The elephant carried me away. I hoped the taxi man would do the same, but no sign of our taxi man.

Ethel and I waited twenty minutes because Ethel thought he might have gotten caught in traffic. Nope. He's a no-show.

We talked to the Thai policeman, who acted as if this were a routine event. The policeman took us down three flights of steps to the lakeshore and pointed to the other side of the lake, indicating there might be taxis there. Under the hot tropical Thai sun, Ethel and I walked about a half mile. But the only taxis are *tut-tuts*, a Thai version of the Filipino jeepney, only with the passenger compartment open-aired. We walked another half mile down the road to a restaurant, hoping to find real taxi. No luck. So we walk back to the tut-tut. One of the tut-tut drivers seated at the long wooden table under the thatched roof seems interested in our problem, while the others are more interested in staying in the shade and drinking beer. With a little bargaining, the tut-tut driver agreed to take us to Laem Chabang for 400 baht. "Which hotel?" he asked as we got in the open back of the tut-tut.

"No hotel," I shouted. "Ship. Big ship. *QE2*."

He shrugged his shoulders. He doesn't understand. But he started the engine. The driver turned his neck, "What hotel?" he asked again.

"Laem Chabang," I said, thanking Kuan Yin that I had remembered how to say the name of our port in Thai. The driver shook his head to say now you're talking. Away we went.

The ride wasn't bad, considering the circumstances. We felt like we were in a pickup truck, only it has a roof. Dirt blew in my right eye and under my contact lenses, but by blinking and tearing, I got relief. Then it started to rain. We got soaked. Ethel looked at me with that look, meaning, "Oh, well we're having an adventure." Over the noise of the blowing rain, the wind, and the rattling of the tut-tut, she shouted, "What about the taxi guys? Will you try to get our money back?"

"You bet, half of it because we did get half the ride. If those guys are smart, they will have folded up shop and left already. If they are there, I'll get the $25. Watch me."

I explained the situation to the taxi people on the dock. It's the same man, a stout dark brown–skinned fellow with red eyes. He can't understand. He tells me to wait. He will talk with the boss. Ten minutes elapse. Another man came. We told the same story. I pointed to my watch and had an inspiration. "The ship leaves soon," I said "Get my $25 or we'll tell our story to the police."

His facial expression suddenly changed. I realized the power of words, or the power of correct words. The first man, the man with the red eyes, returned. They talked to each other in a language I don't understand. They talked to each other in gestures I do understand. The red eyes got redder. Basically, they don't want to pay.

"Who was the driver?" the red-eyed man asked.

"Noi," I replied.

"We can't help. You don't know the driver. We have many Noi. We can't get the money from him."

"Show me some pictures. I'll recognize him. I have a good memory. I know the license plate, too. It was red and had numbers 5323."

Number Two Man frowned and Red Eyes showed more anger than ever. Red Eyes waved me back to the end of the parking lot, where six

Thais, five men and one woman, are squeezed into a little blue car, covered with dust. The woman, skinny as a bean, her face full of eyes, looks real alert and real intelligent, and seems to be in charge. She consulted a clipboard with lists of trips, payments, and next to each, license plate numbers. She shows me the record. It says I paid $30 for a one-way trip! This is false, I assured her. I paid $50 for a two-way trip, plus waiting time. She said in pretty good English, "There is nothing I can do."

I reiterated my story, but it had less effect than ever. They hardened their hearts. Then I remembered the magic words. I pointed to my watch. "Hurry up," I said, pointing my index finger menacingly at Red Eyes's chest. "You have one minute. Pay up, or we discuss the situation with the police."

The magic words worked. The Thai men started shouting at each other in Thai. The woman consulted the clipboard again. Then one of the men in the car offered me $20. Ethel poked me in the ribs, her elbow indicating I should take it. But I'm riding my high horse again. I shook my head no, pointed to my watch, and asked for the full $25.

Red Eyes, who is standing on my left, looked me in the eye. "What you want?"

Oh yes, I forgot to mention that I was a giant among pygmies. They are all small men. I could knock most of these men down with one hand, especially Red Eyes, who appears not only weak, but also under the weather. But what if Red Eyes is a Thai boxer? A Thai boxer can beat a Japanese jujitsu master. I held my right index finger up toward heaven, and then, pointing it at his chest, said, "Pay me $25. It's only fair. Your man Noi didn't wait. We had to walk a half mile to the taxis. Since there were no taxis, we had to ride in the tut-tut and pay. What about right thought, right conduct, right intention?"

From his wallet Red Eyes handed me a twenty and a five. I bowed, folded my hands in the prayer position, and bowed again to him and the people in the car. Everyone smiled.

I worked more for that $25 than I had ever worked for any other $25 in my life, but it was worth it. I'm a hero. Ethel floods me with her admiration. She can't wait to get back to cabin 1041 to give me what she quaintly calls, in Shakespearean terms "her woman's service." Me too. I can't wait.

Day 56
———————
At Sea, off the East Coast of Malaysia,
Headed South in the Gulf of Thailand

IMAGINE *a* SEASON *in* HELL
THREE MONTHS LONG

fter two days on land and the big adventure with the Thai taxi service, Ethel and I needed a rest. Onboard and at sea routines comforted us: We got up late, leisurely ate breakfast in Queens Grill, and snooped around deck in the fresh air and bright sunshine. Aboard *QE2* there is nothing we have to do, but we never have enough time to do it in. Wonderful leisure, a sacred thing. Others on deck share the same philosophy. The decks are hives of inactivity. Most passengers lolled about on deck chairs reading, sleeping, or watching the sea.

By the way, about the deck chair. This incomparable piece of maritime furniture began life onboard the ocean liners as a passenger innovation. Early shipping lines did not provide them; instead, sturdy park benches were bolted to the deck, sheltered from the wind and out of the way of the crew. But passengers, in pursuit of more comfortable as well as movable seating, started bringing from home folding chairs, carpet stools, and steamer rugs. Eventually, the cruise companies went into the deck chair business themselves, renting out chairs, rugs, and cushions for the crossing. Passengers booking a chair had their names inscribed on the small cards inserted into the brass frame atop each chair's backrest. In the days of my youth, during the first five hours onboard, I recall my father running around, making the deck chair reservations with the deck steward, and then running down for table reservations with the dining steward, easing the way, of course, with gigantic tips. That rush ended long ago. Now there are no deck chair reservations to speak of, or dining room assignments. Without any intervention on your part whatsoever, the *QE2* staff sends the information to your room on a small white card.

Waldemar Hansen tried to brief us on what to expect in Singapore and Kuala Lumpur. Since Ethel and I have visited both places before, we think we know it all. As we left the theater, I mentioned, "He forgot to tell them that Malaysia has the world's largest flower, the *Rafflesia*, measuring three feet across and smelling like a London sewer. He also should have talked about Changi Prison, described in James Clavell's novel *King Rat* covering, in detail, what it was like to be a prisoner of the Japanese at Changi. He should have mentioned the world's smallest deer, the mouse deer, which stands only ten inches high when fully grown."

Captain John Burton-Hall announced that we will pass the sunken British ships *Prince of Wales* and *Repulse*, two destroyers deployed without air cover and promptly sunk by the Japanese. The captain also explained that over 150 passengers from the abandoned *Sagafjord* will embark in Singapore to continue their world cruise with us.

"How will we recognize the *Sagafjord* passengers?" Ethel wanted to know.

"They'll complain more about *Sagafjord* than about *QE2*." I answered, wondering if such a thing were possible.

True leisure proved too much for me to bear. I felt a sense of strangeness not going to a lecture. From a pang of conscience I dropped in on the afternoon self-improvement lecture on the topic of humor. The material seemed elementary: exaggerate one characteristic, lead the listener down the path, and then give an unexpected twist. Try to see the humor in everyday life, otherwise life becomes one long dental appointment. An example: "Being a mother is hard these days (common and true observation). If the children are still alive when my husband gets home, I've done my job (punchline)."

Yes, that is funny, but it would have worked better if the punch were changed and withheld to the end. I rewrote the joke: "These days a housewife's job is hard. When my husband comes home, I feel I've done my job, if the kids are still alive."

The lecturer invited four people up to the stage and asked them to brainstorm about what they don't like about the cruise. No problem. The litany seems endless. There they go again, moaning and groaning. When it comes to complaining, these people win. One doesn't like people who cut into the line at the Lido buffet. The other thinks his wife takes too long to dress for dinner. Another, one I can identify with, decries the passengers who usurp his seat on the tour bus when they return from a pit stop. Another woman dislikes people seated next to her who talk during the lectures. She says this while looking straight at the group of five seated at an adjacent table who are in fact talking so intently they don't even hear her complaint. Another woman dislikes how the gentlemen hosts always pass her up. From the looks of her, I can see why. She needs emergency help from Steiner's, the onboard beauty parlor, or perhaps she needs a Muslim veil to cover her atrocious ugliness. Gentleman hosts are not blind. Still another woman whines, a poor soul with that barrel body of middle age, her arms and legs thin, her flesh loose like cooked chicken coming off the bone. She objects to the young women on One deck by the pool who sunbathe in thong bathing suits or wear bathing suits so thin you can see their nipples. Jealousy, thy name is woman!

Mrs. Lonelyhearts. That's who she means. Lonelyhearts. I wonder who's kissing her now? I wonder who's buying the wine?

Talking about problems seems to make things worse. By a chain of linked connectors the audience came up with complaints in abundance. Most things, however, involve the misbehavior of other passengers and have little to do with the crew or the cruise. Don't they know the wisdom of Voltaire: "If you continue to focus on the problems, they get worse." Was Voltaire a Buddhist?

"Next point," said the lecturer. "In good comedy, you have to make fun of yourself." He then asked each person up on stage to name one fault that they have.

Amazing!

Not a single one of them can spontaneously think of anything remotely wrong! Even when coached, the first man, who, incidentally, has a rather large amount of drool running down the corner of his mouth, has to confess that he doesn't have a single fault. That's funny of course. But he's not kidding. That's the joke. He really believes he has no fault. From that moment on, the lecturer called him Mr. Perfect.

The session must break up to make room for this afternoon's bingo. Before they leave, the audience stood up in what must have been the ritual for the other four self-improvement lectures, which I skipped because, not having any faults, I don't need improvement.

En masse the group recited their credo, a modern incantation: "I am healthy. I am happy. I will not let the negative people get me down."

This evening, before dinner, Ethel and I dropped by to talk with Peter, who has been demoted undoubtedly due to the intervention of Rabbi, from Caronia to Mauretania Restaurant. Peter, despite the demotion, looked the best we have seen him. And he has acquired, probably from Mary, the happy gift of gab. Peter explained that he waited on Rabbi for three months on last year's world cruise. "Imagine a season in hell three months long!" Peter has Rabbi's number. "He just does that to call attention to himself. It has nothing to do with the service or with the food. It has to do with him."

Ethel and I nodded our agreement and added that Rabbi's behavior doesn't have anything to do with religion, either.

Dinner tonight has special overtones, for the menu announces it's St. David's Day. I asked Nick, our new waiter who replaced Paul, who St. David was. Nick explained, "St. David is the patron saint of Wales. Tonight we would do well to eat leek soup."

"Why do whales have a patron saint and not cats or dogs?" I inquired using the play-on-words humor not covered in today's lecture. Nick doesn't get it or, if he does, doesn't think it funny. "Those from Wales wear leeks today." Nick glanced around the room, but saw no one wearing leeks.

To make a cowardly amends for what I have said, I ordered lamb basted in honey, made according to an ancient recipe from Wales. St. David would approve.

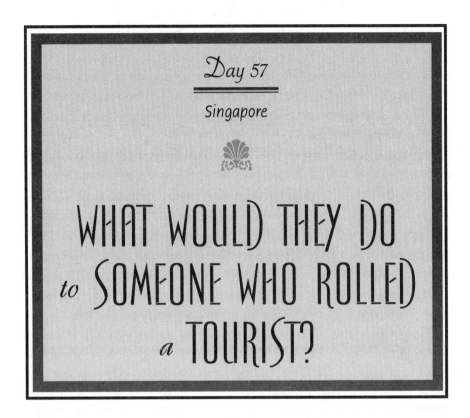

Day 57

Singapore

WHAT WOULD THEY DO
to SOMEONE WHO ROLLED
a TOURIST?

*T*wo years ago we spent a fortnight here in Singapore, staying at the Raffles Hotel in the Palm Court. At that time, Room 102, the Somerset Maugham Suite, was engaged so we stayed in 109, another suite close by. Each morning, when Ethel gave her permission, I set up my portable computer on the white painted wrought iron table under the shade of the palm tree and the Casuarina tree and typed away. Somerset Maugham composed some of his short stories about the East under this same tree. Would that some of his magic would rub off on me?

In the evenings, the ghosts of Rudyard Kipling, Somerset Maugham, Noel Coward, and sometimes Joseph Conrad and John Masefield called me to join them for a drink in the lobby at the Writers Bar. Their call, like the call of the running tide, was a wild and clear call that cannot be denied. I obeyed and nursed my gin martini straight up with a twist, while

Ethel drank the famous Singapore Sling, a sweetish concoction made from gin, cherry brandy (usually Cherry Herring), lemon juice, sugar, and egg white. The egg white gives the drink a slight white foam above the pink, an effect that Ethel likes.

All the aforementioned famous authors have their pictures on the shelf on the right side of the bar, next to the black wrought iron fence that separates the lobby from the main dining room, the Raffles Grill. Some misguided person actually placed the picture of James A. Michener on the same shelf as Conrad. If Michener's picture belongs there, it should face the other way so we don't have to see him among the august company. For some reason, possibly an oversight, my picture does not appear.

Raffles is an institution, not just a hotel. Raffles is one of the few hotels in the world that can lay claim to offering hospitality to travelers for over a century. Opened on December 1, 1887, by the early 1920s it was already known as the historic hotel of Singapore. From 1880 to 1939, when Singapore was known as the Crossroads of the East, the Raffles Hotel label was seen on the steamer trunk of every seasoned traveler. Don't believe me? Go watch the movie on the second floor, which shows Raffles history or visit the Raffles Hotel Museum and inspect the fascinating array of hotel china and silver; picture postcards; old letters, including one from Maugham; and not so old letters, including one from President George H. W. Bush. Maugham's letter, even though he was a retired physician (like some other author I know), is ten thousand times better, more literate and more literary. Enjoy the many period photographs of Singapore and Southeast Asia. That stuff tells the story of Raffles Hotel, the people who made it a legend—they shot a tiger in the Long Bar—and the times in which they lived. "When in Singapore feed at the Raffles, but stay at somewhere else," said Kipling. I say feed and stay at the Raffles.

It used to be that the Raffles had a better, some say much better, reputation than Singapore itself. Singapore now has a good reputation, too. Gone are the days of the opium dens, the death homes where the Chinese went to die, and the stuff you saw in *Mondo Cane*. The transexuals still parade here at night, but Orchid Road now has some of the most famous shopping malls in the world and, of course, Singapore is clean. Spit in public, toss away your cigarette butt, eat on the MRT subway, or jay walk, and prepared to pay a $500 fine. They even fine you if you forget to flush the toilet or get caught reading *Playboy*.

One might say Singapore is overburdened with Confucius-inspired edicts. Since chewing gum is illegal, naughty Singaporeans might offer it after dinner, much the way some film moguls in Hollywood might offer cocaine at their swanky parties. Chewing gum as a form of rebellion. Think about it. Each culture has its own internally defined sense of right and wrong. In New York, having a kilogram of heroin might get you years in prison, especially if your skin's the wrong color. In Saudi Arabia, carrying a quart of Irish whiskey would have a similar effect. In the City of the Lion (*singa* meaning lion and *pura* meaning city in Sanskrit) chewing gum gets you in trouble.

Ethel and I boarded the courtesy shuttle bus heading into the city. Along the way we saw familiar sites: the East meeting the East, with Chinese mingling with Malays and Indians, Tamils mainly. On the street we expect to hear the four languages that have official status—Malay, English, Mandarin Chinese, and Tamil—and we expect to see the subway signs in those four languages. Usually English is first, then Mandarin, then Malay, and Tamil last. We passed Faber Hill (they call it Mount Faber) with its cable car that goes directly to Singapore's secret weapon, Sentosa Island, a giant fun park.

Last time we spent days swimming and visiting the Butterfly Park, where millions of beautiful butterflies alight on brightly colored clothing and ride you around. Also on Sentosa Island they have the Pioneers of Singapore and Surrender Chambers Museum, whereby means of realistic tableaus and audio-visual effects, I learned how the Japanese came over the Malay Peninsula on bicycles and conquered Singapore with a big bluff. The English didn't realize the Japanese were sick and tired, low on food and ammunition; otherwise they wouldn't have agreed to the demands for an unconditional surrender. They certainly wouldn't have agreed to the surrender if they could have guessed the suffering they would have to endure at Changi Prison.

The shuttle left us off at Le Meridien Hotel, situated on the southern end of Orchid Road. Ethel and I had avoided this district on our last visit for fear we might spend all our money. This time we resolved to walk the length of it to see what's there.

We found a place selling pearls. The shop has a beautiful string of natural uncultured pearls with a wonderful pink luster and adequate finish and roundness. Each pearl measures more than a half inch in diameter. The necklace costs only $250,000. Quite a bargain. I offered to buy it for Ethel, but she declined. Too bad men can't wear such things, otherwise I would have purchased the necklace for myself.

Ethel got tired walking, so we took a taxi to the Raffles.

They are booked solid in the Tiffin Room for lunch, but for some reason a waiter pulled us aside, had mercy on our souls, and invited us in, thus bypassing the maître d'. That waiter illustrates again that the little people of this world control things. Later he told me he remembered me from two years ago when I left a gigantic tip. I usually tip 30 percent. It's nothing to me, but to waiters it can be a big deal.

We took our seats among mainly Chinese, but some Malays. Ethel and I are the only Westerners. The Raffles' Tiffin Room opened in 1892. It always was grand and popular, just as it is this day. The restaurant seats two hundred people at fifty tables and used to have *punkahs*, Indian fans, to keep people cool. Now it has air-conditioning. Around 1910 the Tiffin Room closed for a while, but the Sarkies, the new owners, carried on the tradition of serving their dishes at Raffles Hotel main dining room, which later they renamed the Tiffin Room.

Why is this food so famous and why is this restaurant so jammed to this day? It's the food, of course, and especially the curry that brings them in. Tiffin curry's origin traces back to India when men would go to work with their lunches conveniently packed in a tiffin carrier. The carrier, a three-tiered container, usually held rice or *chapati* (unleavened Indian bread), a vegetable dish, and tasty curry prepared by wives or servants. When the British first came to the East, they adopted the same practice, as they preferred to eat hygienic, home-cooked meals. The curry, however, was modified so that it was less spicy. Through the years, tiffin curry evolved into a luncheon spread, which was served in grand hotels in Singapore. These meals often consisted of curry and side dishes of eggs, chicken, prawns, aubergines (Asian eggplant), pickles, and mango chutney, all accompanied by rice, Indian breads, or crackers.

Today's meal is similar and different. Ethel and I experienced multiple dishes, impossible to cover in detail. I will mention the ones I liked the best: baby shrimps, baby samosas, potato salad, bean sprouts, chopped curried raisins, mulligatawny soup, red snapper smooth Indian style, pickled prawn salad, steamed rice, pea pilaf, chicken in tomato gravy, daals, mushrooms and green peas in cream sauce, and of course, for dessert, sweet white Rasgulla pastry balls and their brown honey-soaked counterparts, fine rice pudding (nothing like it), and a massive array of cakes, mousses, raspberry charlottes, sweets, melons, grapes, watermelons, star fruits, pecan pie, and delicious vermicelli pudding.

I returned again and again for more more more. I set a new indoor record for desserts eaten—seven. With the meal we indulged in Taittinger pink champagne, which I feel is the perfect drink for tiffin, or for anything else for that matter. Our waiter suggested we save the cork, for this was a special occasion. What if we did? We would have a house full of corks and they would spill out into the garden, too. Our bill came to 150.92 Singapore dollars to which I added a tip, making the total equivalent to about $138, American.

The rest of the afternoon, probably due to the lingering effect of the champagne, blurs out. We did shop the shops of Raffles, looked in on the Palm Court, and made a reservation for dinner at eight at the Empress Chinese restaurant on the third floor. On the way back to the lobby we spotted Captain John Burton-Hall in a civilian outfit. The captain is here. He's in the right place.

Somewhere I bought a book of short stories by Somerset Maugham and I got his controversial novel *Cakes and Ale*, first published in 1930, about a British literary figure who I shall not name. In a bookstore on Stamford Road I picked up two books on Chinese war stratagems. Looking these over, I see during the next war in April when, according to Mr. Doom, the Chinese would attack Russia, what their strategy will be. Example, which I arrived at randomly by opening the first book: "Kill with a borrowed knife." This means if your enemy's situation is clear, but your ally's stand is uncertain, you should induce your ally to attack your enemy in order to preserve your strength. In dialectic terms, another man's loss is your gain. Specific examples follow, including instructions on how to make the opposing leader think his most capable advisors are traitors. That leader will order the advisors killed with the borrowed knife and the opposing leader will have fewer staff to fight when you attack directly.

The variety of books available here in Singapore daunts the imagination. The people here actually read, just as they do in Hong Kong. The books cost plenty, too. When the demand rises, the price rises also. I spent $111.89 in the Times Book Shop in Raffles City and about $34 in the Raffles Hotel Museum.

Somehow, in a kind of alcoholic haze, we got on the MRT at Raffles City and headed out to the Chinese Gardens by the West 10 (W10) station. The subway looked modern and clean and trains come and go every few minutes. As expected, lots of signs show what you can't do on the train, including eating, drinking, and smoking, but one sign shows a durian, that foul smelling but great tasting fruit of the Orient, with a red line through it. No durians allowed. Ethel and I know why: durian smells like a London sewer, a sordid combination of child vomit, rotted cheese, and stale cow urine that stays in the nostrils, on the fingers, and in the hair for days.

The people take this mass transport for granted, but we don't. Why can't we have this in the United States? For $1 in Singapore we go anywhere in the fair city and get there fast. Ethel and I kept amused watching a six-year-old Chinese girl chin and swing on the overhead straps. Her father nearby beams his approval and delight. Perhaps someday she'll be a star in a Chinese circus.

At W10 we got off and walked a quarter mile to the main gate of Yu Hwa Yuan, the Chinese Gardens. We saw only Chinese here, no Westerners. Some came to picnic and others, the younger ones identified by hand-holding and furtive happy hugging and kissing, for romance. And why not? This is a romantic garden with lots of romantic sights: the cloud-wrapped pavilion; slender, shadowy bamboo trees; bubbling spring over white pebbles; the gallery of tea fragrance; white rainbow bridge; and even the Garden of Romance. Everywhere we see the splendor of oriental gardening that approaches the redemptive qualities of art. We step through the circular hole in the wall and into eternity. We see what Jan Stuart told us about: Large boulders plopped in the middle of grassy knolls. The largest rocks represent mountains and some are wrapped in lucky red to celebrate the new Year of the Rat. Small stone-covered paths wander zigzag through shady groves of bamboo that ruffles in the wind, reminding me of the way *QE2* sometimes sounds, creaking and groaning in rough seas. Flat large yellow stones lead us across pea green ponds to small pavilions in northern Chinese architectural style and to the seven-story cloud pavilion, which we climb to get the panoramic view.

We admired the stone boat, the statue of Confucius, the rookeries of the Garden of Romance, and felt entirely at peace. Man was lost in a garden, and in a garden, by the medieval rules of symmetry, man must be found.

We lingered awhile among the three thousand pots of *penjing*, Chinese bonsai trees situated in Yun Xiu Yuan, a Suzhou-style set of inter-connecting rooms that open on one end into a central garden area. Guarding the entrance stands a 280-year-old lion-shaped *Podocarpus* penjing. Curiously, there is a large collection of jagged irregular granite rocks mounted on wood cut into the shape of the rock. Such rocks would receive no recognition in Texas, but here someone has labeled them as artistic rocks and enshrined them in display cases.

We stopped in the next-door curio shop and the owner sold me a large rounded royal blue hat with gold embroidery and a black braided pigtail that hung from the back. Delighted with the sale, he dressed Ethel and me in red silk robes and took pictures with a Polaroid camera. We look great.

The heat and the walking got to Ethel, so we headed for the tea pavilion where she drank a bottle of water while I admired the variety of drinks available: sugar cane drink, lemon barley drink, soya bean milk, guava, soursop, and winter melon tea. This is indeed the Orient. They do things differently here. And they drink different drinks. They eat different things too, as we discovered back at the Empress chinese restaurant at the Raffles Hotel.

"Want to try some braised goose webs with fish maw?" I asked Ethel.

"No thanks."

She and I stick with duck, scallops, fried noodles, and mango pudding. The waitress gives us a basket with two oranges as a New Year's gift and then she presents the bill, also a gift, only 46 Singapore dollars ($35, American). We liked it so much we make a reservation for dim sum tomorrow.

We tried to make our way back to Orchid Road to the shuttle bus, but for some reason (all that wine at dinner?) we got lost. The night seemed excessively dark and there were less streetlights than in New York or Chicago. The traffic is here still, and in the still night air, the pollution of bus and car exhaust smelled worse. We asked directions from strangers. The first man spoke some language we don't know, maybe Danish. The next man spoke English with a German accent. He just arrived and he was lost too. The next man can't understand what we want and points to a guidebook indicating he is a tourist. The whole scene began to take on a fearsome aspect. The tension mounted like the end of one of those Alfred Hitchcock movies. But then I remembered. If the punishment is $500 for carrying a durian on the subway or crossing the street against the light, what would they do to someone who rolled a tourist? Anyway, I'm well protected. I could hit someone with all the books I'm carrying. Or I could apply some of the Chinese strategies I have learned: kill them with their own weapon.

We stumbled on Bras Basah Road, which I remembered from the taxi-ride morning. We retraced our steps, headed north, and landed on Orchid Road where Le Meridien Hotel was standing in the same exact place where we left it. Our *QE2* bus, alongside, was ready to return us to *QE2*. On the way back to our sheltering mother, we slept.

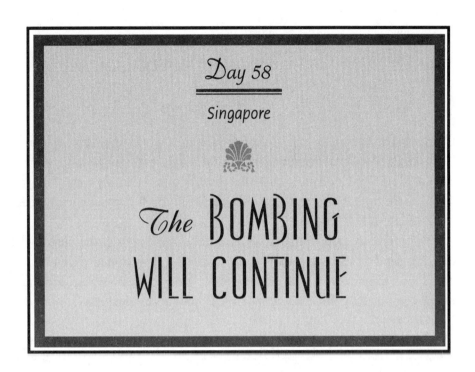

Day 58

Singapore

The BOMBING WILL CONTINUE

*Y*esterday's narrative got out of control. Two thousand nine hundred and nine words covering one day in Singapore! I shall henceforth restrict my typing (it hardly merits the term writing) to two hours per day. "My production is limited," as T. S. Eliot once said. "Writing can wait." I resolve to tone down and loosen up, especially now that our time runs out. One month more of heaven and then we revert to normal human existence, which will include my opening cans of beef barley soup for lunch and my cleaning the dishes after Ethel when I finish dinner. No Colum or Nick will attend us then and no Alex, the restaurant manager, will come around at noon to ask our approval of the evening's menu for dinner. No Simon will bring gin martinis, or uncork famous French wines for us, nor will anyone be seeing at the dinner's end the slightest lift of my finger to bring an Armagnac. A lesson to us all: Our linear time runs on and out. While suns may set and rise again, once goes out our brief light, it is for us a perpetual night.

Ethel and I discussed the possibility of booking a world tour for next year. That might give us a sustaining hope that would extinguish our present gloom. Meanwhile, we must make the most of our remaining time. I must spend more time living and less time reporting on it. I must eat my ice cream while it's on my plate.

Therefore, as an exercise in self-control, I shall restrict the narrative to a thousand words, well, maybe not that little. How about fifteen hundred? And tomorrow, I shall become even more parsimonious, limiting my production to a thousand words or less, the shorter the better, to prove I can do it.

Actually, the other passengers are in bad shape, worse than we are. Ethel and I remain on the world cruise. These others, hundreds of them, depart today. Such a hurrying to and fro above decks and below; such a riotous system of packing and unpacking; such a littering up of the cabins with shirts and skirts and indescribable and unclassable odds and ends; such a making up of bundles and setting apart of umbrellas, of cleaning and loading of revolvers. Only kidding. Guns belonged to an older generation of travelers; Mark Twain's group, not ours.

Rabbi leaves today and so does Mrs. Lonelyhearts. Good-bye, Lonelyhearts. Thanks for the mammaries. Good-bye, Rabbi, you have my forgiveness for, one day on deck, you did apologize by saying, "I hope I didn't inconvenience you too much." Thus, with one brief expression of contrition in the anagogic sense, your holy soul departs from bondage toward eternal glory, from the misery and grief of sin to the state of grace.

Our friends Nathan and Estelle also leave today. We had meant to visit them in the Caronia last night to say good-bye, but we got tied up eating at the Raffles. Luckily Nathan spotted me as I descended the gangway. He pulled my sleeve and shouted with that low-pitched, gravelly voice of his, "Hey, Bernie! Wait up!"

"Nathan, I'll always remember you. You taught me how to shuffleboard."

Nathan pinched my shoulder and whispered in my right ear. "It happened again. Someone I taught yesterday won the tournament. The damnedest thing!"

Ethel and I stood at dockside watching the disembarking forlorn passengers pile into the buses. There but for the grace of God go we.

Are they counting the spoons in Queens Grill now? How does the number of removed spoons compare between the different restaurants? I'll wager more spoons disappear from Mauretania because it has so many more people dining there, but on a proportional basis, I would predict the Queens Grill types take more of everything.

Ethel took charge today. She decided where we go and what we do. The tough choices come up for discussion during dim sum at the Empress. Between the turnip cakes, the rice rolls, the scallops, the chive dumplings, and working up to the mango puddings, we considered visiting the Merlion, a half-fish half-lion statue, that guards the busy Singapore River's mouth, next to the soul of Singapore, the site of the island's oldest trading settlement. Or how about the Empress Place Museum? They might have new exhibits we didn't catch before. Or Clifford Pier, which is always endlessly busy and entertaining. Or Chinatown? Or Little India?

So many choices. So little time. I favored Volcano Park on Sentosa and told Ethel I wanted to see the ten-meter eruption of fire and smoke that they stage every hour.

"Nope," Ethel rejected that suggestion. "We go to the Malay Village."

We took the MRT to Paya Lebar, got off, and walked three blocks along Sims Avenue to a simulation *kampong*, or village, like the ones scattered about the serene, green countryside of Malaysia. Only here I don't see brightly colored wooden houses on stilts surrounded by neat gardens of mangoes, durians, palms, and bananas. Here I see only dull brown wood shops, small restaurants, a bird store, and veiled Moorish beauties. I suppose they are beauties, but with the veils one can't tell. Malay Village, strangely silent, unhealthy and still, lacked something. What? The *Singapore Post* called Malay Village a white elephant and wondered if it had a future. About the future, I can't say. Malay Village certainly had a past; founded in 1985 on twenty-two hectares of land, it was furnished by the

Singapore housing board with a twenty-year lease and considerable public subvention. If it has a present, it doesn't look like much.

What's wrong with the place?

The people stood off. Merchants acted like they didn't want to make a sale. As we entered the kris shop, for instance, they treated us with silence, wouldn't acknowledge our presence, and just stared at us coldly. Even the small brown-skinned children didn't smile.

Then it hit me.

Malaysia is a Muslim state. The people here in Malay Village are Muslims. They think we are the infidel Christians. They think the United States is the great Satan. They hate us. They really do. Remember, history is never over. It continues on and on. Charles Martel (686–741 CE) defeated the Saracen at the battle of Poitiers in 732 and kept the Moors out of Europe, but the jihads continue to the present and probably will continue. This has to be true as the hatred we are feeling is palpable.

Don't believe me?

Read the papers. Witness the latest suicide bombings in Jerusalem and Tel Aviv where teenage Muslim boys blow themselves and others up for the sake of Islam. Remember, Americans were bombed in Lebanon? And what about the World Trade Center? It was bombed too, in 1993. You think that was an accident? Wake up, America! Until you do, no doubt, the bombings will continue. Consider this: to us the Gulf War was about oil, but to them it was about the Islamic religion, which has one billion adherents.

In Malay Village, the Arabian influence is confirmed by the Lagenda Fantasi, a unique multisensory experience that dramatically brings to life legends of folklore, such as Prince Sang Nila Utama, Ali Baba, and Aladdin. This fully automated performance engineered by multi-image projection, surround sound, theatrical tableau, spectacular lighting, and stunning special effects (a holographic genie comes out of the bottle) deserves a look. So does the small museum that offers a walk through on a pebbled path among coconut trees, rice plants, harvesting utensils, and memorabilia like Wayang Kulit, an open air cinema of yesteryear. The village shows authentic Malay households, the glitter and dazzle of a Malay wedding, and comes alive in the living room with lifelike figurines of bride and groom. The cinema tells of the complete marriage customs and ceremony, which looks more like a legal transaction with all the negotiations and document signing. The cinema also has some pretty good footage on Malay games like top spinning, *sepak takraw* (kick volleyball), Congrak, Dam, and kite fighting. The Malay classify the contestant kites into six separate groups, called *wans*: Moon, Peacock, Fish, Cat, Bird, and Western. The kites are highly developed art works with beautiful colors and strange shapes. Some even make sounds as they fly. I liked the Malay kites but the Malay proverbs seemed more like superstition than ancient wisdom. For example: "Do not comb your hair at night or it will ruin your eyesight." Hair and eyes have little to do with each other unless you comb your hair over your eyes or stupidly into your eyes. The other proverbs are so stupid they don't merit mention.

HE CAN'T SPEAK, BUT HE CAN GRUNT HIS MULTIPLE APPROVALS

*K*uala Lumpur, the capital of Malaysia, started as a small tin mining village in the 1820s and grew to an Asian Los Angeles. Just as someone would refer to Los Angeles as LA, they affectionately know Kuala Lumpur as KL. Kuala Lumpur actually means muddy estuary, referring to the place in the center of town where the tin mines are. The blue stannous soil still stands there around the active mines. Two years ago we visited our Hindu friends in KL and, while those friends complained about the Muslims and the Malays mistreating the Hindus, we ate durian with them at their home. I'll bet the neighborhood still smells from that durian. Those KL friends are supposed to visit us.

Clutching my four passes issued by the purser, I headed down the gangway, but didn't see our friends, the Js. Fighting off the taxi drivers, the touts, and the beggars, I walked the dock back and forth three times.

Still no Js. Something must have gone wrong. I went back onboard and told Ethel.

We decided to go to the Batu Caves about eleven kilometers north of KL. The caves, a sacred Hindu shrine, are the site of the famous parade of tens of thousands of self-mutilating pilgrims on Thaipusm, the Hindu day of atonement. They do the main ceremonies in Cathedral Cave while Hindu religion and mythology are illustrated and explained in Museum Cave.

Cancel the caves. The Js are there when we descended the gangway. KL, like LA, has traffic. They got stuck.

Two Filipinos have to carry Mr. J, the former agriculture secretary of Malaysia, like a sack of potatoes, aboard *QE2* because he is wheelchair bound and his wheelchair won't roll up the gangway. Next problem: we have only four passes (the maximum allowed) issued by the ship, but there are five Js.

Using the passes, I took four Js up and then returned again with one of the passes that belonged to Mrs. J, who was already onboard. "Here's your pass," I said with a loud voice to Uncle J, who was standing right in front of the security guard. I slapped the white pass in Uncle J's hand while motioning to the gangway. The guard, without checking the pass, waved us aboard.

It was fun seeing *QE2* through the eyes of our Malay friends. Their wide-eyed amazement at the luxury and the culture and the size and the appointments was obvious. They want to cruise and, unlike Craig and Michelle, they want to cruise with us.

Together we learned how to get around the ship with a wheelchair. It is possible. Every deck had at least one ramp. We even got out to Boat deck using the ramp by the Samuel Cunard Key Club, portside. We pushed Mr. J while we walked on Boat deck under that blistering hot Malay sun. As usual, the people who we passed were sound asleep in their deck chairs; some were snoring loudly. Mrs. J pointed out one woman who was awake.

"Part of the crew, the social director," I told Mrs. J. "As a rule, if they are awake, they are not passengers." I showed them the Sports deck and recalled my triumph short days ago when I defeated over three dozen antagonists to become the shuffleboard champion of *QE2*. The Js wanted to see everything, even the spa, and they did. They even stopped and watched the rehearsal for the Broadway reviews that night, *My Fair Lady* and *West Side Story*. Ethel and I waited patiently while they took in their fill of the shows. Suddenly I realized deep-water passenger carriers were more than ships, more than incredibly wrought hulls. They incorporate distinctive cultural resonances as well. By specific intent, the quality of life onboard conformed to the national character of the owners and the passengers, a maritime simulacrum of its country of origin, destination, or major business associates.

And after we dined in Queens Grill. For that, Alex needed only five minutes notice. Alex put out the wheelchair ramp and Mr. J made it easily into the dining room. Mr. J sat opposite me. He can't speak but he can grunt and he expressed himself with multiple happy grunts. More than the grunts, his eyes told of his pleasure: he widened those eyes, smiled with them, and especially during dessert, rolled them approvingly as he choked on his gâteau St. Honoré. Mr. J cried when he left *QE2*. I don't blame him. Ethel and I will cry too, when we leave.

Showing that crowd around was hard work, so I went to the One deck hot tub to relax. As I wallowed in the warm, frothy water, watching it slop around me and thinking about absolutely nothing, an Australian woman wearing a long white gown came over. Her thin white hand dipped a finger into the water, and cautioned me, "This hot tub is way too hot."

"I like it hot!" I assured her.

She refused to come in and went off to find the deck steward. The tub started to cool and soon the tub was too cold for me to stay in. Ms. Australia didn't come in. She probably went off somewhere to spoil some other passenger's good time.

Bob Lacovara, one of our neighbors, sent a fax from home. *Frontline* did a number on me. They showed me entering the limo while the voice-over announced that I am being investigated by the FBI for Medicare fraud.

Jesus! You would think the FBI would tell me something like that before they told the TV people. That sounded serious. No, that sounded crazy. Was this a hint of future craziness? Should I call the FBI? Should I call a lawyer? Nope! I decided to take the Scarlett O'Hara approach: I'll think of it all tomorrow. I can stand it then. Tomorrow, I'll think of some way. After all, tomorrow is another day.

At dinner Ethel and I sampled the Malaysian soup, which they should bottle and sell as a patented medicine because it opens and effectively drains sinuses. Side effects: burning lips and tongue, and Colum adds, possible runs. I ordered roast beef, explaining to Colum that I am a vegetarian trapped in the body of a carnivore. He approved.

As we pulled out of the harbor I briefed a British couple on the safari they are about to experience in Kenya. The British couple had lots of questions, but Ethel and I excused ourselves. We had to do our job; we had to oversee the departure.

Ethel and I became intensely occupied in the aft of the vessel, controlling the letting go of moorings from the bollards, making fast to the tugs, and then, as the enormous power of *QE2*'s two engines began to throb through to the shafts, safely breaking away from tugs toward the unfettered freedom of the seas.

I explained to Ethel what I learned from Captain Arnott's book about a feature of *QE2* that had caused some controversy: her bulbous bow beneath the waterline. The idea behind this was to create as little turbulence as possible from the *Queen's* bow wave, just as a bulb-headed whale cleaves through the water with hardly a ripple. The purists complained that a foaming white bow wave should be as much a part of the liner as the name of Cunard painted on her superstructure. The speed trials proved the traditionalists wrong. The underwater bulb guided water smoothly away from the ship, cutting down water resistance and increasing fuel economy, yet, one must admit, even today we don't ever get the same impression of speed that a V-wedged prow, cutting sharply into the waves, would produce. Ship designers are now taking the whale analogy a lot further. Our blubbery brethren have corrugated hides, and the latest thinking is that ships should be equipped in similar fashion, with ridges below the waterline. Air bubbles would be released along the forward surfaces, helping the ship to glide along, like a whale, on ripples of air.

At Sea, Strait of Malucca and Bay of Bengal

LOOKING OUT *the* WINDOW REMAINS *the* FIRMEST PILLAR *of* GOOD NAVIGATION

The cruise news and the big talk among the British passengers concerns the divorce.

It's over. Diana and Charles are history. But between them a battle royale looms over her future. Who will get the royal jewels? Will Diana retain her title: Her Royal Highness? It looks like she will continue to be the princess hereafter and will retain her office, staff, and live in a palace, with a big cash payment and a yearly allowance. Tune in next week for more details.

Ethel doesn't know what to do with herself, so I diagnosed her ailment as cruise fatigue. She doesn't want to go this morning to the Lido as she usually does to practice her Spanish. The tapes are getting too hard. The lecture on the bridge by Master Bridge (yes, that's his name—Bridge runs the bridge), the navigator, also interests her not.

I will go to that lecture so I can find out what in the world those guys do with all that time on the deck during their four-hour watches. The answer I learned, I should have suspected: look out the window. "Looking out the window remains the firmest pillar of good navigation," said Bridge.

In this respect, navigating is like practicing medicine. Everyone likes to see all those big machines, but really what counts is the skill of the doctor: his eyes, his ears, his finger tips, and his judgment, not the machines.

We learned about Indian currency restrictions: They can't change rupees onboard at Travelex, and once you have those Indian rupees, you have them forever. You can't change them back to dollars unless you have a currency receipt, fill out forms, and so forth. The old theory of mercantilist wealth still finds a home here in India.

Ethel and Colum had a long discussion about the relative benefits and demerits of last night's snapper, prepared in the Malay tradition. I complained to him that there wouldn't be any living with her when I get home. And I'll bet there won't be any living with me, either.

Sock report: All the socks we purchased in Thailand are OK, except for one that has a slight hole in the right foot's big toe. This means I will have the lot cleaned and will wear them again. Each sock cost only 67 cents. I proudly reminded Ethel of our bet. Ethel said the socks wouldn't last, but they have. Ethel said she is surprised and impressed at my obvious shopping skill. If she hadn't added that last part I might have believed the whole thing. Secretly she wants the socks to fall apart. But I won't let them.

We continued to debate the pros and cons of my sock purchase as we strolled on Boat deck. The sea breeze refreshed us as the second officer of the watch told us that the sea temperature is 87 degrees and the air temperature 84 degrees. We cruised under a shell blue East Indian sky and across an ocean tempered only by light westerly breezes. The sea moisture and the fragrant loveliness of this day stirred us strangely. Yes, there is nothing like it, cruising tropical climes. That's what I love. Pure unadulterated bliss.

As if America and the FBI didn't exist.

Day 61

At Sea, Indian Ocean off the Coast of Sri Lanka

AS TIME GOES BY

*W*ow! I slept like a dead man. Something about the ship or the salt air or the food or the drinks or all that sex knocks me out. Ethel sleeps the same way. We considered the possibility that Nick and Colum add tranquilizing drugs to our food. Nope, Nick and Colum wouldn't do that to us. But I'll bet Nick and Colum would love to do that to the couple two tables down who, according to Nick, have consumed seventeen bottles of gin since we left Hong Kong.

The fault, I believe, laid with her, for she had complained about almost everything: the service, the food, even the lighting in her cabin, which she said was unflattering to her when she applied makeup. Now she focused on her male companion: He didn't love her. He left money to his son and not his entire estate to her. He reeked of too much cologne. He drank too much.

I can tell by the way he chain-smokes his cigarettes and by his accelerated gin intake that his patience is wearing thin. Something bad will happen.

Some sleep laboratories report that, when not clued by the occurrence of light and dark, or day and night, most humans naturally fall into sleep-wakefulness cycles that are twenty-five hours long. If *QE2* were going east, we would lose an hour each day, and there would be lots of zombies walking the decks. But since *QE2* goes west, we actually get an extra hour each day and enjoy a more natural sleep-waking cycle with the twenty-five hour days.

Ethel and I walked out on deck in the morning sunlight, glad to be at sea and happy to be alive. I spotted the sun directly in line with the stern of the ship, so I know we are headed due west. "You're becoming a genuine officer of the watch," Ethel said.

"That I am," I replied in my stiff British accent. "I am the officer of a ship that is the last of a bygone era, a thriving survivor."

News from Israel: More bombs. An exploded bus in Jerusalem. The jihad continues.

You wouldn't imagine that there was any violence in the world looking out our cabin's picture window. All we see there are lots of ships, most of them carrying cargo and most of them headed east, the other direction. That traffic comes through the Suez Canal, via the Red Sea. Ethel and I watched as *QE2* overtook the *Island Princess* (the former *Island Venture*) and left her in our dust—I mean wake, the two V-shaped diverging cataracts of foam at our stern that turn the green water of the Indian Ocean bright blue. There is something extraordinarily beautiful about the wake of a big ship, something about it that looks just right as it extends beyond the horizon to infinity.

The real officer of the watch informed us that today we entered the Indian Ocean, the third-largest ocean in the world. The Indian Ocean averages four thousand meters deep and contains an enormous number of worms in its sandy and muddy bottom. There is a volcanic chain in the plateau at the center of the Indian Ocean, which caused the Seychelles to arise.

I'm in a lazy mood, so I just sat on deck and enjoyed the view and reread *The Innocents Abroad*. It's a good book. But too bad Mark Twain told us practically nothing about the living conditions on the ship. He was too busy criticizing other travel writers and chastising his fellow passengers to have bothered recording what he saw, felt, ate, smelled, and tasted onboard the *Quaker City*. *Innocents Abroad* became a best seller, despite scathing criticisms. Here's one typical example, written by author George

Meredith: "Mark Twain's reminiscence was a piece of crude, heavy intellectual horseplay—an imprudent affront offered to [the] Puritan aristocracy by a roughhanded plebeian jester from Missouri."

The program said that there will be a tea dance today in the Queens Lounge. Ethel persuaded me to attend. Jon, our waiter in Princess Grill, had made the same suggestion, so I agreed. Jon was there and said hello. Jon told us that this tea dance is Viennese, which means he and the other waiters serve only tea. Those passengers who wish something else must go up to the buffet and get it themselves.

Ethel and I headed to the table, nicely arranged under an ice sculpture shaped like a harp, measuring three feet high and melting fast. I admired the berries drenched in red wine, the apple pies, the cakes filled with creams, the fruits, the eclairs, the canapés, the small sandwiches, the cheeses, the hot samosas (the size of a fist), the gâteaux, and the cream puffs next to the hot spring rolls and stir-fry chicken. More food! How can these people eat so much?

We dug in.

The character of the passengers has changed. Even Herman seems healthier and more awake and happy. The gray heads dance with gusto, and it thrills my heart to see so many men and women move together in rhythm to the old big-band favorites: "Charmaine," "When I Fall in Love," "Tea for Two" (as a cha-cha), "Hello Young Lovers," "It's Nice Work If You Can Get It," and "Jealousy." The gentlemen hosts seemed invigorated by something. More puff? A second wind? Admonitions from Captain John Burton-Hall? All, some, or any combination of those things? They are out en force, wearing their small yellow nametags over their hearts. Half are new. The gentlemen hosts dressed informally in slacks and sports shirts with open collars and, except for the tags, you wouldn't be able to distinguish them from the regular passengers. On the other hand, gentlemen hosts are half-breeds, half passenger and half crew. They paid for their trip; not as much as we did, but they did pay.

The British couple next to our table interrupted their tea for almost every dance. They cut many a rug. But when they came back to rest, I saw that the man, who looked about sixty-seven, was severely short of breath. Noting that I have observed his dyspnea, he reassured me not to worry. "I want to die dancing," he said. "It'll be great for me to just click off. But, I worry about leaving her." He nodded to the plump wife at his side who promptly replied, "Don't worry about me. I'll have a new partner within four hours." She then turned to look at the dance floor and pointed out a man and woman having "a go at it," who each looked at least ninety years old. The old codger was standing up and moving out of beat with the music, dancing to the sound of a different drummer. His equally aged wife moved in sync with him. The pair, oblivious to the surroundings, gaze into each others' eyes as they mark their own time. They are in love, grandly and pathetically in love.

But for how long?

When one of this pair dies, their peaceful existence, like that of Adam and Eve in paradise, will come to an abrupt end. I felt a pain in the back of my brain. Tears welled up. The scene touched me so. I'm only drinking Ceylon tea. But I have nevertheless gotten maudlin.

The ship began to tilt and pitch. The dancers know their task has become more difficult, like the trouble inflicted on them by time itself, but, undaunted, they spread their legs some more. They widened their base. They kept on dancing.

Out on deck this afternoon, the scenery has improved a lot. One of the dancers in *West Side Story*, her breasts perfect like doorbells, wearing a thong, paraded her solid animal health. God! She is beautiful, mainly because she has a beautiful behind, from all that dancing, perhaps. She knows it, too, and she isn't afraid to show it by wiggling it about as she crosses and recrosses the deck. While men looked on with admiration, the other women eyed this young nymphette with a combination of hatred and envy.

Back in the room, Ethel and I realized we have new neighbors. They don't argue like Mom and Pop. In fact, they, as far as we can tell, don't talk to each other. But like Mom and Pop, they must be hard of hearing. Our new neighbors play their TV very loud. They like the old classic movies and watch them morning, noon, and night.

Ethel and I recognized, coming loud and clear through the bulkhead, a movie we have seen six times, *Casablanca*. We smiled at each other as we heard the immortal voice of Ingrid Bergman say, "Play it again, Sam. You know. 'As Time Goes By.'"

DOES *the* MOON GIVE YOU IDEAS, BIG BOY?

*U*gh! Today Ethel and I made a sudden discovery: we have less than thirty days to go. We can't protest because it would do no good. Cunard has other plans for *QE2* than to go around the world again this year. Ethel and I have to make the best of the precious time that remains. Therefore, we decided to relax more and do less. In this spirit of rebellion, I decided that I have been getting tied up too much with a schedule. I decided not to go to the word-processing lesson in the computer center. I decided not to go to Waldemar's lecture on India, not to go to Charles White's presentation on "Fishing with the Stars—Bob Hope, Barbra Streisand, Kevin Costner, and others." White is listed on the program as an author, filmmaker, fish behavior researcher, and TV personality. Why would someone list himself or herself as a TV personality? Doesn't White know the Fifth Amendment protects from self-incrimination?

I am afraid I shall have to also miss the profile of the captain of *QE2*. Thus, I shall define myself today in terms of what I shall not do. Negative definition remains OK, and in fact was and is a bulwark of American politics: Elizabeth Dole says she is not a Hillary Rodham Clinton. Senator Benson told us on TV that Vice President Quayle was not President Kennedy: "I knew Jack Kennedy. You are no Jack Kennedy." Thus those people are being defined by what they are not.

Alex, the assistant restaurant manager in Queens Grill (who is not Arnold Schwarzenegger, though he often says, "I'll be back"), gave us the menu for this evening's dinner. I know Alex will return, but I worry if I order Indian food, will I miss the roast beef.

"Have both," said Alex.

Ethel eyed me suspiciously. She doesn't want me to order two main courses. She has no doubt I could easily eat them, but she doesn't want me to look conspicuous.

"Nick knows what I want," I told Alex, handing him the menu. "I appoint Nick my *factotum*. Let him order for me."

In the afternoon, I wrote to my friends Herb and Helen. I stamped the outside envelope with the impressive-looking red-inked stamps that say, "Posted on *QE2*" and signed with my chop from Hong Kong, "Dai Fu Hau." With my letter I put a clipping from the cruise news, which told of a Japanese man who bought a quart bottle of seventy-year-old scotch for £10,000 or about $15,000. No whiskey could be worth that much. No wonder Japan is in trouble.

Thinking about money, I decided I have had too much of it.

So I got my loot from the safe deposit box and brought it back to the room. It's all tied up in wads of bills the size of bricks. I counted out $8,000 in twenties.

You know, there is something very relaxing about counting money, especially when that money belongs to you. Counting money could become a new form of meditation. And just think, with the cash I have here I could probably live in Ambon for a century. Maybe I could buy the island.

Ethel interrupted the counting to show me the new sweater she has just completed for Michelle the Beautiful. I started over. The second time around, counting the $8,000 is just as relaxing. I dropped the better part of my stash back into the safe deposit box and took the $8,000 to the

Travelex, intending to get money orders to send home. The woman there advised an electronic transfer. So at the speed of light my $8,000 sped from the Indian Ocean halfway across the globe to my bank account at the Bay Area Bank & Trust in Webster, Texas. That money traveled that distance (about fifteen thousand miles) for $20, less than 2 cents a mile. What hath God wrought?

I explained to the Travelex woman how much I had enjoyed counting out the money. "Do you get the same thrill from all the counting?" The young red-headed lady looked at me as if I had grown two heads and said, "Not at all! It's just bloody work."

After dinner (which, by the way, consisted of two entrées and double bananas Fosters) Ethel and I, besotted with the ship and out on Signal deck, saw over the vast expanse of water, the moon shining blood red and oblate through the lower atmosphere. Within minutes the moon turned round and orange as it ascended into the dark blue star-studded night sky.

"Romantic isn't it," said Ethel. "Does the moon give you ideas, Big Boy?"

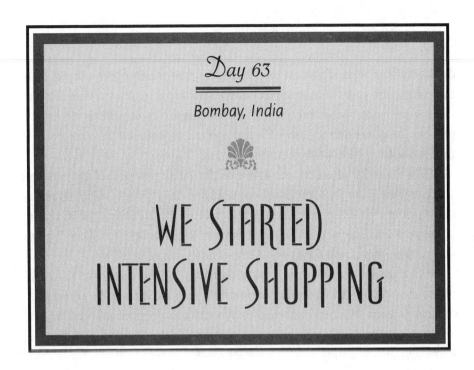

Day 63

Bombay, India

WE STARTED INTENSIVE SHOPPING

*O*K. You want something foreign, foreign-looking things, and foreign-looking people. Something thoroughly and uncompromisingly foreign—foreign from top to bottom, foreign from center to circumference, foreign inside and outside and all around, nothing anywhere about to dilute its foreignness, nothing to remind us of any other people or any other land under the sun. And lo! India arrives.

As previewed, Bombay signals our arrival with a change in the utility water in the toilet. It's filthy and it stinks. The tide isn't high. *QE2* must remain at anchor offshore. We must tender in. But wait a second. It's just not that easy. India is a land snagged in red tape. To get ashore we need special yellow numbered passes, each individually signed and stamped by some official. Our visas from the Indian consulate in New York are not good enough. They told us to have those passes handy for inspection when the police or the army or anyone official asks for them: Don't lose those precious pieces of paper, for without them you can't get back on the dock. Furthermore, if you do lose them, the passes can't be replaced. Furthermore, you must turn them in before the ship can depart. And if there are not the same exact number of passes turned in as were issued, *QE2* will not be permitted to leave Bombay. If, if, if, equaled all of us will be marooned here forever without the passes.

This is India, all right, the India of the "make-work." Make work is work you make so you can have something to do. It is not work that needs to be done and it certainly isn't productive work. In India, the kingdom of make work, the wonder is that anything substantial gets done. Things do get done here, and Ethel and I know how.

Dock passes are one thing; the other is the currency control. You can't take rupees in or out of India. To convert them back to dollars you must have a receipt showing that you converted the original amount legally and not on the black market. In some countries they have a free-floating currency, in some they have a parallel market where you can buy or sell at any price you want, and in other countries, like India, the currency is strictly controlled.

The lines are too long and the stamping and signing and handing and canning take too long. I can't waste my life standing in line. I don't have time to get rupees. Ethel and I entered India without rupees. My impecunious state didn't bother me. I learned long ago that there are many distinct advantages in not having rupees.

Colum told us true. From the tender, as we travel across the bay, we looked at dark brown, opaque water. I have never seen or imagined that a large body of water could become so polluted. It has floating flotsam consisting of pieces of wood, greenish turds in groups, washlines with fecal material, and a door with the doorknob still attached. By the way, a washline is a line of material at sea where the forces of wind and tidal flow are in balance such that the material in question accumulates in a distinctly visible line.

On dock an eighteen-piece band, the men dressed in colonial white with silver trim, received us with English tunes brassily played with an Indian accent. Some lovely lady in a yellow sari trimmed with real gold handed me a red rose and placed a tilak on my forehead, the red beauty mark representing the eye of Shiva. Immediately, the real India embraced us with the crowds and confusion and chaos. We are directed to three different buses. We got on one bus, sat for a while in the uncomfortable heat, and then were told to get off. We must walk on the dock to another bus. Men and women, rusty ones, and boys and girls—all ragged and barefoot, uncombed and unclean, and by instinct, education, and profession, beggars—trooped after us, surrounded us on all sides, and glared at us.

An Indian army officer got on the new bus. He announced that he wanted to inspect all the yellow landing cards. For me this may have proved difficult, because I lost mine already. Before I could panic, the Cunard tour guide handed the soldier a small white Cunard envelope (the same that we passengers use for tips). The major changed his mind; he canceled the inspection.

First stop: the Gateway to India at Apollo Pier. The gateway, a big honey-colored basalt arch in a mixed Muslim-Hindu style commemorates the 1911 visit of King George V and Queen Mary. Bombay is the gateway to India because most of the shipping comes in or goes out from here, so the arch has significance. Engraved overhead are the roman numerals MCMXI.

We got off the bus. Right away the peddlers trying to sell green and blue iridescent peacock feathers assaulted us. The peacock is the national bird of India. It is illegal to sell or export peacock feathers. Even though the people selling them look like they need a break, several square meals, and emergency medical care, we buy no peacock feathers, for we have no rupees.

Two snake charmers raised cobras from woven baskets. Monkeys on leashes surrounded us and little ragamuffin children asked for *baksheesh*. Baksheesh, you recall, doesn't exactly mean tip. It means something for nothing, please. We gave them nothing, for we have no rupees.

Mothers, with malnourished naked children in their arms, bunch the fingers of their free hands together and put them to their mouths, indicating they need to eat. Flies cover both eyes of the children, but neither the children nor the mothers mind. Our hearts go out to them, but if we start distributing money they would mob us. Besides, we have no rupees.

Four hawkers tried to unload a pack of ten postcards for a dollar. I have dollars and bought one pack. The pictures show various sites, including Mahalaxmi Temple for the goddess of luck; the Haji Ali mosque that sits in the harbor and can be reached via a walkway during low tide since high tide floods the access route; Victoria Terminus, the train station; and the Gateway to India arch. Victoria Terminus looks out of focus, as does the picture of Marine Drive. What the hell, each card cost only ten cents.

A man with legs no thicker than broom handles walked on his hands toward us. He beats them all as far as eliciting pity, but again no sale, for we have no rupees.

Another stick man who looks about thirty years old lies across the gutter, his shoeless feet on the sidewalk, his head in the street. Black mud has caked on his bare feet and on his back. The mud marks his face with a diagonal stripe. His eyes are open, but their sense is shut. Their sense is shut just like the sleepwalking Lady Macbeth. But unlike Lady Macbeth, this fellow isn't seeing because he is sleeping. And he is not sleepwalking. He is not moving at all. In fact, he didn't move when a taxi veered inches from his head. This man doesn't need rupees, nor does he want a handout. His problems are over. He's dead.

Next stop, the washing ghats. Most of the *QE2*ers missed a great scene because they couldn't be bothered to get off the air-conditioned bus. At the washing ghats, near Mahalaxmi Station, we watched the extraordinary activity in one of Bombay's main outdoor recreational centers: concrete tubs *en plein aire* where clothes are soaked, scrubbed, and pounded. Hundreds of people, maybe thousands, are washing clothes in filthy black water made the color of light chocolate by the white soap they use. You know what? These people are not working. They're playing, having fun. It's obvious they love pounding and throwing the soaped clothes around and spraying themselves and others. Three small boys wash themselves in one of the concrete basins along with a pile of clothes. The boys squeal with delight as the cold dirty water hits their dark brown bodies and suds them up. Despite the poverty and the squalor, smiles and happy faces are everywhere, except on the face of the supervisor who stands on a platform. He casts a cold eye on me because I am taking notes. I waved. He nodded and smiled and pointed to the three boys. We both laughed.

We passed through an area where the cleaned clothes have been hung out to dry. The clothes look torn and ragged; some display gaping holes in them. They appear hardly worth cleaning or wearing, but they are there. Someone needs them. Someone will wear them.

Next stop, the choolies. These people gave us the word *coolies*. They have been here for three thousand years, fishing in boats that look like they are just as old. Strangely, despite the obvious poor condition of the boats, each boat flies a remarkably beautiful pennant that usually takes the shape of a triangular banner colored brilliant crimson. I asked the guide about this incongruent display of wealth amid such dire poverty. "The flags are the tributes to the goddess," he explained. But which goddess he doesn't know exactly. It could be Kali, but more likely it's Mahalaxmi, the Hindu goddess of wealth and luck.

We passed a Parsi temple. I had some pretty intelligent patients from Bombay who practiced that religion. They worship fire and have two fire temples here in town. No Parsi will pollute the earth, air, or water, so they dispose of their dead in the Towers of Silence. The attendants place the dead body on a grill in the tower and place the chained captive vultures in the same place. In two hours the vultures have picked the body clean and the bones fall through the grate into the center of the tower, where quicklime goes to work on them.

Dwindle, dwindle, dwindle, the Parsi dwindles down. There are fewer than fifteen thousand Parsis remaining from the once bigger community who came here from Persia (Parsi means Persian) in the seventh century. They sought and received political asylum, provided they didn't convert the Hindus. They intermarry now and suffer lots of genetic defects. They can't marry outside the Parsi religion because they are disowned if they do. Most Parsis follow Western customs. They eat from tables and live in individual homes. It would be hard for a Parsi to adjust to the customs of the Hindu and even harder for them to adjust to the customs of the Muslims. No conversions are permitted to this religion, hence two hundred years from now there probably will remain no followers of Zarathustra, the founder (some say reformer) of this ancient Zoroastrian religion.

The bus moved on through dust and dirt and decay, but from the window I saw that most people looked happy and reasonably healthy.

Perhaps they achieve happiness because they accept their fate. They believe the gods, Shiva and Vishnu mainly, have placed them in their present position. If they behave, they will get something better next time around, during their next incarnation. Thus, Indians are on cyclic time, not linear time, as we experience time in the West. What they don't get this time around they might get in their next incarnation. So why fuss? It's all maya (illusion) anyway.

We passed by the slums made of red brick hovels with not a single building bigger than an M5 room and each holding eighteen instead of two people. Not a single building has a straight wall perpendicular to the ground. The kids hold out their hands for money. But what's this? One stone house looks like it's in pretty good shape and four times larger than the others and it has straight vertical walls. It turns out that's where Rudyard Kipling was born, December 30, 1865.

The streets swarm with people and cars and buses. I have a feeling the present situation with the dwindling resources of Earth can't sustain these people. Their future is bleak. I see a wall sign that confirms this idea: "The World Cup cricket match," the sign says, "India's only bright star in the future." Several other signs must have been written by the same cynical author: "Justice is superiour to violence because with justice there would be no violence." Another sign asks, "When will India have heroes again?" Other roadside signs truly puzzled me: "Sometimes all I spend here is my time." Other signs are clear-cut: "Women drive to success on Goodyear." Another: "Women drive to glory on Goodyear." Success? Glory? Which is it? Anyway, why just women? How about men? How about me?

Yes, the Indian people have problems that make our problems, all of them, shrink to insignificance. How can anyone look at this poverty and complain about the air-conditioning on the bus or that the dust bothers their eyes or that there isn't much to see in Bombay? How can our fellow QE2ers get bored so fast and exclaim, "Let's go back to the ship for a drink in the Crystal Bar!"

Bombay has thirteen million people. From the looks of things, two million of those thirteen million don't have homes. They say eight million come into the city each day, five million by train and the rest by car. With the traffic I see, I believe it.

Everywhere multiple signs advertise Indian movies. They are made here in what the guide calls the Bollywood of India. All Indian films have the same plot and yes they have their yearly awards for best picture and best actress and so forth, just as we do. A trip to the air-conditioned movie and the right to sit and watch for three hours costs 7 rupees. Not bad when you consider there are 34 rupees to a dollar. I wonder how long one has to work or beg to get 7 rupees.

Everywhere we go the natives want to take Ethel's picture. Why? We don't know. But they do. Does she look like their idea of what a Western woman should look like? They photograph her alone and also with them. Sometimes they ask me to pose too, but most times the attraction remains Ethel.

We passed the dingy residences on Malabar Hill. The guide described these hovels as elegant homes. They don't look that way to us. Malabar Hill homes are just part of a slum, a slum for the higher classes. We visited the famous Hanging Gardens where I went to the men's room. It stank with the terrible stench of stale urine and dead rats. The gray-white marble floor, wet with backed-up urine, made my feet slip. The other men thought they were back on the ship in wet weather on a slippery deck. One old codger walking ahead of me slipped. I caught him before he hit the deck.

Because the Hanging Gardens aren't much, we walked through them fast, admiring a few ragged topiary pieces that had seen better days. Kamala Nehru Park, opposite the gardens, offered good panoramas of Marine Drive (also called the Queen's Neck because of the way the lights look at night). For a better view the guidebook advised us to climb the three-story old yellow shoe (like the old woman's home in the nursery rhyme). The police there haven't read the guidebook. They won't let anyone over twelve in the shoe. The police are carrying yellow sticks the size of broom handles, so I agreed with them.

Perhaps my luck ran out because I didn't leave an offering to Maha-laxmi at the Jain temple. Jains are those curious people on the streets wearing face masks because they don't want to inhale and inadvertently kill an insect. Every form of life is sacred to these followers of an austere sixth-century Guru Mahavira.

The tour bus refused to start. Our hearts dropped. We're trapped. The

*QE2*ers started to scream. Not to worry. The drivers have been through this before. They got everyone out of the bus, opened the engine compartment, disconnected the air-conditioning, and tried again. Bingo! The engine started. In India there is always a way. You might not know how to handle India, but they do.

Along the road we passed the entrance gate to the Tower of Silence. Up in the air, hundreds of kites or vultures or both circle and circle, probably in search of a meal. The guide explains what my patients had already told me. No relatives may enter the inner sanctum of the towers. The attendants place the body on a grate and let the large captive vultures on chains peck away. Two hours later the body is finished and falls into the pit where the quicklime does the rest. Not for me. I'd rather get buried, preferably in my corn patch. That way my minerals can be transmuted into corn, which the birds can eat. It takes longer, but aesthetically it works better. And the birds still get their due.

The next stop, the Gandhi house (actually the house of a Bombay businessman who let Mahatma Gandhi use it).

There I learned why right smack in the middle of the Indian flag (in the middle white stripe) there is a spinning wheel. The great soul (*Mahatma* means great heart or soul) spun cloth on the third floor of this modest home. On the floor, next to the spinning wheel, lies Gandhi's mat where he rested and sometimes fasted to exhaustion. Next to the mat stands a light green bottle filled with a clear liquid. Gin? Nope. White rum? Nope. Kirschwasser? Nope! It's a bottle of water from the holy Ganges, something Mahatma always kept at his side.

I know Bill Clinton doesn't have a spinning wheel in his bedroom, and if he has a bottle there, it isn't filled with water from the Ganges. The diorama showed the major events in this great man's life. Read about it yourself, if you are interested. You'll always profit by studying Gandhi's philosophy and methods. The thing that impressed me the most was the bonfire of foreign clothes in 1921 and his subsequent admission in open court in 1924 when he pleaded guilty to the charge of treason. Gandhi's explanation brings tears to my eyes: he considered it morally wrong not to be treasonous to an oppressive government. We have many such heroes and heroines in history. The freedom of the world depends on them. It is impossible to praise this kind of courage too much.

The tour ended at Prince of Wales Museum, where we could spend all day just admiring those wonderful Mogul miniatures while, outside the museum, young women well dressed in blue and yellow saris sifted through the trash, separating things. They are so intent on their work, they don't even look up when we pass.

On the way back to the ship I saw lots of signs saying "Welcome to Mumbai" and "I love Mumbai." At the main post office, the place where "Bombay" used to appear has been painted over with the word "Mumbai." Ditto for the main tourist office in the center of town.

The earliest inhabitants of this city occupying the seven interconnecting basaltic lava islands called the place Mumbai after their mother goddess Mumbadevi. The British changed the name to Bombay. But there's a movement afoot to change back to the old name. And why not? Mumbai sounds more Indian and has better historic roots. The old gods never die. They keep coming back, over and over again, like transmigrating souls.

Something is wrong with the tides. *QE2* has to remain at anchor. We can't get to the ship and the ship can't get to us. Passengers must eat lunch in Mumbai. Ethel and I took the shuttle back into town and ate curries at the Taj Mahal Hotel. Masala, a mixture of ground dried spices, forms the basis of authentic Indian curry. The components vary according to the recipe, the main dish, the cook, and the other ingredients. A lamb curry differs from a chicken curry, which differs from curry used with vegetables or prawns (shrimp). Thus, Indian cooking becomes a highly refined art, far, far removed from most Western attempts at imitation.

My lunch proved the point. I experienced the delicate refined and long-lasting subtle flavors and aromas attached to fine curried lamb (mutton Korma), chicken Kavekswe, shrimps, and vegetables. Only the fish curry seemed out of place, not genuine for some reason. All this I washed down with one of the world's most refreshing drinks, a mango milk shake. The all-you-can-eat "curry wagon" costs 250 rupees or seven dollars, American. The mango milk shake cost 60 rupees, or less than $2. We don't have rupees, but they took my American Distress card.

After lunch we hunted for a bookstore and a newspaper. We found both in the Taj Mahal Hotel, just off the main lobby. The books are arranged with the same system I use at home: no order whatsoever, just piled on the shelves. I see *City of Joy* by Dominique Lapierre, that classic epic of love and hope in the slums of Calcutta. The same story could play out here in Bombay, or any other place on this subcontinent. In the store I wandered into the music section. For the first time I appreciated Indian music. I actually heard the drone separate from the raga and I followed the tala. And what luck! We found the *International Herald Tribune*. Amgen closed at 65⅝, up 11⅝ from when we left. My shares have increased in value $607,100.

Tomorrow I shall celebrate my good fortune by giving away lots of rupees. Ethel thought this a good idea, but cautioned, "Don't start until you are close to the bus and ready to leap aboard. Otherwise you'll get mobbed."

We started intensive shopping. I bought a bronze Shiva dancing the Creation of the Universe in an aureola of fire. In a small shop on Lansdown Road, Mangal Arts and Crafts, I got a herd of solid silver elephants for $200 and spent another $200 on silver enamel boxes of excellent quality, workmanship, color, and design. They'll make good Christmas gifts. In the shop we met David Thompson, the assistant manager of Caronia. His friend showed us a wind-up player Victrola that he got for $58, American. I admired (but didn't buy) an excellent, large, highly transparent, yellow spinel for $1,500, on display in one of the shops in the Taj. That was a mistake. That spinel was the bargain of the century. I regret I missed it.

Ethel has tired, so we battled through the beggars, fought off the vendors, walked past the mothers with the naked children in their arms, and made it safely back to the ship.

Unfortunately the hot tub has cooled to below air temperature. That's the latest per the request of the Australian woman—a cold hot tub. It fits right in line with the decaffeinated coffee, the low-nicotine cigarette, the de-alcoholated champagne, sex while wearing a condom, and the like. Reduce the experience. Substitute something milder, less vivid, and fake. That's the modern trend. Anything that advertises what it is not fits into this concept: nonfat milk, tealess (herbal) teas, cholesterol-free omelettes made from Egg Beaters or egg whites, fat-free muffins, low-sodium toast, sugar-free assorted preserves, cholesterol-free margarine, and fruits with low-fat toppings.

Thank God there is nothing modern, dilute, or trendy about India. For all its faults, India is a real experience, the most important real travel experience you can have. You'll love it. You'll hate it too.

A HUNDRED RUPEES MIGHT NOT SEEM LIKE MUCH *to* YOU, BUT *to* THEM THAT'S *an* ENORMOUS FORTUNE

I awoke early thinking about India. India has sacred cows. But the West has its sacred cows too. Only you can't see them. They have to do with scientific materialism, the worship of the machine and material goods as the ultimate providers of human happiness. The social reality for us is that science hasn't solved some of the problems. Yesterday, Ethel and I bet not a single *QE2*er had as much fun as one of those joyous boys bathing at the washing ghat.

Out the portholes, the sun rising in the east looks blood red, just as the moon did last night. It must have something to do with the dust-filled lower atmosphere, something India is good at making.

Naju, a Parsi, dressed in a yellow sari with real gold trimmings, guided us today to the Kanheri (pronounced like cannery) Caves. Along the way she pointed out the orderly way traffic flows despite the large numbers of vehicles. "They jerk your license and fine you 100 rupees if you do something wrong." Naju said this as if to impress us, but of course I know 100 rupees *is less* than $3. How can a fine of that magnitude make any difference?

I pat my back pocket where I have 16,000 rupees, over $500 worth. When I got them today I threw away the exchange slip because I intend to distribute this entire small fortune to the street people.

Naju pointed out the taxis, colored yellow and black, eight thousand of them. They're covered in red dust, like everything else in Mumbai.

We pulled into a station to refuel. The cars parked overnight have accumulated so much red dust you can't see through the windows. This must have been what it was like when the United States had its own dust bowl. Naju said the dust is a big problem and, this time of the year, is the major cause of death. People get bronchitis, can't breathe, and die.

Along the road, motoring slowly through the countryside and all that dust, we saw the same evidence of poverty that we saw yesterday, only worse. People live in rubble on the side of the road, or in shacks packed like wasp nests on top of small hills. Many of the shacks have makeshift walls of torn, greenish brown, thick blankets. Some have no walls at all, just stakes that hold up a shaky provisional roof. Other shelters look like World War I surplus tents, which, incidentally, according to Naju, they are. "There is no end to it—the poverty," Naju explained in disgust and loathing. "These people come every day to the city from their villages seeking a good job and a fortune. But they set up these slums and have no future. When the government a short time ago gave them apartments, they sold them and within a month were back in their hovels."

The shanties look like they are from the California Gold Rush, except they have TV aerials and some have satellite dishes. Naju explained the paradox: "When they get a little money, they spend it on TV and VCRs."

Then Naju added somewhat discursively, "These people know their place. They believe in destiny. They know they need the rich to pay them for services." Then, as a kind of afterthought, Naju said, "Of course, the rich need them too—as servants."

The Kanheri Caves don't disappoint us. These rock-cut temples (109 discovered so far) date from the second century, BCE. The iconography mixes Hindu and Buddhist themes and some of the stupas resemble lingams (giant phalli) of Shiva, an interesting combination.

Most of the *QE2* group just stuck to the first three caves. Cave one remains unfinished because as the monks chiseled it out, they found a crack in the basalt. They intended to make the first cave two storied, but had to stop and start cave two next door. Cave two had two stupas that look like lingams, complete with urethral opening in the heads. Lots of inscriptions lined the walls, but Naju said she can't read them. That's the tip-off that the inscriptions are what Naju considers pornographic. Cave three, the largest and architecturally the most elaborate, looked like an ancient cathedral hollowed out of solid rock, except where the main altar should be at the narthex we found instead (did you guess?) another lingam, which leaves no doubt whatsoever as to what was worshipped here—the phallus. Cave three measured sixty meters long and twenty-five meters wide. Above us, in the third story facing east and directly toward the rising sun, we saw a large horseshoe-shaped window that lights the whole place nicely. Even in the second century, the ancients knew about indirect lighting. On the wall gigantic pillars supported the end walls where we found equally gigantic figures of Buddha. On the front wall the donor couples are carved in relief in the form of men and women resembling Karli figures. The two ladies display excellent breasts that, except for their excessive roundness, look real. This must be a stylized artistic thing, since it is unlikely they had breast implants in the second century. These men and women, staring at us from across the centuries, look happy, contented, sexy, and in love.

I climbed the stone steps and ascended to multiple little villages where many more caves faced small central areas. A little beggar girl, who looked three years old, followed me with her hand out. She doesn't know it yet, but if she sticks with me, this will be her lucky day.

Some caves are quite large and constituted general meeting halls and dining rooms for the monks. My girlfriend and I take the road to the right, the road that looked less traveled by. A sign points to caves 54–109. Time ran out. I saw only twenty-three of the fifty-three caves in the section. We went back.

On the way to the bus I decided this is it. Let's have some fun. I will become the pied piper of Hamelin, making the village children follow me, not with music, but with money.

With the blink of an eye, I signaled Ethel to get her camera ready. The wretched nest of human vermin was already positioned about the bus: rags, dirt, sunken cheeks, pallor of sickness, sores, projecting bones, dull aching misery in their eyes, and ravenous hunger speaking from every eloquent fiber and muscle from head to foot. As I got within ten meters of the bus I pulled several ten-rupee notes from my back pocket and handed them to the little girl who had followed me most of the morning. Momentarily, she stared at the fortune. A quiver of pleasure shook her body. Then she screamed. Then she ran.

Instantly, somewhere in the distance, someone shouted. Within seconds a group of twenty small, malnourished boys and girls arrived, their hands clutching my arms and grabbing as I fished out the next denomination of bills, the fifty-rupee notes.

I sprinkled the fifties over their heads like gentle rain from heaven. They went wild. The wretched nest around the bus uprooted and swarmed like hungry locusts toward me, the press of their hands and legs and smelly lice-ridden bodies. More shouts, louder too. No turning back now. I threw hundred-rupee notes around. They can't control themselves. They wildly, passionately grab the notes from my hand before I can throw them out. The very life is almost badgered out of me by importunate swarms of beggars and peddlers who now hang to my sleeves and shriek and shout in my ears and horrify my vision.

I felt something in my back pocket. I reached back and caught a small spindly hand. From that skeletal paw I squeezed back my money. "Stop," I shouted. "Calm down!" I yelled, frightened and overtired by the riot that I myself desired. Before I could let go of the rupees, the kids started ripping the bills in half. That brought my donation to a screeching close.

While pushing eager boys over and out of my way, I tossed the shredded rupee halves over my right shoulder, ducked down like a football half-back, and plowed through the crowd, headed for the shelter of the bus.

How fragile these people are! One push and they all fall down. Too bad they couldn't wait for the five-hundred-rupee notes. I could have fed whole villages for months, maybe even years. Still, mission accomplished. I feel great. I'm happy.

Meanwhile, someone else is not happy. In fact, someone else is very unhappy. Naju has been screaming at me since I started throwing the fifties, "Don't give them money!" Her livid face had filled with scorn and anger. Her spittle shot in my direction, lost its power, and fell like the gentle rain from heaven over the heads of raging, screaming kids.

Back on the bus, as I sank lower and lower into my seat, Naju delivered the harangue I knew I would get. "A hundred rupees might not seem like much to you, but to them that's an enormous fortune," Naju said, addressing me over the loudspeaker system so that all the other passengers could hear. "Now they will not go to school because they will think they can get much more begging. Those children will now write their friends and tell them that they got money for nothing. When the friends hear that, they will come to the city and increase the poverty and the slums."

On and on, Naju continued in this vein for fifteen minutes, during which she demonstrated to her satisfaction that, by my generosity, I will cause most of the future poverty of Mumbai.

"I hope some of the kids get a square meal tonight," I whispered to Ethel. "They sure looked like they need it."

Bad news. Captain John Burton-Hall announced that the overland group, probably caught somewhere in Deccan, didn't get back yet. We must wait for them. We can't leave at 2 PM as scheduled. Also, something is wrong with the tide for reasons I don't understand. Something about the northern monsoon winds. *QE2* must leave the dock, anchor offshore, and wait there for the overland passengers. Otherwise we will run aground and won't be able to leave for another six, maybe twelve hours.

Seven PM, and *QE2* started picking its way through the fishing vessels in the harbor. The captain missed his party because he had to remain at the helm. Meanwhile, back in our stateroom, Ethel and I had a good time reading various items from the *Times of India*, including information about the crucial upcoming India-Pakistan cricket match. On the surface this is a sports event, but under the surface, it is part of the war between Hindus and Muslims.

More news from the *Times*: A tennis player bombed his competition; an Indian oil tanker sank yesterday in Mumbai harbor killing thirty-six; the gas supply problems are preventing people from boiling water (only those who pay large bribes of 32 rupees [$1] can get their bottled-gas tanks refilled); 638 crore (a *crore* equals one hundred *lakhs*, or the sum of ten million rupees) was lost to the nation for the delay in the decision to import sugar; a woman's marriage has been canceled due to her death (a pity, but death does do that, changes lots of plans and cancels all appointments). She shall have to miss her reception too. And the honeymoon.

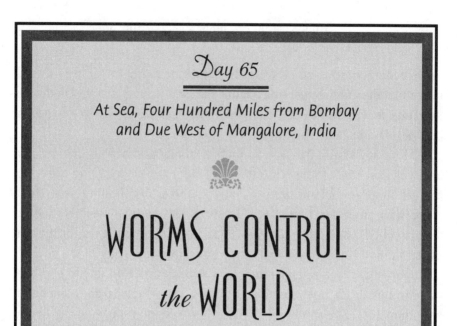

Day 65

At Sea, Four Hundred Miles from Bombay and Due West of Mangalore, India

WORMS CONTROL the WORLD

*C*ruise news says the dollar is up. That's good. But the stock market is down, way down. That's bad. Friday, the market saw the third-largest decline in history. Mr. Doom merits more respect. He might be right. How did the nosedive start? The paper has the explanation. The labor department reported that US nonfarm payroll jobs surged dramatically to 705,000. Normal people would think this great news. Not Wall Street. The Dow dropped 171.24 points. More important, for me, the biotechnology index fell 6.8 percent. Oh well, easy come, easy go.

Ethel and I walked on deck. We looked out over the water and saw no islands, no boats, no nothing, just all that beauty. The vastness of the Indian Ocean daunts our imaginations as does eternity.

Crossing the Indian Ocean by passenger vessel should really be considered an art form. There is already a technical term for doing it right: going POSH. This colloquialism for "grand" or first rate has its origin in the days of ocean steamship travel between England and India. Passengers would, at some cost, book their round-trip passage as Port Outward, Starboard Home. This secured shaded cabins while crossing the unbearably hot Indian Ocean. Abbreviated POSH, it soon applied to passengers traveling first class who could afford luxury.

While Ethel went on deck to read, I went below to spa.

Leonard, looking sleepy but contented, was wrapped in his white terry cloth robe. He's resting in the spa on a white plastic beach chair. Without warning, Leonard shocked me by doing something typically un-British: he asked a direct personal question, "Have you booked the world cruise for next year?"

"As a matter of fact, we talked about it this morning. How about you?"

"I'm booked. But I should like to know who is running it. Cunard and *QE2* have been up for sale, but there are no buyers. They lost millions and millions of pounds and want to get rid of it."

"Another world cruise isn't really a bad idea considering with the cruise miles we have earned and the onboard 5 percent discount, plus the 25 percent discount for early payment, the cabin upgrades, and so forth. We could cruise in our present room in Q2 class for $100,000, the same as we paid this year.

"On the other hand, we could do some freelance travel and return to *QE2* five years hence to celebrate my sixtieth birthday. Then I could write a book like Mark Twain's *Life on the Mississippi* [one of the most disjointed books of our literature], wherein Mark Twain compares a ride down the big river in his youth [part one] with the same ride in his old age [part two]. Naturally, part one is better, much better."

"I hope you'll give me good treatment in your book, Bernie, on both occasions," said Leonard. But he didn't seem worried or concerned. He closed his eyes and fell asleep.

Tonight's my turn to select the movie. I hunted in the film library. The difficulty is picking one we haven't seen. Sometimes we get a film and only during the showing realize that we have seen it before. That happened, for instance, during *Invasion of the Body Snatchers*.

In the film library, an elderly couple from France has the same problem.

Madame picked *Beauty and the Beast*. Monsieur told her, "We saw that."

"My, I don't remember," she said.

"Well, we did."

She put it back.

Monsieur then picked *Flatliners*, wherein cocky young med students experiment on one another to explore what it's like to be dead. Julia Roberts plays in it, in her salad days and pure as a cough drop. Oh, those liquid brown eyes!

Madame grabbed *Flatliners* from Monsieur's hand and put it back, "We saw that one in 1990 when it came out."

Since my new policy is to limit lectures to two a day, I picked carefully. I selected the lecture on the deep-ocean worms. The Indian Ocean on which we are now traveling has a bottom consisting of mud embedded with billions of worms that constitute, believe it or not, the largest single biomass on Earth. The ocean here averages nine thousand feet in depth over an area of twenty-eight million square miles. The bottom water (which incidentally flows in from the Antarctic, not the Arctic, with its protective ridge that prevents cold water from exiting) runs a temperature about freezing, a little above freezing in some places and a little below freezing in others. Every day, all these worms, despite the cold, go to work, eat, sleep, breed, expel wastes (just like us), burrow, crawl, swim, scavenge, and seem to enjoy the whole process. Our lecturer, a world-renowned scientist, explained: "Our studies of these annelids and nemertean worms show that under the best-controlled conditions, animals do what they please. Even in these dark cold waters, they are quite happy." He then advanced the theory that worms control the world.

Amazing verity! I couldn't agree more. But of course this scientist didn't speak in the realm of metaphor, where his clarion truth rings most intensely. He was not speaking of the off-stage oligarchy of real (human) worms that manage things for their own personal profit and benefit.

"How do worms control the world?" I asked.

The answer devolved on a complicated argument that I did not follow, by which he proved that the worms remove enough carbon dioxide from the atmosphere to prevent a big greenhouse effect that would have long ago melted all the polar icecaps and flooded all coastal cities like New York, London, and Rome.

Too bad I didn't get a chance to ask my next question: "If the worms control the world, do they also control the stock market? And if they do, can we get the worms to make the market rise?"

THEY HAD *the* POWER, I FIRMLY BELIEVE, IF NOT *to* DECIDE, THEN *to* INFLUENCE

*I*n the Indian Ocean, between India and the Seychelles, there is a mountain range rising out of a vast undersea plane. That range, called the Carlsberg Ridge, lies below us now, but it doesn't come near the surface and consequently won't bother us. But something else does bother us—our demotion. Ethel and I have demotion angst, a serious disease, but not half as serious as disembarkation angst. Ethel and I are scheduled to leave Queens Grill. We must descend back to Princess Grill. We must get dispossessed to a smaller cabin. Since this is one of the last days in our present accommodation, I shall summarize our experience. But first, I delivered my voucher for the next segment, Mombasa to Rio.

Anne, the purser, asked for the last voucher, Rio to Fort Lauderdale. She said it would help her if I deliver this last voucher now, rather than later. So I gave that to her as well, making a total payment today of $41,109.

Ethel and I discussed the tips. We agreed that it is a wonderful privilege to make people happy by giving them money. I have in mind arriving in Queens Grill and pulling out dollars and letting them fly, the way I did for the street people and the children in Bombay. But Ethel doesn't like the idea. She thinks it would be in poor taste, tres déclassé. So we fell back on conventional tipping via the white Cunard envelopes.

To Val our stewardess: $400. She gave the best and the most unobtrusive service that we received so far. "Call me at six on the dot, little things mean a lot," goes the old song. And Val excelled at paying attention to the little things. She kept me supplied with notepaper, which I devoured like those delicious baby Pacific shrimp they serve at the cocktail parties. And she knew exactly where I like the shampoo and conditioner placed for my bath. (God, I am getting fussy.) Nick gets $200 and Colum $300 because we love them both. But Alex, the restaurant manager who kept us well amused, gets $500. David, Alex's boss, who we hardly saw, gets nothing. No! Maybe $200 would be more like it, just to keep the top man favorably inclined toward us. Tip heavily, I decided. It's a crazy idea, but David and Alex might be able to obtain some kind of reprieve. They might prevent our demotion. I actually believe that they had the power, if not to decide, to influence the determination.

Tips came to $1,600 for this segment. Since we paid $30,256 for accommodation, the total cost comes to $31,856, or $612.61 per person per day. For me, the fairness of any price depends on if you actually get for what you paid, not the absolute amount of money involved. For me, the cost seemed more than reasonable. I would do it over and over again if I could. Ethel would too.

Summary Q2 class in cabin 1041:

Room: Gigantic for sea travel and more than adequate for our needs. If the travelers of old (Dickens, Twain, D. H. Lawrence) could have had the experience, they would have praised it to the skies, far above my poor power. The stateroom's amenities, including the safe, the refrigerator, the walk-in closets, the large marble bathroom with tub, the portholes, the

VCR, all unheard of in days of yore, made this segment a sybaritic pleasure. *Sybaritic* is Ethel's term, not mine.

Food: Excellent in every way: colorful, fresh, clean, tasty, and well presented. We feel many passengers in Queens Grill abused their status by ordering, each night, special off-menu delights for themselves. How can anyone eat all that caviar? Special orders, of course, were their privilege, I suppose, but in doing so I believe that they missed the many fine and interesting dishes on the menu that they would have enjoyed equally well or, perhaps, would have enjoyed better. The menu incorporated food items far beyond the fertile imaginations of any usual tourist. Why not let the chefs decide what they want to make that night? The chefs know what materials are available and they know how they feel. On *QE2*, every chef is an artist. And every artist needs freedom to produce the best results. Get out of their way. Let them work. It is true that Ethel complained the spa items on the menus did not have the calorie counts next to each item as they did in Mauretania and as they should. And Ethel picked up that some spa items were adulterated with high-calorie ingredients like dressings. And we confess that we felt some of the morning coffees at Queens Grill weren't great. To be polite and out of a sense of duty, we emptied our cups anyway. Then we hurried to the Lido to drink usually better, fresher, more flavorful cups of coffee.

Service: Fast and efficient. But not as fast as Mauretania class, but then again, what is?

Entertainment: We went to the lectures and the cultural shows, which far exceeded our expectations. We also did our own thing: watched movies in the room or, when they showed films we had not seen, we watched them in the theater. Do what you wish. Everyone has to please themselves. For us, most evenings, we indulged our personal failings by watching movies. You have something else in mind? Then do that. I'm sure other passengers, for instance, achieved equal contentment playing in the casino or viewing the variety shows or singing along in the Golden Lion Pub or dancing in the Yacht Club or the Queens Lounge or simply sitting romantically on Boat deck watching the moon, the sea, and the stars.

Total value of Q2: Superexcellent. Try to match it anywhere. You can't.

STAND ASIDE—PASSENGERS, NOT CREW, BOARD FIRST

*L*ong years ago in a time out of mind, in a time older than the time of chronometers, after the original continental landmass divided into two parts, India drifted away from Africa where it had been attached at Madagascar, and left in the middle of the Indian Ocean were our granite mountains and our archipelago that the humans of the world now call the Seychelles.

Eons later, about 200 million years ago, when dinosaurs still roamed Earth, we turtles arrived at Mahé, the main island. We saw that Seychelles was a nice place, and made our homes here. We mated every afternoon, peacefully fished and frolicked, buried our eggs, raised families of giant tortoises, and, after a hundred years or so, died. New generations of us turtles took over, but changed our perfect physical appearance but little. Turtles we were then, turtles we remained now, and turtles we shall always be.

Sadly, in 1502, a gang of fierce marauders came with Vasco da Gama to disturb our tranquility, to plunder and pillage. We turtles did not know it, but, in retrospect, that is when our vast, unspeakable sorrows began. The Portuguese cruelly ate us and our eggs, and packed many of us in their great ships to provide fresh meat for their voyages around the world. Eating us was not nice. It was not taking care of us. It was, like so many things we have suffered at the hands of those smelly humans, distinctly unfriendly. The one good thing the Portuguese did was depart without colonizing our islands.

So for another two hundred years, we turtles remained free until the French took possession in 1756. The French called our archipelago Sechelles, in honor of Moreau de Sechelles, the finance minister to Louis XV.

You would think that even a dumb human could see there was plenty here for everyone, but in our backyards the French and English fought great battles over who owned the sand. And, in 1810, when the British had killed enough Frenchmen, the French surrendered. About a century later, in 1903, Seychelles became a British Crown colony. But by 1976, after lots of trouble, we turtles got some freedom back: our land became the Republic of Seychelles.

Ah! That new republic with that wavy red, white, and green flag and that wonderful anthem by Pierre Dastros-Gece. We turtles didn't just like the new republic; we loved it. The Seychellois dedicated whole islands just to us. They made laws protecting us from turtle hunters. Yes, the new masters respected us turtles and we respected them, but still they are human and, frankly, we would like to see them depart. Let things revert back to the way they were when the turtles ruled this land. We did a better job when we were in charge. We will do a better job when we take over again.

As the turtles explained in their most recent manifesto reprinted above, Seychelles had a unique cultural and physical isolation, which accounts for its interesting flora and fauna. But before we discuss that I have to get to more mundane considerations. The *British Times* reported shares in London had a ten-billion-pound nosedive. The Nikkei in Japan dropped 360 points, and similar falls occurred in Hong Kong. Mr. Doom looks smarter and smarter.

On foot and on our own, Ethel and I explored Victoria, the capital of

Mahé. We walked along Lanier Road and then headed north on Independence Avenue and admired the clock tower modeled on Little Ben in the Vauxhall area of London. Another clock in the cathedral habitually chimes twice, five minutes after each half hour and before and after the hour in case you missed the first chimes. For some reason the US government sponsors a cultural house here and also sponsors an open-air art gallery, which the natives love. The signs around the place in Creole interested us because they spell French phonetically, the way it should be spelled. Thus *Musée Historique* comes out *Mize Istork*. *Section de l'administration* becomes *Seksyon Ladministrasyon*, and *Ministère des Affaires Éstrangères* equals *Minister des Zafer Etranger*. If all French were written this way, everyone would have a better chance of saying it properly.

Toyota trucks, each carrying about thirty school kids in the open-air back of the truck, would never cut it in the United States because of liability considerations, but these are the school buses of the Seychelles. A pretty good idea too: open-air transportation in a beautiful tropical countryside without need of air-conditioning.

We visited the Victoria market. Locals are there buying fresh fish and fruits and vegetables and curry powders and lottery tickets for the Seychelles national lottery. The lucky winner of will receive 70,000 Seychelles rupees, or about $14,000, American. On Albert Street, we passed the only traffic light in the whole Seychelle nation. Imagine a country with only one traffic light!

We don't have much time, so we ate lunch at the Pirate Arms on Independence Avenue across the street from the national museum and the post office. Both of us have curried octopus with rice and chutney. Great! For two the tab runs to 103 Seychelles rupees, or about $20 with drinks included. We then rushed back to the bus for the tour.

First stop is the botanical garden, where one could easily spend a week. There we saw the turtles who made and make these islands famous. One of the outer islands has one turtle that weighs 672 pounds. He, like *QE2*, is in the *Guinness Book of World Records*.

Christine, our guide, explained that the male turtle has a concave curved bottom part of the ventral surface called the plastron so he can nicely fit on the female's convex back, her carapace. How nice! Turtles mate during the afternoon, Christine explained, and make a lot of noise when they do. The noise is strange because, although turtles have keen eyesight and good senses of smell and taste, they can't hear worth a damn. Right now it's 2:30 PM; mating time is over, and all the turtles, idle and as still as statues, are resting quietly from all that sexual exertion.

While the turtles enjoyed a postcoital nap (but no cigarettes), we tourists visited the Coco de mer palm trees. These trees, some of which are over eight hundred years old, come in male and female varieties. After about twenty-five years, the female, if fertilized with pollen from the male, starts to bear a large nut, weighting up to forty-four pounds and taking seven years to mature. The male, not to be outdone, has the largest catkin in the plant world. Since Coco de mer is the largest seed in the world, I wanted to take one home, but some kind of government regulation got in the way.

Christine explained that when you peal off the outer shell of the Coco de mer the coconut inside is actually double, so that it looks like a woman's body from the waist to midthigh level. The small brown-black hairs in the (crotch) crease complete the picture of female genitalia. Christine explained that because of this resemblance, the Chinese use the nut as a sex medicine.

"Does it work?" I asked.

"I don't know," Christine replied. "Us Seychelle women have never tried it. We don't need it. We don't have such problems."

"How about the Seychelle men?"

Christine winked. "What the men need is something to tone down."

QE2ers saw still more amazing plants, including the Elephant ear, which is a flower two feet high with a central yellow element the size of a rolling pin. It's no Rafflesia, the gigantic five-pound and three-feet-across flower of Malaysia, but at least it's here and we see at least fifteen of these impressive flowers. A strange subtle fragrance with a citric high note and a beet earth low note emanates from the collection of Elephant ears. Since Elephant ear is such a big flower, I wanted to buy some seeds. But some kind of government regulation got in the way.

We saw the strange baoaba tree in which often dwells the Flying Fox. The Flying Fox is a small mammal that doesn't fly. It just glides by spreading some loose skin under arms and legs, catching the air like a hang glider. The locals soak the fox in vinegar for twenty-four hours to get the fox smell out. Then they prepare a coconut milk curry with the meat as the center attraction. Ethel explained we ate curried octopus at the Pirate Arms. Christine seemed obviously impressed. Christine said, "Seychellois [the locals] love that dish, but the octopuses don't." In fact, one of the current national problems of the Seychelles is the rapidly dwindling supply of fresh octopus.

We saw the star fruit tree loaded with star fruit and the mango tree loaded with mangos and the giant apple tree loaded with what looked like pears and we saw the famous breadfruit tree with fruits the size of basketballs. "Anything you do with a potato [bake, fry, boil, or broil] you can do with breadfruit," said Christine. "But we don't eat them. No taste."

We saw the famous Kapok, a mature ceiba tree, which yields a kind of soft matting, like cotton, that is used for mattresses, sleeping bags, and, more important, life preservers.

It's nice to see the origin of things.

Christine showed us where hearts of palm come from. "Does anyone here like heart of palm in their salads?" Ethel and I raised our hands. "You must be millionaires," Christine announced. "I call this the millionaires' palm," she said, holding the green-gray trunk of a palm tree about twelve feet tall. "You have to cut it down to get the center that is used for the palm hearts, which are mainly consumed by millionaires."

After that, we millionaires headed for Beau Vallon beach, the biggest and, all in all, the best beach on Mahé. It has a long stretch of white sand, fringed by palm trees and studded here and there with massive clumps of gray-brown granite: a spectacular place, especially at sunset.

We met Colum, our waiter, and Simon, our wine steward, and lots of other crew members. I told Colum, "They paid me a high compliment this morning when we tried to board the tenders for shore: 'Stand aside,' one of the security guards said, pointing his finger directly at me. 'Passengers, not crew, board first.'"

"Now you know how we feel!" said Colum. "Sometimes it takes so long for the passengers to get off, we crew members never get to leave."

I don't have a bathing suit. So, I bought one, a beautiful green and yellow Speedo, for $8, American. On Beau Vallon (French for beautiful hill) beach, the girls from the spa, including Katy, the Venus of the clamshell, also known to this humble narrative as Miss Universe, and Elena (who Ethel suspects secretly wishes to become my trophy wife) treated me by removing their tops. They stood there bare breasted in the sun. These ladies don't need breast implants and I don't need the Coco de mer. But with Elena it's more than her breasts that interested me. It's those beseeching brown eyes and that seductive smile, the smile of desire.

"Don't gawk at her," said Ethel as she jerked me away. "You belong to me."

Ethel and I danced at the departure party on Boat deck outside of the Yacht Club. I tried to get down the scene. People. Crowds of them, some in shorts, and gentlemen hosts in slacks and open shirts with yellow metal plates. Music. Male and female vocalists taking turns, sometimes doing a duet, like "Unforgettable." The massive ship with teakwood deck. The soft, smooth, blue tropical sea stretching to infinity. Fresh tropical breezes with a breath of perfume in them. The regularly irregular mountains overlooking the town of Victoria, silhouetted against the western sky that began to change color as the sun settled. And in that sky, two sets of clouds, vast and silent and still fleecy white cumulus that ride at about three thousand feet, and, higher up, the ice-crystal cirrus clouds that look like streaks of white cotton candy against a bright blue field. Drinks. Orange fruit punch, well doused with rum.

Just when I think I have it down, the scene changes: As the sun descends below the mountains, the greenery turns black, and details blur. The mountain ridges become two dimensional, thin and frail, against the background sky, like a Hollywood prop. In the west, the lower clouds first turn from white to yellow then to pastel orange and then, I kid you not, beet red. The upper clouds remain the same white for a while, then go through the identical polychrome sequence of color changes, but on closer inspection, the part of the cloud facing west colors first and is lighter than the part facing east. And talking about east, I see it is darker than the west, but only the part of the sky hugging the horizon appears deep purple, above that blue, then beryl, and above that a remarkable cerulean.

Minutes later all the high clouds turned color again: first rose, then crimson, with the sea in a V-shaped triangle, the point at the ship and the wide part covering all of the distant shore, reflecting the sky's brilliant crimson like a dense ruby port, creating the wine dark sea that Homer spoke of.

As *QE2*'s diesel electric engines rumbled to a start and the deck began to vibrate, I matched Ethel's footwork, whirled her this way and that with surprising agility. The song is "Moon River." Strict time waltz, and very smoochy.

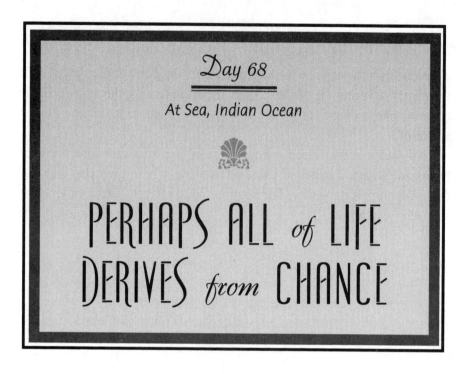

Day 68

At Sea, Indian Ocean

PERHAPS ALL *of* LIFE DERIVES *from* CHANCE

*T*he program arrived under the door this morning. But cruise news did not. I told Ethel they decided that the stock market news was so bad they didn't want to print it. Once again, too many choices present themselves. I decided to stick to my determination and limit the lectures to two hours per day.

Professor Don Kurtz promised that the most beautiful and amazing astrophotographs of galaxies and nebulae ever taken will be shown, explained, and included with the latest results and pictures from the Hubble Space Telescope. Professor Kurtz hails from the department of astronomy at University of Cape Town.

After Kurtz, I'll listen to Waldemar speak about Kenya, and that's it for me for the day. The rest of the time I will spend reading on deck, thinking, sitting on Boat deck admiring the sea, and looking over the stern at the wavelets produced by *QE2* as they diverge into V-shaped cataracts of foam. I shall admire the churned water making a beautiful pale white aquamarine ribbon the width of the ship, a ribbon that stretches from here to eternity.

"What's the first thing you'll do when you get home?" Ethel asked.

"Inspect the garden. How about you?" I asked.

"Guess."

"Pet P.J."

"Right!"

Alex wanted to know if I am that neurosurgeon discussed in the cruise news who operated on the wrong side of the brain.

"No, I am not. But anytime anyone is operating on the brain, it's the wrong side."

Alex felt that I was on the lam, but he didn't know why. "I am on the lam, like so many of your customers. But I'm not telling you why," I said.

Alex was referring to the famous case of Rajeswaris Ayyappan, 59, mother of the more famous Indian film star Sridevi Ayyappan, who traveled to New York City to the famous Memorial Sloan-Kettering Cancer Center to get the wrong side of her brain operated on.

"How can such a thing happen?" Alex asked.

I replied, "I don't know. But I have a theory. The neurosurgeon was burned out. He didn't have the guts to quit, so his inner dog or his unconscious mind, whatever you wish to call the jumble of underlying motives embedded deep within the human psyche, helped him out. The proof is that this was the second time this year he operated on the wrong side of the brain."

A flash of recognition. Alex understood. "That may happen to me," he said. "I see myself punching someone out."

"No, Alex, with you, it might happen more poetically—you might flambé a customer. That would have more symbolic significance."

Alex nodded pensively.

The astronomy lecture proved remarkably interesting. The crowd loved it too. Professor Kurtz started with this joke:

The British sea captain gets word that there is a light off the starboard bow. The captain tells them to radio the light and tell them to bear off. The message comes back, "Bear off yourself!" The captain turns red, puffs out his chest, and personally sends the next message. "I am a captain in the Royal Navy. Bear off!" The reply came quickly, "I am a retired seaman. Bear off and be quick about it." More incensed, the captain sent, "I am a battleship. Bear off!" The reply, "I am a lighthouse."

Authority must yield to reality. That's the moral.

Ethel asked Kurtz, with all the galaxies and all the stars, what would the probability be that there is an Earthlike planet out there. The answer is highly probable. But Ethel failed to follow up with another question: What is the chance that the Earthlike planet has oceans on which cruises a vessel like *QE2*? The answer, probably unlikely because *QE2* is unique. There will never be any other ship quite like *QE2* in the whole vast universe.

After the lecture, the gray head next to me, a man in his eighties, wanted to know if he fell asleep during the slides. I told him, "I don't think so. But I'm not sure. I know there was some steady breathing coming from straight in back of me, but you seemed OK."

"Rather chaotic up there," he observed, motioning to the picture of the Milky Way galaxy still on the screen. "Seems like all those galaxies got mixed up by chance. Maybe our own existence also derives from chance."

I shook my head in agreement. It took him eighty years to figure this out, but it took him less than a minute to say it.

The old guy got up stiffly and said apologetically, "I can't stay for Waldemar's lecture. I know I'll fall asleep."

Suddenly I realized that science approached philosophical problems (like the notion of existence and its meaning) indirectly, but pretends it isn't doing so. Religion approaches the mysteries directly and doesn't pretend. Science knows it doesn't have the answers. Religion knows it doesn't have the answers, but pretends that it does. Also, science tends to explain things in terms of tautologies, making science appear smarter than it really is. Example: one elderly woman asked Kurtz what holds the galaxies together. Gravity, he told her.

"But what is gravity?" she retorted.

Kurtz, shocked by this abysmal display of ignorance, said, "You know. The same force we have here on Earth. The force that holds the galaxies together."

Kurtz explained this quite confidently, but I hope deep in his heart of hearts he knows not a soul alive knows what gravity really is. The same basic scientific ignorance applies to time, matter, and energy. Sure, we can measure those things (any fool with a watch can tell you what *time* it is, but who can tell you what time *is*?), but we don't actually know, all in all, what we are dealing with or what we are measuring.

Science fascinates me. Nowhere else do you get such wholesale speculation from such a trivial collection of facts. Further, if we have that kind of difficulty with simple physical things, then what about love, tenderness, devotion, or loyalty, and so on? We shouldn't be so proud of what we've done or what we know, for behind the pretense of knowledge lies ignorance vaster than the oceans, vaster than the universe.

At dinner, Alex announced, "A call from the States for you, Dr. Patten. It's a woman. She made me promise not to say she was a woman. She made me swear I wouldn't say that in front of your wife. I am sorry to get you into trouble like this, but I had to tell you."

It's a woman all right. But she isn't calling from the United States. It's Anne, the purser. Anne said she thinks it would be rather inconvenient for us to move to 1079, down in Princess Grill. So why don't you just stay where you are? "OK with me," I said.

Anne added, "Furthermore, 8184, your Penthouse Suite, may become available in Cape Town. We may move you then. 555 Fifth Avenue will have to approve."

"OK with me," I said. "And thank you."

In the spa, Leonard wanted to know when I'm coming back to eat with him in Princess Grill. I have to give him the bad news: "We might stay in Queens Grill."

"I wonder why?" he said, puzzled. "Cunard never does things for you unless the company has something in mind."

"Perhaps it is because I give big tips," I said.

"If you don't mind, Bernie, tell me how much you tip."

I told.

Then Leonard told me his tipping routine. He gives $50 each week to his steward and to each of his waiters. To the woman who brings around the petit fours after dinner, he gives $25 every other week, "since nobody tips a person like that." Leonard tips his wine steward $25 every week, because he drinks a bottle of wine each night, but he feels he doesn't get that much service from the waiters because each day he has the same thing to eat: one boiled egg for breakfast, a salad for lunch, and only the main course for dinner. "Yet," he complains, "the weight keeps increasing."

Nick looked worried. He confessed he worries about our transfer. So does Simon. To be frank, we worry too. We would rather stay than move. They would rather we stay than move. It's all up to 555 Fifth Avenue.

At dinner Alex explained how the gentlemen hosts get the job. They come from some recruiting firm in California. They travel free and get $10 per day for drinks. They obviously have money and nothing to do. Alex said he will do that job later on when he gets brain dead. This doesn't jive with what I heard before about the gentlemen hosts paying 10 percent, so I shall have to check.

Alex, upset that we might be leaving, wanted to do something special for me, so he made bananas Foster. This is a dish I make at home, so I will critique his version. He used white sugar. I use brown. He says they used to use brown but it made the syrup too thick. He flames and tops off the bananas with chocolate. I use a touch of cinnamon and a sprinkle of lime juice to give it some zap. Alex agrees and offers to do that. No, I want to experience it the way he does it.

"Pretty good," I told him. "You get an A because I'm in a good mood." Then I added, "Undoubtedly, Alex, you were eager for my critical appraisal."

"Not really," he said. "It's a numbers game. Some passengers you please. Some you don't. Hopefully, you please more."

"Wow, that disappeared fast." Alex stared at my empty plate.

"No great pleasure lasts long," I said smacking my lips and wondering what Alex would think if I asked for another bananas Foster. No need to bother. Nick, my factotum, stepped in and ordered for me: "The same again."

IF YOU RESPECT US, WE KILL YOU

*M*ombasa is thoroughly ugly, cramped, squalid, uncomfortable, and filthy; just the style of cities that have adorned this country since Adam's time. And Mombasa has no redeeming features.

Ethel and I made our way along Moi Avenue. She photographed the gigantic aluminium white tusks (the symbol of Kenya) that arch across the street. The Muslim section along Kenyatta Avenue, named after this nation's first president, looked unspeakably dirty and crowded, worse than Moi or Nkrumah Road. Crowding the streets on the shaded side are beggars, who beg forever yet never collect anything; wonderful cripples, almost distorted out of all semblance of humanity; vagabonds driving laden asses; porters carrying dry goods boxes as large as cottages on their backs; and peddlers of grapes, hot corn, pumpkin seeds, and a hundreds other things. They are yelling like fiends while others sleep happily, comfortably, and serenely among the hurrying feet, the famished dogs, and the insistent flies.

The sidewalk broke up and then stopped. The place started to look dangerous, so we gave up and headed back. Along Moi Avenue we ate at Rick's Casablanca, near the general herbalist shop. In Kenya herbalists are licensed as health professionals and prescribe remedies.

Rick's Casablanca sports a lot of local color with some, come to think on it, too many, young black women cruising about. Ethel refused to eat. While she drank mineral water, I ate a Nile fish that tasted great. Lunch for the two of us cost only 600 Kenyan shillings ($12, American), drinks included. We continued walking past the down-and-out New Palm Hotel, whitewashed against the sweltering tropical sun. The sidewalk is in terrible shape, with multiple breaks, rubble in the path, water, and mud. In addition to the dust, the air fills with acrid blue smoke exhausted from numerous buses, vans, cars, and trucks, but few motorcycles. I realized how important emission control laws can be. Kenya has none, or if it does, no one obeys them.

They do have the best beggars I have ever seen, lots of them with leprosy. Some have their fingers completely eroded off so that only the palms of their hands remain. They stretched out their mitts. Afraid to go near them, we gave nothing.

For 200 Kenyan shillings, we engaged Ali, a Muslim guide at Fort Jesus, a historic landmark of East Africa. Ali, of course, is Shiite, the more radical type of Muslim. His name comes from the fourth-century Muslim caliph Ali, one of Muhammad's first followers. Ali (the original Ali, not our guide) got control via assassination, his reign characterized by unrest and civil strife, and he died at the hand of an assassin. The Shiite believes in jihad as the sixth pillar of Islam. Shiites don't want to force conversion, for that is forbidden by the Koran. The object of jihad is to gain political control of societies and run them in accordance with the principals of Islam. The basic creed is brief: there is no god but Allah, and Muhammad is his Prophet.

Ali said the tour lasted thirty-two minutes. Ali said Mombasa is 95 percent Muslim. My guidebook says 85 percent. Vasco da Gama came to Mombasa in 1498 and within a week antagonized the locals. After some fighting, the Portuguese took over in 1593 and built, using orange and yellow corals mined from the sea, Fort Jesus.

Ali made me nervous. He talked too much about the brotherhood of man. "All men are the same before God."

"But what about the women?" I asked.

"The Prophet said women were of no importance."

My nervousness increased as Ali covered the nature of Ramadan, Islam, surrendering to Allah's will, and so on. But I began to relax when he mentioned that he liked the idea that the United States protects Kenya from invasion by Uganda. Ali personally doesn't want to fight. He's afraid of guns.

Ali showed us the quarters where the Portuguese kept the slaves. Ali lectured us about the injustice of taking fathers and mothers from their children and looked at us strangely, as if we were in some way responsible. Then we visited the small decrepit museum that had some old pottery and other junk. The main attraction was a skeleton in an opened grave. "These old bones are obviously Christian," said Ali. "The head faces west. A Muslim head would face north to Mecca." And then, as a kind of afterthought, Ali told us that tomorrow everybody on the street who is Muslim will wear white, himself included. "We Muslims own this country."

"*Pole, pole.*" Ali pulled my arm. "That means go slowly. In a tropical country, if you go fast, you fall down. In Europe you go fast to keep warm."

We passed over the bastion and looked out of the parapet to the old harbor from which the dhows plowed the Indian Ocean. A teenager saw my T-shirt, which has a large kiss mark in red and these words in French: "*Embrace moi, je parle francais.*" The teenager wanted to know what *moi*, the president's name, was doing on the shirt. "Just a coincidence," I explained. "*Moi* is French for *me*. "My shirt says 'Hug me, I speak French.'"

The kid didn't understand. He asked again, "Why is *moi* on your shirt?"

I pulled a fifty-shilling note from my pocket and waved it in the air. "Why is Moi on your money?" The kid shrugged his shoulders and looked out at the sea. Then Ali invited us into the old town, the place where Waldemar Hansen told us not to go because it was too dangerous. Ali tempted us, "Come see da Gama's home. It's still intact."

"Is it safe?" I asked.

"Of course, I protect you!" Ali said with the unsettling smile of a con man.

What the hell! It's broad daylight. And, we have Ali. He will protect us. Right?

The old section looked tired and run down, down and out. A real slum, much worse than downtown. The home of da Gama looked old, but not old enough to be from the sixteenth century. Ali pointed out some wood carved doors that have seen better days and showed us the former British police station and a home for Somali refugees, sheltered by the United Nations. "You heard of the United Nations?" Ali asked. Ali's eyes have begun to bulge. His teeth look excessively large, like a wolf about to devour a piece of meat. It was then I knew we had made a mistake of a rather large magnitude.

Meanwhile, as we descended further and further into the Muslim quarter, the graffiti on the whitewashed walls and on the sides of the buildings got worse and worse. "Malcolm X" written in red, then lots of red Xs, three feet tall and two feet wide, appeared everyplace. Some have "Malcolm" written across them and some have the "Malcolm" on the left side and some just have the "X" and no Malcolm at all.

That's OK. I'm not afraid of Malcolm X because I read his autobiography (really written by Alex Haley). Malcolm X didn't seem bad. Besides, he's dead.

Deeper into the quarter: "We hate U.S." and "If you respect us, we kill you" and "Americans go home" and "Death to America." At least the signs didn't call us the great Satan, like Ayatollah Ruhollah Khomeini.

We arrived at a deserted cemetery. A sensation chilled me, a kind of terminal air-conditioning.

Ali shouted.

"No need for alarm," Ali assured us: he's calling for his friends.

From nowhere, six Muslim men appeared. What are they doing here in the cemetery?

The six men and Ali laughed and yelled things to each other in Kiswahili. Every once in a while they made furtive sideward glances at Ethel and me. They're with each other, together, but for what?

Ethel, busy taking photos of the wooden doors, the old buildings, and the kids on the street, noticed nothing wrong. But I figured it was time to end the tour.

"How much do I owe you?" I asked.

Ali's reply stunned us: "Two thousand shillings. We quote prices in dollars. Your tour cost $200, but I'm letting you go for two thousand shillings."

None of this made sense. Two hundred dollars would come to 10,000 shillings, not $2,000, which would amount to 2 million shillings, or $40,000, American. Either way, Ali sure is one hell of an expensive tour guide.

Ali's friends have gathered around while Ali and I have a mutually supportive conversation to resolve our differences and disagreements. I spotted some things that helped me reach a conclusion: Two men have sticks at the ready, and one man, who was rather gaunt and grisly, carried in his right hand a large yellow rock, probably part of the coral from Fort Jesus. Ali himself, though smiling, had clenched his fists. I wondered what it feels like to get killed in a cemetery. Probably, it's uncomfortable. It would be better to continue cruising on *QE2*.

Discretion is the better part of valor. And I have taken the better part.

It pays, sometimes, to just pay. I handed Ali 2,000 shillings. His eyes popped out. While Ethel and I slipped away, the other men and Ali started arguing.

"Why did you let him do that? The agreed price was 200 shillings, I heard it. You could have beat him up." Ethel was irate. She hates to be taken.

"Get real!" I said while looking back down the dusty road. We were safe. The muezzin was calling the faithful to prayer.

"Didn't you see the signs on the walls? You think they're joking? They want to kill us. Besides, there were seven of them. They had sticks and rocks. I could have handled them one at a time, but all at once, no way."

Ethel shook her head and pointed an accusatory finger my way, "They cheated us and you let them."

"Yes, they did. And yes, I did. The money is nothing, $40. Just thank Allah you're still alive."

It's a good lesson: the difference between religion in theory and religion in practice. A striking discrepancy that we witnessed that is well shown in novels like *Palace Walk*, a majestic and capacious accomplishment, rich in psychological insight and cultural observation, by Naguib Mahfouz, the Nobel Prize–winning author from Egypt. The novel shows the treachery and deceit of Arabs and Muslims. Read it and don't ever forget it.

The night show of native dances was no good. The dances were not beautiful, and the dancers, ditto. The costumes were not beautiful, and the singing, ditto. The music was just a bunch of noise. This show was a total artistic nothing, a failure. At the end of the show, Andrew, the social director, said, "Well, now wasn't that different?"

What else can you say?

The crowd agreed and gave a very unenthusiastic clap. *QE2*ers have an abject prejudice against seediness, however ennobled.

Day 70

Mombasa, Kenya

NO OTHER METHOD
of TRANSPORTATION
INVOLVES THIS KIND *of*
NAVIGATIONAL INSOUCIANCE

*T*oday, at dockside, I fell in love with a black woman. She stood there stiffly, rigidly straight, six feet sex (I mean six feet six) inches tall, gazing, not at me, but at infinity. The carriage of her neck had that charming touch of youth and unfamiliarity. Her jet-black skin felt warm and smooth and slightly slippery. She didn't mind that I touched her. Her puffy African lips moved not, smiled not. Someone had shaved her entire head and powdered the scalp red. Such coloring I had seen before among the Samburu, a Kenyan tribe that lives just south of the Ethiopian border. The shaved red head means this woman, usually as a prepubescent girl, was engaged to marry and has already had her clitoridectomy to tone down the tendency (the elders say) of women from that tribe toward promiscuity.

Yet, my new love was anything but prepubescent, for she showed full womanhood. She wore a small red napkin around her neck and a larger red cloth with vertically positioned black stripes as a loincloth. Above her waist she stood naked. In her hands she carried a flagon of palm wine. Were these the breasts that launched a thousand ships? The most beautiful breasts I have ever seen were there at my eye level, bared to the open air. Her breasts stuck out like two oversized doorbells. While she stood there, still as a statue, I pinched the right nipple, the size of a black Greek olive. It hung lower than the left, as it should. I cupped the left breast; it was slightly fuller than its mate, and in the natural order of things, exactly right.

A native man, wearing khaki pants and a dirty white shirt with green stripes, stepped protectively between the black lady and me. This short fat bum with a bald head and yellowed teeth, which reflected years of dental neglect and hundreds of packs of cigarettes, noted my admiration and whispered to me with sour breath, "She's for sale, like so many African women." His voice was low pitched, raspy. The price: $1,000.

"I don't have time to haggle. The ship leaves soon. Tell me your best price," I said.

"You can have her for $300."

I glanced at the woman. No response. She didn't care. She stood there indifferent. To her, the price signified nothing, nothing at all. This was as I expected.

"Listen," I said. "She's no good to me unless I can get her aboard. I have to check with the officer who controls the gangway. Don't sell her to anyone else. I'll get back as soon as I can."

The gangway officer didn't like the idea and wouldn't help. The Filipinos loading cases of Heinekin beer into the hull on Five deck liked the idea, but they couldn't help; they were busy. Frantic, I went back onboard. I tried to think of a plan. I went to the baggage master on Two deck. He said he couldn't help; he had no labor. I knew Ethel wouldn't like the idea of sharing our stateroom with another woman, but it would only be a minor inconvenience, for a little while, say twenty days, until we got to Fort Lauderdale. Sooner or later, come to think on it, I would have to talk to Ethel. I just couldn't surprise her. I couldn't have her discover me and the black lady in the stateroom in flagrante delicto. If Ethel knew in advance, things would go better. If she agreed, things would go even better.

Ethel didn't like the idea, but didn't veto it either. I asked Val, our stewardess, for advice. "I have Franklin, my pantry boy. He could sneak her aboard for you. But if she's that big, two Filipinos would be better. Wait in your room. I'll see what I can do."

Twenty-two minutes later, Franklin arrived with a friend. The three of us went down to the dock. The black lady and her owner hadn't moved. The owner was glad to see me again. The lady didn't care one way or the other. Franklin couldn't restrain his admiration. "She's beautiful! Look," Franklin said, standing on his tiptoes. "She's taller than I am, must be six foot."

"Don't feel bad, Franklin. She's taller than I," I said, standing tall besides the black beauty and holding my hand high with my palm flat and facing downward to dramatize the level of the top of the lady's red bald head.

I peeled out the fifteen twenty-dollar bills and counted them into the hands of the owner. When the last bill landed, the owner said, "I want $400."

I grabbed the money. "No deal!"

"Three hundred fifty," he said calmly.

I should have expected this. Wherever there's a man selling a woman, there's trouble.

I turned to Franklin and his friend. I shook my head and pointed my index finger toward the ship, indicating that we should go. And I would have left the black lady standing there at the dockside in Mombasa, Kenya, if the owner's mouth of dental neglect hadn't nodded and whispered, "Three hundred, OK."

Franklin and friend carried my black lady aboard *QE2*, to the general admiration and occasional disgust of the other passengers. "How much did you pay for her?" one man snickered. "Three hundred dollars?"

"Three hundred shillings would be more like it."

And so the black lady stands sullen, silent, and immobile, no ray of lovemaking in her eyes. She leans against the wall of our cabin, 1041, projecting her bare breasts into the open space that hangs over our twin beds. Every once in a while, in a moment of distraction, especially in the evening when the room grows dark and bleak, I turn and see her in the corner and startle. After some time, Ethel and I will get used to the extra passenger in our seagoing home, but not yet.

My next problem: what to do with her when we get to the States?

At lunch I bragged about my new girlfriend and invited Colum and Nick to come see her. Naturally, after I gave them details about the breasts, Nick and Colum got interested. David, the manager of Queens Grill, said ten years ago Mombasa never looked that bad. He hadn't been to town for ten years and was shocked by the deteriorated streets and the run down appearance of Mombasa. The place has changed for the worse. And by the way, David asked, "Can I borrow your black lady for an evening? I want to have some fun with her."

David made me think of an important question. Where did all that World Bank money go? It was supposed to go to building up the infra-structure in Kenya, but it looks like it might have gone into private jet planes for President Moi.

I put my new plan into effect: strict limits on lecture time and more time for fun and frolic. All I ask of life is a bunch of books, good food and drink, a great ship, movies, leisure time, a rising stock market, lots of dreams, and love. I decided to start the new policy immediately after this afternoon's lecture on the sex life of worms and fish.

Six women entered the theater during the afternoon lecture on the sex life of deep-sea worms. They sat in front of me. One said to the other, "Where's the movie? This looks like fish."

"Fish!?" the other exclaimed, making a poison face. They left.

But you know, I wonder if they aren't right. The lecture is boring. Why am I filling my life with un-fun things and un-fun people? After all, our time on *QE2* draws to a close. Soon the saddest view that would ever confront us will appear in our porthole: the sight of tugs shepherding the ship to our final pier at Fort Lauderdale.

The unexamined life is not worth living. I must raise the question: attending all those lectures—is it, perhaps, an attempt to allay hedonism's persistent guilt? Why can't I just discover a blessed idleness and peace, a kind of Buddhist nirvana right here on *QE2*? Now that Ethel and I have united with the crew in a miraculous symbiosis, why not embrace an escapist philosophy? And thus, it came to me. The most significant and most delightful element of cruising is its aimlessness. That is why we return to the port of embarkation: we have no real objective, no purpose, and no responsibility. No other method of transportation involves this kind of navigational insouciance, the absolute inessentiality of the voyage, the pursuit of nothing but pleasure. From now on, I will try to embrace indolence, eschew haste, and laze in the pleasant nautical limbo on this multitiered pleasure palace, *QE2*. I shall place strict limits on anything that menaces my joyous inactivity.

Alex had good news and bad news. He showed me an article in *Time* that said the *Journal of the American Medical Association* published a study that confirmed my research. The bad news was that Trafalgar House would sell *QE2* to the Dutch.

"Don't worry, Alex," I tried to assure him. "Cunard fought commercial battles at sea for 120 years, and the company knew how to roll with the ocean swells and survive until the trade tides turned."

My new hedonism started at dinner. I decided to attempt a new *QE2* record. I ordered four desserts. Nick brought them out fast, one after another. I devoured the syllabub, then ate the tiramisu, after which followed the chocolate Marquesa, and last, the bread pudding.

Nick and Colum appeared at the table, Nick on my right and Colum on my left. They held papers on which they have written my Olympic scores, perfect tens for the new event I am founding, dessert consumption.

At Sea, Mozambique Channel between
Mozambique and Madagascar

MADAME, I AM TERRIBLY SORRY YOUR STEWARD DIED *and* WAS BURIED *at* SEA

A large Indian group appeared on deck. This Indian invasion requires a special menu and special Indian chefs aboard sounds funny to me. There is also some sort of new requirement on how the animals are killed to conform to some sort of Hindu religious thing.

In Florida we had lots of elderly gray heads who stayed for the high adventure of crossing the Panama Canal. Then in Japan, the Japanese; in Hong Kong, Chinese; and in Australia (God help us), those rowdy Australians. Now the Indians have joined up, probably to sail to Cape Town. Except for my black lady, I don't think we have any Kenyans.

Anne called from the purser's office. 555 Fifth Avenue approved our staying in Queens Grill and will move us to the penthouse sooner than expected. The transfer will take place at sea on March 19, between Durban and Cape Town.

OK, today I shall try to have a real cruising experience. I took to the deck chair and a book in a quiet stretch of the sheltered Boat deck on the shady portside. *The Innocents Abroad* amused me between my glances through the railing at the endless sea. Funny thing, the ocean. All that water. The waves have a hypnotic quality that makes it possible to look at them for hours without any good excuse. I feel the soft breeze on my right (bow side) cheek and hear it whisper hints of strange tropical nights and breathtaking sunsets amid the wind song and deck creak and the glissando of hull riding through water. I sniff the air. The air has a breath of perfume in it and a touch of kerosene from the Bunker C fuel we burn.

Gigantic sea leisure imposes on me, envelopes me in a kind of protective cocoon. These things and more fulfill my cruise expectations to perfection. A seascape compels me more than a landscape. Why, I don't know. But it does. Perhaps it is because the sea, as Victor Hugo said, lacks the somber sadness of right angles. But I do know while sitting on the deck chair and gazing at the sea I feel immeasurably at peace. Perhaps I might abandon this meager work and write a book called *How to Sleep*. After which, if it sold, I might attempt a book on *How to Eat on* QE2, and then, *How to Screw*. They say write what you know. Beyond that, without considerably more research, I cannot go. Before, for instance, trying to write my magnum opus, *How to Gaze at the Sea without a Twinge of Guilt*, I would need a whole lot more experience.

Waldemar Hansen gave the lecture on South Africa. I'm not going to repeat it here. If you wish to know about it and the Boer War, Cecil Rhodes, diamonds, Jan Christian Smuts, Dr. Christiaan Barnard and the first heart transplant, apartheid and all that, go to your nearby lending library and mention my name. Tell them you want to read about the Cape of Good Hope and how Natal was named by Vasco da Gama, the Portuguese navigator who sailed along this stretch of coast Christmas Day 1497, and therefore christened it "Terra Natalis," land of Christ's birthday. Since I'm in a lazy mood, I'll be hanged if I tell you why they call the state across from the Vaal River, Transvaal. And I definitely won't inform you about the Protea, the national flower of South Africa, which actually looks like it contains the transmigrating soul of a tarantula. Find those things out for yourself. I'm on vacation, dreaming while looking at the wild sea foam, listening to the sea yelp and sea howl, two sea voices often heard together. Or better still, read something intelligent about this land. Read *A Sport of Nature* by South Africa's Nobel Prize–winning novelist, Nadine Gordimer. Then read Alan Paton's classic *Cry, the Beloved Country.*

I broke away from my sea trance to go to the interview of Geoffrey Hudson Coughtrey, penthouse butler. I want to learn about the penthouse before we get there. I want to be prepared for all that luxury.

Right away I liked this guy. Geoffrey calls himself a freelance butler, just the way I call myself a freelance scholar. He doesn't drop names the way I thought he would. Well, not too many names, that is. Eleanor Roosevelt told him if he must stand outside her room, she would prefer he got a chair and sat down. Geoffrey loved Mrs. Bessie Wallis Warfield Simpson, the woman who led King Edward VIII to abdicate his throne. Geoffrey even made a pilgrimage to Mrs. Simpson's grave in the same cemetery where Victoria lies. (Victoria didn't want to be buried in Westminster; she preferred to lie with her beloved Albert.)

The caretaker said uncomplimentary things about Mrs. Simpson and said she was among the lesser royals. He refused to show Geoffrey the place. Thus, our penthouse butler couldn't leave the rose he carried, or his note, which read: "You don't know me, but I believe I knew you."

Geoffrey preferred being freelance rather than in private service, because the butlers he knows in private service have "led rather closeted lives."

One trip, at her behest, Geoffrey had to clean the countess's diamond ring in gin each night, and then there was the time he constructed a life preserver for a lady's pet pigeon. During a recent interview for BBC, Geoffrey and the royal butler were asked the question, "If the queen asked you to put a log on the fire, would you do it?" The royal butler said, "No, that's for the handyman to do." Geoffrey said he would simply pile the log on. Why not?

I can see Geoffrey delivering a condom to one of the penthouse suites late at night. Why not? But I imagine he would deliver the condom with flair, on a covered silver platter.

Sometimes the customers irk Geoffrey. For instance, when the idle rich come onboard and he hears them in the hall saying, "I wonder if we'll have the same servants we had last year?" Or how about the time when the midship steward died. Geoffrey attended the funeral, and had just come from the sea burial. "Madame, I am terribly sorry your steward died and was buried at sea," he consoled, whereupon the woman inquired, "Where's my laundry?"

Geoffrey touched on some points that seemed to make Brian Price, our cruise director, uneasy. Hence, we got no elaboration on: "When *QE2* hit that rock outside Boston, the captain worried, but it turned out it wasn't his fault. Then there was the time we dropped the propeller. We were in the Bermuda Triangle and had to drift. I was on leave during the ninety-foot wave, but I was on board when *Caronia* hit that lighthouse. We all evacuated to the navy station and had a grand time because the drinks were so cheap."

Geoffrey forgot to mention the time when, in an Atlantic gale, the *QE2* anchor tried to leave the ship, and, in the process, gashed a hole in the hull. These stories I know. No doubt about it, *QE2* has suffered her share of sea troubles. But no consideration could move me to put down several paragraphs of dry facts. And why defame the ship I love? Oh well, what the hell. I'll briefly relate the most recent disaster, just to prove that I can: Misfortune came to *QE2* on a cruise a few months after her 1992 world cruise. She was sailing west along Vineyard Sound off the New England coast, bound for New York. Shortly before 2200 on August 7, while passing south of Cuttyhunk Island, the captain, pilot, and officers on the bridge felt a rumbling, heavy vibration. The ship shook. The captain's first reaction was to think that the ship had struck a floating object or that there was a problem in the engine room. Captain Woodall stopped the ship and ordered some of the crew to emergency stations to inspect for any damage. From other parts of the ship it was reported that the vibration was either less noticable or not even felt. Some passengers seated for dinner noticed a slight discomfort, but it was not enough to stop a group of waiters in the Columbia Restaurant from singing a happy anniversary song to a celebrating couple. There was no panic, and most people were untroubled by the incident. The evening cabaret continued. The musicians played on, and, in the casino, the roulette wheel kept spinning. Meanwhile, information was received on the bridge that there was water in some of the double-bottom tanks that should have been empty. It was then concluded that two freshwater tanks, one saltwater ballast tank, and an empty fuel tank had been breached. Calculations established that the stability of the ship was not in any danger, and that any ingress of water could be taken care of with the water ballast pumps. The captain notified the coast guard by radio, and was told the liner must anchor nearby for further investigation until the coast guard was satisfied that there was no danger to passengers or a threat of oil pollution to the environment. My brother, Jim, says that local mariners, such as himself, could have advised the captain that running *QE2* fast through the area would have caused enough squat to lower the hull and scrape the bottom.

Tonight, while most passengers watched the nightly entertainment, consisting of Renato Pagliari (billed as an international singing star) and dance champions Chris and Tracey Milburn, seventeen die-hard amateur astronomers and one professional astronomer, Professor Don Kurtz, rendezvoused on Sun deck (also known as Helicopter deck) at 10 PM to stargaze. Stargazing is like sea gazing, but instead of looking at the sea you look at the stars.

Unfortunately, clouds obscured the stars and we saw only Sirius, which is 8.57 light-years away, meaning we are looking back into history and seeing what happened to that star over eight years ago. Besides this remarkable fact, Professor Kurtz explained several other things, like why the moon looks upside down while we are in the Southern Hemisphere. We are upside down looking at the moon from below. In fact, down here they talk of the Rabbit in the Moon, not the Man in the Moon, because upside down, from the Southern Hemisphere point of view, the face of the moon looks like a rabbit. We also learned why the stars rise vertically, or seem to rise vertically, near the equator. We also learned about the phenomenon, as I have already noted, of the sun setting faster in the tropics, and he explained, and I understood for the first time, the phenomenon of the green flash.

Want to know about such things? Take the next world cruise.

SIC TRANSIT GLORIA MUNDI

In accordance with my new policy of fun and frolic, I spent the morning loafing. The hot tub and the pool alternated in pleasuring me until the sky turned black and it started to rain. People fled the open deck as if it were the end of the world. Not me. I jumped in the pool and two German men followed. The storm worsened. The sea got rough. The pool got rougher with white caps and foam all over the place. Large amounts of water spilled over the aft starboard corner of the pool. Then it poured. Very little of the rain is getting me wet because most of me is submerged in the pool.

Wow! The rain is cold. It woke me up and it woke everyone else. The deck has cleared, so there are just we three men in the pool, having a grand old time amid the teeming rain and the pool water sloshing this way and that. The wind began to blow and we all got salty sea spray flung in our faces and spume blown up our noses. One of the Germans yelled something I didn't understand, but the way he said it, I knew he was

425

having the time of his life. Me too. The rain intensified. It's midday, but it looks like night. Maybe they're right: it is the end of the world. But if it is, that's the way I want to die, having fun.

I shouted to the Germans, "Don't worry. We're waterproof." They laughed. But I knew they didn't understand. Correction—they didn't understand the words, but they understood my emotional message, my elation. They understood the spirit, the joy and pleasure of swimming in the rain.

A flash of lightning! I examined the sky critically. I'm waterproof, but I'm not lightning proof. The sky that projected aft of Sun deck looked jet black except when fierce bolts of lightning crackled out of the clouds. Boom! The thunder followed, right after the flash. It's real close, so close I smelled the ozone. Between flashes, with the stygian darkness, the swirling wind, the torrential rain, and the sea foam splashing in my eyes, I can't see much. The Germans have the same problem. For an instant, they looked concerned, but shrugged their shoulders. They have been under fire before. Me too. We just keep splashing, trying to stay afloat.

I resolve to get out of the pool as soon as the lightning strikes something on the back of the ship. Otherwise I'm not leaving. I'm having too much fun. I started singing "Singing in the Rain," except I substituted the word *swimming* for *singing*.

The Germans sang too; they sang off key, but, amazingly, they knew the tune and the words. Suddenly, the rain stopped. The wind blew from the other direction. *QE2* had achieved frontal passage. Almost instantly, the sky cleared with patches of blue showing through. Within five minutes, the sun shone brightly. But the other passengers stayed hidden. Do they fear the wet deck? Do they think the lightning will return? Or more likely, did they go for drinks in the Chart Room or the Crystal Bar? Not a bad idea. My German friends and I ordered some single-malt *QE2* presentation scotch from the deck steward and enjoy them while we have One deck, the pool, and the hot tubs all to ourselves under the blue sheltering sky.

Back in cabin 1041 I stared at myself in the mirror. I lectured the image. "You're addicted. You may as well feed your addiction. Your only hope is to work off the stuff gradually."

So I fed my addiction. I went to the lecture about UFOs.

Professor Kurtz told us up front that he doesn't believe in UFOs. He thinks that they are just a big hoax. Yet, he told us that four million Americans swear that they have been kidnapped by UFOs. And most of those people swear that they, in the process, have been sexually abused. (Although impressive, this number *is less* than the 6,408,206 Americans who have seen and talked with angels.) Conclusion: there may be more angels out there than UFOs.

Given Professor Kurtz's skepticism, I decided not to tell him that my personal abduction concerned Venusians who captured me and took me into their vagina-shaped spacecraft where seventeen of them, all looking exactly like Marilyn Monroe in her prime, forced me to have sex over and over and over again.

Tonight in Queens Grill, we have Irish foods. I ate positively the best corn beef and cabbage I have ever eaten. It's hard to imagine that it is possible to make something so humble and so lowly so good, but the *QE2* chefs did. Simon, our wine steward, suggested a Bushmill Irish whiskey to go with the corn beef. Anything alcoholic is a good idea, but I knew if I drank Old Bush, Colum wouldn't like it. Bushmill, although you would never know it from reading the label, comes from United Kingdom–controlled northern Ireland, and Colum comes from Dublin in the republic.

To avoid political conflict I ordered a Paddy's, but they don't have it onboard, so I settled for a big stiff John Jameson, made in Bow Street, Dublin (pronounced by Colum as *Doo-blin*). I added a spoonful of water to the potent drink to bring out the flavors and to prove to Simon and Colum and Nick and Alex and David that I am a temperate man. But when that one was finished, I realized that I had not been fair to Simon who is, after all, British. Simon needed to be appeased. So I ordered a Bushmill and made Simon promise, as part of the professionalism of his position, not to tell Colum that I drank the "creature" produced in Belfast.

I confess that I have a great affection for strong drink, but lest you believe that I drink too much, please be informed that I do have a personal rule to control my intake: I never drink more than I can lift.

The following message, received from the New York office, interrupted dinner:

"After assessing *Sagafjord* in Subic Bay, following the engine room fire she sustained on 26th February, 1996, we have decided to bring this date forward and withdraw *Sagafjord* from service with immediate effect. . . . Many of you have very happy memories of cruising onboard this fine ship and will be saddened to learn of her earlier than anticipated withdrawal from service."

It doesn't take much to kill a ship. One fire and *Sagafjord* is dead. Let's take a morbid look at the deaths of some of the other great ships:

Titanic—with a three-hundred-feet gash in her hull, sank in less than three hours on April 15, 1912, on her maiden voyage after hitting an iceberg in the North Atlantic.

Normandie—the world's largest ship—on February 9, 1942, sparks from an acetylene torch ignited a bunch of life jackets and mattresses. The fire spread rapidly, destroying a good part of the ship, but the total destruction was the result of firefighting equipment because numerous tugs, fireboats, and land-based firetrucks pumped tons of water onto the burning hull, causing *Normandie* to capsize. Twenty months and $5 million later, the uprighted ship sold to the scrappers for a mere $161,000.

Caronia—the Green Goddess, also known as the millionaire's ship, while under tow during a storm to a Chinese scrap yard, wrecked and sank off the coast of Guam.

The first *Queen Elizabeth*—became a floating attraction in Port Everglades, Florida, a business that ultimately collapsed, allowing C. Y. Tung, a Hong Kong shipping magnate, to buy *QE1*. Tung's intention to renovate and refurbish her as a floating university was nearly complete when a mysterious fire broke out on January 9, 1972. The giant liner turned on her side, burned for days in Hong Kong harbor, and became a total loss.

Queen Mary—now reportedly for sale, transformed herself into a floating hotel in Long Beach, California.

Lusitania—in her time the largest ship afloat (launched in 1907 at 31,550 tons), remains one of the most famous of all Cunarders. After eight years of commercial service, she was torpedoed on May 7, 1915, off the Irish coast. She went down in eighteen minutes with 1,198 souls aboard.

Sic transit gloria mundi.

AND WHAT DO ZULU WIVES DO *for* YOU? THEY MAKE BEER

Some passengers who got up early saw the helicopter land on the Sun deck. Customs agents and the harbor pilot got out and the chopper took off. Captain John Burton-Hall had ordered the deck cleared of people and things because last time some cushions or something got sucked up into the engines and the helicopter couldn't take off again. Those who got up early also saw the release of thousands of blue helium balloons. They also saw the scuffle between *QE2* and the *Island Princess*. The *Princess* beat us to port, but, since we had reserved the berth before she did, *Island Princess* had to stand aside while *QE2* pulled in ahead. Rumor had it the captain of *Island Princess* didn't like the idea.

Ethel and I walked down the gangway to the greeting of a seventeen-piece orchestra playing "When the Saints Come Marching In." The musicians are all black, except the leader.

Alex (not our Alex from Queens Grill, another Alex) guided us through the countryside along modern roads lined with wind-maimed trees, north to Shakaland in KwaZulu-Natal territory. He said that we are lucky. "Because the perpetrators have to work during the week, most of the Zulu violence occurs on weekends." Politicians on both sides are the major targets. So far no tourists have been killed. This past weekend another politician bit the dust. "The human violence is nothing," said Alex. "More people have been killed this year by flash floods. Some flash floods had crests of nine meters. As usual, the poor took the brunt of nature's fury. They are the ones who build along the river banks their shacks of wood and tin and waddle and mud."

Harsh nature proves Africa a cruel continent. And talking about cruel: We passed by the Shark Board, a government organization that tries to control the sharks. The sharks can go ninety kilometers upstream and take a man in pretty fresh water. The Shark Board deploys four hundred nets along the coast to keep the sharks out and the surfers in. The problem is magnified during the annual sardine run, when millions of sardines make their way along the coast, followed by the game fish that eat the sardines, followed by the sharks that eat the game fish.

Miles and miles of sugar cane, the crop that saved the Natal economy, passed by just as corn would pass for miles upon miles if we were riding through Kansas. Alex said there are many market gardens here, and so there are. The soil looks black and rich. The gardens belong to the Indians whose ancestors came to work the sugar cane plantations. Indentured for four years, they broke their backs to earn (in the 1860s) ten shillings a month. And after their labors, they were offered free trips home. Most didn't leave.

Anyone not white in the old Union of South Africa was considered coloured, including the Indians. True, the Indians had one of the three houses of parliament—one for Indians, one for people of mixed blood (coloured), and one for whites. Indians might consider themselves a little better off than the Kaffirs (a contemptuous term for blacks), who had no parliament whatsoever.

In 1893 Gandhi (an attorney at the time) was forced out of the first-class section of the railroad at Pietermaritzburg. That treatment led him to choose a life of fighting for the rights of others, based on a technique called civil disobedience, which he learned by reading an essay by Henry David Thoreau. Thomas Jefferson said, "The government is best which governs least." Thoreau said, "That government is best which governs not at all." The essay "Civil Disobedience" had a tremendous effect on oppressed people the world over. Not only was it the major document used by Gandhi in the struggle for Indian independence, but also, half a century later, Dr. Martin Luther King Jr. used it as the handbook of the American civil rights movement. In 1962 the Reverend Trevor Bush, fighting apartheid in South Africa, noted, "Thoreau's influence in South Africa has been extremely important in our struggle to win rights for the oppressed nonwhite population of our country." All that's part of the past since April 1994, when the whites voted apartheid out of existence. One could argue that the vote constituted a mere formality since the system of apartheid rendered government impossible, with its Pass laws, the Group Areas Act (each of the four racial groups—black, white, Indian, and coloured—had to live in designated areas of each village, town, city, and dorp), the Riotous Assemblies Act, and so on.

You see, the blacks got tired of the post office opening envelopes addressed to newspapers. They got tired of the secret police and of the *sjambok*, a special whip, and of the plastic bag over the head, the heavy boot on the spine, and, in the more sophisticated cities, of the electric shocks. So the blacks got AK-47s to make some points about their problems, and when the AKs didn't do it, they used UZI .45 submachine guns, Belgian FALs, limpet mines, SAM missiles, and CD cluster bombs. Now the African National Congress (ANC) has discovered that power is like freedom. You must fight for it every day. And so the ANC, not the whites, now fight the Zulu.

Nothing is new to those who know history. The violence in Zululand is usual, for theirs is a bloody culture. The Zulus made war on the English in 1879 after the English provoked them. Bitter fighting resulted in massive deaths on both sides. The Zulu traditionally mopped up their enemies by killing the defeated tribe's women and children and goats and chickens. The cattle, the major form of Zulu wealth, they herded off. The English got the same treatment when defeated, and strangely the Zulus got the same treatment from the English. When the English won a battle, the Zulu wounded were killed and gutted in traditional native fashion to free those Zulu souls to go somewhere. I wonder where they went and how gutting got them to that place faster.

In 1870 only five to six thousand Zulus were left, but now they number over six million, 14 percent of the population of South Africa.

Alex likes the Zulus. I can tell by the way he praised their bravery in battle: "Zulu war technique is very thorough and very professional." Some things he doesn't like: "The national flower of South Africa is the Protea; the national flower of Kwazulu is the plastic bag."

Alex droned on about one battle after another that took place in these hills. But the evidence of any battle is slight, a few markers on the side of the road. The grass has covered all. The passengers ask the conductor, "What place is this. Where are we now?"

I am the only *QE2*er awake listening to all of this. Ethel, at my side, has drifted off. I can tell by the way the Japanese couple in front of us have their heads lolling on their chests that they sleep also. A glance in back and to the side shows the couples in those seats asleep as well. Too bad. They missed the story about John Donne, the white man who became a Zulu chief, sort of like Kurtz in the *Heart of Darkness* by Joseph Conrad. John Donne had 49 wives and 117 children.

Shakaland is actually a collection of beehive huts that were once the set for a TV movie on the Zulu. Instead of demolishing everything, they converted it into a tourist attraction and a Protea Hotel, which consists of a bunch of huts. Each hut has a very un-Zulu larger-than-life-sized bed, the kind that can be purchased only in America, and a toilet, a small refrigerator, a VCR, and so on. Despite all that, the hut gives the feel of Africa and helps a Western visitor adjust to a situation, which under less happy circumstances would be intolerable.

The cars in the parking lot, incidentally, don't belong to the tourists. The Zulu own them. After their dance, they hop in their cars and head home.

Although the facility looked fake, the people are not, and Blessing, a real Zulu, showed us around. We learned about the many-wives concept. Blessing thinks it's a great idea because there is a surplus of women. The wives cook and clean for the husband while the husband provides for the wives. Right now the bride price is eleven cows, higher than in Kenya where it is two cows—three if the woman in question could make good beer. Since a cow costs 800 rands, a Zulu wife costs 8,800 rands, or $2,444. Considering that the Zulu current annual income averages less than $100, I concluded the Zulu value women highly. Of course, that's only the purchase price. Maintenance runs more. And what do Zulu wives do for you?

They make beer. That is their one supremely important mission in life. Blessing showed us the chief's number one wife making beer. The beer ferments overnight in large oven-glazed clay pots. In the morning, the wife strains the stuff through a reed mat and it's ready to drink. At the beer drinking ceremony, the head wife drank first to prove the beer was not poisoned. Then the chief tasted it for quality. He approved the beer and praised the quality. With a nod of his head he gave permission for the head wife to pass the beer around. The QE2ers don't like the idea of drinking from the same gourd, but, to be polite, a few do. Me too.

There must be some mistake. This beer tastes wretched. If the chief thought that this was great quality beer, he would just love Pabst Blue Ribbon. Because the beer is a sacred thing, number one wife insisted that all men uncover their heads when drinking the beer. The religion of South Africa is rugby, but the religion of the Zulu is beer drinking. I hope I don't get sick, but I know it is likely that I will, having seen the truly vile sanitation used. Fortunately, the beer spilled on Ethel and she didn't have to drink it. It looked like white-beaded vomit as it caked on her Bermuda shorts.

At lunch, the sanitation also wasn't up to snuff. I asked for corn and the woman picked it right out of the pot with her dirty hands. She's married. I can tell. Among the Zulu, married women wear red hats and cover their breasts. The unmarried women wear headbands made of brightly colored beads and don't cover their breasts—a form of advertising.

Next, we have to inhale the smoke of burning heather. This is supposed to do something for us, help us contact the gods, but it mainly made our eyes water. We coughed. The assistant witch, a young woman covered with white sandstone and bare breasted, put her whole face in the thick smoke. She inhaled deeply and shook her head in ecstasy. Inhaling smoke, as it is among the American Indians and among over one hundred million American cigarette smokers, is serious business.

The Zulu dancers looked genuine, and their dance, like that of the Samburu, came right out of the Stone Age. The Zulu let only the unmarried women dance. I like the way those bare breasts shake like bags of jelly—nice effect. We should try it at home at garden parties and barbecues.

Zulu culture: Only the men sit on the sofa, the women on the dung floor. Men go first into the restaurant to clear the way of danger. They carry their *assegai* (an iron-tipped spear weighing two pounds) while the women carry the babies, water, food, and so on. Zulus never arrive on time. They talk loudly. If invited to a party, they show up with six uninvited friends. Zulu men have no problem requesting leave to attend their mothers' funeral three years in a row; they shake thumb to hand, not hand to hand; and they call the greeting to the chief, "Bayete Ndlovu! (Hail, oh great elephant)," not the more informal "Sawubona, Bhuti? (How's it brother?)" The Zulu maintain their own prejudices: they call the whites ice people; whereas they consider themselves sun people. Here's what they say about whites: "Listen, if your ancestors spent half the year with the earth so frozen you had to work, work, work to keep from starving during winter, you would be crazy too."

On the way back to *QE2* we took a short tour of town. Durban, South Africa, looked like Brisbane, Australia, and doesn't look like Mombasa. Ten years from now when the Africans fully take charge the scenery will change. Mombasa went downhill. Durban will do the same. Even now, while whites and blacks still share power, Alex says things have deteriorated. Many more people are on the street selling things. The crime rate has skyrocketed.

Guess what? The plans for the Toronto post office got forwarded here and vice versa. So Durban's post office has a roof that can withstand five meters of snow and Toronto has a post office whose roof, during its first winter, collapsed. Waldemar told us the same story about the Brisbane post office. Could that have happened twice?

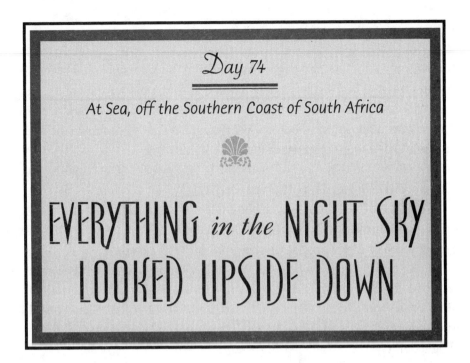

Day 74

At Sea, off the Southern Coast of South Africa

EVERYTHING in the NIGHT SKY LOOKED UPSIDE DOWN

Today we moved from 1041 up to the penthouse 8184. We decided to talk to Geoffrey, the penthouse butler, and to Val, our present stewardess, to make sure things went right.

Geoffrey said we should pack everything except what's in the closets and then "give us a whistle."

I decided to test his mettle. "Geoffrey, you'll find lying on the floor in our old cabin a black lady that I picked up at dockside in Mombasa. I'm afraid she's in no shape to walk herself up here. You'll need two men to carry her up."

Unperturbed, Geoffrey turned from fixing the curtain on one of our two picture windows, a smile on his face. "Right! We'll handle her, sir!"

Geoffrey was glad we were coming to him. Val, on the other hand, was sad that we were leaving her. She tried to hold on to us with some interesting conversation about the port, the weather, the prior world cruises she experienced, and a discussion of a few of the current passengers she takes care of. One woman, for instance, stays in bed all the time and will not eat. This passenger has stayed in the ship's hospital twice so far this trip and had just left a hospital in California before she got on. Val said this bedfast woman refuses to tell the doctors what's wrong or why she had been hospitalized before. Val thought, "That's not fair to the doctors who have to go on what amounts to guesswork."

I assured Val that most of medicine is guesswork: "Don't worry Val. The doctors can handle it. They're used to it."

Another of Val's charges spends her days and nights in her room, taking all her meals there. Val said she sleeps at odd hours so it's hard to figure when to clean up. "Does she go to port?" I asked.

"No, but one night when she got an invitation to dine with the captain she left the room. She stayed only for cocktails and came back to dine in the room again. This is her sixteenth world cruise. She probably has seen it all." Because the woman's behavior resembles that of Phileas Fogg, Jules Verne's character in *Around the World in Eighty Days*, I wondered if this woman was British.

"No," said Val. "She's American—from California."

"California. Oh, right! That explains it."

And then there is that British couple (Lord and Lady ——) who have separate, adjourning rooms. Val offered to open the connecting door, but neither one of them wanted that. Some mornings Lord —— will go out and next door, knock on the door, and ask his wife what she planned for the day. If he likes the plan, he sticks with her. If he doesn't, he doesn't.

"Yes," said Val. "Sometimes, especially in England, marriage is really a matter of convenience. But for me, what's the sense of being married if you don't sleep together?"

And Val has a passenger with Alzheimer's disease. The guy doesn't know Val from one minute to the next, even though she repeatedly tells him her name and repeatedly shows him her gold badge with her name printed on it in bold black letters. "I have to order his meals for him. Otherwise, he won't eat. Sometimes I get him up to the dining room and tell the waiter to order for him and make sure he eats something. Bless his heart. It's not his fault. But I do blame the woman who came with him. His daughter hired her to look after him. As soon as the ship sailed, the woman announced that she was going to cruise and we haven't seen her since."

"There's hope." I told Val about Herman, who has made a remarkable recovery. Herman now looks ten years younger and walks around the deck with a purpose. The other day, I even held a reasonable conversation with him about the weather.

After lunch, we went to 8184. As if by magic, all our bags stand there. Our clothes have been neatly hung in separate closets, one closet for Ethel and one for me, and each as large as M5. My black girlfriend lay unconscious on the floor behind the blue sofa. This new stateroom represents the ultimate in comfort aboard, except perhaps for the double-decker suites, Queen Mary and Queen Anne. P.J., our cat, would love this place. The room has a sofa and a table with three chairs in the sitting space. P.J. would try all the chairs and the sofa and curl up on the most comfortable one. Or P.J. would lie on the sill of one of our two picture windows from which we see the sea stretching out before us for seven miles, a figure I arrived at knowing the height of the Sun deck above sea level and the diameter of the Earth and the principles of tangential geometry. I'll describe the penthouse when and if I have the time. Right now I wanted to do my laps in the outdoor pool on One deck.

Ethel didn't like the idea of my going around the penthouse hallway in my bathing suit. "What will Geoffrey say?"

"He'll say nothing, of course. Remember he's a gentleman."

"OK. What will Geoffrey think?"

I headed down to the open decks and the pool in my bathing suit. A nippy wind blew down from the north. It's so cold it looked like the passengers have deserted the ship: no one occupied the chairs on Boat deck, nor was there even one hardy soul on the Sun deck, Sports deck, or One deck. I have the decks to myself. I am master now.

The hot tub felt gelid so I can't go in, but the big pool has retained tropical heat and a smoky mist rose into the cold air, giving me the feeling that I am bathing in some thermal spring in Rotorua, New Zealand, or Hot Springs, Arkansas, or the baths of Cuomo in Puerto Rico. Now you know my personal failing. If I were in reach of a pool, a river, or the sea, I would swim in all weathers in all countries. I can still run a mile too. But I am as discreet as an actress about my age.

When I returned to 8184, I saw that Geoffrey placed canapés on the table, some of them with salmon. P.J. would like that too. I brushed the crumbs from my lap and got up to dress for dinner.

We needed more electrical outlets. Paul, our other penthouse butler, got an extension cord for us and showed us an American-style plug hidden behind the blue and white curtains. Paul said I can plug my electric tooth-brush into the bathroom socket for shavers. He knows because that's what he does. Full contentment with our new room—new view, new status, and new staff follows. Heaven exists. This is it, this is it, this is it.

We skipped the entertainment and not because it isn't good. We know it's great, but we just don't go for things like that. Instead, we attended stargazing on the Sun deck. Captain John Burton-Hall has put out the ship's lights so Professor Kurtz and the group, about thirty strong, can see the stars better. Everything in the night sky looked upside down because, by Northern Hemisphere standards, it is. The night was clear and the stars remarkably beautiful. Just think, everyone of the billion billion trillion atoms in us came from a celestial inferno, a star. In a very real sense we are children of the stars.

For the first time in my life I clearly saw the Milky Way. I understood the relationship of the Milky Way to the orbiting Magellanic Cloud (named after the first and most famous world-cruise enthusiast, Ferdinand Magellan) and I got the meaning behind the dark blobs in the center of our galaxy: they are giant dust clouds composed of gases and debris, measuring hundreds of thousands of light-years across and casting a long shadow our way. When we look at them, we look back into history 107,000 years, when the light from those stars started its journey toward Earth. Professor Kurtz pointed out the Southern Cross and showed us how to determine true south by following the long axis to the southern pole star. I see the stars slowing, rising and falling, rotating around this point, and I finally understood that Earth's rotation makes the stars seem to rotate, except the ones lined up with the two polar regions of Earth. They seem fixed.

God! I am an ignorant man. What else don't I know? Our experience today seemed perfect. But I know it was not perfect. It couldn't have been perfect. Life is not perfect. And it was life.

Cape Town, South Africa

HERMAN WIPED HIS GLASSES SO THAT HE COULD SEE EVERYTHING THAT DEBBIE HAD *to* SHOW

A fifteen-piece band, and twice that number of what looked like Dallas Cowboy cheerleaders complete with pom-poms, white and purple fur hats, and Nancy Sinatra marching boots, greeted the *QE2* playing "Down by the Riverside" and "Hello, Dolly."

For reasons known only to God and perhaps God's representative on *QE2*, Captain John Burton-Hall, the ship had a twenty-three–degree list to starboard and stayed that way all day. Ethel and I felt like we walked into the funhouse at the amusement park, with the hollow blue penthouse hallway bending to amuse us, turning our world slightly aslant and making us think.

439

Think? About what? About the precarious nature of things.

Out on deck we saw in the distance, rising above the city, a flat-topped Table Mountain. Sometimes this mountain, during a sharp southern wind, develops a fine gossamer cloud that covers the top and drapes over the side—the tablecloth.

What country of the world has three capitals? You guessed it. South Africa. Cape Town is the legislative capital. Pretoria is the administrative capital. Bloemfontein is the judicial capital, although there is a move afoot to change that.

Before we left the ship for the morning tour, Captain John Burton-Hall announced a change in departure times: *QE2* will leave Cape Town tomorrow at noon and not at 2 PM, as previously scheduled. He explained that the day we were to arrive in Rio was a holiday, so we have to depart early to get there earlier. That didn't sound right. Something else made him change the schedule. What? Tonight at dinner, we'll ask Alex.

We rode through the countryside with Barry, our guide, a happy sort of fellow. He smokes kif or kef or whatever they call Indian hemp here. I smelled it on him. It's like marijuana, but stronger.

Proteas lined the road, sometimes growing wild, but more often growing in gardens. There are over four hundred varieties of this flower. Proteas are so beautiful, have such vibrant colors, and are so big, I wanted to grow them at home. Besides, they look good enough to eat. In fact, in the Middle Ages most flowers were cultivated not for their beauty, but for their nutritional content. What would a Protea taste like?

I told Ethel, "Keep a sharp eye out for seeds, particularly for the largest variety, *Protea magnifica* (*barbigera*, also know as the woolly bearded Protea, or Queen), which has a large white furry center with a black spot the diameter of a marble and is surrounded by three tiers of red petals, each with a white furry border embroidered on them." Actually, I would have settled for *Protea cynaroides* (the King or Giant) with a large white disk surrounded by flame-shaped red, yellow, and green petals.

The bus stopped at the Afrikaans Language Monument. The new flag of the Republic of South Africa, the one selected after multiple suggestions from the public, flew overhead. It's beautiful and unusual: a black triangle on the staff side with a yellow fringe and many other colors. The colors refer to aspects of South Africa: the blue for the sky, the green for the vegetation, white for peace, red for the bloodshed for freedom, and black for—you can tell.

Seeing that flag reminded me of Nadine Gordimer's description of the first time it flew: "We watched the flag slowly climb, still in its pupa folds, a crumpled wing emerging, and it writhes one last time and flares wide in the wind, is smoothed taut by the fist of the wind, the flag of South Africa."

Alex told me I was politically incorrect because the flag pin I had worn in the Queens Grill was the flag of the old regime. Wearing the old flag, an unprepossessing collection of three horizontal stripes, from the top down—orange, white, and blue—made me look like a reactionary.

The gift store at the Afrikaans monument has flag pins with the new flag. I bought one. Tonight I shall be politically correct. The paper that comes with the new flag pin said, "South Africa—the Republic's new flag is ethnic in design and concept and heralds an era of optimism, progress, and peace for all its varied race groups." Wouldn't it be nice if that were true?

Roughly in the center of the Afrikaans Language Monument there is a hillock or acropolis, consisting of clusters of round granite rocks. These rocks, some with rounded tops, others with fissures and clefts, look like they are part of the oldest landmass on this planet, which, incidentally, they are. They resemble small replicas of Paarl Rock, the nearby massive rock formation, which usually glistens like a pearl as the early morning light hits the morning dew. Looking out from this great height to the valley below and then across to the granite mountains across the way, I realized the landscape looks like Greece. South Africa is as far south of the equator as the Mediterranean is north of the equator. Therefore the climate here and that of Greece should be roughly the same. If that's true, then the weather should be right to grow grapes and produce some reasonable wines. It is.

Next stop, the KWV, the largest wine cooperative in the world. Here we listened to the usual speeches about grapes and vines and how the wines are made and stored. They told us that wine can be a multisense experience: taste, smell, sight, and touch. "But what about hearing?" I asked. "You left that out."

"Clink your glasses and give a toast."

I did, "To big ships, and big dreams." My auditory sense is satisfied. They store the wine in imported oak, because in South Africa domestic oak grows year-round and thus ends up too porous to hold the wine. They showed us massive oak vats that they call by strange names: Big Bill (an oak cask), no relation to Bill Clinton; Mrs. Bill next to him, no relation to Hillary Clinton; and baby Hillary (a small cask), no relation to Chelsea. Talking about the Clintons reminds me that America is usually the country with the biggest and the best of everything. But here that isn't true. Here they have the biggest vats assembled in the world. I counted five of them, and each, I am told and do in part believe, holds 207,302 liters of wine. That means I could show up every day for seventy years and get three liters of wine to drink and still have 130,652 liters left in the vat.

"Forget it," said Ethel. "If you drank three liters of wine on day one, you would be still asleep on day two."

We learned all about making ports and sherries. By now, I knew the process by heart. Especially the twin processes to make sherry. But if you think I'm going to waste my time telling you about stuff like that, forget it.

At lunch, I ate with our driver and with Barry, our guide. Barry isn't touching his food and barely drank his wine. He had gout last week, and he couldn't touch, much less walk, on his right big toe. He has just partially recovered. The way he talked I gathered he fears gout more than cancer.

Birene, an old Brit with a twinkle in her eyes and an energetic voice, sat next to Barry and told us her tale of woe. She crossed the Atlantic on *QE2* during the shakedown voyage last year, a voyage now dubbed the cruise from hell. "Passengers slept on the chairs in Queens Lounge for several nights. The pools were filled with junk. They kept *QE2* at sea, because it couldn't meet safety and health standards. There we were, circling about the North Atlantic while the crew tried to get the ship into shipshape."

While *QE2* circled, Birene fell and got a concussion. The doctor sent the bill to Cunard. As expected, the Americans, unhappy with their cruise, did what the Americans usually do. They sued. The case will come up shortly. Birene didn't sue. She accepted cruise miles for her trouble and now she finds herself back again for another try. "Everyone got sacked," said she, as she sipped her cream of wild mushroom soup. "The Germans went home and five hundred Englishmen came aboard to get things fixed. The first voyage after a maiden voyage can be an adventure."

"Did the toilets flush?" I asked.

Birene smiled, "Yes, but the water was black."

Back at the ship, we're listing more, about thirty degrees. Alex didn't know why, but Ethel and I thought it was kind of fun. "We could skate downhill from one end of our room to the other."

"Ask Geoffrey to get you some skates."

Alex suggested that there is another reason that we will leave early tomorrow: money. Alex thought South Africa's money-starved new government raised the port fees and Cunard decided to take off.

Somehow Alex and I got into a discussion about death. I explained that death was blackness, nothing but pure terrible blackness that went on and on and never ended until the end of the world. At least I thought it was. Naturally, since I had never been dead, it was hard to be sure.

Alex said he knew a surefire way to determine if I were dead.

"How's that?" I inquired.

"The best test would be to wave a plate of steak Diane, Château Talbot, plus a glass full of Glenmorangie twenty-year-old single-malt scotch before your nose when you are in your coffin. If a breath of life were left in you, you would sit up and eat and drink. But if you smelled the steak and the wine and the scotch and did not stir, then they could just nail down the coffin lid and be certain that you were truly dead."

"Great wisdom!" Ethel affirmed. "Sex and money he can take or leave, but when it comes to food, he would kill."

I took a long pull on my Château Mouton Cadet and said, "Alex, from now on, you're my factotum too. You and Nick can order for me. Both of you understand me."

The show tonight, entitled "Cape Carnival Folk Show and the South African Woolens Fashion Show," like in ancient Gaul, was divided into three parts. Part one was a fashion show, displaying an original white satin Muslim wedding gown that had a bunched amount of material in the front, reflecting the overall pattern of the woman's silhouette. Part two, even better, a statuesque tanned woman in her twenties named Debbie who held the title Miss Bikini of South Africa. Debbie, wearing lots of gold jewelry and not much of anything else, strutted around the stage, gyrating her bottom, and puffing out her rather ample chest, proving conclusively that she deserved her title. The total cloth used in the bikini was less than one-tenth of a square meter and about one-millionth the amount used in the Muslim wedding gown. Debbie came down into the audience to give us a close-up view. The other men and I roared our approval. Even Herman was impressed. Herman wiped his glasses so that he could see everything that Debbie had to show. Yes, Herman, our demented Herman, now indulged in perverse pagan pleasures, nasty, lowdown, and dirty. Part three of the program, unique in its own rank, included Muslim singers and dancers in weird and beautiful suits of green and yellow. The audience joined hands with them and sang "Auld Lang Syne." For one brief moment things were as they ought to be. We were at peace with Islam. Everyone was happy.

Day 76

Cape Town, South Africa

BOTH THESE LADIES ARE HOT, VERY HOT

*G*eoffrey, our butler, advised us to take the shuttle to the waterfront shopping mall. We did because no one would ignore Geoffrey's advice.

Heard on the shuttle bus: "Ask Larry about that. Peter doesn't know anything."

"Who's Larry?"

"You know, the fat one." Thus do the passengers identify crewmembers. I wonder if the crew does the same to us.

At the waterfront, we found the Victoria and Albert Hotel, a marvelous three-story white and gray-blue colonial-style Victorian relic that could easily pass for a museum. It reminded me of the Raffles in Singapore with its air of faded Victorian gentility. We can't stop at the hotel bar that over looks this picturesque harbor, and we can't stop at the marine museum. We don't have the time. Instead we headed into the market.

Here the lottery prize is two million rands, about $56,000. Perhaps I can develop a new theory of estimating the wealth of a country by finding out what the people think represents a large sum of money. In South Africa the sum amounts to five times what it amounted to in the Seychelles, which, in turn, exceeded the top prize in Indonesia.

Talking about money: I changed $60 at American Express. They gave me 3.8 rands to the dollar, .2 more than Travelex onboard. The change man wanted to know why I didn't change my money onboard *QE2*. As usual, I really can't explain. "Laziness," I said. "Simple laziness." And you know what, that explains a lot of what I do, that and simple ignorance. The American Express man informed me that yesterday in Cape Town *QE2* passengers spent over a million dollars and the ship itself took on three million dollars worth of provisions.

"Hey, look at this. The money has elephants on it," I said to Ethel as I handed her a red twenty-rand note. The twenty has a momma, a papa, and a baby elephant, and a big picture of an African elephant. Even better, the fifty-rand note has lions—a momma and two cubs drinking from a stream. A big daddy lion with a full mane stares intelligently and contentedly out at us. He has eaten. I can tell. The ten-rand note has a green rhino with two horns, and a mother and daughter in the background with the enlarged face of papa in the foreground.

Ethel and I inspected the supermarket. They have bunches of Protea for sale for 17.5 rands and quinces (Cydonian apples) for one rand each, and ostrich filet for 7.5 rands to the pound. You don't see that in the States. Nor do you see the vast collection of frozen foods for cats and dogs. Yes, for cats they have tripe and chicken livers, whole lamb livers, steak and kidney pasta, beef, and turkey. The frozen-food–pet-food brand that appears most popular is K-9. And here's another thing you might miss in the States: hundreds of Venus flytraps are on sale for seven rands for a flowerpot full. I love this meat-eating plant and should have brought some back to eat the fruitflies in our room. Actually, the presence of flies in our room doesn't bother me at all. I consider it a good sign that no one has sprayed the hell out of the place. If the flies stay alive, the habitation might be safe for us.

Back on *QE2*, on A stairway, while waiting for the elevator, we met David Thompson, who, as usual, has bought so much junk he has trouble carrying it. He shook his head. "I don't know why I buy all this stuff. My mother will kill me."

I tried to assuage his guilt, "You could perhaps open [notice how I now, in true British fashion, insert a word between the helping verb and the verb proper] a museum."

"A restaurant is more like it. My ambition is to own a restaurant. I'll display my collections from all over the world. I intend to call the restaurant Tables of the World, like the old Mauretania was called."

Without the Venus flytrap, I killed two fruit flies with my hand while waiting for Ethel to finish with the bathroom. "Hurry up," I yelled. "We have work to do."

We headed out to deck to supervise the departure. I handled the letting go of warps from the bollards while Ethel kept her eye on the attachments to the tugs. There's a fog about, so QE2 sounded three times that loud foghorn. Simon, our wine steward, is out here working with us and recording the scene with his video camera. Louis, our friend from Scotland, spotted us on deck with Simon, who as usual wears his wine steward outfit. Louis said, "I see our alcoholic American friends travel with their wine steward."

"Not a bad idea!" I told Louis. "We might hire Simon to follow us around and keep us supplied."

A woman on deck insisted she bought a Coco de mer carving in a Bombay bazaar. Nobody corrected her. She turned to me, "When the ship takes off no one checks to see that your seat belts are fastened." I agreed. Also heard on deck: "People move from one country to another because conditions are so terrible all over." And: "You can observe a lot if you look." And: "It's no exaggeration to say the undecideds could go one way or another."

A few miles offshore, fog completely enveloped QE2. It's eerie. We can see nothing but gray in front, in back, and all around. QE2 sounded its foghorn every few minutes and the landscape of fog and the deep groan of the horn thrilled me. You can't get this at the Hilton. Nor at the Hilton can you get the sway and creak and groan of a ship. QE2 is back in her element—cruising the ocean sea. The fog horns of other ships and boats sounded answers. Their sounds appeared to be various distances away and from the differences in sound must have come from different-sized ships. The small ones, I imagined, have higher pitch and less loud horns. We can't see those ships, but we know they're out there. I hoped we didn't collide. The captain must have that same hope, for he slowed QE2 down. We crept along for seventeen minutes. Then stopped. The best thing to do in a dense fog is to stop and sit. The best thing to do among icebergs is the same. If *Titanic* had stopped the way so many other ships around it had stopped that fatal night, it wouldn't have hit the berg. The berg might have hit it. But nothing would have happened.

Only about thirty sea gulls followed us out of Cape Town Harbor. In the old days when QE2 used to dump the garbage overboard, thousands of gulls would follow the ship in and out of port. In fact, some people said you could tell the quality of a ship's food by the number of gulls. Instead of stars, perhaps, we should use the gull unit to appraise a ship's cuisine. Two thousand gulls might be tops. That reminds me of the ship unit of appraising a woman's beauty, the Helen. If Helen's beauty launched a thousand ships, then the beauty of a woman that could do that would amount to one Helen. These days, however, we might have to resort to measurements in micro-Helens, as the case may be, or fall back to a row-boat standard to accommodate some of the elderly beauties onboard. On the other hand, we have experienced a new influx of rather young South African women who measure and exceed the one Helen standard. Some even rate two or three Helens, like Sally and Mary, the two women I met in the hot tub today.

Sally is a big woman, but well proportioned and sexy. Mary is small but could compete with Debbie for the Miss Bikini title. Both of them are hot, I can tell. They are very hot. Both Sally and Mary worried about the sign on the hot tub that warned, "Those using immune suppressant drugs and those who have immune system difficulties should not use the tub." I assured them, "If you are normal, don't worry."

Sally smiled and gave me the eye. "I am normal," she said. "How about you?"

I have to tell her that I'm married and therefore off limits. "We can be discrete," Sally said.

While I tried to figure who was "we"—she and I, or she and Mary—

Sally looked away and, with her eyes, followed the deck steward (the same who serviced Lonelyhearts) as he crossed to bring some gray-headed woman a drink. I scratched my chin and found myself wondering what it feels like, during intercourse, to be a woman, and whether their pleasure is keener. It must be. Why else would they be pushing so hard? Sally turned her face to me. "Don't use your body as a briefcase to carry yourself around. Use it to live with. Last chance before we go after that deck steward." I shook my head no.

Mary and Sally didn't move. I left the tub.

Sally will connect with some man soon. Mary will connect with some man soon. Since they seemed to work as a pair, perhaps, both will connect to the same man—soon.

5 PM QUICKIE *with the* TENNIS INSTRUCTOR

J finished *The Innocents Abroad.* Toward the end, Mark Twain ran out of things to say, or he was lazy and satisfied, or he had a bad case of homesickness, or cruise fatigue, as the meager entries in his notebook prove. What a stupid thing a notebook gets to be at sea anyway. Please observe his style:

> Friday—Morning, dominoes. Afternoon, dominoes. Evening, promenading the deck. Afterwards, charades.
> Saturday—Morning, dominoes. Afternoon, dominoes. Evening, promenading the decks. Afterwards, dominoes.
> Sunday—Morning service, four bells. Evening service, eight bells. Monotony till midnight. Whereupon, dominoes.
> Monday—Morning, dominoes. Afternoon, dominoes. Evening, promenading the decks. Afterwards, charades and a lecture from Dr. C. Dominoes.

Ethel thought she might have cruise fatigue but she isn't sure. She didn't seem to have any specific symptoms, such as not enjoying dinner or thinking the ship boring, and her notebook has retained its usual sparkle:

Monday—Got up, washed, breakfast, lunch, dinner, show, went to sleep.

Tuesday—Got up, washed, breakfast, lunch, dinner, show, went to sleep.

Wednesday—Got up, washed, breakfast, lunch, dinner, show, went to sleep.

Thursday—Got up, washed, breakfast, lunch, dinner, movie, went to sleep.

Ethel stopped writing today (Friday), discouraged. That may be the prodrome of cruise fatigue. I shall keep her under close observation.

My own account is more personal and more thrilling than Twain's or Ethel's: "We go to breakfast at nine, Lunch at one, Tea at four, have sherry and canapés in our room at seven, dinner at eight."

Geoffrey asked me to review his manuscript *No More Nuts* and to listen to the BBC program on butlers. The program, as usual for this sort of thing, had little or no information. We found out nothing. We learned nothing. The public wants insipid stuff like that and that's what it gets.

No More Nuts is different. It says something. I read the manuscript and decided to mull things over, outlining the theme, the structure, the plot, the characters, the development, and the truth of what Geoffrey wants to communicate. I must do some serious thinking before I offer suggestions.

A book is often a complex thing. Writers like Geoffrey work long and hard trying to get their book right, fashioning out of chaos, in the torment of their souls, something intricate, intelligent, interesting, and occasionally beautiful. A critic of books should exercise the same due diligence in evaluating books as was exercised in creating them. Without a complex analysis, a reasonable conclusion cannot be reached.

The big news in the *British Times* concerns mad cow disease. Ten cases of proven transmission to people occurred according to Professor John Patterson, who added that it is impossible to "put a precise figure on risk." Leading microbiologist Professor Richard Lacey—one of the first to issue dire warnings about the potential dangers of BSE (Bovine Spongiform Encephalopathy, the human brain–disease equivalent of Creutzfeldt-Jakob Disease)—predicted that there would be a rapid rise in the incidence of Creutzfeldt-Jakob Disease (CJD) in Britain. Slaughtering the national cattle herd could cost twenty billion pounds, an awful lot of money, and one doesn't know out of whose pocket it will come. France, Belgium, and Germany have imposed bans on beef from Britain. But Agricultural Minister Douglas Hogg condemned the French move as "quite unnecessary and probably illegal."

I can tell by the way Hogg talks that he is mad. The European commission will take up the matter tomorrow. Meanwhile, Alex assured us that *QE2* uses only American beef.

I will attend five lectures today. One on the Battle of the Wales should give me insight to the problems of Princess Di and Charles, one will be Waldemar on Rio, one will be Brian Price interviewing Waldemar on his life and times, one will be "Do Animals Think?" and the last one will be "Does South Africa Have a Chance to Survive?"

As I headed to the theater, I passed a woman in a wheelchair. She is propped up by a slot machine and is too weak to pull the handle or press the button. Her paid companion, at her direction (the nod of her head), does that for her. The handicapped get no special privileges: she loses just like everyone else, but because she has a go-between, she loses slower.

For South Africa the prognosis looked grim. For Mandela the prognosis looked grim: he has just had a heart transplant. Each month in Soweto 160 murders happen, an equal number of rapes, and about the same number of attempted murders. The murder rate exceeds that of the United States by a factor of six and there is a pretty good chance that some, perhaps most, crimes are not reported. Therefore, if anything, these grim figures represent underestimates. The official death rate from crime is 57 per 100,000, meaning that crime, not cancer or heart disease or stroke, is the most common cause of death in South Africa.

After the lecture (attended by over a hundred South Africans), one person in the audience after another got up to talk about healing the wounds and correcting the mistakes of the past. One man, the owner of a factory employing fifteen hundred, said as if he were communicating some great revelatory truth, "The blacks work just as hard and are fully as capable as the whites." A tourist mentioned that he and his wife traveled around South Africa recently and found in the *dorps* (villages) and the countryside (they avoided the black cities for good reason) nothing but evidence of a peaceful working society. An Afrikaans-speaking farmer got up to say the blacks work well with him. He added that he felt the reason for all the trouble was the British. They left South Africa with a constitution that made apartheid legal. "The fault lay with the British," and no one else. But this farmer did concede that the other part of the problem was the South African police. "Nine-tenths of them spent their time enforcing apartheid. Now that that is over, they don't know how to control real crime. Over half the force has resigned. Those who remain— one quarter are under investigation for corruption."

Desmond Tutu, the Nobel Prize winner, has the job of sorting out the crimes of the past regime and determining what to do about them. His commission possesses extraordinary powers and can, without warrants, break and enter to obtain information. Is this a good idea, replacing one police state by another?

The Battle of the Wales is another thing. The divorce will happen. Di will get the jewelry, a home in the castle, an office, some servants, but she will lose her HRH (Her Royal Highness) title. Di fears the Royal Marriages Act of 1772, which provides that the children may be withdrawn from her. Di has problems, as she told us herself on TV, with bulimia and depression. She likes to make nuisance calls, and, get this, according to the lecturer, Di might be an *oiler*. An oiler? Whatever that is. But her life, like life on a ship, has settled down into a routine. Here's an abstract of Di's personal diary:

9:00	Brush teeth.
10:00	Shield children, especially Prince William, so they have some sort of normal life and don't become crackheads.
11:00	Health club workout, including tennis instructions, followed by private massage.

12:00	Lunch with gal pal, including a quick flirt with the Pakistani heart surgeon in the next booth. Invite him to candlelight dinner.
1:00	Aromatherapy (bring check for 15,000 pounds).
2:00	Visit children's hospital.
3:00	Talk with agent about buying a deserted island.
4:00	High colonics administered by Reeves, the butler.
5:00	Quickie with the tennis instructor.
6:00–8:00	Make crank calls from the coin telephone on the corner (the fun part of the day). Include one to Camilla Parker-Bowles. Tell her that her face bears a close resemblance to a mad cow.
8:00–8:30	Dress for dinner. Wear the diamond tiara.
9:00	Dinner with heart surgeon. Romance after.
11:00	More crank calls, if time permits.

Day 78

At Sea in the South Atlantic

IF ONLY WE'D STOP TRYING *to* BE HAPPY WE COULD HAVE *a* PRETTY GOOD TIME

The seas turned rough last night. Through our picture windows we saw whitecaps and steep swells extending to the horizon. The pitch and roll has downed a few of the passengers. Nowhere near as many as before, for we are all old salts now. Or at least we are salt substitutes. Ethel inquired, "What is an old salt substitute?"

"An ancient mariner, in industry parlance—An old salt is a person who sailed the seas for a living. An old salt substitute is a person substituting for an old salt—a person who sails the seas for pleasure."

Like the sea, the Dow rose and fell and then rose again proving, J. P. Morgan correct. When a reporter asked old J. P. what he predicted for the stock market, he said, "The market will fluctuate." Now that *QE2* has moved further west, closer to the New York Stock Exchange, we get the closing averages much sooner, the day after rather than two days after.

The faster arrival of general information doesn't do me any good. I need specific information about my stocks. But do I really care? I'm afraid not. I am happy as a clam. No care from the outside world can interfere with my bliss. Even if I lost my three million dollars, it would bother me not at all. It's all illusion anyway—maya. The rapid way that values increase and decrease proves that the values are not substantial or real.

Every year, if you are still alive, a birthday comes. Mine came today. I decided not to do anything since I overdosed on the five lectures yesterday. Now that we're short timers, Ethel and I have become quite particular about how we spend our time. We just want to play and have fun and drink and eat.

About eating: I decided that, since I was still gaining weight despite my self-imposed deprivation of not eating desserts at lunch, I would eat whatever and whenever I wished. "The diet wasn't working so why should I do it?"

"You really have a talent for self-deception," Ethel pointed out. "You stopped eating desserts at lunch, but doubled up, at times quadrupled up, on them at dinner."

"Indulgence—for me that's what the remainder of this trip will be all about."

My indulgence began by my eating for breakfast a filet mignon cooked medium rare, plus fried potatoes with onions, grilled tomatoes, and a plate of exotic fruits, which included finger bananas, kiwis, strawberries, blueberries, pineapple, papaya, melon slices (orange and green), and passion fruit. I also drank a glass of fresh-squeezed orange juice and a cup of coffee. Breakfast, often a neglected meal at sea, need not be neglected by the astute passenger. The menu routinely offers anything you can think of, including roast beef. I usually enjoy the fruit plates and maybe a crepe with béarnaise sauce and small Pacific shrimp in it. But some days I'll eat banana pancakes or blueberry pancakes or a toasted bagel with salmon. So far I haven't dared to order the caviar for breakfast. That would be too decadent, even for me. Nor have I ever ordered roast beef. Eight-ounce filet mignons are enough for me.

Talking about beef, I regret to inform you that, according to the cruise news, the report on British beef is not good. The European Commission said, because of the health risks, the bans on British beef were legal. British producers are devastated. Large firms and cooperatives compound the problem by announcing their intentions to boycott British beef and buy beef elsewhere. But is this information reliable? I have my doubts because another error appeared in the cruise news' daily quiz. How would you answer this question? "Who among American presidents had a doctorate?" The quiz answer was "Woodrow Wilson was the only American president with a doctorate." What about President Clinton, who holds a doctorate in law from Yale?

For my birthday Ethel gave me two presents: T-shirts, one blue and the other white, commemorating the world cruise, and a Halcyon Days enamel box with the words inscribed, "It had to be you." The scene glazed on the box's top shows a man and a woman on deck, next to a *QE2* life preserver. The couple is toasting each other with martinis. He wore tails and she dressed as a flapper with a low-cut blue evening dress and darker blue headband. She held her cigarette on a long black holder, away from him and the cocktails, and gazed into his eyes. In the background the painter set the sunset, purple and rose on the horizon with an occasional seagull over head. "It had to be you," words by Gus Kahn and music by Isham Jones. First performed in 1924. That's the way we feel. Romantic and twentyish, uniquely elegant and exclusive. Time—our youth—it never really goes, does it? It is all held in our minds for as long as we want it to live.

The Halcyon Days enamel box touches me. I love to see on that mellow creamy glaze a man and a woman together, toasting their love. The enamel reminds me of a bygone era of fastidious and festive living, when no small domestic need was thought trivial, no personal foible frivolous, and every object played a significant role in the gentle drama of domestic life. A time before TV when people actually felt feelings, had real affections, and knew real emotions. A bygone era that persists in certain eddies and back waters of the modern world—a bygone era that persists, thank God, on *QE2*.

To celebrate my birthday, Nick, Colum, and Simon came to 8184 for sherry and canapés and to admire the black lady. I pointed out the quality of her breasts. All agreed she looked great, but Colum seemed shy. I believe his experience with women limited. Nick said the other Queens Grillers show off their purchases and a war of jealousy goes on every night that we don't know about. "If so," I explained, "the war is over. I own the winning item."

Simon agreed and told me David, the Queens Grill manager, wanted to borrow the lady for exhibit, as a joke of course, as a joke.

I felt strange serving drinks to the waiters who knew so much more about how to do this than I. Simon detected my difficulty and took over. Simon poured sherry for everyone but opened a Perrier for himself. I offered my favorite toast. "To joy, and fresh new days of love." Then I explain that recently I have been thinking of changing my favorite toast: "To big ships and big dreams." Ethel and I sipped sherry as the men told us about their lives.

Colum just answered an ad in the paper and got the job as a waiter on *QE2*. Colum has been here two years, with St. Patrick's Day his anniversary. Nick has been sailing six years. Simon beat them all with eight years at sea. None of them wish to make the sea a career. I get the feeling Nick and Simon will drop out soon to work on land and settle down with wives and, eventually, children.

I'm in a writing mood, so I did a review of Geoffrey's manuscript, *No More Nuts*, and I also made a stock market letter for Alex. The critique went in an envelope with Geoffrey's manuscript. The stock market letter went in a Key Club white envelope labeled: "To: Alex Seymour, From: Santa." I hand delivered both.

After dinner, Ethel and I stumbled back from Queens Grill. Stumbled, I said, because we overdid the soufflés by having eaten two of them, a chocolate and a Grand Marnier, and we overdid the drinks with the sherry and the bottle of Château Lafite Rothschild 1976 and the twenty-year-old single-malt scotch, and the nightcaps of Grand Marnier. As I fumbled with the key to 8184, I heard a cricket chirping its strident mating call.

"A cricket! Good luck in China. The Chinese keep them in diminutive cages in their homes as pets," I said.

I looked down and saw the cricket right there on our penthouse door. I told Ethel about the cricket that I saw today at poolside. "I worried about him. But now that I know there is another cricket onboard *QE2* I feel the poolside cricket might have a chance to find a mate after all. He might, in fact, find his mate right here in our penthouse suite."

Ethel pulled the sleeve of my tux and, smiling, pulled me close to her. She reached her right hand down and grabbed my crotch. "Why not, Big Boy? That's where I found my mate."

At Sea in the South Atlantic on Passage to Rio de Janeiro

OCCASIONALLY I HAVE BEEN KNOWN *to* EAT LUNCH *with* MY CHAUFFEUR. WHY NOT DINE *with the* CAPTAIN?

Q E2 moved north toward the equator and experienced a warm wave. Most passengers haven't registered the weather change so the decks, though quite pleasant, remain deserted. Before doing my laps I warmed up in the hot tub. Just as I was getting up to leave, a young woman dressed in a red bikini strolled across the deck. She was one of those old-time tawdry blondes, with a drink in one hand and a cigarette in the other. She put on the hot tub's edge a plastic cup that had in it her golden light liquid, which looked like ginger ale without the bubbles.

"What?" Miss Red Bikini pointed her cigarette at my chest and exclaimed, her speech slightly slurred. "I've been waiting all week to share the hot tub with you and you're leaving."

"I'll be back. Time for my swim."

But after I did my laps, I changed my mind. Miss Red Bikini was the type that attracted me like a magnet. In ten seconds I knew that I had fallen. But had I fallen for her or for the red bikini or the two necessary props of decadence that she carried, the cigarette and the drink? All those things conjured images in the thin air, insubstantial images of long blonde hair falling onto dimly lit shoulders; white teeth against soft lips, warm and big and red as a cushion; the slope of rounded breasts cupped against my hands; suntanned thighs; and bright gasping orgasms, followed by the faint musky smell, an expensive perfume mixed with a bluish haze of cigarette smoke that hangs over everything like a mist over a lagoon.

All that stirs me strangely. But I know I am merely cunt struck—attention passengers, we are now channeling Henry Miller. Cunt struck! That's all. And I know the cure: I had better leave. Miss Red Bikini, who had watched me the whole time I was swimming, waved with another cigarette in her right hand, a dimpled hand that I wanted to cover with fiery kisses. She shouted across the empty deck, "Where are you going? Come here!"

I pointed to the pool clock indicating I had to go.

"See you tomorrow," she shrieked.

Commotion. The ship abuzz. Today a country fair will take place in the Grand Lounge. The crew is excited too. Multiple signs posted in hallways, elevators, the library, and stairwells announced one thing or another: games of chance, plus crystal ball readings, a haunted house, auctions of Cunard memorabilia, games of quoits and darts, food and surprises, raffles, tombola (a British gambling game resembling Lotto), tug-of-war, and fortune telling. "Don't miss it. Bring plenty of cash."

This annual world-cruise event benefits a preselected charity. The fair is similar to those held each year during the summer months in towns and villages throughout England. This year's recipients will be Children First in Greenock, Scotland, and Zoe's Place (for disabled children) in Liverpool, England. The fair has become a tradition on *QE2*. Over the years hundreds of thousands of dollars have been donated to charity. As part of the fair, five hundred dollars gets you appointed guest chef of *QE2*. That lets you select the menu for tonight and you get your name on that menu recording the fact that you're in charge.

That appealed to me. Despite the fact that it would immortalize my name on the Queens Grill menu, Ethel vetoed the purchase as too expensive when she actually feels it is too ostentatious. I'll have to fish around for something else equally silly to spend my money on.

Our penthouse suite has no hot water and the cold water doesn't look drinkable because it has lots of little black particles in it. Is *QE2* trying to ease the transition from ship to shore by making things for us difficult onboard? Since the water is so bad, I can't take my morning bath. Might as well go play shuffleboard.

Bob saw me around the putting green and shouted, "Well, well, Doc. To what do we owe this great honor?"

I cupped my hands over my mouth and shouted above the whine in the rigging, "No lecture today."

"Lecture? I thought doctors knew everything already. Why attend a lecture?"

"We do know everything." I announced to Bob and the gray heads assembled, some of whom, I note, are holding the stick menacingly, like a Zulu spear. "I go to lectures out of force of habit. I'm addicted, an information junkie."

Bob pressed me into immediate service, organizing the couples into teams and supervising the players. He told me that he misses Nathan. I missed him too. "Meanwhile, Bob, you're stuck with me."

Right away I came up against the problem of cheating. Peter, middle aged with gray hair and barrel chest, bothered me in particular. Peter the cheater.

Very suspicious! Peter slipped the disks away before I got down there to add his score. Then he told me his version of what the score was. One time I turned my back and found Peter adjusting the tally board on the bulkhead. The gall! He put it up twenty points for his team. "What the hell are you doing?" I asked.

"You missed. On the last frame black had a Plus Ten and had pushed yellow into the Ten Off, so my team gets another twenty points."

"Are you sure?" I asked rather lamely, knowing that Nathan would have said, "Cut the shit you goddamn lousy cheat!" Nathan would have charged in there and pushed the score right back to where it belonged. Numerous times the contestants stepped over the line for their shots, giving themselves an advantage. Bob shrugged his shoulders. What can you do? Bob and I consider that a minor, dinky, insignificant sort of honest cheating. It's the dishonest cheating that bothered us. Finally, I put my foot down when Peter's team lost eighteen to seventeen. Peter looked at me and said, "No, Bernie, we have a tie, seventeen to seventeen." He pointed to the scoreboard where, sure enough, it said seventeen to seventeen, when just two minutes before I myself had placed the red and black pointer on eighteen to seventeen.

"Nope," I said. "That says seventeen to seventeen because you just moved it that way. I have the scores written down on my notes in my pocket. Want to see them?" The notes, of course, which everyone has seen me making during the games. The notes have nothing to do with the scores, but constitute the raw material I use for the construction of this narrative. Peter backed down. The winning team roared. To them I am a hero. To Peter I am a loathsome enemy. Now I know what Lincoln meant when he said you can't please all of the people all the time.

At lunch, Alex handed us the evening menu. Nothing on it appealed to Ethel. Does she have cruise fatigue? If so, it worked out better that she got it now and not in January when we started. We speculated on the subject. She thought maybe her stomach got upset by all that water she drank before she noticed the black spots.

Lunch measured up to the usual high standards of Cunard cuisine, so I don't need to tell you about it. Just imagine a dinner served at 1 PM and you would have a good mental picture of our lunch. Today, for instance, I enjoyed a Mediterranean seafood cocktail for starters (starters is British for appetizers). I followed that with beef consommé, with real chunks of beef and real barley. I cleared my palate with a cooling watermelon sorbet. Then I ate half of a baked chicken, seasoned with Provençal herbs and spices. The chicken melted in my mouth. Spiced potatoes, broccoli, and carrots accompanied the chicken. To make up for lost time and to advance my project of waist expansion, I had two desserts, a hazelnut gâteau and three scoops of creamy rich rum raisin ice cream. I finished with cappuccino. Not bad, right?

That's the usual lunch, yet I don't believe that I have had the same thing for lunch. In other words, the menu varies so much and offers so many different choices. I have selected a different entrée, and in most cases a different soup, sorbet, and appetizer, every single day for the last seventy-nine days.

Ethel and I bought two plastic white hats to get in the mood for the fair. The hats are the kind the barkers wear outside the old circus sideshows. My Uncle Tommy had one that he wore on the job. I memorized his spiel: "Step right up, ladies and gentlemen, witness the most extraordinary sights, the Giant, the Elephant Man, the Bearded Lady, the Fat Lady, the Midget, the Wild Nigger, the Pin Head, the Alligator Boy, and the Half-Man–Half-Woman." The Half-Man–Half-Woman was my favorite. He/she always stood in the last booth, which was always the most crowded. This freak, a morphidite and a miracle of science, was divided completely in half—the right side was male and the left side was female. The costume on the right was a leopard skin and on the left side was a brassiere and a spangled skirt. Would we see such a side show at QE2 country fair?

Ethel and I stepped into the Grand Lounge. The crew has transformed the place into a congested group of displays, stalls, and other attractions. The atmosphere smacked of a carnival. Ethel bought a T-shirt from our waiter, Nick, who looks quite different out of uniform. At the center of the room Brian Price, the cruise director, kept announcing rolls of the wheel of fortune, telling us what we might win for a two-dollar bet. Ethel pointed out that we can get a liter of Harvey's Bristol Cream Sherry and urged me to take a chance. "No thanks," I told her. "We might win. We have too much booze already."

The wheel of fortune spun and some other passenger collected the

Harvey's. A surefire way to insure that you don't win is to not take a chance. Next prize was one of those coveted red Cunard umbrellas. We didn't bet because we have a blue one that came with the penthouse suite. Instead, I pulled the roll of bills from my back pocket and started spending. I paid $100 for a tour of the radio room and the bridge. No chance involved. I considered it equivalent to purchasing a tour. Then I bought a tour of the kitchens with Jonathan Wicks, *QE2*'s executive chef, as our guide, and then I bought a tour of the engine room to be given by the chief engineer. All of the tours are to take place at some future time, hopefully before I get off.

We spotted Monsignor Foley circulating amid the noise, fun, and good cheer, selling straw chances for prizes. He's such a nice guy. One of these days I might go hear Mass, but I'm so busy now that I don't have time.

What's this? A dart game. "Too bad for them," I told Ethel as I purchased six darts, the maximum number of darts allowed for starters. "They won't let me play after I throw these." Bang, bang, bang—all bull's-eyes. I won a white Cunard cruise hat. Now I have three hats. Bang, bang, bang—all bull's-eyes. I won a toiletry set. I pulled out two dollars for more darts. My money is rejected. They won't let me play anymore.

Next, we bought ten chances for Hamilton, the teddy bear who traveled around the world with Captain John Burton-Hall, and we took ten chances on the Rio at Night tour. We've done that tour before. We could suffer through it again. Actually, Ethel could suffer through it. She doesn't get the same thrill from looking at all those seminaked dancers go through the history of Brazil in two hours at Plataforma Uno.

Ethel didn't want to go through the haunted house, so I went alone. Tracey Milburn, dance champion, *QE2* dance instructor, and done up as a pretty good Vampira, met me. Come to think on it, with that smugly evil smile she makes a great Vampira. Then a butler dressed in tails (younger and taller than our own butler, Geoffrey) took me through a narrow warren of horrors. It's dark and twisted in back of the stage, among the dressing rooms. Dry ice–generated mists obscuring my view, and the ship kept moving to unbalance my feet. Now and again, ghouls and other fiendish things popped from closets or coffins or from nowhere at all to squirt me with water, hang cobwebs on my head, or blow hot air in my face. The whole thing is not too scary, just fun, until the waiter lifts a silver platter revealing a starkly bloody human head. I startled, but then realized someone cut a hole in the tabletop and the head belongs to a crewmember. He is still alive. I can tell by the way his tongue kept darting in and out, side to side, and then licked his cherry red lips. Amazing! The crew did so much with so little by being creative and imaginative. They did so much with so much energy and verve.

Besides darts, I had another sure win: the quiz on human anatomy. Two dollars for the entry got me a bottle of champagne. I doubt any non-physician would know the odontoid process from the loop of Henle to the islets of Langerhans. In a way, my entering this contest might be considered unfair by some. But the barkers said I'm entitled to capitalize on my knowledge, just like anyone else.

Back at 8184 the hot water still didn't flow. If *QE2* is trying to help us in making the transition back home by teaching deprivation, I wonder what deprivation they will have in store for us next.

Looking forward and slightly port through our two picture windows, Ethel and I watched the sun go down. Professor Kurtz was right. The decline in these tropical latitudes lasts but a few minutes. While sipping our champagne, we watched the sun turn from yellow to orange and then become an oblate disk with slight crimson at the fringes as it, our own and nearest star, plunged and penetrated the regions of the lower atmosphere. All of a sudden, for about seventeen seconds, just as the orange faded out behind the horizon, I saw, for the first and probably the last time in my life, the green flash. Only what I saw didn't appear as a flash so much as a green disk, like the sun, with the rounded part of the disk on top of the horizon and the truncated part at the water's edge. The green was a bright, sharp green, lighter and brighter than a shamrock and more fleeting.

An invitation slipped under the door. This time it's from the officers, requesting the pleasure of our company for cocktails in the wardroom. These invitations, I forgot to mention, have been arriving fast and furious. Usually we reject them, because we are trying to remain privately and romantically by ourselves. On this segment many invitations came from the jewelers aboard who wish to introduce us to the joys of purchasing gems in Rio. Those we discarded without reply.

Even though we would like to, we can't go to the officers' party. We have a conflict: tomorrow we dine with the captain.

Wipe your hand across your mouth and laugh. Yes, I said we would dine with the captain. Why not? Twice last year, in a moment of paternalistic indulgence, I ate lunch with Trent, my chauffeur. If I can eat lunch with the man who drives my limousine, why can't I have dinner with the guy who steers the ship?

THREE SHIPS SET OUT *to* SAIL *the* OCEAN BLUE. ONE CAUGHT FIRE. NOW THERE ARE TWO.

*A*fter midnight today, March 25, 1996, Zulus cannot legally carry fighting sticks, batons, or spears, their traditional weapons. Zulus say that their rights are being infringed. What will happen? No one knows. Correction, you know. On the basis of what you know about the Zulu warrior culture and the history of Natal, how likely will it be that the Zulus will lay down their weapons?

Ugh! More trouble afflicts the British beef industry. McDonald's announced it would stop selling burgers for four days while it disposes of its British beef and gets beef from elsewhere. The loss of revenue from those Big Macs alone amounts to over £22 million. Wimpy and Burger King will follow.

Despite the beef crisis, and probably oblivious to it, our penthouse cricket made progress. He now occupied the forward stairwell between the penthouses and the Boat deck. Whether he found a mate or not, we don't know. He still crickets, so I presume he still wants companionship. Talking about that, I saw on the same stairwell a thin middle-aged woman passenger (who shall remain nameless) and a much younger officer, an engineer (I can tell by the purple band in his epaulets), headed up to her penthouse room. She looked under the weather, severely so considering that it was 10 AM. Romance looms in her immediate future. I can tell by the guilty look the officer gave me as I marched up the stairs behind him.

At breakfast, I told Colum that we didn't take a chance on winning a champagne breakfast served by Geoffrey in the penthouse. We can get that any day. We prefer to come down to Queens Grill for a real breakfast served by a real waiter. Colum agreed and thanked me for the compliment. Besides, breakfast for us now goes automatically. As soon as we arrive, we get our orange juices, coffees, fruit plates, and then order the rest of what we like. It's better that way. No one has to think. Nick and Colum just order for us as our factotums. Not a bad idea, since thinking has become somewhat difficult, especially in the mornings, due to all that booze at night.

I couldn't resist the first lecture. Judy Cornwell, an actress who appeared well known and well regarded by the British among us, talked about "Sex, Sensuality, and Fat Ladies." Judy should know about the topic. I've seen her on deck making eyes at the men, myself included. She definitely weighs enough to pass the fat test. Despite the extra weight, she looked sexy. Some fat women do. Making love to them, I imagine, might not be all that bad. Sort of like jumping on a waterbed. Making love to a skinny woman gives just the opposite effect: I once made love to a fashion model. It was like being in bed with a bicycle.

Just kidding. Judy told that joke, quoting the writer Anthony Burgess. She told it to warm up the audience, which, incidentally, consisted of, you guessed it, fat ladies. Judy pointed out the absurdity of the current crazy standard of female pulchritude and the tendency of every culture and every age to alter and modify the human body to meet supposed standards. In Victorian times, the ladies liked that wasp-waist appearance and they sacrificed a lot of health to get it. Internal organs shifted under pressure, lives shortened, breathing was impaired, and a number of the ladies swooned and fainted as a consequence. When anesthesia came in, they resorted to operative removal of the lower rib cage, usually the last two ribs, to make room for those displaced abdominal organs. Some women (I could name names but won't because a few are still alive and famous in their own right) swallowed little blue gelatin capsules that contained ova of tapeworms. The ova developed into big adult tapeworms and the ladies lost over sixty pounds from the worms. This practice, though effective against obesity, had to stop because of the health hazards involved. There were dire warnings from, of all places, the American Medical Association.

Judy's lecture gave me an idea. Why not write a book titled *At What Price Beauty?* I could tell of the lily foot deformity in China, where little girls had feet so small from being bound that by the time they became adults they couldn't stand up, much less walk. And what about liposuction? Breast implants? Chin implants? Cheek implants? And all those diet pills and the addictions that they have caused? Marilyn Monroe checked out for the last time in 1962 due to an overdose of reds (seconal), which she took because she felt nervous and couldn't sleep because of overdosing on blues (amphetamines), which she was taking to reduce the size of her fanny. As far as I could see, there was nothing wrong with her fanny. Most of the problem was with the media. They show pale, thin, really sick-looking girl-women as the beauty standard. Take Princess Di, for instance. Only after her confessions do we realize that she struggled with bulimia and tried, several times, to kill herself. Perhaps we should go off the gold standards of beauty and behavior.

For some reason, I thought of Mae West. "Come up and see me some time. I won't tell." The Royal Air Force named its life preservers after her. Well, not really after her—after her breasts or the bra that contained those breasts, which incidentally arrived five minutes before her body. "Is that a bra or a life preserver?" some man asked Mae. "Both. Check them yourself, Big Boy."

Two men in the balcony started talking loudly. Judy shouted up at them, "Excuse me! Excuse me! You and I can't talk at the same time." The crowd of fat women broke out into claps and cheers. The men left.

One Scottish woman (by now I can tell where they come from by their accent) next to me said to her friend, "I still would rather be thin. It's uncomfortable being fat. I am trying to think less of food by doing more reading."

Fat chance that reading more will thin her down. A diet, more than books, would be of greater benefit. My experience has been that the more I eat, the more I weigh. Now that I am off my diet, my weight has zoomed up. I have gained seventeen and a half pounds since we started. And I am hell bent to gain more.

At noon we went to see the Great South Atlantic Swim-Off, part of the charity fair. Brian Price, our cruise director, looked tired but had been swimming only fifteen minutes. Swimming at a reasonable pace, I know one can do 168 lengths of the outdoor pool in an hour so. I bet $100 that the three of them—Brian, Tracey (dance champion), and June (*QE2* librarian)—will do $168 \times 3 = 504$ lengths of the pool. Tracey and June look like they are swimming much faster than Brian, but I'm betting they will fade and all three will swim at about the same rate. But because the weather turned bad, Ethel and I didn't stick around to find out. It started to rain and a fierce wind came up. Passengers headed in to the bars for shelter, but poor Brian, Judy, and Tracey had to continue swimming.

No thanks, I would rather remain a passenger. At least we can come out of the rain when we want to.

Later in the afternoon, on the way to the spa, I met June. She thanked me for my support. They raised over $1,000 with the swim and the total laps amounted to 756. She complained that the salty water burned her eyes and asked me to take a look at them. Her eyes looked fine to me. I assured her that she would recover. June showed me the tally sheet. Brian swam 168, exactly what I predicted, but the ladies averaged 293 between them, outdoing him by far, so I lost the bet.

At 7:17, Paul, our other penthouse butler, came to escort us to the captain's party. The first stop was the captain's office, situated forward of the penthouse suites. This office, as large as a penthouse suite, has windows that face the bow, but the curtains are always drawn, just as they were tonight.

The deck steward (Mrs. Lonelyheart's fling), dressed in a Ritz hotel uniform, greeted us with champagne. The same people who own *QE2* own the Ritz hotel. Next, John Burton-Hall greeted us. We said a fast hello, thanked him for inviting us, grabbed some canapés, and moved on.

The captain's cabin: Fully carpeted, with thickly upholstered chairs and couches, indirect lighting, neat little table lamps, and velvet curtains framing the small portholes. Plush, but not regal. In the background I heard the noise of machinery and the noise of the propellers rising above the waves. Ethel and I headed across the room to the other side to the captain's desk, in the front of the room on the starboard side. The desk faced the stern. He has an inbox and an outbox. The inbox is full; the outbox is empty. Poor soul. If you have an inbox and an outbox, you can't be free.

Displayed throughout the cabin are pictures of the captain and Marie, his wife. One shot showed her holding a pet monkey. The monkey loves her and she loves it—all that is instantly obvious from looking at the picture. I wonder what story lies behind the monkey picture? The captain's TV, no bigger than ours in 8184, is white like ours and plays videos, but his also plays CDs. Ours doesn't.

Along the starboard wall this sign embroidered in red letters on white linen held the captain's prayer: "Fair weather and following seas." Along the port wall I found several autographs of the reigning monarch, Her Majesty Queen Elizabeth II. The autograph from 1954 shows strong vertical strokes, as if invisible metal wires pulled on the top of each letter. Some distance away from the Elizabeth signature and separated from the name by a space stood a capital *R* (for Regina, Latin for queen), written by the same hand and exceeding the heights of all the other letters, except the capital *E* that begins her name. But as the signatures get more recent, there are subtle and not-so-subtle alterations. The most recent signature (1994, I think. I couldn't take notes because my hands were full of Mumm's champagne and salmon canapés) showed the letters slightly more irregular in form but still oriented vertically without a slant to the right or left. The *R* now was directly attached to the Elizabeth signature and looked distorted, almost illegible as an *R*. More like a cursive minuscule *n*, written as large as a capital letter.

What does all this mean? I wish I knew. Where is the graphology expert when we need her? Why didn't I take her course when she gave it between Singapore and Bombay? If I had, I might make more sense of the queen's signature and the changes. Right now I think I see, *the Queen* and *Elizabeth* saw themselves early on in her reign as slightly different entities. Hence, the separate *R*. Now that the two personalities are joined, she feels more comfortable in defining her existence by her title and the duties of her role. It is a part of herself and she is a part of it. That leaves us with the recent distortion of the *R*, which looks unreadable unless you knew what it should be. What's the significance of the distortion of a capital *R* to a small *n* written large? I'll leave that for you to figure out. If you don't get it, write to me and I shall tell you my ideas on the subject. Go head and think about this. Thinking will do you good. Hint: I used to know the answer, but have forgotten it.

We adjourned to the captain's dining room, just aft of the Mauretania Restaurant. The captain stood and grabbed a large bell that had been at his right hand, which I hadn't noticed. He offered a toast to the queen. I went ahead with it, even though I don't believe in royalty. I'm a democrat in the original sense of the word, a believer in democracy. If you believe in democracy, I don't see how you can believe in monarchy. So for the nth time in my life I did the socially acceptable, but hypocritical, thing. I toasted the queen.

Then Captain John Burton-Hall bowed his head and said, "Gray and windy—the future of the company is in doubt. We wait with bated breath the takeover of the Trafalgar House." He hoped that the organization taking over Cunard would continue the cruising tradition and *QE2*. That I can toast too, without reservation or hesitation. But I admit I'm worried because it sounded like the captain was worried about this. I don't understand any of it, but I shared his concern. John Burton-Hall then told us that this is the twentieth captain's dinner on this year's world cruise. He measures out his life, not with coffee spoons, but with dinners. "And," he continues to toast with a sigh of relief, "the last for the refugees of the *Sagafjord*." What about the Sarafjord passengers?

Captain John Burton-Hall lifted his head and looked straight at the clock on the far wall. "Isn't it frightening the way time goes by," he said grimly. Mechanically, I lifted my glass to toast this last profound remark. I was also toasting the fact that *QE2* has a seasoned philosopher at the helm.

But then I retracted the glass realizing that despite all the Mumms and the Marques de Riscal white wine and the Château Fonplegade red wine and the Armagnac I had consumed, and despite the pleasant mental fog of all those drinks—that one doesn't toast the evaporation of time. Just recognize its quick passage and make the most of it. Never celebrate its passing.

During dinner, at his request, Ethel sat next to the captain. She has forbidden me to detail the conversation with him because she feels a lot of what was told to her was told in confidence. And so I draw a curtain over the narrative at this point in time. But I will tell about the monkey picture.

When John Burton-Hall and Mrs. Burton-Hall were in Guatemala, a monkey became attached to her and followed her around. When it came time for them to leave, they realized they couldn't take the monkey with them, so John Burton-Hall had to abandon it. By the way he talked about this, Ethel says, he still feels guilty. I wonder if the monkey also has regrets. If so, it would prove that monkeys not only think, but they also love.

Ethel came away quite impressed with the captain. Being absolute ruler of a floating empire as immensely comprehensive as the latest *Queen Elizabeth* (the ship) demands, as well as a lifetime skilled in seamanship and doctorate degrees in diplomacy, joke appreciation, advice to lovers, drinking, table talk, speech spouting, handshaking, and a thousand other skills. Captain John Burton-Hall had all those things and more.

While Ethel had the captain for her dinner companion, I had someone equally as exciting, Lillian Lessing. She and husband Frank experienced the *Sagafjord* trouble. The way she tells it, at 10:10 in the morning, while the ship was 200 miles south of Hong Kong and 180 miles east of Manila, a fire broke out in the engine room and destroyed the electrical-generating equipment. All passengers reported to lifeboat stations and waited there for three hours for the abandon-ship order that never came. Instead, the fire had been extinguished and the ship was left to drift without power, water, or utility water. On day three they got the portholes opened, so some ventilation occurred in the cabins. Some passengers slept in their rooms with doors opened and others slept on deck. The only hot meal was barbecue for dinner, prepared on the deck. No water, no toilet, no lights at night. Think about it! To get to her cabin she had to be guided by a steward with a torch (British for flashlight). They even packed in the dark and one of her bags got lost. She was lucky because some other passengers had three bags lost. Cunard offered a refund, transportation home, cruise miles for another or other cruises, or completion of the cruise on *QE2*.

Mrs. Lessing felt they signed too fast, under duress, and will get more when inquiries (inquiries is British for investigations) are made upon their return. According to her, five hundred passengers abandoned their world cruise, about one hundred and fifty transferred to *QE2*, and another hundred and fifty transferred to the *Royal Viking Sun*, the other Cunard ship that is still making the round-the-world trip.

Three ships set out to sail the ocean blue. One caught fire. Now there are two.

Rio de Janeiro, Brazil

IN HER OWN WAY, I BELIEVE, SHE LOVED ME BACK

$\mathcal{T}$he *QE2* shuttle bus left us off at the Copacabana Palace Hotel. We walked past the H. Stern's store. The H stands for Hans. Hans's stores are ubiquitous. Last time we visited Rio, we got taken to H. Stern's, so, we have resolved not to get taken there again. Taken in the literal sense, because H. Stern provided free transportation from our hotel. And we got taken in terms of cheated. H. Stern's makes the shortest-lived jewelry in creation. The bracelet I bought Ethel looked great for a week. I recall thinking when one stone fell out that we could get it reset, but two hours later three other stones disappeared.

Old gypsy motto: "Sometimes you get the bear and sometimes the bear gets you." The difference between the bear and H. Stern's is that at no time do you ever get H. Stern.

Talking about our last trip to Rio reminds me that in those days the cruzeiro lost value every day. The hotel adjusted the room rates upward according to the inflation rate, usually 10 percent per week. Taxi drivers carried correction tables to apply to the stated fare on the meter. I forget how many cruzeiros you got for a dollar, probably three thousand. Anyway, one day as I sauntered through the lobby of our hotel seeking cruzeiros, a strikingly beautiful brown woman, dressed in a floral dress with a décolletage that would knock your eyes out of their sockets, stopped me and said in French with a Portuguese accent, "Vous-voulez coucher avec moi?" I frowned and waved her off. She repeated the next time in English with a Portuguese accent, "You want to sleep with me?"

"No!" I shouted so loud it was as if a gunshot had gone off in the lobby. People turned and stared at us. I cupped my hands over her left ear and whispered, "No sleep, all I want is to change money."

"I do that too." She snapped her fingers. From nowhere appeared another sharply dressed and exquisitely made-up woman of similar age, maybe two years younger, clutching a fistful of dirty cruzeiros. God knows where those bills had been and what those bills had seen. Her cruzeiros looked real and her rate was 30 percent better than the bank rate. She assured me that she was not making a black market. She was making a parallel market. There's a difference: The black market is illegal, but the parallel market is not. "Parallel market: It's sort of like a black market, but with a different name," she explained. The woman was a prostitute, a black marketeer, and a spin doctor all rolled into one.

Today I won't deal with black market or parallel market currencies. Today I won't deal with prostitutes. Today Brazil seems untamed like a jaguar. Jaguars are OK from a distance. But today, I'm timid. No jaguar for me. I prefer a house cat. But in those old days, the world and Rio seemed innocent, easier, more friendly, and safe. Now it doesn't. Perhaps it's I, not Rio, who has changed.

The Meridien Hotel hasn't changed, except new currency bills are posted over the cashier. They call them Reals and they sell for about the same as a US dollar. The sign about the room rates increasing every day has disappeared. The government has inflation under control. Just like the old times, we ate at the Café de la Paix. Ethel was too tired to walk along the Avenida Atlântica to Marios, where the *churrascarias* specialize in barbecued meats.

After lunch, Ethel and I walked along Copacabana. I inspected the bodies beautiful belonging to the Cariocas (as the inhabitants of this fair city like to call themselves) as they walked along the beach. No, they don't walk. They move to rhythm, the bossa nova beat of "The Girl from Ipanema." Ipanema is a goddess, the mother-goddess from Macombe who lent her name to the song and to the beach next to Copacabana. Some of the girls gave me those telling sideward glances, but most, like the girl in the song, kept their eyes staring forward as they marched into the sea. They don't know that I love them. The older women returned my stares with a thankful smile as a rule. The young are beautiful. The old are beautiful. But the old are more beautiful than the young. Consequently, I know that my old age has begun.

I can't swim on Copacabana Beach because the water has too much raw sewage in it. We detected a gigantic stench. I don't know much about beaches, but I do know shit when I smell it. So we walked farther down along Avenida Vieira toward Leblon, a higher-class beach with the Sheraton hotel at its end. On the way we visited the fort at Ponta do Arpoador and saw the military museum there. The bunkers haven't changed and everything reminded me of Boy Scout camp. Even the commande's room looked like the office I had when I was the senior patrol leader of Troop 170 in Queens, New York. Come to think on it, Boy Scouts and soldiers have a lot in common—flags, mess halls, sleeping dorms, marching songs, dirty jokes, and communal games. Only the military doesn't have adult supervision. Perhaps that's why they tend to do that nasty killing thing. We saw the bombs that were used in the silly border war with Paraguay and we saw the shells that they dropped on Copacabana during the coup d'etat engineered by the generals.

Along Ipanema Beach the water looks much better, aquamarine in fact, like a gemstone at H. Stern's. Ethel guarded my stuff while I went in. We walked back. Ethel almost died of sore feet and we soon retreated into the sheltering arms of *QE2* and Queens Grill with Nick, Colum, Simon, and Alex to comfort us. After dinner Ethel collapsed into bed. I went to the samba show by myself.

Samba is samba, and the soul of Rio. They have fourteen samba schools in Rio, each of which takes learning samba quite seriously. Every year at Carnival a fierce competition takes place to see who is the best.

As in the beauty contests at home, a lot remains in the eyes of the beholder, but there is a universal appeal, especially to the men.

On *QE2* the samba show started with the traditional singing of "The Girl from Ipanema" (which I mentioned is a bossa nova, not a samba) and "Brasil, Brasil" (notice they spell their country's name with an *S*, not a *Z*), a true samba.

A couple commenced their dance. They are from the blue samba school: That's the name of their school, Blue Samba. The woman, the samba champion of the world, wore a white gown with white satin ledges, embedded aquamarine jewels, and layers of ostrich feathers. She held a blue and white flag, and swirled the flag around the stage as she danced. She and her partner flawlessly swayed to the music, making wider and faster gyres, gesturing gracefully with outstretched hands. She held a most expressive face, with eyes squinting into the distance and mouth opened in a wide horizontal smile, revealing glistening, straight, bright white teeth. They are voguing, and for a moment, they transformed themselves and those who dreamed with them, into the king and queen of CAR-NI-VAL!

The announcer told us that this was the team who won this year's samba prize. The previously reticent audience went wild. But they went even wilder during the next act.

Four beautiful women arrived—sinuous, shimmering resplendence. Close up and real—in three dimensions, on stage, one at a time, they danced their version of the samba. They are *mulatos* (mulattoes), dressed mainly in their brown skins, as scantily dressed as the women on the beaches in this wicked city.

Each mulato showed her stuff and made her bottom whirl and shake. The *targas* disappear in the frenzy and we thought we were looking at naked orbic flesh. The sensuality—the sight of all that female beauty, all that reproductive potential—awed some, intimidated others, and even frightened a few. Raw sexuality, with large gyrating hips and rounded brown bottoms—some *QE2*ers can't handle it. Not me. I volunteered, at their requests, to dance on stage with them. With the insistent beat, and under the spell of my beautiful partners, it all came back, the lessons in samba gymnastics. I pushed myself to the edge, straining every nerve, muscle, and sinew of my body. I don't need a thalium stress test to see if my heart is OK. The samba tested my heart instead.

My partner and I moved faster and faster in widening circles, driven by a kind of primitive frenzy that I know has its origin, pure and simple, in some out of mind and out of time mating ritual. I shook my bottom faster than the ship's propeller spun. The audience went wild with cheers and claps. My mulato beauty turned tail, faced the audience, and moved her frenzied backside into my face. It shimmied and shook to the wild samba beat. I responded by pushing my arms and legs and pelvis faster and faster. I grabbed her waist and now she and I moved around the stage doggy style, my favorite position. My brow filled with sweat. My breathing became rapid, regular, and deep. My pulse pounded in my head as if I had run twenty-five miles cross-country. But I'm with her, moving in unison and on the beat, showing my stuff. Then she stopped and turned around. She hugged and kissed me, a big wet kiss, one on the forehead and another on the cheek and, with the audience cheering us on, my mulato delivered another kiss on my mouth. Her lips were big and warm and soft and smooth. Unforgettable!

By instinct, I reached around with my right hand and grabbed the right cheek of her behind. I'm in her arms now and happy and willing to die. I don't care who comes or what happens. She didn't resist. In fact, she nudged closer. The idea of this warm female body seeking to slake its appetite on me affected me like the thought of an avalanche. At that moment, I knew I loved her and, in her own way, I believe, she loved me back.

A jazzy sadness quivered in her nerves. She bit her lower lip and wiggled that beautiful bottom, her private treasure, at me as she disappeared behind the reredos of backstage.

After the show, exhausted and sweating, I made my way past the Golden Lion Pub and headed back to the penthouse. "Was that you?" one British woman asked and then answered herself without my having to respond. "You are quite a dancer. Have you received formal instructions?"

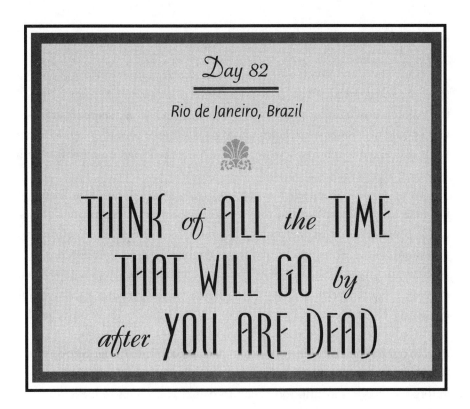

Day 82

Rio de Janeiro, Brazil

THINK *of* ALL *the* TIME THAT WILL GO *by after* YOU ARE DEAD

*T*he biotech index has declined 10 percent. I could have lost my shirt, but, strangely, I am so relaxed that I don't care.

Aloisio Mendez acted as our tour guide today. He commented about the slums as the bus sped by. He called them *favelas*. Somehow that special name makes the slums of Rio appear better (more romantic really) than the slums in Cape Town or Bombay. Before we could learn about the favelas, the lady on Aloisio's left interrupted him to complain that the air-conditioning was too cold. Others thought it not cold enough and complained when Aloisio turned it down. Under a roar of general protest, Aloisio adjusted things back the way they were, whereupon the lady on his left complained again. Aloisio fiddled with her private nozzle, an act that can have no general effect whatsoever. Amazingly, that made her satisfied. She, like so many other passengers, just needed some TLC.

481

"OK, about the favelas," Aloisio tried to start again, but some men in the back interrupted: "You're too loud! Turn it down!" Aloisio adjusted the volume down, and down some more until the group seemed satisfied and I could no longer hear. I was about to ask him to turn it up again when I got distracted by the two women on my left who were embroiled in a private conversation.

These ladies occupied the top end of the social range in England because they both spoke the dialect called *Fraffly*, based on the aristocratic pronunciation of the word *frightfully*, as in "Weh sue fraffly gled yorkered calm." Translation: We're so frightfully glad you could come. Another distinguishing feature of this speech is the ability to talk without moving the lips. (Prince Charles is an ace at this.) Other examples of Fraffly, or Hyperlect as it has also been called, include "How fay caned a few" (How very kind of you) and "Good gawd, is thet the tame?" (Try to translate this yourself. Hint: it has something to do with the time.)

The woman at the window had "embarrassed herself" the night before by "having a little too much to drink," and then requested of the barman something no proper women would ever request.

"Naturally, part of the fault lies with the barman. He should have cut me off," she told her friend in a voice so loud that the information about favelas got drowned out and lost forever. Her aisle-seat friend, showing once again how, when they wish, the British can express themselves powerfully and very directly, admonished in crisp Hyperlect, "The barman had nothing to do with it. When you drink too much, you get drunk. That's what happened. It's your fault and none other."

Ten million people live in Rio, the city of contrasts. Twenty-five percent in favelas, and most of them up to no good. Aloisio believed the Catholic Church bears part of the responsibility. He said the poor make more and more children because they don't practice birth control. Then the parents send the kids out to get whatever they can, wherever they can, whichever way they can.

It all started in the sixteenth century when a Portuguese navigator mistook Guanabara Bay for the mouth of a river (the entrance to the bay is narrow) and named the site Rio de Janeiro, or River of January. Guess what month that navigator arrived? Right.

Thus, Rio has been a mistake from the beginning, a marvelous mistake. The Cariocas themselves call it *Cidade Maravilhosa*—Marvelous City. They ought to know.

Aloisio opined that the biggest problem here is that the people don't follow rules. The laws are not enforced. Compulsory education, for example, has been on the books for years but the government doesn't force parents to send children to school. No one pays much attention to the traffic laws either because they are not enforced. Hence the high accident rate. And the women are just too loose, and on and on.

Aloisio is right. Cariocas need more discipline. But if they got it, they would stop being Brazilian and start being German. The way Cariocas see it, fewer rules means more fun.

We stopped at an overlook where I got one of those marvelous drinks called the Guarana. They had them on the beach yesterday, but I didn't get one because it was natural, not pasteurized. Here they had the pasteurized brand, Guarana Brahna. It tastes better than Classic Coke and has a remarkable freshness, like a guava and passion fruit combined. While I drank, an old British woman wearing a large white hat asked in her Yorkshire accent, "Did we see you samba last night?" She gave the answer before I had a chance. "You were great! Some said it wasn't samba. But we're here in Rio where they invented it. They should know."

I bought her a Guarana Brahna, assured her that samba was samba, and told her my secret. "At Salvador da Bahia for two weeks I suffered through a samba gymnastics course at Club Med."

The bus wended its way through narrow cliff-sided roads that the British, once hoping to make tremendous profits that never materialized, built long ago. We passed lush green valleys steeped in brilliantly colored tropical flowers: hydrangea, hibiscus, and bougainvillea. Sharp, steep ridges ribbed the countryside and it was cloven with narrow canyons, and here and there on the heights, rocky upheavals climbed, mimicking battlements and castles. And out of rifted clouds came broad shafts of sunlight that painted summit and slope and glen with bands of fire, leaving belts of somber shade in between.

Our mountain destination was Petropolis, a city about forty miles from the center of Rio de Janeiro. Emperor Pedro II of Portugal named this town after himself and established his summer capital here in the cool hills of the Serra dos Órãqos, or the Organ Hills.

We stopped at the cathedral and paid respects to the mortal remains of Pedro and his queen, his daughter, and the daughter's husband. In a side chapel, which breathes a powerful sulky sadness, full-length, life-sized, and lifelike statues of all four royals lie on the coffin lids. The king felt cold and stony, but looked great. The queen felt cold and stony, and looked ugly. Someone had misnamed her Isabel, a name that derives from the Irish queen Iseult La Belle, or Iseult the Beautiful. It must be awful dark inside those tightly sealed stone sarcophagi—inky black. Pedro, the former king, I'm afraid, lies there in a terrible inky blackness that goes on and on and never ends.

Then we visited the Museu Imperial housed in the Summer Palace. We put on slippers to go through the palace and helped polish the floors in the process. I saw a nun dressed in white. She looked seventeen, too young to be a nun I would think. She had no makeup and wore horn-rim glasses. Her upper lip had a mustachio, but on her left-hand ring finger circled a wedding band. Just like every other nun, she was married to Christ. And proud of it. How come Christ gets so many wives and I don't?

The history of Pedro and Isabel: One day Pedro was king of Brazil. The next day he was not. Sort of like what happened to Nixon. A bloodless revolution. The king had to go home to Portugal via a clipper ship. Nixon had to go home to California via Air Force One. And soon Ethel and I will experience a similar demotion when we leave *QE2* and have to go home to Texas on Continental Airlines. Pedro had to forsake Brazil, Nixon had to forsake the White House, and we shall forsake our constant quest of sun and sumptuous living as our floating resort hotel, *QE2*, surges across the ocean seas without us. All transitions of that ilk, luxury to less, hurt. What does it prove? It proves that kingship and office and luxury all have their ephemeral qualities, especially in these parlous times. One thing strikes me with a force it never had before: the unsubstantial, unlasting character of fortune and fame. Too many fall from great and good for you to doubt the likelihood, as Robert Frost says in his famous poem "Provide, Provide." These people, Pedro and Isabel, struggled feverishly through life, toiling like slaves in kingship, in oratory, in generalship, in politics, and in literature, and then lay down and died thinking in happy possession of an enduring history and deathless name. Well, two little centuries fluttered away, and what is left? A crazy inscription on a block of stone, a stony statue, which stuffy antiquaries bother over and tangle up and make nothing out of but a bare name and a crude story. Before this day I had never heard of Pedro II. And after this day, I shall forget him.

But I won't forget his crown. Pedro was in such a hurry to leave, he forgot his crown. In a display case it sits, flashing 639 diamonds, 77 pearls, and gold weighing over three pounds.

Lunch took place in a Norman-style hotel called Palácio Quitandinha. We had nothing but praise for this meal that included the caipirinha, a famous Rio drink, made with cachaça, ice, sugar, and lime juice. Cachaça, the perfect alcoholic beverage of Brazil, packs a wallop. After two cachaças I kept feeling myself sliding under the table. The food included *xinxin* (pronounced *shing-shing*), a chicken stew cooked with ground dried shrimp, hot spices, and dende oil. The meal closed with port, an old Portuguese tradition. I had two glasses. But lest you think me a lush, the glasses in true Portuguese tradition were thumb sized, no larger.

Colum spent his day hang gliding, an activity infinitely more dangerous than viewing a summer palace, but probably safer than drinking caipirinha. "Please don't do that again, Colum, until we get off in Fort Lauderdale. Now that we have you trained, we want you around serving us as our waiter." Then I thought of something. I assured Colum, "I know what's going on. I used to do dangerous things. It's part of growing up, proving oneself a man."

Colum looked at me appreciatively as if I had risen several notches in his estimation. The effect lasted a moment more until I opened my mouth again. "But, now that I'm rich, I don't want to die." I declined the notches I temporarily gained and lost a few more.

"On your advice, I guess I'll cross hang gliding off the list," said Colum as he handed me a chocolate eclair, my third dinner dessert. "When I get to Barbados, I'll sky dive."

Ethel and I went on deck to see the sail away. The ship has a new complexion, more brown and younger, Brazilians speaking Portuguese.

Eight young boys already played basketball on the Sun deck court. I hope they don't hog the outdoor pool tomorrow. The crickets went on deck to see too. I counted twenty-two. Are they multiplying? Are they eyeing new crickets that came aboard today, bodies and faces, mostly out of curiosity but in some cases with lust in their hearts? Do crickets love? Do crickets think?

No program arrived under our door tonight. Ethel wanted me to call the cruise director to find out why. Ethel claims she can't plan her day without that valuable document, the daily program that usually lists the sixty-seven activities you could do if you wanted to do something besides read on deck and watch the sea go by. While I'm talking with Brian, she wanted me to ask how they decide what the drink of the day is. Does Brian do it? Does a committee do it? Does anyone ever order that drink or drink it? Without a program, we'll never know what tomorrow's drink of the day will be. Incidentally, today's drink of the day is history—a Green Goddess (vodka, Midori, blue Curaçao, and orange juice for $4.25). The official after-dinner drink today is also history—German Coffee (made with Kirsch for $4.25).

Pretty soon Ethel and I will be history too. And if that doesn't make us sick, think of all the days *QE2* will cruise, and all the places it will cruise to, and all the interesting people who will cruise with it, walk her decks, sit in the Queens Lounge, drink in the Crystal Bar, and eat in Queens Grill after we have gone. And pretty soon, you too, dear reader, will be history. And if that doesn't make you sick, then think of all the time that will go by after you are dead. The single best thing you can do for your health is have fun. Enjoy yourself now just in case death is a blackness, nothing but pure terrible blackness, that goes on and on and never ends.

Day 83

At Sea, off the coast of Brazil

HOW MANY CREPES MUST ONE MAN FLAMBÉ *before* THEY CALL HIM *a* MAN?

*T*wo hundred and fifty-two passengers got on yesterday. Where are they? The passenger density appeared no greater, so just as many must have got off (the British say *got* instead of *gotten*, for they consider *gotten* a rather quaint Americanism). The number of people onboard might not have changed, but the type of people did. Young boys hogged the hot tub. Only one tub worked, so I had to share it with them. Unlike the rowdy Australians, they're well behaved. But it's not like the old days when I, all alone in the hot tub, watched the sun go down.

The ship's lecturers got ahead of the program by talking about the duty-free Disneyland of St. Thomas. I'm not interested. Neither is Ethel.

We're headed to the Caribbean that we know so well, a group of islands shaped by two people whose influence still pervades everything: Columbus, who named most of the islands, and Conrad Hilton, who opened them to tourism. Columbus really wasn't all that great. He thought the Earth was round, all right, and proved it by going west to get east. But Aristotle knew that fact already and had estimated Earth's size only a little smaller than it really is. Columbus got it smaller too, though much smaller, about half the actual size. Consequently, Columbus thought if he sailed three thousand miles west he would land in the Indies, and his misnomer, West Indies, persists to this day.

Columbus died relatively forgotten and out of favor with the Spanish court because of his repeated requests for titles, lands, and money, and the fact that he never brought back much gold. His bones lie on the island of Hispanola, one of the four Greater Antilles islands, also named by him. History remembers him for the discovery of the New World, but history forgets that when Columbus landed people were already there to greet him. Why didn't those people discover America? Or ask the question another way. How could Columbus discover something that already not only was discovered, but also was inhabited by indigenous Americans dating back over twenty thousand years? Those people who stood on the shore of El Salvador when Columbus sailed in that bright sun-drenched October day in 1492 held in their hands rolled leaves, which they called tobaccos; one end they set aflame, from the other they inhaled blue smoke. These were none other than the ancestors of our modern cigars and cigarettes. From that humble beginning, while Spain conquered the New World for a while, tobacco conquered the Old World, probably for all time.

The *Nina* with 60 tons, the *Pinta* with 60 tons, and the *Santa Maria* with 120 tons could all fit into the Queens Grill. Recall that *QE2* is a 67,000-ton ship. *QE2* is 279 times bigger than all of Columbus's ships put together.

I decided to keep the narrative short and just have fun. Let's break out the booze and have a ball. Let's get wild. Being in the Caribbean will help. Anyway, try as you may, you have to get passionately interested in small things to say much about the Caribbean. And one can only wax eloquently about sand and beaches so much. The idea is just to get out there and enjoy them. Before I do that, I shall summarize the history of the Caribbean:

Columbus discovered the islands. Spain exploited them. European powers fought over them. Many islands changed hands many times. Then the islands fell into a deep sleep. For the most part, they are still sleeping. That sleep, an endearing feature, explains why these islands are the relaxation centers of the United States.

Today, as usual, I steamed myself. Two couples came in and started complaining that the room was too hot. They wanted the steam to be cool and asked Elena to cool it down. Elena explained that steam rooms were supposed to be hot.

The woman among them, who spoke with a British accent, asked me, "How long have you been here?" Without giving it much thought I said, "Eighty-one days."

"My God," she exclaimed. "How do you stand it? Do they bring your meals?"

Miss 91 in Queens Grill discovered after dinner as she got up to leave that she had put her dress on backward. The plunging neckline was actually at the rear and the button back of the dress was at her front. She stood up, right in the center of the fish bowl (the sunken central part of the Queens Grill dining room), and made a scene, screaming that she didn't know what to do. The ruckus was so loud that Bob, across the way, awoke briefly.

To cover the lady's exposed front, Alex removed his jacket and put it on her backward so that the sleeves of his blue blazer made her look like she had acquired a straightjacket. Alex escorted her out, both arm in arm, saying, "See, now we're a pair." In response there were a few isolated pockets of clapping from those passengers able to put their drinks down, after which the chatting and drinking and eating, with the same firm concentration of an army of fire ants, resumed.

Freud tells us nothing happens by accident. The ninety-one-year-old lady probably was making some kind of unconscious protest about dressing up so often. If she is like us, she has probably dressed formally more often on this cruise than she has in her entire life. Every day at sea is a formal-attire day in which I must wear my tux or my dark business suit to dinner. Some days that we have been in port and have departed early also became formal. We averaged three formal nights a week. When I get home I shall continue the practice, of course. And I shall also require, I told Ethel, an appetizer, soup, a sorbet, and a main course, a dessert, and coffee at lunch and dinner. If we can't continue sailing, at least we can pretend. She agreed, provided I give announcements over our home loudspeaker system about lifeboat drills, starlights, phoenixes, priority ones, and, of course, the ship's navigational reports at 9:30 AM and 1 PM.

Alex made crepes for us. They were delicious. In his honor, I sang a song for him in a Texas accent, "How many crepes must one man flambé before they call him a man? The answer my friends is writ in the wind."

Day 84

Salvador (Bahia), Brazil

YOU BOILED the WRONG EGG!

*A*lex showed us a memo: "To all Masters of Cunard ships. Cunard has for the last 30 years used exclusively U.S. beef and will continue to do so. No danger exists in getting mad cow disease aboard ship."

I told Alex we knew it was American beef because American beef tastes better and feels softer. He seemed slightly offended by this, so I added, "When the passengers find out it is American and that American beef has been banned in Europe for years because it has been raised with [God, forbid!] hormones, they'll wish it were British."

Alex answered, "That's OK. In the event of an inquiry, I'll just make up a new memo that Cunard has, for the last thirty years, used only Argentine beef."

Ethel and I got up at 6:30 and reported at 7:00 for breakfast to catch the tour of Salvador, Bahia. As usual, the H. Stern's car waited for *QE2*ers at the dockside ready to take them. No one is interested. They had been taken too much already.

The first stop was the Farol da Barra fortress, which is now a lighthouse. The guide, whose name I didn't get because she didn't give it, told us not to drink the sugarcane drink the street vendors sell. I hope those vendors don't speak English because she insulted their drink right in front of their vending machines. They have their own gasoline-powered grinders right there at curbside. They feed the raw sugarcanes directly into the hopper, grind them up, and spit out the stuff into your glass. "The drink has street dirt," the guide explained. "Don't touch it. In the country, you may drink it, because in the country the dirt is ecological dirt, cleaner dirt."

The guide, a middle-aged, somewhat baggy white woman with powerful bifocals, through which I saw magnified blue eyes, spoke with a German accent, though she insisted she was born in London and moved to Salvador at age three.

Just as in India, the street hawkers surrounded us with offerings, including multicolored ribbons from the local church, Igreja do Nosso (Senhor do Bonfim). Tie these around your wrist three times and let them fall off naturally and your three wishes will come true.

"Does it work?" I asked.

The hawker replied, "I don't know. I tried it only once. It still held on to my wrist after a year, so I cut it off."

The unnamed guide explained the *figa*, which we see universally depicted in the jewelry. It is a fist with the thumb placed between the second and third finger. It is supposed to ward off the Evil Eye. I have a different idea. But I'll leave that to your imagination. Hint: Make a fist. Put your thumb through the crack between fingers two and three. What does it resemble? Why would a culture originally from Africa think such a symbol held supernatural power?

Because of some rifts in Earth's plate tectonics, which I don't understand, Salvador divides into two parts: the lower town (lower plate) and the upper town (upper plate), consisting of the peneplain, an ancient land surface eroded down to sea level and then thrust upward. Steep streets link the two parts. But the easy way to get from one to the other is to use the Carlos Lacerda elevator, a device first installed 140 years ago and refurbished in 1966.

At the top of the elevator, in the upper city, we stood at the lookout point near the city hall and peered out over All Saints' Bay, or *Bahia de Todos os Santos*. I thought of that warm humid day, November 1, 1501, when Amerigo Vespucci, a semiobscure Italian navigator, sailed in and marveled at Recôncavo, the ninety miles of lush, tropical coastline surrounding the bay. Sometime later, in 1633, offshore about one hundred yards, the Portuguese built the sturdy Forte de São Marcelo. Its three-feet-thick stone walls, designed to withstand invasions by the Spanish and Dutch, have withstood the test of time.

I wonder if Amerigo realized that his name, not Columbus's, would denote the New World. A contemporary mapmaker wrongly thought Vespucci discovered the whole of the South American continent and, in the most literal way, put his name on the map. When he learned of his error, the mapmaker, one Martin Waldseemuller, took the name off, but by then it had stuck. Vespucci himself preferred the name *Mundus Novus*, Latin for New World.

We visited the great baroque church of Igreja de São Francisco and the smaller third-order church next to it. The main church amazed us all, even jaded old me. Every inch of available space has a carving in wood, which has been gilded over with real gold leaf. What wealth must have been placed here. What wealth is still here. Stupid me thought the Franciscans who built this church took a vow of poverty. The vow did not extend to their churches. Poverty is for the people. Wealth is for the Holy Mother Church. The marbles and the statues and the woods and the blue tiles (*azulejos*—we have seen them everywhere the Portuguese have been) came here from Portugal as ballast. But the gold was sent from here to Portugal and then worked there into leaf. Part of the gold then returned to Salvador again. This church, this cathedral, this thing they sank so much money and energy and slave labor into was, for them, what the space shuttle is for us—an icon of the age.

Salvador was another place where the very life was almost badgered out of us by importunate swarms of beggars and peddlers, who hung in strings to one's sleeves and shrieked and shouted. But we know by now how to handle them. Ignore them.

Did you know angels have sex? They must, for the many angel figures on the church walls clearly show male and female genitalia. Do you know angels get pregnant? They must, for two angels have swollen bellies and full breasts. But the archbishop didn't like what he saw, so the boy angels got mutilated and the girl angels got skirts. The mutilation team didn't have its heart in the job because many of the angels with full sexual organs are still on display in the little dark nooks and crannies of the nave and transept.

In a side aisle, the natives prayed to the statue of St. Antony. He supposedly finds stuff that's lost and also takes care of the poor. Every Thursday, his day, the poor line up outside along the south wall and receive gifts from those who wish to get some credit in heaven for works of mercy. Besides taking care of the poor, St. Antony can also get you a husband. First ask nicely. Then, if you don't get results, steal his statue and hang it upside down in a well until Mr. Right pops the question. Please return the statue so the next user can get her man.

The group moved along, despite the aged bodies, through the cobblestone streets of the old town. QE2ers seemed more vigorous these days. Why?

Along the way we saw the pillory where the slaves were beaten and sometimes killed. The noise of all that screaming and all those lashings disturbed the rich families who lived nearby, so the government moved the pillory up the hill to the monastery.

Rounding the corner of a dour building, through one of the narrow streets that beelined straight down to the harbor, we caught the sudden sight of *QE2*, our nurturing mother, transfixing us with awe. Why does she, anchored some distance from the shore, inspire such admiration from people who just left her short hours ago?

The scene reminded me of Xenophon's *Anabasis* (*Expedition*) when the men first caught sight of the sea. A great commotion arose, with shouts of "The sea! The sea!" Spears were raised and thrown in joy, but the commotion frightened the donkeys and the carts fell over the edge into the gorge below. Thus, in 300 BCE, something primitive and important was awakened by the sight of the sea. Our group felt it also.

After a long climb up a long hill, we entered the Igreja da Ordem Terceira do Carmo. Right in the middle of the convent stood another pillory. The guide explained, "Yes the monks owned slaves. Yes, the monks beat and killed them too. Some debate took place on whether slaves had souls.

Can you imagine that?" our guide asked, the scowl on her face showing her disgust for the monkish behavior. "The Catholic Church didn't know if black people had souls," the guide nodded her head and scanned the group. I sensed something else coming, so I didn't say anything. I just kept my eyes attentively on her. She was getting her courage up.

"I may as well tell you, the new archbishop is a cardinal who may become pope. Only a few very religious people like him. I don't. He can't leave the native religion alone. *Candomblé* is mainly white magic; magic for good, not for evil," she explained.

"This bishop won't let them practice their candomblé. Last year he tried to stop the 'washing day' ceremony. The second Thursday of January the women of Bahia, in traditional multitiered white lace costumes that look like birthday cakes, walk in joyful procession from Nossa Senhora da Conceição, near the harbor, to the Igreja do Bonfim. Once there, they set to scrubbing the square and church from top to bottom, decorating it with flowers and fairy lights. Then starts songs and dances lasting until the early hours of Sunday morning."

"What happened?" I asked, as if I couldn't guess.

"Despite the bishop's prohibition, the ladies marched and washed, same as usual."

The archbishop hasn't got much experience with women. When they want to clean, nothing can stop them. He sounds a lot like Noah Webster, who was by all accounts a severe, correct, humorless, religious, temperate man and not easy to like, even by other severe, religious, temperate, humorless people. This archbishop, who, incidentally, is also the archbishop of all of Brazil, figured large in the current news. Not only does he take stands against the African religion, a faith deeply rooted in the hearts of the people, he doesn't let cripples marry: "He forbade a paralytic man and a woman who loved each other from marrying because the man is impotent."

Several elderly couples looked at each other knowingly and clasped hands. They understand love, happiness, joy, and romance are all about and within us. Potency has little to do with it. If potency were required for marriage, half the couples on *QE2*, I imagine, might be forced asunder.

"The papers have made a lot of hay on this case. TV shows have discussed the pros and cons ad nauseam. The bulk of public opinion sides with the couple in love and against the bishop. Several Protestant sects have stepped forward to offer the marriage."

Our nameless guide gave her opinion that couples in love should be permitted to marry. "What do you think?"

The *QE2*ers, romantics at heart, want the couple to marry. They want them to live happily ever after. They want everything Christian in this place scraped off so that the pagan spirit can float free. They also want to kill the archbishop. So do I.

Monks used to run a hotel here in the Carmelite monastery but discovered the hotel didn't pay, so they abandoned it to a group of investors who made it a five-star hotel. The investors proved to be involved in Mafia money laundering, so the government put a stop to it.

Back to the ship and lunch at Queens Grill. The sherbet today is quite unusual: mandarin orange with coffee beans on top. The beans crunched when I bit into them and the coffee flavor came out strong on the tongue and palate. "Colum, this is the most unique sorbet that they have ever made for me." Enthusiasm daunted my respect for English. A thing is unique or it isn't. Nothing can be most unique.

Colum said that the sorbet chef is running out of ideas and is just winging it. He knows I'm keeping track of the whole business.

After lunch, I headed down to the gym to weigh in. I tipped the scales at 167.5 pounds, a gain of more than seventeen pounds. Nice work. At least I have accomplished something on this trip; my waist expansion program is a success. As I got off the scale, a man on the exercise bike next to the scale called me the Samba King. "See," I said to Ethel, "they still remember." The biker assured Ethel that I was great. "They should sell dances with you for $25 for the charity fair," he said. "All the ladies would pay."

Ethel asked as we got in the elevator, "When will you samba for me, Big Boy? I can pay more."

"It's not that easy. I need inspiration."

"You mean I don't inspire you?" Ethel pouted.

"You do. But not in the same way as those beautiful brown bottoms."

Ethel was satisfied. This explanation was, after all, the truth.

The crew show starts tonight at midnight so Ethel and I took a nap. We set the ship's telephone alarm to snooze, and before we knew it, an hour and a half had gone by. The phone rang and it was time to dress for dinner, hit the movie afterward, and then dash to the Grand Lounge to take in the show. Nick Barker, our Queens Grill waiter, started things right with his rendition of "I Just Called to Say I Love You." He sang professionally, intently, with great voice and style. Nick gave Ethel his camera and she kept clicking away, getting him on film. Then we heard Kaye Horgan, wine stewardess, sing "The Way We Were." First class. But Paul Mason kept us in stitches with his jokes between acts. The humor is dry and witty, typical British. Sometimes I laughed so hard I thought they might eject me. Other times I laughed so hard I fell off my chair.

Some examples:

A man goes to the doctor because his hearing has suddenly gotten worse. The doctor looks in the patient's ear and says, "What is this suppository doing here?" The man says, "You solved two problems. Now I know where my hearing aid is."

Again:

John Major and the queen are riding in a horse-drawn coach and the horse breaks wind. "I am so sorry, Your Majesty," says John Major. "That's quite all right, John," says the queen. "I thought it was the horse."

Mason hit the Queens Grillers hard. He should know them because he has, for many years, waited tables in Queens Grill:

A man in Queens Grill orders two eggs for breakfast, one scrambled and one boiled. When the order comes out, he looks displeased. "What's wrong?" asked the waiter. "You boiled the wrong egg!"

That was the joke that made me fall off my chair. No one else laughed at it. Another:

A man bought a chain saw that the salesman guaranteed would cut down 250 trees a day. The first day it cut 250, but the second only 230, and the third day, even fewer, 210. So he took it back to the store. "Let's have a look at it," the salesman says as he pulls the cord. The customer says, "What's that noise?"

One last one:

The husband writes his wife a note: "If you wish to make love tonight, pull my willy [that's what the British call it] once. If you don't wish to make love tonight, pull my willy seventy-six times."

Day 85

At Sea

CELEBRATING TWELVE WEEKS CRUISING on QE2 and STILL TALKING to EACH OTHER

*W*e awoke and made love. Sex at sea remains a unique experience for many reasons. I like the way, after our full fury has been spent, we lie there still connected while the ship continues moving up and down. We feel the bed fall away from us like an elevator falling fast, and then stop and rise again, pushing us closer together, all in the rhythm of the sea, the ancient mother of all life. There is a sensuousness to the thing, something hard to describe, but it's there. It is as if *QE2* embraces and makes love to us at the same time that we make love to each other. A kind of orgy involving a ship.

Ethel wanted to know if I will still be a sexual dynamo when we get home.

"Doubtful. Here the sea air stimulates me or something. Perhaps, it's because there's nothing better to do."

Ethel thinks that if it is the sea air, maybe we could put it in a can and sell it. Whoosh! A man punctures the can, the sea air rushes out, and the couple falls into bed. "Great sex. That's why they keep coming back to cruise." Ethel said, slipping on her pink panties.

They do keep coming back. Cruise statistics prove that once you cruise you want to cruise again. Exit polls show more than half the people leaving the ship intend to return. And the polls show a significant percentage of passengers have sex within hours of coming aboard. We number in both those categories.

Ethel and I lingered so long in bed we almost missed breakfast. Alex thought we overslept. I didn't disillusion him. Then he served a *Queen Elizabeth 2* Crew Problem/Solution Notice on us. (This is the form that goes in the crewmember's record. Three of these and they get the sack.)

The notice, under the heading Specific Nature of Problem, said that we "Nearly missed breakfast. Out too late at night." The category checked is Timekeeping. It's only a warning, so I relaxed. It won't happen again, I assured Alex.

More gifts arrived, including a bouquet of flowers and a note from Captain John Burton-Hall saying what a privilege it was having us onboard. And, more significantly perhaps, was a gift from hotel mangager John E. Duffy, a beautifully glazed black enamel quart of highland malt Scotch whiskey, distilled and bottled in Scotland by Morrison Bowmore Distillers at Glen Garioch. Against the black background appear in brilliant gold letters "QE2," indicating that the ship had gone into the Scotch whiskey business. *QE2* had always dispensed the finest old blends (as I know so well), but now the prestige and selling power inherent in *QE2*'s name has been distilled into promoting the world's most exclusive scotch. At eighty-five proof and for $25 a bottle, it's guaranteed to be at least twelve years old, so it may have a fair claim to the title. But the proof would be in the drinking, and when it comes to scotch, my suspicions run high, especially when the brand in question is a blend and not a single malt.

This is the presentation scotch I've been trying to taste, but Simon, our wine steward, didn't wish to get some for me. Could Simon have been protecting me? As a drink it still remains elusive, because Ethel won't let me open the bottle. She thinks I should wait until we get home.

In a way, each of these gifts has a note of sadness in them. We have sailed—no, we have *steamed*—no, we have *diesel-electriced* for twelve weeks—have seen many different countries, and have experienced a variety of cultures. Our enjoyment and our memories have happened. They are part of a now nonexistent past. The cruise continues in the immediate present into the as yet nonexistent future, during which the whole thing will end. There's the rub: it has to end. And the idea of it ending has put us in a bad mentality. But, you know, we're not the only ones.

"Hate Week," Geoffrey called it. "The last week of the cruise the passengers get out of sorts and have all types of small complaints." Also, the panicky packing has started. One man, Sir Michael Rosenberg, had his private chauffeur get on in Rio to do the packing. Perhaps I should ring up Trent, my chauffeur, and have him board in Barbados to do the same for us. Geoffrey said Hate Week is especially difficult this trip because the *Sagafjord* people are still complaining, and the original *QE2*ers are complaining about them. "They should be grateful they are still alive. After all, there was a fire in the engine room and, with all that fuel, the whole thing could have exploded."

Paradoxically, as our time narrowed, some people became more friendly, some women became more aggressive, including Miss Red Bikini, who the gods have hallowed by putting all of the beauty of the race in a single face and body. Alas, the blonde with the red bikini has abandoned me in favor of the deck steward, the same steward, as I told you, who got off Mrs. Lonelyhearts before she got off in Singapore. Some loves were never meant to be. But doesn't Miss Red Bikini know the crew plays a game to see who beds the most passengers? Actually, the way Miss Red Bikini looks at the deck steward with that slow feline smile, full of passion and desire, indicates she wants to help increase his score. Let the deck steward have her. Homer, if he ever came back, would be proud of me. No fighting over beauty. No fighting over a woman's love.

Five passengers assembled on Two deck in the midship lounge for a tour of the engine room. Company policy forbids this, but since we have paid $100 each to the ship's charity fund, we get a tour.

All the people gathered for the tour are (what else?) Queens Grillers. I introduced myself to two of the men, telling them that they, like me, drink martinis for dinner.

"There aren't many of us left," said Sir Michael Rosenberg, the wag, who looks like his picture should adorn a bottle of Schweppe's tonic water.

Chief Engineer Gillan showed us around and answered questions. The power plant runs on diesel electric, which arrived in 1986 or 1987, and cost one hundred million pounds. Holy cow! Can that be possible? One hundred million pounds sounds like big money to me. Could he have meant one hundred thousand pounds? Nope, that figure sounds too low. One hundred million pounds it must have been. The diesel engines drive the generators, which power the engine with ten thousand volts. Each of the nine engines weighs 120 tons. The new power plant saves 35 percent in fuel costs over the old steam turbines.

We put on ear protectors and headed through the watertight doors into the belly of *QE2*. Large machines frighten me even though I consider myself a worshipper of the machine. The noise, despite the earplugs, is deafening. The smells aren't as bad as I expected, only a slight whiff of machine oil and certainly no smoke. The vibration seemed minimal. Down here the ship is steady as a rock.

We passed some sweaty Filipinos who have disassembled one of the diesel engines. Gigantic pistons hang out of the engine's guts. Massive electrical cables surround us, going this way and that. Chief Engineer Gillan explained the current flows at 3,000 volts around the ship and various transformers reduce it to room-serviceable 220 and 110 volts.

I asked if the magnetic fields generated by the currents have adverse effects on health and Gillan said, "Everything has an adverse effect on health."

I asked if the wires are balanced, so that the current goes both ways and the magnetic fields would cancel out, leaving no net external field. He said scratching his head, "I don't know. Do you have a heart pacer?"

We ducked through another watertight door and entered a room that looked much older than the previous room. I noted many layers of yellow paint on the equipment and made some notes related to the narrative. Gillan guiltily admitted that this room has not changed since 1969, the year of *QE2*'s maiden voyage. We inspected the flash evaporators that make freshwater out of seawater and make boiler-feed makeup (whatever that is), water for the cooling water systems, and for washing and drinking. The evaporators, with the assistance of the reverse osmosis units, provide one thousand tons of freshwater each day. The evaporators are covered with thick layers of yellow paint and some rust. The old evaporators look like the explanation for the black spots that sometimes exit the faucets of our penthouse suite. We worked our way aft and saw the gigantic driveshafts that looked a yard in diameter (but actually measure fifty-nine centimeters) and must be over eighty yards long. They connect to the variable-pitch propellers that turn at the constant speed of 144 revolutions per minute. Each shaft has been covered with towels and blankets to keep the vibrations down. We even walked down to the end of the ship where the driveshaft leaves the hull and connects with the propellers on the outside, under water.

We didn't tour the sanitation system nor the sewage disposal plants, completely self-contained and sealed, and located on Eight deck. We didn't see the fuel, IF 380 (Bunker C), which they heat under pressure to 140 degrees centigrade for injection into the cylinders. At room temperature, *QE2* fuel looks like road tar. *QE2* goes about fifty feet on a gallon of Bunker C and *QE2* consumes about 380 tons of Bunker C per day! The total power output equates to three thousand medium-sized family cars or ninety-five megawatts of electricity, enough to light the city of Southampton.

Do you know why the engineers, on their epaulets, have purple stripes between their gold stripes? The reason goes back to the *Titanic*. The engineers stayed aboard and faced their certain deaths to keep things running as long as possible, giving the others a better chance of escape. All engineers went down with the ship and King George V decreed, from that date on, that the Royal Purple will be worn. Tears come to my eyes whenever I hear this story again, a story of real heroics like this, and then I feel a kind of pain in my forehead. The purple pays tribute to the engineers as heroes, which they were.

John E. Duffy, the hotel manager, threw a cocktail party for us and thirty others. The party took place in his amidship quarters on Two deck. It was fun and I saw lots of familiar faces. Peter the cheater was there. Naturally, I snubbed him. Hilde wanted to know why I don't show up for shuffleboard anymore. I told her because of the lectures. "I can't do both."

We reminisced about Nathan. Hilde misses him in a way, though she didn't like his take-charge attitude. "He even kept score for me. He didn't realize I didn't care about the score."

We loaded up on free Mumm champagne and I loaded up on shrimp. And then, when we were fully stuffed and drunk, we headed up to Queens Grill for dinner. Simon had chilled a Le Montrachet, probably the world's best white wine. Because I'm in a generous, expansive (Irish) mood, I offered Alex a glass. Considering the bottle cost $280, I valued his glass at $35. What the hell, that's what great wines are for—to share with good friends.

At the end of dinner, Ethel announced she can't leave the ship. She will stow away in Alex's cabin and go on to Southampton without me. Alex agreed with the plan, "The idea is reasonable and it won't cost much."

Nick and Colum served us with a special surprise: a fruitcake, on which the chef has written "Celebrating 12 weeks cruising on *QE2* and still talking to each other."

Not only are we still talking to each other, but as soon as we got back to the room, Ethel pulled off my pants, caressed my willy one time, and pushed me into bed.

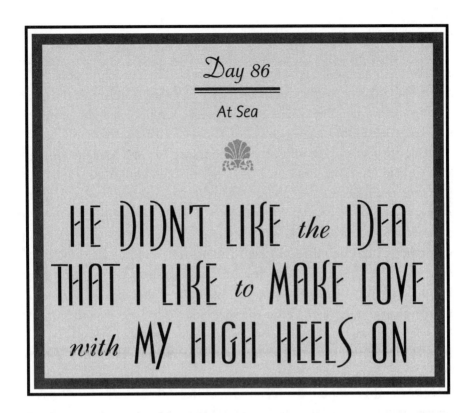

HE DIDN'T LIKE *the* IDEA THAT I LIKE *to* MAKE LOVE *with* MY HIGH HEELS ON

*J*ohn Major, we read in the British papers, announced a crackdown on louts. I asked Alex what a lout is. "You mean you don't know?"

While Ethel decided to stow away because she can't leave *QE2*, I decided to make the most of my remaining days aboard. I went to the new shuffleboard championship. Dudley and Grace won fair and square. Grace was in excellent form today, sometimes scoring thirty-four points in a single frame. Grace is amazing. That's why we called her Amazing Grace. We all sang her song. Now Grace will be the most sought after female partner and Dudley will be the most sought after male partner. For shuffleboard, that is. Since Miss Red Bikini broke off with the deck steward and came back to me, I have been restored to the coveted position of number one male sex object in the hot tub and on One deck.

After the tournament, I wanted to go to the Interdenominational

Divine service run by Captain John Burton-Hall just to see what happens and to be able to say that, one Sunday, I went to church. Geoffrey had other plans for me. For two hours, we chatted about his autobiographical manuscript *No More Nuts*.

Geoffrey tells interesting stories about how he and Dora, his girl, got into trouble after they crashed a party at the USO club in Singapore. Or that time when Dora got a cab by walking in the back door of the Ritz and then walking out the front. Dora died of cancer, but Geoffrey thinks of her every day. And there were those stories of the Beatles who stayed up all night and day and the Duke and Duchess of Windsor and how Geoffrey, now the senior bedroom steward reigning supreme in *QE2*'s penthouses, began his Cunard career as a commis waiter in the *Aquitania*'s tourist-class dining saloon after the war. He told me that decorum was so lax that he and his dining room colleaguers indulged in all kinds of impertinent horseplay with their inexperienced emigrant guests. Including the outlandish trick of—wait a second! Those stories belong to Geoffrey and I can't tell them here. He will put them in his own book, if he can get the time to write one, and if he can give it the proper application, and if he can develop the proper discipline. I told Geoffrey: "Heaven knows I haven't done much writing in my life, but when I have, it's been an absolutely strict discipline, as all serious writers that I know have done. You do so many words a day, say, one thousand."

Being a mentor does put one in some strange situations. I heard myself tell Geoffrey that, because it might interfere with the writing, he should take care not to drink too much. Geoffrey agreed he would try. And I agreed in June to write him to check on his progress or lack of progress.

Recall that the sign in the captain's quarters prayed for "Fair Weather and Following Seas." Instead, we got foul weather and headwinds and rain and lots of ocean motion. *QE2* has entered the equatorial regions where there is continuous congestion of weather systems. Ethel turned pale and went to bed. She felt cold and looked weak, tired, and pitiable. I tucked her in under two blankets as she refused my usual remedy for mal de mer: a stiff drink. "If I drink something, I might vomit," Ethel moaned.

"Wouldn't that help? Hippocrates said emesis cures nausea."

Ethel closed her eyes as I gazed out our two picture windows. Islands of storm floated over the sea, contorting in spasms of white-topped wrath. "I wish I could tell you there is better weather ahead, but there isn't. More trouble is coming. Great sheets of rain, thick and dark and monotonous, continue to float across the white-capped sea."

Ethel didn't respond. She was asleep. The ship lurched and, despite the blankets, she rose one foot from the bed, proving that in a rough sea, a bed might stay put, but its hapless occupant might not.

Despite the weather, I swam in the outdoor pool. Of course, it's rough—but fun. One of the old Germans joined me. He tried to swim but floundered. I almost had to rescue him, but he managed to grab one of the ladders and pulled himself out. I continued to swim for a half hour, loving every minute of it. Rain splashing the face, waves three feet tall rising and falling, white caps too, and swells, just like the real ocean. I can't get enough of this, and I can't get this at home.

After the swim, I met Miss Red Bikini in the One deck passageway where she had waited for me. "Where were you today?" she said as she blew a pink bubble with her chewing gum. Her lips had that puffy look that I liked, like Michelle Pfeiffer. Then she took a drag on her cigarette and spoke while exhaling, the smoke punctuating her speech and suggesting a world of utter decadence, "I missed you all day." Jesus, she had a mouth that made smoking look sinful!

I invited her to come with me to the spa. Miss Red Bikini's real name is Charlotte. She works in Washington, DC, as a librarian. She came along by invitation as a lark. A fascinating woman. She is traveling, she said, with a man who is no longer interested her. Although registered as husband and wife on the ship's manifest, she assured me they are not. "All he wants to do is read and drink and sit on deck in the sun and snooze. We still share the same cabin, and we're friends, but that's it."

Charlotte and I whirlpooled together, swishing around in unison in the rough water. There is nothing, absolutely nothing, worth doing half as much as simply messing about in ninety-three–degree water in the whirlpool of a ship that was frantically tossing in rough seas. Playfully, she pulled me next to her. Close up Charlotte's face looked wrinkled, older—but not bad, understand, just different, as blood looks different when viewed under a microscope. "What about the deck steward?" I asked.

"Didn't work out. He didn't like the idea that I like to make love with my high heels on. I need someone more open and more flexible. Someone I can respect. Someone more intelligent. Someone like you, Benny. Besides, last night I had a dream. I was in the pool. You were wearing your green and yellow Speedo and jumped in."

What harm is there in having a woman friend? I promised I'd meet her at the hot tub tomorrow. Meanwhile, I must do some serious thinking.

Back in penthouse suite 8184, Ethel still lay abed and fast asleep. I woke her for dinner. After dinner she collapsed again. How can anyone sleep so much? Is this a psychological reaction to having to disembark? Or does she have a virus? Is she seasick? If I believed in doctors, I would have taken her to one. Ethel did have enough energy to read over tomorrow's program. Just in case she recovered, she circled the things she wanted to do.

What's this? The program said that it had a purposeful printing error. The first passenger to tell Angela Behrens of the mistake will win a bottle of champagne. Ethel can't find anything wrong. She handed me the program knowing that I will find it instantly for I have a knack for that sort of thing. It's like proofreading. I wrote a note to Angela:

3/31/96 9:17 PM

Angela—The sun rises in the AM and sets in the PM, not vice-versa.
Bernard.

I rushed my answer down to Angela's office and handed her the note. She held a bottle of Mumm in her hand and shook her head. "You should have rung. I was just going to Four deck to deliver the prize. Believe it or not, the champagne has already been won."

But the error set me wondering. What if the sun did rise at night? Would the morning be night and the night be morning? And suppose light and dark were reversed, would we flick a switch to turn on the night? And would it all matter? Chances are we would adjust to it quickly and everything would be the same again.

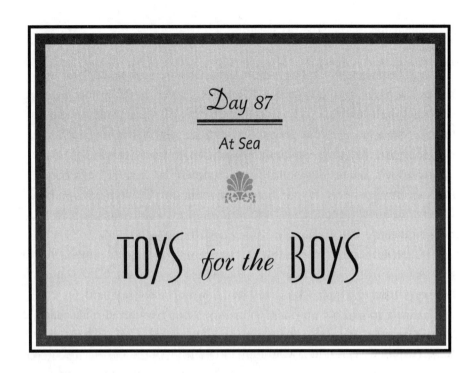

TOYS *for the* BOYS

*T*he sun rises in the southeast and sets in the southwest. Therefore, we have passed into the Northern Hemisphere. *QE2*, for the fourth and last time on this world cruise, passed the equator. The captain issued us our last certificate for crossing. We are now sailing through the horse latitudes, named from olden days when horses traveled by ship at these latitudes because the good weather helped assure that the horses arrived in good shape.

Since the trip draws to a close, I decided to pay my bill. The breakdown looked reasonable: $31 for photos, $525 for laundry, $100 for haircuts, $284 for tours, $498 for shopping (Ethel only, I paid cash), $383 for phone calls, and $87 for books, making $1,908. The rest, $3,413, went for booze. Cunard gave us the onboard credit of $4,000 and another credit of $300 for being in the penthouse. So after subtracting our credit from our bill, our out-of-pocket expense, excluding tips, was $1,021 for three months of cruising.

And talking about money: Bob Lacovara the space engineer who is house-sitting for us just sent a fax telling me that American Express wanted to talk with me. Thus do the realities of life intrude on the fantasies. American Express probably wants to rasp about my not having paid their bill for the last three months. From now on I'm calling it American Distress. Would they cut off my credit? Who cares. I have $35,000 in cash, more than enough to pay my bill, tip Geoffrey, Paul, Nick, Colum, and Alex generously, and still have a sizable hunk left to wire back home.

While at the cashier, waiting for them to count my twenties, I heard a passenger from Russia arguing with the purser. "I need $2,000 now. It was easy to give you money, but when I want it back it's hard."

I volunteered that they could use my money to pay the Russian. "I want hundred-dollar bills, not twenties," he snarled. That's what the passenger wanted. And that's what they gave him.

Another man got irate because they have billed his wife for the room she is in. He wanted one bill for the two rooms and didn't want wifey to be bothered. The purser explained that since he and his wife have separate cabins, they had separate charges assigned to each cabin. "Don't bother my wife. Give me a single bill." That's what the passenger wanted. And that's what they gave him.

The big event today was the tug-of-war.

I arrived at 3:30 on deck, but hundreds of crew and passengers beat me there. I had to stand in back, left peering over multiple shoulders and heads. As they are called, the teams assembled. They stood with rope in hands and at the whistle pulled against each other with all their might. It was the Kinky Pirates against the Drunken Sailors, and Toys for the Boys (a team of women from the Secret Service, named so because they are in hotel services and spend most of their time cleaning rooms without acknowledgment or recognition [tips] from the passengers) versus the Ladies from Queens Grill. Drunken Sailors won, and so did Toys for the Boys. Deck hands, recruited on the spot, quickly and unexpectedly lost to the Caronia waiters and the Hotel Stores. I saw the reason: The deck hands, who looked six times stronger than anyone else, wore street shoes, which slid along the deck. The other teams came prepared with sneakers that gripped the deck firmly. Thus does superior equipment succeed in winning a tug-of-war, just as it succeeds in winning a world war or any other kind of power struggle.

Elimination trials continued. Most of the passengers drifted away, leaving only an important few of us behind including John and Geri Notman, acquaintances from Queens Grill. They are with me at my side, in the front line now, cheering the Piss Artists, the team of waiters from the Queens Grill. The team has Nick and Simon as anchors. We Queens Grillers stick together. Slight acquaintances are always more than they were when people meet in unexpected places. My loyalty to Queens Grill was somewhat irrational though since I had spent more time in Mauretania and Caronia. Why didn't I root for them?

Two Tons of Fun fought the Untouchables. The Secret Service's Toys for Boys and Revenge Four and Powerhouse and the Transformers and the Starlights and Big, Fat, and Balding and Thirteen Days (until leave in Southampton) all duked it out.

The competition intensified. Caronia waiters were disqualified. John and Geri can't figure it out, nor can I. Something serious I suppose. But who knows? Then the Mauretania waiters were disqualified for cheating. The emcee announced, "This is not funny; cheating will not be tolerated." Then, as if by way of apology, the emcee added, "It's nice to want to help the teams, but rules must be followed." The officers stationed new judges on both ends of the deck to inspect the teams.

Interesting! The crew has shown the same behavioral dysfunction as the passengers did during the shuffleboard championships, with one essential difference: with the crew, the rules will prevail and the cheaters will not. Despite the warnings, the judges, "by unanimous vote," disqualified the Queens Grill waiters, known to the world as the Piss Artists, for "having fifteen people on the team, six more than permitted." Thus, by default, Powerhouse beat Queens Grill. Finally, after ninety minutes of other eliminations, we got to the finals.

The Aquas, who came from nowhere, looked strong, in fact, too strong. The Aquas looked artificially constructed of any crewmember who might be an asset in a tug-of-war. Another instance where muscle, weight, and fat counted, and nothing else. Their appearance smacked of cheating or unfair advantage or both, and the crowd of passengers, noting that the crewmembers of Aquas, beside the naked quest for power, had no organic affinity toward one another, resented this fact, seeing it for what it was. To make matters worse, the Aquas strutted around the deck, showing their muscles and thighs, smirking, shouting at the crowd. They boasted that they were sure to win against those weak-willed women on the Toys for the Boys team. It sure looked that way. Toys for the Boys were half their size, had one-fourth their weight, and one-tenth their muscle. Can you blame me for hating the Aquas? I detested their overconfidence, their hubris. I thought of that poem "Casey at the Bat." A poetical ending, that's what I wanted. I wanted the Aquas to strike out. John and Geri wanted that too. In the old days aristocrats like John and Geri would just lop off their heads. They can't do that now. More's the pity.

But they can boo. "Down with the Aquas! Aquas, boo!"

Instead of disapproval, hisses, and ridicule, by contrast, the crowd cheered for the women's team from the hotel accommodation Secret Service. "Toys for the Boys! Yeah! Kill 'em! Toys for the Boys! Yeah! Kill 'em!"

The whistle blew. Within seconds, before we had a chance to shout, "Come on Toys, come on," the Aquas found themselves pulled off the deck. They couldn't believe it, nor could we. But it happened, as if the Toys for the Boys had a secret baby elephant working for them.

While the ecstatic crowd cheered, the Aquas demanded another chance. Make it two out of three pulls. "We weren't ready. After all, it's the championship."

"OK," said Toys for the Boys, being real sports. Why not give the Aquas another try?

Both teams lined up. The whistle blew. Another pull! Whoosh! This time it's worse. The Aquas are jerked right off their feet. They lost again. And they lost for good. For a full three minutes, the crowd screamed, clapped, and cheered. The underdogs won. How delightful! And what is better: there is no joy in the hallowed halls of power where the Aquas' team was put together. The mighty Aquas have struck out, defeated easily by Toys for the Boys, a team of runted, disgruntled ladies who in silent service clean the rooms of *QE2*. These gals don't look like much, but they sure can pull.

Captain John Burton-Hall invited us to another party for the full world-cruise passengers and members of the World Cruise Society. With a sigh of relief we heard it would be the last. Are we cloyed? Surfeit? Or just satiated? By now you must know the scene: "1996" written in ice. Festoons. Trays of crab claws, shrimp, mussels, canapés, caviar, and ice-cold vodkas. Marvelous Peking duck rolled into wheat pancakes and smeared with plum sauce. Whirling dances to tunes known around the world. More vodka and caviar. Joy. Happiness. Good friends. Fun. Festivity. Amusement. Diversion. Whirlwind good times.

How fast they fade!

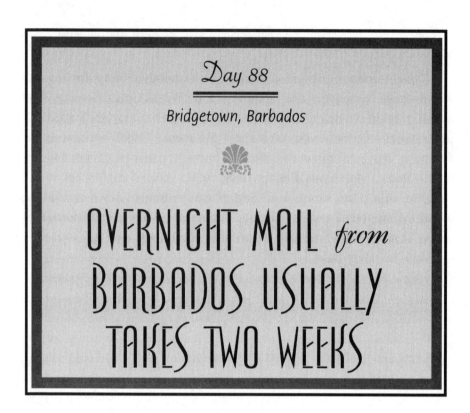

Day 88

Bridgetown, Barbados

OVERNIGHT MAIL *from* BARBADOS USUALLY TAKES TWO WEEKS

*W*e awoke and found ourselves docked in Barbados next to Club Med's ship, the *Horizon*. Across the way was P&O's *Princess*. One of the guidebooks, I forget which, said you can tell the seasoned cruise passengers from the unseasoned, because they don't get up to see the ship come into port. If that's true, we're seasoned, well seasoned. Not only would we not get up to see that, we also wouldn't even think of it.

Three other ships—that means stiff competition for taxis. All those tourists sure do get in the way.

Ethel changed her mind. She wants to leave the ship. She wants to see and pet P.J. I'm indifferent. Sure, I wish to pet my cat, but I'm happy here and I will be happy at home. And if I were home, what would I do? Probably go out in my boat.

Charlotte (also known as Miss Red Bikini) passed us, heading in the opposite direction and leaving a wake of smoke and perfume two yards wide and ten yards long. Smoke and perfume has always suggested a world of utter decadence that attracts me like a magnet. Charlotte's dazzling sexy beauty makes me catch my breath. "Did you see her?" Ethel asked.

"Who?"

"That woman who just went by. She's your type."

Crewmen have lowered the lifeboat. An examination on safety at sea, the practical third of the examination took place alongside the ship in the harbor. Geoffrey, our penthouse butler, failed the test. He told me why, "I have trouble giving orders." Along the deck, we passed sleeping passengers. One of them, on the One deck aft, had an 0 sign. This means his head is back and his mouth opened to form a rounded opening that looks like an 0. Physicians have ways of appraising the physical state of people while they sleep. The 0 represents the state of least decrepitude. Following that and getting worse is the Q sign, where the 0 has the tongue hanging out of the mouth to simulate a Q. And last is the fly sign, where the flies alight on the open mouth, whether it shows a Q or an 0. I saw no fly signs, although 0s and, more rarely, Q signs do appear. Bob, the Queens Griller who usually falls asleep at dinner, sometimes has a 0 but nothing more serious. The thought occurred to me that Bob might sleep less at dinner if he drank fewer martinis. Perhaps I should talk to him about this. But, who am I to reprove a drinker? Last night Bob was fast asleep while still chewing his food. That constitutes, I believe, a new and previously unreported sign whose significance remains, at this moment, moot. Chewing is an extraordinary complex action, and I found it amazing that someone could sleep and chew at the same time. But Bob can and does. He must swallow too; else he would have, long ago, choked to death. Sleep eaters—well why not? Sleep walkers, sleep talkers, and sleep eaters are of imagination and all compact: they all do things in their sleep.

In a symbolic gesture presaging her return to domestic concerns, Ethel removed the withered flowers from one of our three floral displays. Her right arm got covered with deep yellow pollen. In an instant I realized where Geoffrey got his yellowed pinkie finger: the flowers.

Ethel doesn't want to have anything to do with the Chase Vaults and the mystery of the moving coffins that has attracted visitors to Barbados for over a hundred years. The moving coffins are at Christ Church. I'll let her have her way and go with her to the beach. She'll soon tire of sun and surf and then I'll suggest an island tour, which will conveniently swing by the Chase Vaults. Once there, I intended in ten minutes to solve the ancient mystery of why and who moved these six-hundred-pound lead-lined coffins without disturbing the sand around them. Numerous deacons and well-thought-of public figures in Barbados have attested to the fact that the coffins moved. No earthquakes occur in Barbados, so that is not the explanation. But recall that deception is a kind of specie that one has to plan carefully, especially in marriage where one's actions are often so transparent to a practiced partner who has lived decades with you. I might get away with visiting the coffins, but I know I won't get away with both seeing the coffins and visiting the place where George Washington stayed.

Yes, Washington slept here in Bridgetown. The father of our country visited as a tourist in 1751, accompanied by his half brother, Lawrence. Lawrence, afflicted with tuberculosis, needed a rest. The trip combined tourism with health. Pretty economically too: they paid £15 a month for accommodations, exclusive of liquor and laundry. Lawrence Washington served in the British navy in the Caribbean on the flagship of Admiral Vernon, after whom he named his estate in Virginia, Mount Vernon. When Lawrence died, George inherited the place and kept the name.

George Washington kept a detailed daily diary, even more extensive than this one you now have in hand. In his diary, he mentioned how much he loved Barbados. He and Major Gedney Clarke (whose home they occupied) and Lawrence viewed the sights of this fair island from a coach drawn by six horses. Of one such excursion George wrote: "We were perfectly enraptured with the beautiful prospects which every side presented to our view fields of cane [George spelled it *Cain* with a capital *C*], Corn [another capital], Fruit Trees &c [his sign for *etc.*], in a delightful Green."

Perhaps Washington was an insular maniac, a person (like myself) who finds islands irresistible. The mere knowledge that they are on an island, a little world surrounded by the sea, fills these people with an indescribable intoxication.

The Clarkes passed the Washingtons en route to the Carters, who in turn led them to the Crofton's, where George got smallpox and spent the next three weeks at death's door. George made history by recovering, a rare event in those times and in anytime, since smallpox usually proves fatal. The smallpox episode made a lasting impression on Washington, for when Jefferson suggested that a vaccination for smallpox might help prevent the disease, Washington ordered every single man in the Continental army vaccinated. The rest, as they say, is history: Smallpox killed many more British soldiers than it killed Continentals. British soldiers were not vaccinated because the British medical establishment didn't believe in vaccination. British doctors have, I think, on this issue subsequently changed their minds. Hence, smallpox, this little RNA virus, working for the American side, literally won the Revolutionary War for us. Not a single vaccinated Continental soldier died of smallpox, a predictable result since smallpox vaccination is 100 percent effective, so effective that no case of smallpox has occurred any place on this planet for over a decade.

History is replete with stories like that. I love them, the insignificant events that turn out to have significance beyond anything ever imagined. And since history composes itself from contingent things, events that don't have to happen, one wonders what would have happened if George Washington had not come to Barbados, or if he had not gotten smallpox, or worse, what would have happened if he died of smallpox here in Barbados? Who would have won the Revolution if smallpox had killed an equal number of British and Continental soldiers?

As predicted, many tourists jammed the taxi stand, pushing and shouting as usual.

The ninety-one-year-old woman from Queens Grill (the one who put her dress on backward) stepped ahead of me and told the dispatcher, "I want a taxi now! I feel sick!"

The dispatcher is used to all that and the likes of her. He just shook his head, and said quietly and firmly and politely, while motioning her back, "No. If you're sick, go back to the ship. Otherwise, you'll have to wait."

Miss 91 is no longer aboard *QE2*, where they have to fall for her baloney. To the dispatcher she strangely resembled an ordinary mortal. "Now!" she commanded.

The dispatcher ignores her and motions the next in line into a taxi.

Although Miss 91 stepped back, other people did not. They kept pushing ahead and jumping into the cabs before they got near the stand. The Barbados police tried to restore order but *QE2*ers remain, as we all should know by know, difficult to discipline.

A large bin of garbage just removed from the ship started to roll toward the dock edge. It just missed some tourists. A Filipino grabbed it as it was about to tip into the water. He saved it from a watery grave. While watching the bin, we almost got run over by a large truck carrying cases of Heineken and Coors beer. Waiting for a taxi in Barbados can be quite hazardous.

Miss 91 tapped me insistently and viciously on the back, saying in a raspy voice, "Your elbow is blocking me. Stand aside."

I solved the problem by moving six inches, something she could have done if she wanted to. Why didn't she? Because she wanted to show that she was still alive. She wanted to further define her miserable existence by causing trouble.

I persuaded a driver to take us to the marine park for $15, American. Be careful here. Barbadian currency, worth half that of American currency, is also called the dollar. Make sure you know what dollars you are talking about.

Before our taxi pulled out, Miss 91 pulled open the left front door of our taxi and, without asking the driver's permission, hopped into the front left seat. (They drive on the left here so the steering wheel and the driver sit on the right.) The driver asked, "Where to?"

The raspy voice replied, "I don't know. Where are we?"

He repeated his question while looking at her a little strangely, "Where do you want to go?"

She replied, "I don't know, I told you!"

He motioned for us to go in the backseat. "These people want to go to the marine park. Do you want to go there?"

"Goodness, no. I have a sore arm. And I can't swim."

"Come with us into the countryside. After I drop them off, I'll bring you back to town."

"No, I can't afford it."

"But, I haven't quoted a price."

"I don't care. I can't afford it, whatever it is. Let me out." Whereupon, Miss 91 pushed the door open and jumped out.

On the way, the driver told us that he avoids the older passengers who come from the big ships. "They cause too much trouble with lots of phony complaints. Mon, they talk. Make you look bad. Some say you take their money. Old mon keeps saying I took his money. Next week he find it in drawer. Look at me."

Our driver took his eyes off the road, turned around to face us, but in the process he turned the wheel and swerved into oncoming traffic. He caught himself and jerked us back into our lane, avoiding a front-end collision with a blue pickup truck. He continued, "I have a wife and five children. Tourism is my business. Do you think I would cut my own throat?"

Our driver, Hector, proposed a tour after we have had our fill of the beach. He said he will pick us up and drive us around the island. "We'll see the botanical gardens and then swing by the Chase Vaults."

Ethel frowned. She smells a rat. But Hector pointed on his map to how the vaults lie right in the path going back to the ship. Great! We agreed on the price of $70 American and agreed to meet him in the marine park parking lot at 2 PM. But, recall, we have been through this before in Thailand. I told him, "If you don't arrive by 2:15, we leave." I didn't pay in advance. That way we won't wait more than a quarter hour, no matter what.

While I swam at the marine park, Ethel paddled (paddled is British for waded) in the turquoise water. We walked next door to the swanky Coral Reef Club for lunch.

I started with chilled guava pineapple juice. Why can't we get nectar of the gods at home? Then I had crabmeat salad, shrimp salad, tunafish salad, pizza, quiche Lorraine, followed by roast beef, chicken, baked kingfish with herb butter, apple strudel, and a papaya. I ended with cappuccino. After eating each item I commented to Ethel about the taste, color, aroma, consistency, and freshness, and compared that item to the fare on *QE2*.

"Are you becoming a foodie?" Ethel asked.

"Not at all. It is impossible to become what you are already."

I charged the meal. Twenty minutes went by before the downcast waiter returned with a puzzled look on his face. "No work, Mon. Platinum card too. First time I seed that. Captain tried. Still no work."

I paid in cash. Now what? There are only two serious diseases: lack of cash and lack of credit. Of the two, the latter is more serious than the former. Ethel thought while we are at it, we should celebrate the disgrace of a refused platinum card by having another go at one of those expensive wines, which we can't afford. "Good idea," I said. "How about La Tache, one of the great red burgundies of the world? We can get it in Queens Grill for only $380 a bottle."

Hector didn't show. We took another cab, which appeared from nowhere at exactly 2:15 and took us back to the ship. I accepted the judgment of fate: I'll never get to solve the Chase Vault mystery.

In view of the financial emergency, I hooked up my portable phone and called American Distress. I dialed #18 and sure enough the operator came on. Within ten minutes I had a callback number in Barbados. I can call anywhere in the world. The portable phone operator seemed reluctant to inform me that the calls cost 62 cents BBD per minute. She couldn't understand my enthusiasm for the fees. I didn't tell her it's a far lower rate than the ship's $50 BBD per minute.

Sure enough, American Express had cut off my credit. I pleaded with the American Express agent. No dice. I pleaded with the supervisor. No dice. I explained I have had an American Express card since 1969. So what? I explain that I'm away on the world cruise and didn't get any mail. Too bad. I explained that I had previously charged and paid over $100,000 to the card this year alone. Yawn. Then I thought of something: "I'm writing a book about the world cruise and will have to include a section on how you cut off my platinum card line of credit."

The supervisor said, "Dr. Patten, we understand that the amount of money involved for you is trivial, but we need a check for $8,600 before we can reactivate your card." They suggested I send the check from Barbados by overnight mail. "But overnight mail from Barbados usually takes two weeks."

Meanwhile, my card will remain no good, a serious inconvenience, because I wanted to use it to buy a beachfront home on Magens Bay in St. Thomas.

The post office closed at 4 PM, but a policeman got them to open up and process my letter. How's that for service! He said it was nothing special. He was trying to think of a way to talk to the cute black beauty who ran the post office. I gave him the excuse. The two of them remained talking tête-à-tête as I walked back to the ship. If they do marry, American Distress was the cause.

Next, I called Vince. He confirmed the breast implant companies did me dirty on the TV program. Somehow they made it look like I didn't believe in my own research. I do, of course, perhaps too much. They showed me getting in the limo. Instead of hearing me say "TV is junk food for the mind," the audience heard a voiceover say that the FBI was investigating me for Medicare fraud. So, maybe when I get back to the States, the FBI will be there to put on the cuffs.

Tonight we went to the pirate party and barbecue on Helicopter deck. The full moon hung overhead. Soft Bajan (the native term for Barbadian) breezes waft across the dance floor as we strutted our stuff to tunes played by the full *QE2* band. The crowd was exuberant. They are trying to make every minute of pleasure count. And as specialists in that particular field, they are doing great. Even Leonard is out there with a girlfriend. They are cutting a rug. And Louis and Margaret, Dave and Bobby, John and Geri, Charlotte and the man who is not her husband do the same. Charlotte is puppyish tonight, leaning on his shoulder and smiling. They probably patched things up, at least for tonight.

While Ethel and I did the rumba, I gazed up at the crystal-clear ocean night. Orion was there with his shimmering jewels of Betelgeuse and Rigel, and I wondered at Sirius, the Dogstar, the brightest body in our heavens, about which I knew nothing until Professor Kurtz came along. The full moon still has a rabbit in it, not a man. Suddenly I realized the moon and Earth and where the sun went down are lined up exactly. The thrill of it sent a shiver down my spine. Tomorrow Earth's shadow will ellipse the full moon and we will witness an eclipse. This is the first time that I have ever predicted an eclipse.

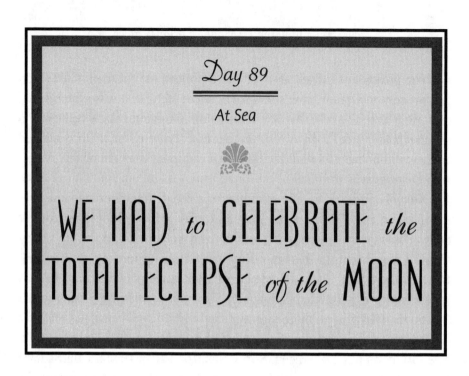

Day 89

At Sea

WE HAD *to* CELEBRATE *the* TOTAL ECLIPSE *of the* MOON

*B*efore we leave the ship I should review the penthouse.

The room we have, 8184, has two enormous picture windows that look out over the sea and over a lifeboat, on which we sometimes see, especially in the early morning, Filipinos checking something. Ethel hopes they are not checking out our morning mating techniques. And if they are, that we meet their standards.

This penthouse suite is misnamed because it is not really a suite: It doesn't have a separate bedroom with a door that can be locked. Instead, the bed, a king-sized one bigger than the total space of our entire M5 room, occupies an alcove on the forward side adjacent to, but not physically separate from, the living room.

Of course, we have the usual TV and radio and tape player and refrigerator and private safe. The walk-in closet measures about the size of M5 and so does our bathroom, which in addition to a large tub and marvelous white marble walls has gold fixtures for the tub, sink, toilet, and bidet. Our sitting room encompasses three chairs and a sofa with a small table, on which each night our butlers, Geoffrey and Paul, place a silver platter filled with canapés. (Geoffrey also puts the newspapers, the *Time* magazines, the faxes, and the letters on my bedstand so I don't miss them.) The new thing here is our own bar, with cabinets loaded with genuine lead-crystal wine and water glasses. The refrigerator has Perrier water and soft drinks, which we have used when we entertain. In fact, our penthouse rooms are the first rooms in which we have felt entirely comfortable entertaining other passengers or crew. With the other rooms on other lower decks, we always knew there were other, better accommodations higher up, and we wondered if our room might not measure up to our friends' tastes. With our penthouse we knew we were in, with the exception of the double-decker Queen Mary and Queen Anne suites, the best accommodations *QE2* had to offer.

I also have a large desk area to work at and at this moment have over twenty books within easy reach of my computer. Drawer space far exceeds our needs and most of the drawers have remained empty. Tomorrow when I make up the tips, if I feel up to it, I'll go over this segment's costs, which exceeded $3,000 a day. All in all, the penthouse rooms are the largest, most modern, and best rooms we have occupied on *QE2*, and they are the ones we like the best.

Ethel and I picked up the picture taken during the dinner when we celebrated twelve weeks aboard. It's only a photograph and will soon fade, but it did capture us each looking marvelously healthy and happy, and it captured Nick and Colum, our handsome and happy waiters, who in the picture, as in life, continue to hover over us, sheltering us in their protective arms. If Ethel or I are cloyed or surfeit, it doesn't show. If Nick and Colum are overworked, resentful, jealous, or displeased, it doesn't show.

Poor Jonathan Wicks, *QE2*'s executive chef. He slipped in the kitchen and broke a bone. These days he hobbles around deck with a cast on his left foot and in his right hand he holds a brown wooden stave for support. At lunch, he came by to talk with us, claiming he has endured "all the possible dirt" about his condition. That is, he thought he had.

Mrs. Rodrigues, at the next table, said, "You look like a shepherd, Jonathan, but where are your sheep?"

Wicks replied, "You ate them last night, madam."

Whereupon, while I was eating apple strudel with the rich vanilla sauce dripping down the corner of my mouth, I attempted to console him, "Ethel and I don't care where your sheep are. Sheep or no sheep, we will follow you to the ends of the Earth. A person who can cook the way you do should be considered a British national treasure."

Dave, my friend from computer class, said it's time for the cruise to end. "When trivial things start bothering you, it is time to move on and do something different before you start behaving like some of the others."

I asked Dave how he felt about the world cruise, since he and Bobby have stayed in the penthouse and eaten in Queens Grill the whole trip. "It was a vast cultural experience that you cannot duplicate for any price."

Leonard visited and had canapés and a drink of Perrier before dinner. Unfortunately, he is one of those Lloyds of London "names," whose losses have been several times over the cost of a world cruise. "Is there no limit to the liability?" I asked while munching some salmon-coated caviar.

Leonard, his mouth full, shook his head no.

"Can't you get out of it?"

No again. "Asbestos, there doesn't appear to be an end to it," he opined. "And now it's breast implants."

"You pay for that too?"

"Yes, Lloyds insured implants. I think too many."

Ethel and Leonard meticulously went through each and every party, tea, cocktail reception, and gift that they have received during the last eighty-nine days. The gifts coincide exactly, except for the farewell flowers from the captain and from the cruise director, Brian Price. We thought Leonard, from the same sources, will receive his sweet bouquets a few days before he gets off in Southampton. Leonard said, "Over two hundred people crashed the party with the captain the night before last. There are only about a hundred and seventy-two real world cruisers. That party had more than five hundred."

"Hey, Leonard, let's go up to Boat deck starboard-side to look at the moon face-to-face. There will be an eclipse tonight."

"I rather doubt it, Bernard [Leonard always pronounced my name the correct way, BERnud, not berNARD. And why not? I wouldn't call him leoNARD]." And then he said in that crisp authorative British English: "If there were to be an eclipse, the ship's program would have announced it."

I explained the geometry that made the eclipse mandatory. Leonard was convinced.

Ethel remained skeptical. "Eclipse? No way. All that booze has finally pickled your brain." So Ethel stayed behind. And missed the eclipse.

On deck, Leonard and I saw the rounded shadow of Earth eat out the moon's light, changing it from white to rosy red, like a fire burning low in a huge stone fire pit, and eventually blackening it altogether. A total eclipse. Millennia ago Aristotle saw that happen and concluded that because Earth's shadow on the moon was round, the Earth must be round as well. With periodic visits, Leonard and I followed the thing, the moon's mystic play of shadows twining and twisting and dancing as if they were alive in the night sky. By eight o'clock the total eclipse was over and the moon had lifted out of complete shadow but remained in the penumbra of Earth, looking red, then pale and copper, and then yellow. After dinner the full moon had reacquired its usual bright white complexion, proving in the end, that history, the world, the moon, this solar system, all of it, belongs to us, because more than any other animal, we understand it. Not only that: certain of us who pay attention to lecturers like Professor Kurtz not only understand it, but also can predict eclipses. Amazing! And of course, although our credit is low, it's a reason to celebrate.

Credit low? That's an exaggeration. Our credit is zero. But still we had to celebrate the total eclipse of the moon with a special wine, a bottle of La Tache. And how about a few rounds of twenty-five-year-old scotch?

What will tomorrow bring, sorrow or anything other than joy? What if it's winter's chill, rain, storm, or summer's thrill? Tomorrow's still the future. This is today!

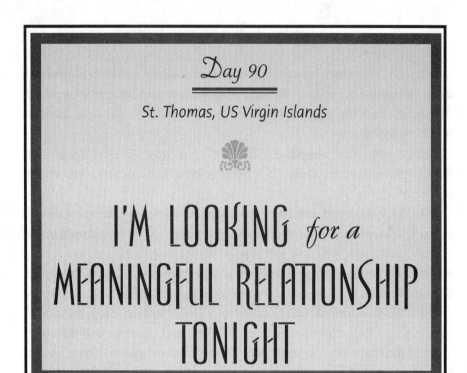

Day 90

St. Thomas, US Virgin Islands

I'M LOOKING *for a*
MEANINGFUL RELATIONSHIP
TONIGHT

*W*e couldn't land at St. Croix because Hurricane David had flattened the area, swiftly transferring much of the island's landing pier into the Caribbean. So we had to tender to Charlotte Amalie (pronounced by the locals with the accent on the first, not the second, syllable, just like the original Dutch pronunciation), capital of St. Thomas.

St. Thomas must be the patron saint of shopping. There are shops everywhere, each bearing the great names of our materialistic society like Cartier, Ebel, Gucci. The perfumes, capable of taking the stink out of life, floated out of stores and on through the street, Safari (Ralph Lauren), Arpege (Lanvin), Tresor (Lancôme), Gio (Armani), and Dune, Poison, Tendre Poison, Diorissimo, and Miss Dior (last five by Dior).

I bought four bottles of Dune because it was billed as "un parfum de sérénité aux notes florales océanique" (a perfume of serenity with oceanic floral notes). I resisted the pull of AH Riise liquors and their tasting bar where some of the male members of our crew were already plastered. You avoid them too: there are no liquor bargains in St. Thomas.

Outside Riise's store one woman from *QE2* talked to another about the cruise from hell that cost Cunard £7.8 million. Don't the pearls, emeralds, diamonds, tanzanite rubies, transparent tourmalines, translucent sapphires, necklaces, baubles, bangles, and beads interest her? Can't she see them glitter and shine? Why can't she act normally and shop like the rest of us? That shakedown cruise ended long ago. Why continue bitching about ancient history?

For $8 Ethel and I got a cab and headed right to Magens Bay beach, one of the best, if not the best beach in the world. Along the way, I noticed something: the Virgin Islands are part of the United States of America, but they drive on the left side of the road. Yet the steering wheel is on the right. It all works, just like anything else that people agree on.

We went to the right place, because some *QE2*ers and most of the crew were there at Magens already, all huddled in the bar because it was raining hard.

While they watched the rain and drank prodigious quantities of beer, I swam the entire length of the bay. Inebriate of rain am I! And debauchee of damp. The feel of tropical rain teeming on my head. Reeling through endless turquoise water, I plunged along. It's like I'm taking a shower and a bath at the same time. Delicious! Between the heaves of the storm there was a stillness in the air, and like Dune, a breath of serenity with oceanic floral notes. Though mankind cannot return to Paradise, at least Magens Bay offers sanctuary to us exiles, a reminder of Paradise.

Halfway across the two-mile stretch, I noticed that enough rain had fallen to form a three-inch layer of freshwater on top of the briny water of the bay. Interesting effect: I'm gliding in a layer of freshwater, but, since the bay is salty, theoretically I'm not.

I'm also not swimming alone. Millions of little green fish are swimming with me. Every once in a while, they get agitated, frightened by a much larger fish splashing through the water in back of them. The little fish took off, literally jumped out of the water, flew above the surface at an altitude of two to four inches, and then, after having made a flight of about nine feet, fell back again into their watery home. How do they do it? I don't know. They can jump. But are they really flying? They do flap their fins furiously fast as they travel through the air. I saw them. I kid you not. They flap as if their very life depended on their remaining aloft. Which, I suppose, it does.

A king pelican came to their rescue. He dove two feet into the water. Coming up, the pelican had the big fish in his beak. The pelican floated on the soft rolling sea swell, in the pouring rain, and eyed me with contempt as he tried to swallow the big fish, which was making a giant bulge in his neck. Finally the fish went down. The pelican turned to me and seemed to be saying with his round bulging eyes, "You dumb fuck. Didn't you see that big fish next to you? Why didn't you go for it?"

That's what it's all about. Isn't it? One species eating another. Nature, we soon find out on closer inspection, is not a groovy way to channel wholeness, but really more like *Nightmare on Elm Street.*

I turned onto my back and started kicking furiously to show the pelican that I can do something he can't. The moment he flew away, the little fish started flying again. New power—it was I that moved them. By kicking hard, I can make them fly. It's fun, an innocent source of amusement. The little green fish probably think my legs are two other big fish that could menace them. But they can't figure out why some of their numbers are not getting eaten. Enjoying my new authority over fish, I made thousands of them fly around my head. I know I can't tell Ethel about the experience, for she would think it in bad taste to tease such cute little innocent creatures of God.

When I reached the end of the bay, I hit the shore and walked back. The rain was cold and hard and it stung as it hit, and the wind cut like a whetted knife. But I felt great. In fact, I felt more alert and more awake than I had ever felt before.

Ethel waited under a tree and got soaked to the bone, so we headed to the bar and had piña coladas. I ate a hot dog and we both had the homemade mutton stew, a Magens Bay specialty, which was just as good as the Queens Grill cuisine. No, it was better, because we're cold and wet and hungry.

"I see by the paper they caught the Unabomber," said Ethel.

"Thank God, it's over. I was worried because I fit the FBI profile—I graduated summa cum laude from an Ivy League school and have a science background."

Ethel downed her colada and ordered another. "Having majored in chemistry, I'm sure you can make a bomb." She pointed an accusatory finger at me.

"Chemistry may have been my major, but my real interest was love. Therefore I would never bomb anyone."

"Not university professors, perhaps, but you bombed Dow and the other implant manufacturers," said Ethel. "Anyway, I knew you weren't the Unabomber. You're not so much of a loner as he was."

*QE2*ers sported on deck their recently acquired St. Thomas T-shirts, some of which say interesting things: "A man is like a tile floor. Lay it right the first time and you can walk all over it for the rest of your life." Another, worn by Charlotte: "I'm looking for a meaningful relationship tonight."

Back at the penthouse, Monsignor Foley visited and discovered that in our bar we have real leaded crystal. He admired this as he drank his twenty-five-year-old Macallan single-malt Scotch whiskey. Foley is a jolly soul who shares with Geoffrey, our butler, an affection for strong drink. I like them—all three.

"You know, Father, I wished, during the world cruise, that I had gone to Mass at least once, but I didn't. I was too busy." Foley understood. There is no sin he would not forgive, especially with a single-malt in hand.

Then we got the bad news: Captain John Burton-Hall came on and announced, "I have had word that the *Royal Viking Sun* ran aground near Accaba. The ship hit a coral reef in the Red Sea and is taking on water, but the pumps are holding. Passengers have mobilized at the lifeboats, but have not yet needed to abandon ship. More details will follow."

Holy cow! Holy mad cow!

Three ships set out to sail the ocean blue. *Sagafjord* caught fire. Then there were two. Another hit a reef, *Royal Viking Sun*. And now of three, remains but one.

WAS THAT *a* PIG *of* ILL OMEN?

*G*ood Friday and we are about to be crucified, after which we descend
into hell and (I hope) after that rise again. We got ready for the
descent by packing. The baggage master helped by taking my five cartons
of books and the six-foot statue of the black lady out of the penthouse and
away to I know not where. These items joined massive amounts of other
stuff called "unaccompanied baggage," which will get to us I know not
how, I know not when. *QE2* has taught me her lessons well. Don't worry.
Someone will do the job.

We also made a list of all our purchases. If they wanted, US Customs
could make it a nightmare. US law is complicated. Every country has its
own little exemption or gimmick. American Distress made it easy for me
to decide what to do with all my cash: pay the bills and tip. I have one
regret. When I pay in cash, I get no frequent-flyer miles, the only real
advantage of paying with the American Distress card.

I won't have to declare that I have $5,000 or more of monetary instruments, because I don't have it. Wait a second! What about the three million dollars' worth of Amgen stock I have in my pocket? The customs flyer said stocks and bonds must be declared or they are subject to seizure. My problem is that I didn't declare the stocks going out, so if I declare them coming in, there might be questions and trouble. I put the certificates in an envelope and addressed it to myself. I placed two stamps on it. The stamps show two beautiful, obviously female angels, against a starry background. Into your hands, oh my most beautiful angels, do I commend my three million dollars.

I've had problems like this before. Once, on returning from France, after I had already handed in the form with nothing to declare, customs told me they had a tip that I was carrying a large amount of currency, or currency equivalents, and they wanted me to come clean, make it easy for myself, and avoid more trouble. Otherwise they would take my bags apart, find the money, seize it, and prosecute me. "Come on, Doc. Make it easy for yourself."

"Search away," I said handing the man a large leather bag while I clutched close to my side my attaché case that contained the money and the bearer bonds. The customs agents opened everything in front of them but found nothing. They were too intense and too excited to think about the attaché case. Come to think on it, why mail my stock certificates? I might try the attaché case trick again. It worked once. It could work again. I only have three million dollars to lose and maybe some jail time.

The problems of disembarkation, our problems, shrink to insignificance compared to those problems experienced by the passengers on the *Royal Viking Sun*.

"That Cunard luxury liner," said the *British Times* today, carrying one thousand passengers and crew on a round-the-world cruise, was towed into port after hitting a coral reef in the Red Sea. So far, so good. Except *Royal Viking Sun* is not a liner. It is a cruise ship. The reporter probably doesn't know the difference.

"Passengers, including 54 Britons and 450 Americans, donned life jackets and went to lifeboat stations after they took on water and began to list following the impact last night." This story has no byline so I can't tell who implies that the lifeboat stations took on water. This example of sloppy writing proves that even British journalists sometimes can't get down a decent clear English sentence. Notice how Americans outnumber the Brits almost ten to one.

The article continued, "Tugs towed the ship to the Egyptian port of Sharm el-Sheikh as the company announced the rest of the 116 day cruise would be abandoned. Passengers were told to expect compensation for the abrupt end to the cruise, which cost upwards of 21,500 pounds, due to end April 29."

God! This writing's jumbled! Shame.

"Cunard Spokesman Peter Bates said the passengers were 'all safe, there are absolutely no injuries. They are reasonably happy, considering what they have been through.' An operator at the international control centre in Stavanger, Norway, which controlled the rescue operation, said, 'engine power was lost after the collision, pumps were used to expel the water and put the ship back on an even keel as passengers mustered at life-boat stations.'"

But, what about the coral?

"Officials at the Mohamed Nature Reserve, a protected area of coral reefs at the southern tip of the Sinai Peninsula, said they were checking to see how much damage had been done to the coral."

I told Ethel, "Three ships set out on world cruises. Only one made it."

"Not yet. We haven't finished," she replied.

"You're right. In fact, I missed the lesson of *RVS*'s misadventure, the lesson of my own story, the conflict between nature and humanity. The sea, a symbol for nature, is indifferent to people. Alternately cruel and kind, teasing or menacing, the sea is as heartless as a cancer. Consequently, survival is often a matter of chance. Humanity's struggles are grimly ironic, because accidental death always hovers nearby and, that failing, certain death always awaits us farther on. The careful reader would have realized what I didn't: the contingency of their existence, the precious tenuousness of life. The universe, toward us, recognizes no sense of obligation."

I can't muster enough energy to go to Brian Price's lecture on the construction of *QE2*, nor can I go to Waldemar's on customs rules. My experience with government dictates that attending a lecture on the rules wastes precious time. The government itself doesn't know the rules. Most rules are ignored or not enforced. They are too complex or too stupid or both. And the rules change so often it pays not to keep up with them. I resolved to just do something more useful with the time like sleep, or sit out on deck and admire the vast and shimmering sea, or swim in the One deck pool, or soak in the hot tubs or whirlpool with Charlotte.

Wait a second! A notice in the daily program said that those who purchased the tour of the bridge should assemble on Boat deck A stairway. I sensed a mistake. Advertising like that will produce a bunch of queue jumpers. That's what the British call them. We would call them something else. Louts? No, that's not it. Line breakers? Maybe. Sons of bitches? Yes.

Twenty-two people showed up for the tour, but only ten have paid. No one seemed to know who paid and who didn't, so they had to take us all.

The first stop was the radio room. Only one officer was on duty. He kept getting interrupted by phone calls. He showed me the TV and told us we just got hooked up to CNN. The color image of the man sitting next to me one table forward and one table to port in the Queens Grill stared out at me with that haughty supercilious smile of his. I thought that guy might be a TV personality. Now I know he is. Actually, he looked better on TV than he did in Queens Grill. Probably it's the effect of makeup, and the lack of the multiple drinks he usually has in the lounge before he and his wife enter the restaurant.

"Everything used to be Morse code and radio, but now it's satellites," the officer explained. "Satellites for communication, satellites for navigation."

"So why don't they call it the satellite room?" I asked. "Because tradition carries weight, especially on *QE2*. And getting a navigational fix by satellite is fundamentally an efficient, but soulless activity."

The harassed radio officer showed us a floppy disk from the computer that downloads the daily news. From the disk they print out directly onto paper in the print shop and distribute it. This explained the sometimes incoherent and occasionally jumbled news that we get: no editorial control.

He showed us the Cunard communication net, wherewith everyone on the Cunard ships can talk to everyone else through the New York office, which represents the center of the net. We then got a demo of how to fax to Norway. But during the demo, a call came in from France. It sounded clear as a bell and the French sounded authentic, so I know they didn't just stage the call.

On the bridge, Richard Bridge, the navigator, showed us around. The interlopers have lost interest. They wandered about, talking to themselves and making it difficult to hear. Bridge showed us the radar clutter, which picks up waves up to 96 miles away, where the horizon ends. The radar's actual range is 160 miles, so part of the radar goes right off the curve of Earth and into space. No wave clutter in space. Bridge and the group looked out the window. The horizon narrowed and widened, and dipped and rose, and at all times its edge was jagged with waves that seemed thrust up in points like rocks, reflecting themselves clearly in the jumbled hash on the radarscope. "But how do you tell the wave clutter from a small ship?" a Spanish-accented voice in back asked. Bridge smiled, and with his right index finger pointed to his right eye. "We look out the window. And the human eye always beats radar and the human mind always beats the autopilot for common sense," he added. We've heard all this before so we are not surprised that things haven't, in the last few weeks, changed.

Bridge then set the course for 302. "Once the course is set, the autopilot would continue to steer the ship 302 no matter what, into other ships, even into America. It's that dumb!"

Bridge loves *QE2*. I can tell by the way he talks he loves her more than he loves his own country. I'll bet one day, perhaps soon, he'll be the master here.

Bridge showed us the big wave damage on the bow. The wave bent the steel and "set down the deck," but "they built *QE2* for North Atlantic service so it can take it. Other ships can't, especially those of recent vintage." Bridge rolled his eyes. He was, I believe, making reference to the *Royal Viking Sun*, which was commissioned December 16, 1988.

The Spanish voice asked, "What was it like when that ninety-three-foot wave hit?"

Bridge said, "An estimated four thousand tons of water hit the ship. The wind was force-ten, about 140 knots, before the anemometer blew off. I had never seen anything like it. I just stood here my mouth agape in awe of the terrible forces of nature."

Tonight in Queens Grill, everyone seemed to have had more than usual to drink. The Mr. and Mrs. Gin Drinker, a couple down the way, were quite drunk even before they sat down to eat. As usual, a row broke out, this one more intense, over the woman's usual complaint that Mr. Gin Drinker had not left his entire fortune to her but had divided part of it among his two sons. On and on she went deriding him in a most unfortunate way, mentioning again the now-familiar litany of offenses, which included, of all things, drinking too much and wearing excessive amounts of cologne. Finally, Mr. Gin Drinker could brook no more abuse. He got up to leave, stumbled along about fifteen feet, and then, Blam!, hit the deck.

Rodrigues, at the table next to us, the Puerto Rican who lives in Nassau, the Bahamas, and who always dresses in a two-toned suit like Ricky Ricardo, saw and heard it all, and cried out, "Starlight! Starlight!"

Nick and Colum got Mr. Gin up.

"No bones broken," Rodrigues stood up and announced to the people in our little dining alcove.

Mrs. Gin Drinker, either unaware or unconcerned that her husband had fallen, lit a cigarette, put it in the ashtray, and pushed back her seat, but couldn't rise. Nick and Colum rushed to her side and helped her leave the restaurant. Later Nick came back and stubbed out the cigarette and took the uneaten food away.

Rodrigues put a mechanical pink pig, the size of a small dog, on his table and turned it on. The pig walked around and squealed oink-oink all over the place.

I cupped my hands over my mouth and yelled above the racket, "It's making a lot more sense than you do, Rodrigues."

"He's a pig, but he doesn't eat as much as you do, Doc."

Rodrigues grinned and turned the pig around so that it didn't go over the side of the table. Was that a pig of ill omen? Or was it a lucky pig?

Miss Edith Russell's lucky mechanical toy pig kept a baby quiet in the *Titanic*'s lifeboat number eleven. Her pig played "Maxixe" whenever its tail was twisted. The pig and Miss Russell survived the sinking of the *Titanic* and both returned safely to New York. That was a lucky pig.

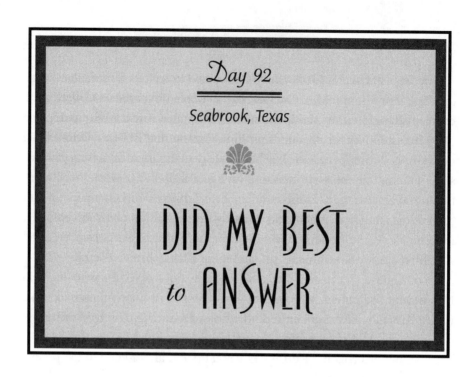

I DID MY BEST to ANSWER

*I*t was fun. But we're home, home from the sea.

The customs man said the regulations were so complex they couldn't figure them out. Anyway, Congress had forgotten to renew the law, which covered tariffs and trade. In the absence of anything better to do, they simply charged us 10 percent above the usual allowances. He wasn't interested in money, stocks, or bonds. Instead he wanted to discuss a novel he had just gotten around to reading: Mark Twain's *Adventures of Huckleberry Finn*. I had heard of it.

Trent looked the same. But he said we looked different. Healthy and more tan. He should know. He owns a tanning salon.

P.J. looked the same. She was waiting for us in the driveway and accepted eager pets.

I talked with the FBI. The dumb fucks didn't even know they were investigating me. The agents said that the TV show must have made it up. That's great. I'm going to make some money suing someone.

As predicted, the overnight check to American Express from Barbados didn't arrive. If you want fast service in the Caribbean, you have to wait for it. I stopped payment on the old check and wrote a new one.

Our neighbors, Vince and Lennie, came over and asked, "What was it like aboard?"

I did my best to answer.

EPILOGUE

You know, I shall miss the *QE2*, but there is one advantage about being home that I am rotten glad of: there ain't nothing more to write about. If I had known what a trouble it was to make a book, I wouldn't have tackled it. And I ain't going to do that no more.

INDEX